C.CINNAM
FIL.VARIÆ
P.SEIDLITZ
S.CORIAND
SULPH.SUB

More Than the Music

More Than the Music

Hank O'Neal

Fort Worth, Texas

Library of Congress Cataloging-in-Publication Data

Names: O'Neal, Hank author
Title: More than the music / Hank O'Neal.
Other titles: Texas music series (TCU Press)
Description: Fort Worth : TCU Press, 2025. | Series: Texas music series | "More Than the Music is an unusual musical memoir."–Introduction. | Includes bibliographical references and index. | Summary: "More Than the Music features twenty-seven unique jazz stories – stories that came about through my own experience. Most of them began so long ago, even as far back as the 1950s during my teenage years. In those days, jazz was still the new kid on the block, at least on my block. It was something most people knew nothing about – including me – so I watched, listened, and learned. By the time I reached New York City in 1967 and began aging out of my twenties, many of the people who had previously just been names on records or in books were now people I had met, worked with, and were getting to know on a personal level. I've picked out thirty-one terribly talented and fascinating music-oriented men and women with whom I had more than a simple working relationship; these were people who helped shape my life, some in significant ways. Once, they were all well-known – some only in the music world, others far beyond it. Their stories are detailed in twenty-five chapters from when time moved a little slower – before we were bound by TikTok's clock or 280-character tweets – because, once upon a time, we weren't always in such a hurry. I have purposely mixed it up. While most were jazz musicians, others came from different worlds: a CIA director (Edwin M. Ashcraft), a famous movie star (Clint Eastwood), a noted poet (Allen Ginsberg), a famous industrialist (Sherman M. Fairchild), a legendary talent scout and social activist (John Hammond), a Pulitzer Prize-winning composer and academic (Mel Powell), and the world's foremost music festival producer (George Wein). And yet, it was the music that brought all of us together, and I consider myself very lucky to have known them"– Provided by publisher.
Identifiers: LCCN 2025031700 | ISBN 9780875659305 hardback
Subjects: LCSH: O'Neal, Hank–Friends and associates | O'Neal, Hank–Biography | Sound recording executives and producers–United States–Biography | Jazz musicians–United States–Biography | LCGFT: Biographies
Classification: LCC ML385 .O56 2025 | DDC 781.65092/2 [B]–dc23/eng/20250718
LC record available at https://lccn.loc.gov/2025031700

Fort Worth, Texas

TCU Box 298300
Fort Worth, Texas 76129
www.tcupress.com

Design by Bill Brammer
Cover design by Adrienne Martinez. Illustration © Mertingen/Adobe Stock.
Photograph courtesy of the author's collection.

For the **Unknown Person** who, in the fall of 1938 in Kilgore, Texas,
sold my mother the wrong record that, fifteen years later,
launched my musical journey that continues to this day.

This is the record.
To learn how this came about just turn the page.

Indian Love Call

In 1936 MGM released *Rose Marie*, a motion picture adaptation of the 1924 Friml/Hammerstein/Harbach operetta of the same name. The movie featured Jeannette MacDonald and Nelson Eddy, possibly the most beloved romantic duo making movies at the time.

It is unclear when or where my parents saw *Rose Marie*, but it may have been at the Morris Theater in Daingerfield, Texas, or more likely the newly opened Crim or even the Texan in Kilgore. My mother enjoyed light classical music, was something of a romantic, and loved Jeannette and Nelson's rendition of "Indian Love Call" in the movie.

The movie was as popular as its two stars and in 1937 the two screen lovers recorded "Indian Love Call" and it was released as a Victor Red Seal, 4323-A. A year later, in the fall of 1938, the same song was recorded by Art Shaw and His Orchestra and was released on Victor's inexpensive Bluebird label. The Victor Red Seal probably cost $1.00; the Bluebird was but 35¢. And the version by Art, soon to be Artie, Shaw was on the other side of what became the biggest selling hit record of 1938, Cole Porter's *Begin the Beguine*.

Kilgore was not a metropolis then or now, and the likelihood of the store that had a handful of records for sale having a stock of Victor Red Seal classical or semi-classical recordings was remote. But they would have copies of the biggest hit of the day and "Indian Love Call" happened to be on the other side of Bluebird 7746-A. My mother asked for "Indian Love Call" and the clerk sold her the only version that was in stock.

Fast-forward to 1954. I was a fourteen-year-old in Syracuse, New York. I loved music and was allowed to play my parent's records on the Victrola in the dining room. I mostly played my father's 12" Red Seals of Beethovens and Bachs and Chopins—but one day I opened an album of 10" records and played a few. One of them was "Indian Love Call" by Art Shaw and His Orchestra with a hot vocal by Tony Pastor and nothing was ever quite the same.

Contents

NOTE

The date following the names is the year in which my first interactions with these friends and artists began.

Introduction

More Than the Music is an unusual musical memoir. It features a number of jazz stories that are mostly just known to me, as well as profiles of some of the most celebrated performing artists, but an almost equal number are less well-known and in 2025 exist mostly in obscurity except in the memories of those my age or even older. I've also included profiles of a number of nonmusicians or, at most, skilled amateurs, but people who made a difference not only in my life but for the performance, recording, and preservation of the music. In a number of instances, belated as it might be, this is a thank you note to many of these men and women.

Most of these memories were formed long ago, some in the 1950s, when I was a teenager. In those days jazz was still the new kid on the block, at least on my block, something that most people knew nothing about. Much of what they did know was nasty and lurid, related to marijuana, alcohol, hard drugs, and the crimes and awful stories that were manufactured and spread by the likes of racist sociopaths like Harry Anslinger and his political friends. I looked past this and just listened to the music, and by the time I found myself in New York City in 1967 and began aging out of my twenties, many of the people who were just names on records or in books were people I'd met and was working with and getting to know better and better.

I've picked out thirty-two extremely talented and fascinating music-oriented men and women with whom I had more than a simple working relationship, people who made a difference in my life and in many instances influenced me significantly. Once upon a time all these men and women were well-known; some only in the world of music, others far beyond that world. Their accomplishments were real and justly celebrated, as they should have been. It has been many years since I first encountered them, and in 2025 all the full-time musicians are deceased, but four of the nonperforming artists are hanging in there. While some may be mostly forgotten, they have not been forgotten by me.

I have purposely mixed it up. Yes, they are mostly jazz musicians, but there is also a director at the CIA (Edwin Ashcraft), a famous movie star (Clint Eastwood), a noted poet (Allen Ginsberg), a famous industrialist (Sherman M. Fairchild), a legendary talent scout and social activist (John Hammond), a Pulitzer Prize–winning composer and academic (Mel Powell), and the world's foremost music festival producer (George Wein). And it was the music that put all these diverse people together with me.

So here are twenty-seven stories from when time moved a little slower than it does today, and you didn't have to fit in with TikTok's clock or two-hundred-eighty X-like twitter critters. Because once upon a time, we weren't in such a hurry.

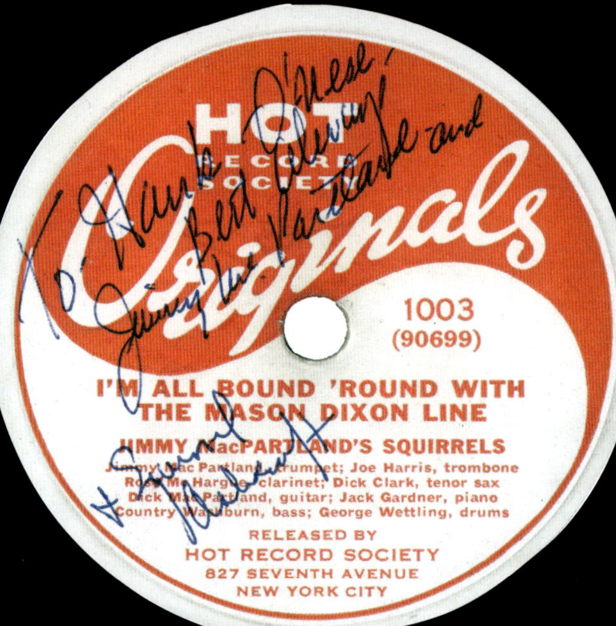
HOT
RECORD
SOCIETY
Originals
1003
(90699)
I'M ALL BOUND 'ROUND WITH THE MASON DIXON LINE
JIMMY MacPARTLAND'S SQUIRRELS
Jimmy MacPartland, trumpet; Joe Harris, trombone
Rosy McHargue, clarinet; Dick Clark, tenor sax
Dick MacPartland, guitar; Jack Gardner, piano
Country Washburn, bass; George Wettling, drums
RELEASED BY
HOT RECORD SOCIETY
827 SEVENTH AVENUE
NEW YORK CITY

HOT
RECORD
SOCIETY
Originals
1004
(90697)
ORIGINAL DIXIELAND ONE-STEP
JIMMY MacPARTLAND'S SQUIRRELS
Jimmy MacPartland, trumpet; Joe Harris, trombone
Rosy McHargue, clarinet; Dick Clark, tenor sax
Dick MacPartland, guitar; Jack Gardner, piano
Country Washburn, bass; George Wettling, drums
RELEASED BY
HOT RECORD SOCIETY
827 SEVENTH AVENUE
NEW YORK CITY

1

E. M. Squirrel Ashcraft

September 20, 1905 – January 25, 1981

IF YOU ARE LUCKY, AS I HAVE BEEN, there are often a number of people you encounter in your formative years who make important impressions on you, set you in the right direction, and influence you in many different ways, sometimes positively, sometimes negatively. It turns out I was lucky, and many people have helped me in many ways, almost always positively, beginning with my parents. But along the way there have been countless others who were mentors in one way or another and often set in motion hundreds of thousands of events and circumstances that would flow through the years and become whatever my life became and, as time passes, continues to evolve. Perhaps the most important influential mentor in my early twenties was a man with an unusual name, Squirrel Ashcraft. This is how it happened.

In January 1963, I reported for my first day of work at the Central Intelligence Agency. That is a crazy story in itself but outside the scope of this musical memoir. For the next ten months I was in and out of various CIA training courses, and in the midst of the Clandestine Service training program I was suddenly and unexpectedly pulled out of the course, returned to Washington, and assigned to the Office of National Estimates (ONE), a small think tank–like division within the CIA that produced National Intelligence Estimates, then the single most important type of finished intelligence issued by the intelligence community. These estimates were created for those men and women at the highest level of government, from the president on down.

When I was told of this change of direction I was stunned and probably blurted out something like "But I'm only halfway through the training program, why is this happening?" To which I was told, "Because they need you at Headquarters."

I had recovered a little and said to the officer in charge, "Sir, I'm twenty-three years old, untrained and inexperienced, how could anyone need me at Headquarters?" The answer was unexpected and maybe made sense to someone, just not to me. It was a staffing problem, and someone thought my African studies minor might be useful until the CIA recruiters could find a forty-five-year-old PhD to take my place. In 1963, people with training or interest in African studies or matters related to Africa were not nearly as pervasive as they are in 2025.

I was only in the office from November 1963 until May 1964, seven short months. But it was long enough to seal my fate and set in motion everything that still swirls around me today. The reason for this is not because of anything I did or didn't do.

I had to serve in ONE using my real name, Harold L. O'Neal Jr. This meant I was on every list that mattered of known CIA employees, which in turn meant the likelihood of me going overseas as a Clandestine Services operative was less than zero. As my seven-month tour of duty with ONE was coming to an end in May, my career outlook was looking forward to moving from a desk in one office to a desk in another and becoming an analyst in some other division. This was the kind of job I had no interest in, and I let the people in the Office of Training know it. I told them I'd resign before I'd sit behind a desk all day. This got their attention, and one day in late May I was told someone may have come up with a solution.

OPPOSITE

Jimmy McParland's Squirrels records autographed by Squirrel Ashcraft and Jimmy McPartland. (Author's collection)

One of Squirrel's best records with the Princeton Triangle Jazz Band from 1928. The song was his composition. (Author's collection)

If they would have me, I was to be assigned to the Office of Operations, a small but interesting division that functioned in an operational capacity in the major cities of the United States. The operatives in the field used their true name and even had a credential that identified them as a CIA employee. It was a very exclusive club; at any given time there were probably less than one hundred credentials in circulation.

I was somehow accepted, and on a day in June 1964 I made my way to 1717 H Street Northwest. It was a nondescript building that was probably razed and replaced long ago because it was about two blocks from the White House, and as time has passed this commercial backwater has become a more desirable location. But for me, even though it was a long commute from McLean every day, it became a very desirable location.

The CIA had a few floors in the building, and I made my way to the appropriate one. I stepped off the elevator and came upon the requisite guards and security. I showed my badge and asked directions to the director's office. I'd been told someone would meet me there and brief me in on what I was supposed to do. They were waiting for me inside the barrier, gave me a cursory welcome, told me I was going to meet the director, say a few words, and spend no more than five minutes with him, after which they'd take me to my office. I was told to take a seat, which I did, next to an attractive lady who I later learned was named Anne Redman.

All I knew was that the director had a long name that sounded like he was in the social register, Edwin Maurice Ashcraft III, and that he'd come from the Chicago office. It turned out he was very well socially registered. I sat and waited, people came and went, some saying things like Mr. Ashcraft thinks this or that. Finally, an older man emerged, I later learned he was the deputy director, John McConnell, and I heard him use the name "Squirrel" in referring to the director. I leaned over to gatekeeper Anne and asked, "Does the director play the piano?" She gave me a puzzled look and said, "Yes, at the Christmas Party." This is when it dawned on me this might be more than a five-minute meet and greet.

Today, if you type Edwin Maurice Ashcraft III into a search engine, you'll get a few hits, one or two that relate to his government service, and a few more that are tied to his family law firm, Ashcraft and Ashcraft. If, however, you type in Squirrel Ashcraft, you get a bunch of hits dating back to the 1920s when he was a hot pianist in Chicago, and at Princeton where he was a member of the Princeton Triangle Jazz Band. In 1964, however, he was as elusive as Garbo. He'd been as high visibility as anyone in Chicago up to World War II and for a couple of years after he returned from his tour with the Office of Naval Intelligence. But in the late 1940s he'd more or less vanished, and the legendary Monday night jam sessions at his home in Evanston, one of the most coveted local invitations for over a decade, vanished into mists of cherished memories for those lucky enough to have been there. And in June 1964, he was the director of Domestic Operations of the Central Intelligence Agency and had been since the mid-1950s.

The five-minute meet and greet turned into three or four hours. I had records Squirrel Ashcraft had made in the 1920s and 1930s, knew about the musical side of his life, and was the first person who'd turned up at the CIA who did. And so this scheduled five-minute professional interlude turned into a seventeen-year adventure that in many ways continues to this day.

Though forgotten today, Squirrel was a legendary figure in the world of jazz, at least into the mid-1970s, but much can be lost and forgotten in a quarter of a century. Other than some older musicians, he was, for example, the only person I knew who had heard Louis Armstrong and King Oliver at the Lincoln Gardens and had known and associated with a host of other legendary players from the 1920s who were just names in a book or music in the grooves of old records to me. He was the kind of man who could make a simple telephone call and tell John Hammond, Neshui, or Ahmet Ertegun I was OK, and they'd welcome me warmly. The same was true of any number of musicians of a certain age, i.e., the Austin High Gang, and their musical associates or disciples.

He was the first jazz artist I ever heard perform in an informal setting, that is away from a concert hall or club where I was a paying spectator. By that time, he was in his '60s, hadn't played regularly for years, never had been a first rank player anyway, and now had an affliction in one of his hands that affected his dexterity. But for someone of my age and limited experience, it was more thrilling to be standing two feet from a legendary figure in his living room than hearing a great pianist from the top balcony in Carnegie Hall.

He was also the man who first introduced me to an active jazz musician, in this case Jimmy McPartland. Later, he would introduce me to many others, and simply because he made the introduction, I was accepted by these men and women without question.

A little background is in order. Squirrel was born in Evanston, Illinois, in 1905. His family was socially prominent and well situated. As a teenager in the early 1920s he discovered jazz and became as deeply involved with it as possible. He was active in Chicago in the same way John Hammond was in New York, and he met many of the up-and-coming young jazz musicians in that city long before they had become prominent, befriended them, helped them whenever possible, and continued doing this for years and years. I witnessed this largesse on many occasions.

Squirrel came east in the late 1920s and attended Princeton. He played both piano and accordion, was part of Princeton's Triangle Club, wrote songs, recorded with the Triangle Club Jazz Band, was known to and played informally with such legendary figures as Bix Beiderbecke, and even corralled the elusive cornet player one night, convincing him to record with the Princeton band. It almost came off, but not quite; Bix was there when everyone fell asleep but had vanished when they awakened. He continued at Princeton but eventually returned to Chicago in the early 1930s and took up his post in the family law firm.

He opened his home to every jazz musician who could find their way to Evanston, and hundreds did, usually on Monday nights. The sessions at Squirrel's featured a who's who of whoever was in Chicago at the time. He began to record these proceedings around 1933 with a primitive recording system that improved as years passed and better equipment became available. Until he left for World War II, hundreds of private discs were made, sometimes with the help of his friend John Steiner. Steiner eventually issued some of the goings-on on Paramount 78 rpm discs and later on 10" LPs.

World War II closed down the Monday night sessions; Squirrel was inducted in the US Navy and assigned to naval intelligence. After the war, he returned to Chicago, his law practice, and the music and recording began again, this time not only on discs but on a crude tape recorder that used paper tape. The music didn't last long, however, because in the late 1940s Squirrel was selected by the fledgling Central Intelligence Agency to run its Chicago field office, and the music slowed down once again. He was so good at the CIA game he was urged to become the director of all domestic operations in the early 1950s.

Squirrel accepted the challenge, closed down the house in Evanston, moved to Washington, and vanished into another world, his whereabouts unknown except to the musicians and friends with whom he kept in touch. There were no sessions at Squirrel's massive apartment in Washington. When I arrived on the scene in 1964, his piano sounded a bit like one would find in a Charles Addams haunted house. But that was soon to change.

Suddenly there was someone around who knew his past and even had some of those old John Steiner-issued Paramount records and Princeton Triangle Jazz band 78s to prove it. I was the junior guy in the Office of Operations, but I always had immediate access to the director because of the music. This is when I learned that love of jazz of a certain sort can cross *any* cultural divide, regardless of age, race, or anything else.

It didn't take long before the piano was tuned and regulated, and informal musical gatherings began. The first was with Jimmy and Marian McPartland, and two wonderful local Washington musicians, clarinetist Tommy Gwaltney (who founded and owned Blues Alley) and guitarist Steve Jordan. Squirrel got his hands back in shape, so he could spell Marian when she wanted to relax and, just like in the old days, everything was recorded.

Informal Sessions

With Ormond Downes, Howard Kennedy, Rosy McHargue, Jimmy McPartland, Joe Ruston, Bob Zurke, Jane Ashcraft, Zutty Singleton, Peanuts Hucko, Jean Enzinger (Bach), Jimmy Dorsey, Gloria Faye, and Bobby Hackett. (Author's collection)

Jimmy Dorsey's birthday party at Squirrel's home. (Author's collection)

Very Informal Sessions

Howard Kennedy and Rosy McHargue. (Author's collection)

Joe Rushton and his motorcycle. (Author's collection)

Playback after a recording. (Author's collection)

Squirrel Ashcraft on clarinet. Could it be Frank Teschemacher's? With Jimmy McPartland and Gloria Faye. (Author's collection)

The recording machine circa late 1930s. (Author's collection)

Home Recordings

Informal sessions recorded by Squirrel Ashcraft, John Steiner, Fuzz Pearson, and others. (Author's collection)

Piano Solo
by
Jess Stacey
Improvisation and
Embraceable you.
Ashcraft.
DATE

audiodisc
recording
blank
NEW YORK, • U.S.A.
78RPM
Zurke - Blues -
Boogie-woogie type.
1938—
RECORDED AT 78 R.P.M. 33 R.P.M. • OUTSIDE-IN • INSIDE-OUT

Genuine
TRU-TONE
RECORD
JAZZ ME
Title
FREEMAN
RUSHTON, HOWE WILSON
Recorded by ASHCRAFT
WESTERN PRODUCTS, Inc.
CHICAGO, ILL.
U. S. A.

78
Lateral
TECHNICAL
RECORDING
SERVICE
P. O. Box 5911
CHICAGO, ILL.
copy
YOU TOOK ADVANTAGE
Jack Gardner
-17-45

Home Recordings

Informal sessions recorded by Squirrel Ashcraft, John Steiner, Fuzz Pearson, and others. (Author's collection)

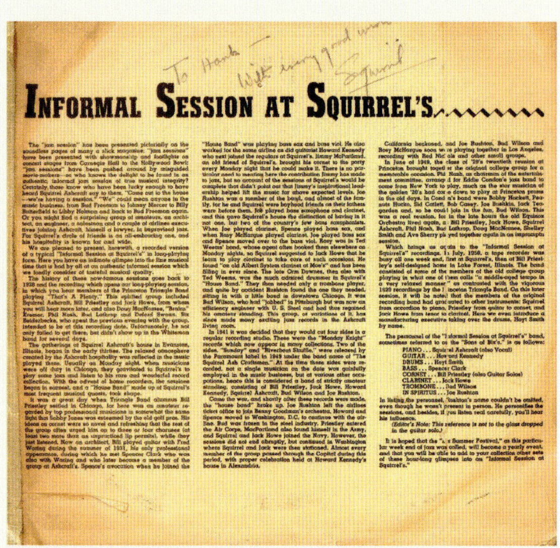

To Hank — With every good wish Squirrel

INFORMAL SESSION AT SQUIRREL'S

The "jam session" has been presented pictorially on the soundless pages of many a slick magazine; "jam sessions" have been presented with showmanship and footlights on concert stages from Carnegie Hall to the Hollywood Bowl; "jam sessions" have been pushed around by misguided movie-makers—so who knows the delight to be found in an authentic informal jam session of true musical integrity? Certainly those know who have been lucky enough to have heard Squirrel Ashcraft say to them, "Come out to the house—we're having a session." "We" could mean anyone in the music business, from Bud Freeman to Johnny Mercer to Billy Butterfield to Libby Holman and back to Bud Freeman again. Or you might find a surprising group of amateurs, an architect, an engineer, a salesman and a couple of airlines executives joining Ashcraft, himself a lawyer, in improvised jazz. For Squirrel's circle of friends is an all-embracing one, and his hospitality is known far and wide.

We are pleased to present, herewith, a recorded version of a typical "Informal Session at Squirrel's" in long-playing form. Here you have an intimate glimpse into the fine musical time that is had by all at an authentic informal session which we fondly consider of tasteful musical quality.

The history of these now-famous sessions goes back to 1928 and the recording which opens our long-playing session, in which you hear members of the Princeton Triangle Band playing "That's A Plenty." This spirited group included Squirrel Ashcraft, Bill Priestley and Jack Howe, from whom you will hear more later, and also Doug MacNamee, "Brains" Kramer, Phil Nash, Bud Lathrop and Deland Swann. Bix Beiderbecke, who spent the previous evening with the group, intended to be at this recording date. Unfortunately, he not only failed to get there, but didn't show up in the Whiteman band for several days.

The gatherings at Squirrel Ashcraft's house in Evanston, ...

Informal sessions at Squirrel's #1. (Author's collection)

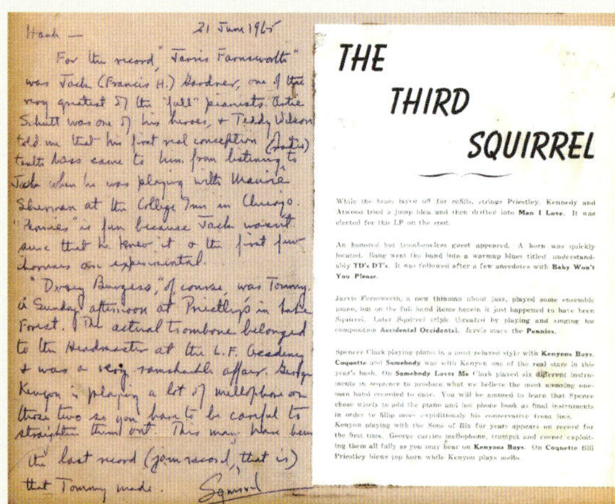

Hank — 21 June 1965

For the record, "Jarvis Farnsworth" was Jack (Francis H.) Gardner, one of the very greatest of the "full" pianists. Artie Schutt was one of his heroes, + Teddy Wilson told me that his first real conception (Fatha) tenth bass came to him from listening to Jack when he was playing with Maurie Sherman at the College Inn in Chicago. "Pennies" is fun because Jack wasn't sure that he knew it so the first few choruses are experimental.

"Dorsey Burgess," of course, was Tommy. A Sunday afternoon at Priestley's in Lake Forest. The actual trombone belonged to the Headmaster at the L.F. Academy + was a very ramshackle affair. George Kenyon is playing a lot of mellophone on these two so you have to be careful to straighten them out. This may have been the last record (jam record, that is) that Tommy made. Squirrel

THE THIRD SQUIRREL

While the brass layed off for refills, strings Priestley, Kennedy and Atwood tried a jump idea and then drifted into **Man I Love.** It was elected for this LP on the spot.

An honored but tromboneless guest appeared. A horn was quickly located. Bang went the band into a warmup blues titled understandably **TD's DT's.** It was followed after a few anecdotes with **Baby Won't You Please.**

Jarvis Fernsworth, a new thinman about jazz, played some ensemble piano, but on the full band items herein it just happened to have been Squirrel. Later Squirrel triple threated by playing and singing his composition **Accidental Occidental.** Jarvis stars the **Pennies.**

Spencer Clark playing piano in a most relaxed style with **Kenyons Boys. Coquette** and **Somebody** was with Kenyon one of the real stars in this year's bash. On **Somebody Loves Me** Clark played six different instruments in sequence to produce what we believe the most amazing one-man band recorded to date. You will be amused to learn that Spence chose wisely to add the piano and hot phone book as final instruments in order to fillip more expiditiously his conservative front line. Kenyon playing with the Sons of Bix for years appears on record for the first time. George carries mellophone, trumpet and cornet exploiting them all fully as you may hear on **Kenyons Boys.** On **Coquette** Bill Priestley blows top horn while Kenyon plays mello.

Informal session at Squirrel's #3. (Author's collection)

Second Session at Squirrel's

SONS OF BIX'S

TOP: l/r: MARY (piano) and SPENCER CLARK (bass sax and string bass), John and Nina Satterthwaite, JACK GARDNER (piano), BUD WILSON (trombone), Lloyd Laflin, HOWARD KENNEDY (guitar), MARIAN McPARTLAND (piano.) LOWER: Jane Ashcraft, Crick Priestley, BILL PRIESTLEY (cornet, guitar), SQUIRREL ASHCRAFT (piano), Gilmer Black, Anna May Laflin, JACK HOWE (clarinet). Photo JIMMY McPARTLAND. Not included: JOE HALLA (guitar), HOYT SMITH (drums), PHIL ATWOOD (bass.)

The record SECOND SESSION AT SQUIRREL'S continues a series made at the Bix Summer Festivals held annually by Chicago musicians who knew and were highly inspired by the cornet of Bix Beiderbecke. Bix became a loved friend playing frequently, sometimes professionally, with these men. The music they play today they acknowledge to owe still a great debt to Bix's inspiration.

Bix's genius was expressed in creating a definite leading horn style which was melodic and incisive. No comparable melding of the horn's potentialities had preceded him. As a result large numbers of hornmen have carefully investigated Bix's style. Some of his contemporaries, now twenty years after Bix's last note, retain the facility of phrasing like he did or using a tone like his. The Festival music makes especially interesting listening because one realizes that occasionally Bixisms in solos or in arrangements are intentional, and then the question arises, "are they kosher Bixisms?" You can decide.

Our first SESSION recorded was a salute to Jim McPartland, the original Son of Bix. Among other invaluable services he performed was the flicking of the photo above.

Our present SESSION is a salute to Doc who happened to be living with Priestley during the period of the 1951 Festival. Doc called the tunes.

There are other qualified hornmen who would fit well in the spirit of the Festival. We hope in the future to have Andy Secrest, Red Nichols, Sterling Bose, Eston Spurier and Bobby Hackett as guest conductors. There is evidence in molded plastic that Cathcart, Sherwood, Wiggs and Windhurst might enjoy themselves too. We hear some about the Bix sounds on the coasts, in England and Australia.

Unfortunately we are too late to call upon Harry Johnson; but we can include a little of Harry on a private recording in a future SESSION as we included a bit of Bunny this time. Aside from the men we have mentioned there is an interesting example of the Bix sound on Henderson's SINGIN' THE BLUES, where Rex Stewart simulates expertly the original Bix chorus. McKinney Cotton Picker John Nesbitt playing across from Bix in the Detroit Greystone Ballroom, admired the Sound enough to make it his style. And don't forget that fellow Tommy Howell on the Fred Gardner U of Texas OKehs.

Other Bixology: Sutton and Stacey have recently recorded Bix piano compositions. George Cooke has created a Bix Memorial Program which has had several radio presentations and is collecting memorabilia to be housed in the Library at Davenport. George Hoefer is working on a biography. Amy Lee has an unpublished book-length poem on the Bix story. Eddie Condon included some mighty nice Bix anecdotes in the recent Condon TV shows. Dr. Jack Owen influenced the reissue on V-Disc of the trumpets of Harry Johnson on HANDFUL OF STARS and Red Nichols on DANCING ON THE CEILING and the cornet of Hackett on his "SINGIN' THE BLUES.

Informal sessions at Squirrel's #2. (Author's collection)

Informal sessions at Squirrel's #4. (Author's collection)

With Jimmy McPartland, Dick Barrett, and Marian McPartland at 3900 Watson Place, Washington, DC, in 1966. (Author's collection)

The first "new" informal session was eventually issued as a record that was given away to anyone who wanted one. I cut my recording teeth on Squirrel's Ampex F-44 and two Electrovoice microphones. This is how I once described that first recorded informal session:

On May 1, 1966, I set up a tape recorder under Squirrel Ashcraft's piano and recorded all the music that was made that night by an interesting assortment of musicians and a few months later assembled the recordings and produced a record entitled *More Informal Sessions at Squirrel's*. I even assigned it a catalog number, MIS 1. If you look on page A432 of Tom Lord's *The Jazz Discography,* it is listed.

The session was indeed informal, and pictures I took that night prove it. Squirrel and Marian McPartland are at the piano, Jimmy McPartland is on trumpet, and Dick Barrett plays his guitar in the background. The music rarely rises above the level of charming, but this is the first record I ever "produced" and it is not even a production. But it was the first, and I'm told you always remember the first one. It didn't even have a printed jacket, just a generic white jacket with a large sticker, one that had to be wetted and applied to the empty jacket cover by hand. This is how the label appeared:

Over the next decade, Squirrel and I produced about ten records with MIS catalog numbers. I recorded his retirement party, we issued some of the private recordings he'd made in Chicago in the 1930s, and in the 1970s we released recordings made at his Princeton Class of '29 reunions featuring a band of old, older, and sometime younger musicians known as The Sons of Bix. Each band had at least one ringer. Max Kaminsky, Bob Haggart, and Maxine Sullivan appeared at one time or another, but these records also fell into the utterly charming category.

Labels for the first More Informal Sessions release in 1966.

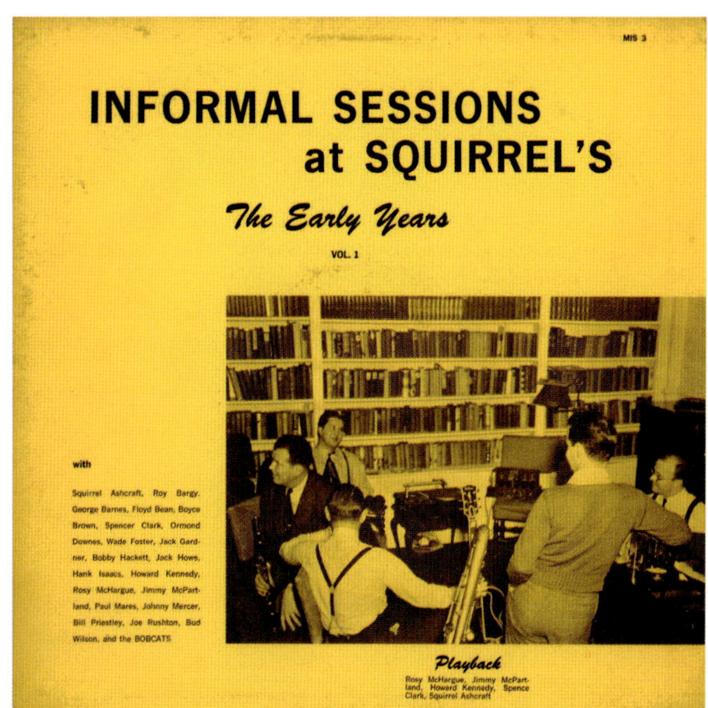

The first LP release of informal sessions from the 1930s. (Author's collection).

My Recording Academy membership card. (Author's collection)

The Central Intelligence Agency encouraged me to transfer to the New York City office in 1967, and I did so in June of that year. Squirrel made certain many of his musical friends would welcome me when I arrived. Two of these were John Hammond and George Avakian. I dipped my toe into the NYC music scene cautiously, but one thing I was encouraged to do was to become a member of what was then known as the National Academy of Recording Arts and Sciences, now better known as The Recording Academy, the people who give out the Grammy Award on a glitzy network broadcast every year except when COVID shut them down in 2021 and 2022. Then they came back strong, and the 2025 edition was highly praised.

In order to be accepted for membership you had to be qualified in one or more categories and the only category remotely possible for me was record production. Of course, my production credits at the time consisted of three privately issued records and one real record that hadn't been issued. But I sent in an application, had a few friends vouch for me, probably Hammond and Avakian, and I became a member and remain so to this day. It has been nearly a sixty-year run.

It was pretty simple then. To put it in historical perspective, *Sgt. Pepper's Lonely Hearts Club Band* was voted album of the year for 1967, Aretha won for "Respect," Elvis won for Best Sacred Performance, Bill Cosby won for Best Comedy, and Duke Ellington won for Best Instrumental Jazz Performance - Large Group or Soloist with Large Group. And there were only forty-eight categories. Of those winners, two Beatles and Bill Cosby are still alive. But let's go back all those years to a time where no one breathing then is today. There was no broadcast, there were not thirteen thousand members, and the first ceremony I attended was held in a very ordinary ballroom in a midtown hotel in New York City.

Listening back to the old acetate and aluminum recordings from the 1930s, Squirrel reminds me of a pianist like Frank Melrose: A great deal more passion than technique, but good enough to get the job done. He was a better than average amateur in those days, could easily hold his own with his peers, and could provide good accompaniment to A-list artists when it was required. I remember him telling me that one night the entire Bob Crosby band came out to his house for a Monday night session. The thing that pleased him most was that the first complaint was from a neighbor whose house was three blocks away. And he got to play with the band when Bob Zurke was doing something else with a glass in his hand.

Squirrel's influence in the jazz world was not as a pianist. He was always behind the scenes and, eventually, way behind the scenes. If Eddie Condon couldn't get a liquor license to open Condon's, Squirrel could make the call to the right person so it could be worked out, despite the checkered past of some of the club's owners. If a certain player were down on his luck, there would be a check in the mail. There were any number of people he supported for life. He was a safety net for many of the first generation of jazz musicians and probably some of the second and third. My guess is he was a safety net for a lot of people I didn't know about, musicians, old friends down on their luck, or even a struggling bullfighter.

After he officially retired in the late 1960s, Squirrel spent less and less time in Washington and more time at his home in Spain. Sometimes a year would pass and I wouldn't see him, except perhaps to see him off on either

The CIA retirement party with various CIA employees and jazz musicians, including Jimmy McPartland, Tommy Gwaltney, Billy Taylor Jr., and Eddie Phyfe. (Author's collection)

the ocean liners *Michaelangelo* or *Rafaello*, his favorite modes of transportation between New York and Spain. When in Spain, he had little time for music, but toward the end of a letter from there, dated November 12, 1969, he says, "We are listening, which we do seldom at all, to Miles' Sketches, and I wish so very, very much that Bix could have heard it . . . We think about you often. Please write the whole story." I'm not sure I ever did, but in the 1970s and early 1980s, he had a burst of musical energy, at least every June, for half a dozen years.

In 1975, Jack Howe liberated a funny little band, affectionately called The Sons of Bix, from cornetist Tom Pletcher. Jack was an amateur tenor saxophone player who'd been part of the Princeton Triangle Jazz band with Squirrel in the 1920s. He augmented the SOBs with Princeton alumni musicians, aided by the likes of Spencer Clark, Bob Haggart, Max Kaminsky, Maxine Sullivan, and others. The band only had one certain engagement each year: to play a class reunion at Princeton. The band played at every reunion until at least 1982.

Squirrel actually played a little piano on all the dates until 1981. I recorded the performances, which, as often as not, were presented in tents. Squirrel and Jack then chose their favorite tunes, and I arranged for a few LPs to be pressed up and distributed to the dwindling faithful. The records are often spirited, but not landmark recordings. The records were a friendly souvenir, but little more. Much to my surprise, some of them have been listed in Tom Lord's landmark publication, *The Jazz Discography*.

The 1979 Bix Festival at Princeton LP. (Author's collection)

In those years, if I had to be in Washington for whatever reason, Squirrel's Watson Place apartment was always open, whether Squirrel and his wife were in residence or not. I haven't stayed in a hotel in Washington since 1960; but to confess, I only went back a few times after Squirrel died in 1981. One of the last times I was there was at the urging of his wife, Patter, the former Mildred Winslow. She telephoned in the mid-1980s and said she was cleaning out files and had found some correspondence from me in a box of music-related junk in the back of a closet. Would I please come down and save all these found items from the trash collector? I was also urged to pick up the crank-up Victrola with the bamboo needle cutter that was now stored in the basement. I'd first seen it at an old filling station somewhere in Virginia in the mid-1960s, offered the owner ten dollars, which he was happy to have, and had passed it on to Squirrel so he could play his old Hot Five 78s as he played them in the 1920s, when they were fresh and new. I was happy to have it back, and it still works just fine.

I drove down, had a nice visit with Patter, and loaded all the papers, the boxes of stuff she'd found in the closet, and the old Victrola in the back of my car. I had a last look around and never went back, but stayed in touch with Patter until she became ill and her Alzheimer's progressed to the point where she didn't know who I was.

When I got home after that last trip, I had a good time looking at the correspondence, the old clippings from the 1930s and 1940s. At the bottom of the box I saved from the trash man, I found the bell of a battered cornet, with a note from Jimmy McPartland. This was all that was left of the cornet Bix had given Jimmy when he replaced Bix in the Wolverines. This was the kind of thing that turned up at Squirrel's house. And I'll bet things like that don't turn up too many other places. For years and years, the bell of the horn hung from a sprinkler pipe near the ceiling of my home/office at 830 Broadway, but in 2018 I took it down and donated it and some other Bix-related material to the Bix Beiderbecke Museum in Davenport, Iowa. The museum and the bell survived the most recent flood, but it did have to be evacuated to a higher floor.

Squirrel Ashcraft was a kind and generous man who touched the lives of many men and women in a positive way. When he found time to touch a piano, it was equally positive. I never heard him play the blues.

The bell of the horn on display at the Bix Beiderbecke Museum in Davenport, Iowa. (Author's collection)

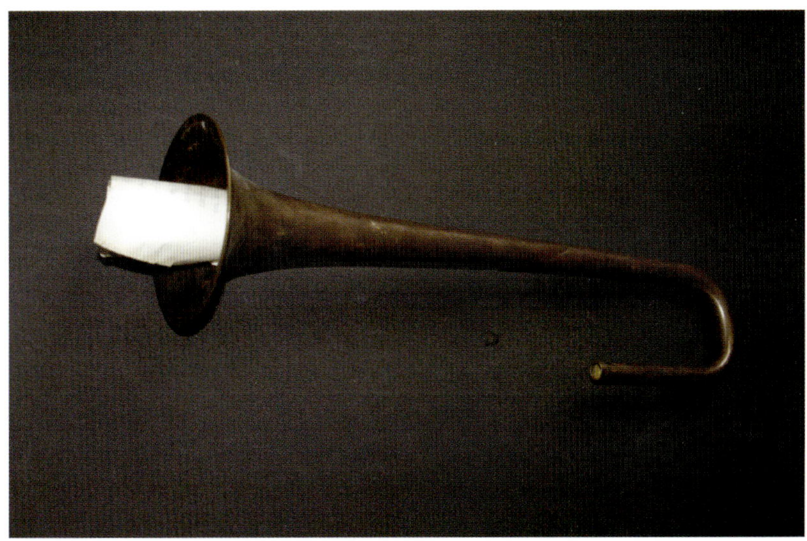

The bell of the Beiderbecke/McPartland trumpet with a note from Squirrel. (Author's collection)

THE GRAPHIC ART OF PAUL BACON

THIS IS NOT A COMB, OR HAVE PENCIL, WILL TRAVEL

Hank O'Neal

2

Paul Bacon

(December 25, 1923 – June 8, 2015)

IN 1999 I wrote an essay entitled, "This Is Not a Comb or Have Pencil, Will Travel." It was about my friend Paul Bacon and was for a catalog accompanying an exhibition at the Sordoni Gallery entitled *The Graphic Art of Paul Bacon*. He even made a tiny drawing to accompany it.

Twenty-six years later it is still all true and in part reads as follows:

Music made the difference. It did for Paul Bacon, it did for me, and I pity the person for whom it didn't. And it made a difference for both of us early, as teenagers. With some people it is even younger—it has to if it's going to shape your life. You hear something you've never heard before, and somehow, unexplainably everything connects, everything stirs within you and you're never the same. Those first sounds, exciting, visceral, heart-pounding sounds begin a process that never stops—that stays with you forever. For some, the music is the dominant force in their lives, they become professionals, music is their life. For others, it becomes a driving avocation—for most just as listeners, for others as producers, or—for a lucky few like Paul—as a semi-pro performer who plays for the sheer joy of it.

For me, the sound I'd never heard before burst forth from an old Artie Shaw Bluebird 78 rpm record, one my mother bought by mistake in 1939. I heard it years later, by accident, in 1953. Paul Bacon got his first taste a few years earlier, in 1938, when he heard a Chick Webb Decca. Shaw's band played an old operetta classic, "Indian Love Call," in a way that astounded my thirteen-year-old ears; Webb's band was even hotter playing a new Benny Carter arrangement of "Liza", the Gershwin standard, by then nearly ten years old. And neither of us was ever the same. Paul once wrote, "Jazz is powerful stuff, it usually seizes you at the same time as sex, and it is deeply affecting to many of its converts throughout their lives—enough so to make bearable a slight alienation, but whatever the emotional responses to jazz are, wherever they come from, they are unifying in their strengths."

You meet people along the way because of the music, people with whom you might not otherwise associate, people who can and do shape your entire life. I know it happened to me, and I know it happened to Paul Bacon. I don't know about today, but once upon a time, in the 1930s and 1940s, being a serious jazz fan was almost like being in a secret society, with its own passwords, language, and codes of conduct. People who passionately liked what then was called "hot" music congregated in "hot clubs," and these clubs were all over the world from New York to Paris to Bangkok. Jazz enthusiasts would come together, listen to records, sponsor concerts by their favorite artist, or whoever was available, and sometimes even issue records.

A legendary hot club congregated regularly on Monday nights in Newark, New Jersey, and in 1940 one of its hottest new members was Paul Bacon. Another member was a friend who lived not far away, Phil Stein, and yet another hot jazz fan was Phil's striking teenage sister, Lorraine. Paul recently referred to her as the glamour-puss of the Newark Hot Club, but that was long ago, and the same Lorraine is now the Glamour-Puss of the Village Vanguard, which she sternly oversees since the death of her husband, the club's legendary founder, Max Gordon. Someone else for whom music made the difference.

OPPOSITE
The Graphic Art of Paul Bacon, 1999.
(Author's collection)

It was always the music, a shared, not so secret passion, that brought these three people together, not the Newark Bears, even though they were a pretty good baseball team in the early 1940s, fielding the likes of Tommy Byrne and Hank Sauer. Hot jazz, the hotter the better, was the common denominator. An old Jabbo Smith record, *Sweet and Low Blues* or maybe *Decatur Street Tutti*, scavenged for a dime in a junk shop, could and did forge a common bond among impressionable teenage listeners, a bond that could and did last a lifetime. Even with Jabbo, jazz, at least a certain kind of jazz, could bring people together and keep them together forever.

The Record Changer, May 1948. (Author's collection)

If you speak with those who know Paul well, they all will tell you he could always draw. By his own admission he had skills, just no particular vocation, no way to translate his skill into a decent meal. He was just another teenager without direction, but within a few years, he found the vocation and got better as the years went by. Yet according to those in the know, he started off pretty well. His situation reminds me of something one of Joe Venuti's cousins once said to me, when I asked him if it was true Joe was born on a ship coming from Italy to America. "Yeah," he replied gruffly, "and he was playing pretty good when he got off the boat."

Paul's first drawings were made for the *Newark Hot Club's Jazz Notes*, Bob Thiele's *Jazz,* and other small magazines, but his search for a life's work was rudely interrupted; he was just the right age for the Marines, and the Corps proved it for the next three years. Paul traveled extensively during his stint with the Marines, kept his pencil in his pocket but with very little opportunity to use it, except to hand letter various items for officers and, after the war, create some stands for a service band while he was stuck on the island of Peleliu waiting for transport back to Newark. His experiences overseas were undoubtedly broadening, but unlike Peggy Sawyer, he didn't come back a star. He left as a youngster passionate about music and art and came back the same thing.

Unknown, Seymour Berg, Alfred Lion, unknown, Paul Bacon, and on the floor, Lorraine Stein Lion (later Gordon). (Author's collection)

It was now April 1946. Things were relatively peaceful in the world, and Paul Bacon, along with a million other GIs, came home looking for work. He had a fantasy of working at a drawing board doing super fine hand lettering, when suddenly Hal Zamboni, who, with his brother, had a Bauhaus-influenced design studio in midtown Manhattan, took him in. Almost overnight, the fantasy became a reality. Zamboni encouraged his young apprentice, sent him to classes with Lewis Daniel, gave him varied assignments, and paid him thirty dollars a week for his time. And it could have ended there, doing basic design work, illustrating magazines, creating advertisements. But it didn't, because of the music.

The Newark Hot Club was pretty much a thing of the past, the war chewed up millions and millions of old 78 rpm discs during the dreaded shellac drives, more records were being reissued, and LPs were just around the corner. But by 1947, there was a new focus for the faithful, a wonderful monthly publication, *The Record Changer*. This inexpensively produced magazine featured articles, reviews, and (best of all) sales of rare records. There was also one extraordinary independent jazz label. Although not exactly thriving, it was doing well enough to regularly issue 78 singles and albums, which needed designs. The label was Blue Note, and Paul's jazz pal and onetime model Lorraine Stein was now Lorraine Lion, married to Alfred Lion, who had founded the company in 1939 with Francis Wolff.

His life began to fall into place, a Paul Bacon design suddenly appeared on *Sidney Bechet's Blue Note Jazzmen*, and more, many, many more were to follow. But then something else happened, primarily because even though Paul loved Louie, Bix, and Jabbo, he wasn't what was known in those years as a mouldie fygge, someone who just liked music from the 1920s. He also liked Fats (Navarro), Dizzy, Monk, and Miles, and this caught the attention of Alfred Lion, who suggested to the two proprietors of *The Record Changer*, Bill Grauer and Orrin Keepnews, that his young designer friend might make a fine modern jazz critic, one who could relate to the old and the new. Bill and Orrin were wise enough to pay attention to their elders (they were still in their twenties and Alfred was at least thirty-five), and took on the kid, as Alfred had suggested. Since Paul was gainfully, though modestly, employed elsewhere, he was expected to provide reviews for a very nominal fee (often just being allowed to keep the record he was called upon to review).

Bill and Orrin ran *The Record Changer* on a shoestring budget, but they were destined for bigger things—and dragged Paul along with them without so much as a whimper. By the time the little magazine ceased publication, Bill and Orrin had begun producing reissues for RCA's new label "X" and launched their own Riverside label. Many of the initial releases for "X" and almost all of the Riversides featured cover designs by Paul Bacon. In fact, Paul eventually became chief designer for Riverside in its early and middle years.

It was fun to design jackets for jazz LPs, and it undoubtedly provided a much-needed creative outlet, but it was not possible to pay many bills with the meager proceeds derived from a few jackets a month. Yet the jazz connection ultimately led Paul to the design field where the demand for his work soon allowed him to open his own

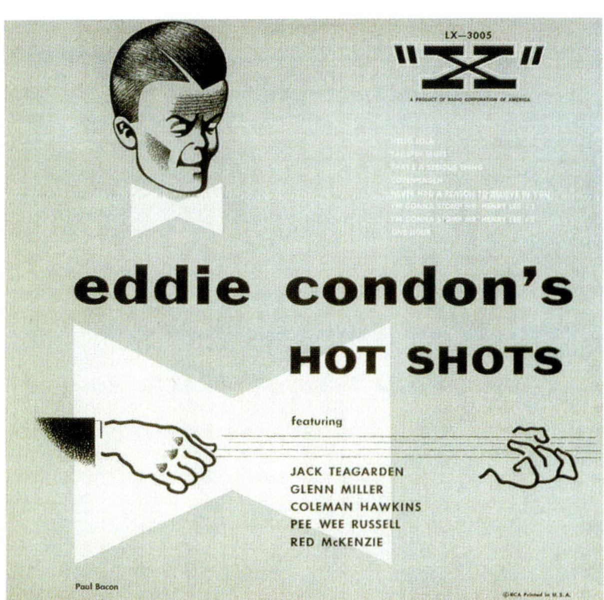

Two early "X" LP cover designs by PB. (Author's collection)

Two early Blue Note cover designs by PB. (Author's collection)

studio, raise a family, pay the mortgage, and do all the other mundane things to which most people, even the finest creative artists, aspire—at least when they are honest with themselves.

In 1950, Bill Westley asked Paul to provide some illustrations for a book about chimpanzees he was writing. The art director of E. P. Dutton, the publisher, asked if the artist could possibly do a dust jacket to complement the drawings. The artist could and did, thus producing the first of thousands of dust jackets that grace many of the most notable books of the second half of this century. *Chimp on My Shoulder* was a modest success, and in 1999 it is best remembered by Paul Bacon and the Internet. Bibliofind.com currently lists seven copies in varying conditions with prices ranging from $12–$45. In the description of one of the copies can be found the following unsolicited testimonial: "The text is clean, Paul Bacon's illustrations are wonderful, bright and clean."

Muggsy Spanier once sang, "You're bound to look like a monkey when you grow old," but Paul didn't have to worry. He started out with the monkeys, so there was no problem winding up that way—the chimps had, after all, provided the beginning. Still, there were no other immediate freelance jacket designs on the horizon, and Zamboni was still his home base.

A year or so later, however, prior to Riverside or label "X", Bill and Orrin, who paid his bills by being an editor at Simon & Schuster, had the idea to package a record with holiday literature. They needed some action on the cuff and asked Paul to produce a dummy for the overall package. It must have been a good one; the art director at Simon & Schuster, Tom Bevans, asked, "Who is this guy?" and the work started to come in. There were enough clients to open his own studio in 1955, and he worked for anyone who would call. He confessed, "If they had a dime, I'd draw." But it's not that simple.

Paul's career in jacket design started slowly but built steadily, never stopped, and is now in its forty-ninth year. He hit the big time in 1956 with Meyer Levin's *Compulsion*. He'd done important books before, but this was the first he'd been given that everyone knew was going to be a bestseller before it was issued. Paul's design made its way to the movie titles, but unfortunately without proper credit.

There are some legends about Paul. One is that he is able to carry on three conversations simultaneously while hand lettering a book jacket. Another is that he is in such control of his mind, eye, and hand that he can not only recall obscure typefaces from memory but improve on them in the process. The most noteworthy is that Paul has read all the thousands of books for which he designed dust jackets. And it's true. In his words: "I've read them all, even the junk. If there was a key to a book, something that would be considered a graphic key, then I was going to find it myself. I knew it was buried somewhere in the manuscript. The publisher would send me a manuscript to see what I'd do. It was a much more carefree at the beginning, there were some restraints, but there was also a sense of freedom."

His friend and longtime associate, Harris Lewine, recently said, "Paul could read a manuscript and no matter how good or bad it was, could find a kernel of honesty and would try to replicate this on a jacket. The graphic key often revolved around Paul's personal identification with something. This might be completely beyond the quality of a so-so novel, but would mesh with the quality of the better writing in it."

Paul once commented, "It was all very informal in those days. I'd read the manuscript and think about it, and make some sketches. I often went to a place with a sketch under my arm. The publishers were very honorable, and it was a relaxed way to make a living, even though the life of a freelancer is never carefree. They usually kept me away from the authors, they didn't want me to get too close to them." The publisher didn't want the author to influence the jacket design.

This is borne out by Joseph Heller, who recently said of Paul, "He's done all my jackets, other than that I don't really know him. We'd meet occasionally at a book party, say hello and shake hands. I liked him because the publisher liked him. With *Catch-22* there were several things that came in before Paul's. I'm never shown a design until the publisher finds something exciting; and Paul has always been original, surprising, and wonderful." *Catch-22* was in 1961, and thirty-five years later Paul designed the dust jacket for the sequel, *Closing Time*. This is what Paul said about that, in the liner notes for an album featuring Nat Adderley, for which he also designed the booklet cover:

"One of the perks of living long enough is if you're around and don't quit, you get to do things like create a Nat Adderley cover in 1958 and 1996, or create the original design for Joseph Heller's *Catch-22* and then thirty-three years later design the jacket for the sequel, *Closing Time*. You don't get to do it very often but when the opportunity comes it is very gratifying to have the opportunity of being involved with a Nat Adderley or Joseph Heller after thirty years is kind of great. Everyone is getting a little thin on top, but that's part of the deal."

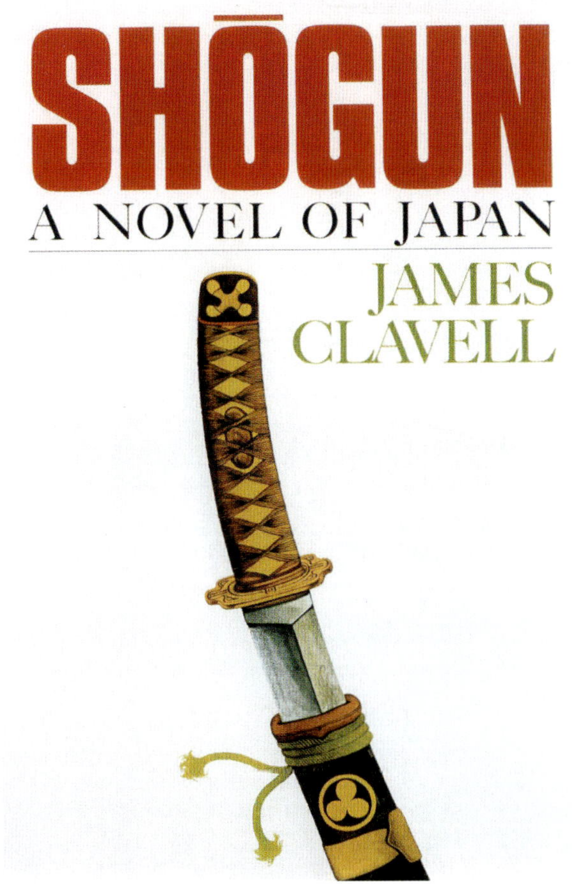

Shogun dust jacket by PB. (Author's collection)

Neither Heller nor Bacon mentions that it took a good deal of work on Paul's behalf to get to the final *Catch-22* jacket. The first sketch, featuring a hand and finger proffering a universal gesture, scandalized all concerned. The dangling red hubba-hubba man that appears on the dust jacket was in the next sketch, and many subsequent sketches, but it was a long road. With each sketch, Heller's name and *Catch-22* grew and the little red man shrank, until the final version emerged. Harris Lewine: "Paul never gave up. Most illustrators would've given up, but he would never say 'go away.'"

Paul Bacon's "big book look" emerged about the same time. It is unclear if he developed the concept on his own, but Paul popularized it and became famous as a result. The "big book look" was the antithesis of dust jackets up to that time, with type laid over an illustration and a wrap-around spine. Paul's dust jacket featured the name and title in the large typeface at the top of the jacket and

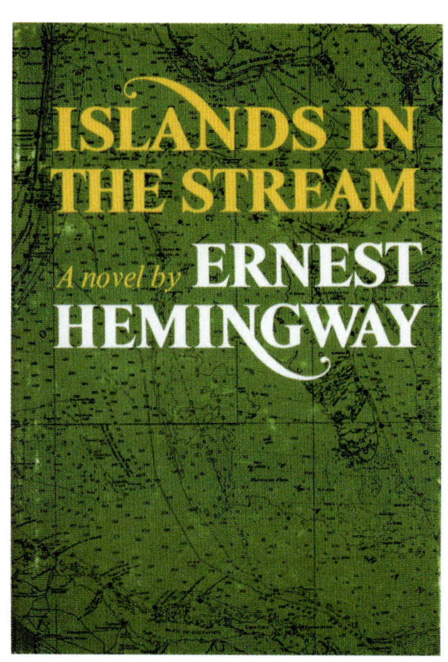

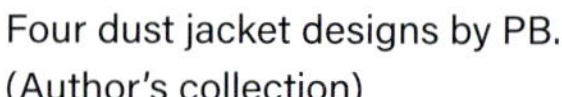
Four dust jacket designs by PB.
(Author's collection)

a centered spot illustration of the field of white, black, or solid color. This was the form often used for a noted author. For an author's first book the concept might be reversed—a larger illustration might be required to catch a bookstore browser's attention.

The range of his work is remarkable. The forty-four selections highlighted in this exhibition, from *Chimp on My Shoulder* to *Thomas Jefferson and Sally Hemings: An American Controversy* have something for any taste: blockbusters, cult favorites, literary classics, scandalous titles, and more. I'm amazed at the prominent authors and books listed in this catalog. One could list these books and pose the question: what do the following forty-four noted writers have in common? And then you could make a longer list, many hundreds, and ask the same thing. The easy answer is that most of these books might be found in a good public library, but the right answer is they all have dust jackets created by Paul Bacon—in common with thousands of other books.

Other questions to ask: Apart from the "big book look" what is unique about a Paul Bacon design? What sets them apart? Joseph Heller used the words "original surprising and wonderful." True enough—but his designs also show a quiet but elegant simplicity, a clean, focused utility. In the language of a bopster, words that Paul would understand and appreciate, "The Scene Is Clean." Yet, one must remember, Paul may appreciate bop, but he doesn't play it. Lots of notes, played very fast, funny harmonies, insider music. That's not the kind of music or art he creates. The line of the New Orleans-tinged music featured in a Paul Bacon performance is much like that of his dust jackets—sparse, accessible, to the point, and completely lacking in gratuitous ornamentation. Just as there are no heaving bosoms on Paul's dust jackets, his music-making is not embellished with nonmusical effects—each note counts.

Just before I wrote these words I went to a shelf and removed six books by E. L. Doctorow. In chronological order: *Ragtime, Loon Lake, Lives of the Poets, World's Fair, Billy Bathgate,* and *The Waterworks*. Paul designed the jackets for the first five and the cover illustration for the sixth. I've read the books; he found the graphic key to each and translated it into assisting design. He also found a marvelous graphic key in *The Waterworks*, maybe the best of the six, but the publisher used only the illustration (which Paul says he'd like to redraw).

The wish to redraw the horse-drawn trolley is indicative of Paul's consummate professionalism—he wants his work to be correct, and he'll fight for it. Quietly. Harris

Visions of Cody dust jacket by PB. (Author's collection)

Lewine calls him a "self-effacing fighter," an artist who was not schooled in any traditional manner but who emerged from the fine arts background of the times.

Take a look at Jack Kerouac's *Visions of Cody*. What sets the design apart, what makes it a Paul Bacon design, is his understanding of the book, his presentation of Jack Duluoz and Cody Palmer in a seamless linear landscape that begins with the spine and continues across the front of the book. Lester and Billy, a diner, automobiles, the two main characters, and the record label for the Musicraft release of Dizzy Gillespie's "Groovin' High," which presumably both characters were. Or look at the leaning trumpet player on the cover of Ross Russell's *The Sound*. Someone once said, "You can't judge a book by its cover, but they clearly hadn't seen Paul Bacon's dust jacket for *Visions of Cody*."

What about his other primary design activity, covers for 78 rpm albums and LPs, as well as CD booklets? Paul's other artistic jazz life was in full bloom for a dozen years, roughly 1947 to 1959, hibernated for a few years, and then took off again in the mid-1980s. It would, of course, be possible to ask the same question about jazz musicians as about writers: What do the following two hun-

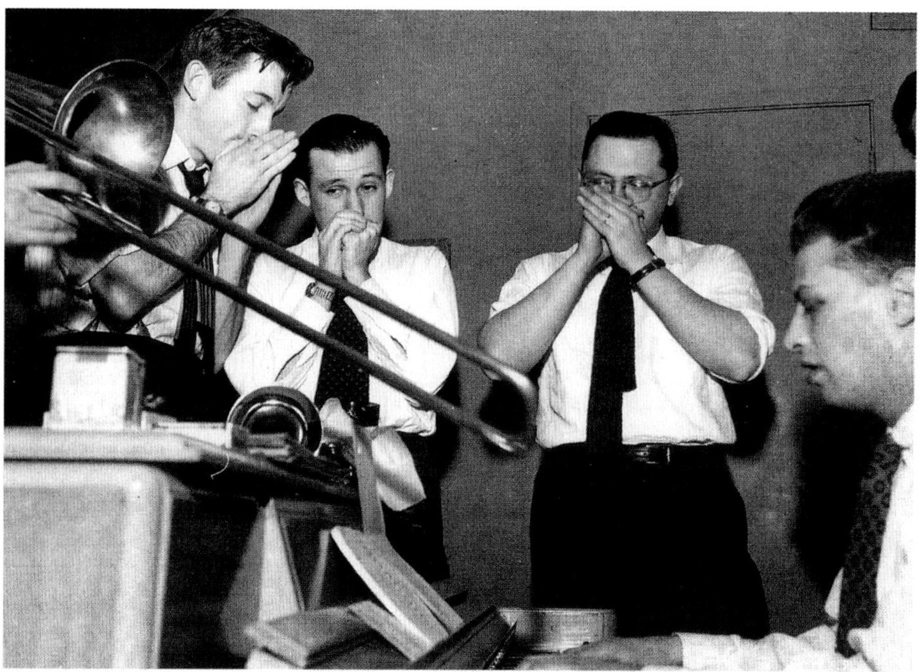

Conrad Janis, Paul Bacon, Orrin Keepnews, Bill Grauer, and Bob Greene. (Author's collection)

dred noted jazz artists have in common? It would be a laundry list of the great ones from the pioneers in New Orleans and Chicago to young artists of today. Or maybe the number is three hundred, but it doesn't matter. He did the work, remarkable work, creating designs that are the equal of his finest dust jackets. There is, however, one important difference: Paul knew and still knows many of the musicians. With the dust jackets it was them and us, but with musical projects and musicians it was us and us.

Orrin Keepnews tells the story of signing the legendary Thelonious Monk to Riverside. He and Bill Grauer made certain they took Paul along to the meeting. They knew (and knew Monk knew) that back in the 1940s when some of New York's alleged finest critics suggested that Monk should go downtown, against his wishes, Paul was one of the people who put up the money to gain his release. This is not to suggest that Monk signed with Riverside because of Paul's presence, but there was nothing wrong with the insurance—and Monk signed the contract.

Paul set standards for LP jacket design. He was, after all, there at the very beginning, and his work for Blue Note, Riverside, and RCA's label "X" has become as legendary as is the music released on those records. And what made his early work so remarkable was that he had a different signature style for three different companies—simultaneously.

A Paul Bacon Blue Note design was instantly recognizable in the early 1950s, as was one for Riverside or "X." Even a casual glance at a jacket in a bin at Sam Goody's, or even Big Joe's on Forty-Sixth Street, would say Paul Bacon, but it would also identify the company. Which was the idea, because even though the product issued by each company was jazz, it was often very different. And the same rule applies to the album covers as the books, he listened to them all. The main difference was that Thelonious Monk's *Mysterioso* LP required about forty minutes of listening, with repeated playing a distinct bonus, while three hundred ninety-eight pages of convoluted Kerouacian prose set in tiny type on the pages of *Visions of Cody* took a little longer to digest. Paul claims he read quickly. Not that quickly.

Then there's Paul's purely musical life, the life of a jazz musician playing the most lowly of instruments, a comb, amplified by a sheet of cellophane and a microphone. A certifiable genius like Thelonious Monk had a hard time finding gainful employment. What if you are an enthusiastic art director with a comb? It would, of course, be possible to make another list of musicians, equally long, though perhaps not quite as diverse, with whom Paul made music for half a century. In the dog-eat-dog world of live jazz he managed to survive with a hot comb and mostly sentimental vocals—just the right combination of sweet and hot. But his musical work paid few bills and was not particularly gainful. Thank goodness he had a day job and owned the studio. If there was a session and it had been a particularly good night, Paul could be grateful that, as he pulled himself off the bandstand just in time to make it to the office, the only person who could fire him was himself.

Paul was a tentative performer, and it all began with the same gang that revolved around the Newark Hot Club, *The Record Changer*, and the assorted record labels for which he produced album designs. Bill Grauer was the primary culprit. He organized regular Friday night musicales at the home of his wife's parents, 425 Riverside Drive (yes, that's where the name of the record company came from). Grauer was an unabashed champion of the comb as a hot jazz instrument. A small comb, a bit of cellophane, the ability to hum a tune, and a sense of rhythm and timing were all that was required.

Some people don't approve of the comb as an instrument, and before he began his career Paul Bacon was solidly in the anti-comb camp. He went to a musicale and "put up with this old-fashioned stuff sneering inwardly all the while, unwilling to do anything but observe." Then a funny thing happened. Grauer suggested he try it. He did, and he found he was a natural if there ever was one. He went every Friday night, creating musical mayhem with Grauer, Conrad Janis, and four guys named Bob: Greene on piano, Thompson on washboard, Sann on banjo, and Lee on jug. The Hot Club of Riverside Drive was often overloaded with combs, but all the participants had a little more hair in those days and kept one handy. On at least one occasion Orrin joined Paul and Bill for a comb trio, and complaints were heard as far away as the Jersey shore.

As time passed Paul got a little serious about his music making and even appeared on a record in 1951; four selections with cornet player Carl Halen, which were eventually released on Riverside. In his own words: "I sang on 'Heebie Jeebies' and 'Dr. Jazz.' They didn't let me sing on 'Willie the Weeper' or 'Cake Walking Babies from Home.' I got paid $5.00 for bull frogging it. There was only one microphone at the little Columbia University studio and I had to stand on a wastebasket to get close enough to it to be heard."

Then there was The Washboard Five, and The Hot Damn Jug Band of New York, and much traveling in search of musical activity (in and out of New York City, but rarely much further than New Jersey or Connecticut). By the late 1950s, however, the Paul Bacon studio was much expanded, there were seven employees, and with the added responsibility, Paul cut back on his musical activities. But he always kept his comb in his pocket, ready for action either improvised or loosely scheduled.

A most pleasant bit of musical action occurred in the 1960s when he found himself at the justifiably legendary Earthquake McGoon's in San Francisco. "Turk Murphy was playing 'Shake That Thing' and somehow I got the courage to let him know I had a comb and he asked me to sit in. When we finished he said, 'Don't go away' and then Clancy Hayes came over and said, 'I thought everybody in the Mound City Blue Blowers was dead.' We played for the rest of a great night."

Bob Greene rekindled Paul's interest in live performance in 1976 when he put together a band he called The World of Jelly Roll Morton, a group that recorded for RCA Victor and was scheduled to perform in Carnegie Hall. And so Paul and his comb and supply of cellophane wound up on the stage of that hallowed hall and he never looked back.

In 1980 another friend, Charlie Sonnanstine, told him about a band that was being organized to play straight New Orleans jazz just for fun. A bit later came the chance to play at The Cajun, a New Orleans–style restaurant in New York City. The job was to last eight weeks, but in one form or another it has lasted nearly two decades. Tuesday nights at The Cajun with Stanley's Washboard Kings often is musical magic. The small bandstand comfortably holds about seven guys, but I've seen as many as fourteen crowded into the space. On the right night, it's as good as anything in town, and there's some pretty good stuff in this town.

Paul is a modest guy. He doesn't say much about himself, and my guess is there are two main reasons he doesn't. One is there's just too much to remember, and if you focus excessively on your past achievements, there probably won't be many in the future. Equally important, he learned long ago that while you're talking it's difficult to do anything else. And in an ever-lengthening career, which so far has merrily combined literature and music for six decades, there is still much to do. His pen and comb are still poised ready for action. If you live long enough, are creative enough, and keep your wits in order you can accomplish a great deal. Paul isn't inclined to ramble on, he once wrote the barest of biographic details about himself onto scraps of paper purloined from an unsuspecting West Coast innkeeper. A barely adequate Aubrey-like *Brief Lives* entry.

Thelonious Monk Orchestra at Town Hall LP jacket by PB. (Author's collection)

1985 Floating Jazz Festival poster by PB. (Author's collection)

A Vision Shared dust jacket by PB. (Author's collection)

1995 Oscar Peterson Tribute poster by PB. (Author's collection)

The foregoing offers a few more details, but the following outlines for those who are concerned a few biographical specifics taken from the two scraps of paper he once gave me:

> *Paul Bacon was born on Christmas Day in 1923. The Bacon family is very old and dates back to 1640, with Michael Bacon in the Dedhem, Massachusetts. The family grew, parts of it prospered and others didn't. A few members achieved some success in fields as diverse as civil service, architecture, growing roses, or even acclaim in book jacket design. Paul was educated at various schools and finally graduated from Newark New Jersey's Arts High School in 1940. After a couple years of seasoning, he joined the Marine Corps in April 1943 and remained with this organization, visiting assorted Pacific and Far Eastern locations, until April 1946. He returned to New York City and got busy with his pencil and a comb.*

Paul's career can, of course, come crashing down in a moment if the Internet makes books redundant, CDs become microchips that don't need booklets, lawsuits force cigarette manufacturers to cease using cellophane, and Speert stops making nifty combs. All very unlikely, at least for the time being. It's been a good ride, Heller and Hellman in the morning, Morton and Monk at night. And even if the Testrossa didn't make it out of the garage, the clunks that did are still chugging along just fine.

More recently, I wrote the following:

I don't remember when I first met Paul. I'm pretty sure it was in late 1975 or early 1976, because St. Martin's Press had decided to go all out with my new book, *A Vision Shared,* and hire the most prominent book jacket designer in New York to do the job. I didn't make the connection at first, that the Paul Bacon who was doing my dust jacket was the same person who'd done all the X, Riverside, and Blue Note covers I'd been collecting and looking at since the mid-1950s, but I figured it out pretty quick. And now as I look back on it, I think we connected about twenty years earlier. This is the story.

In January 2025 it is sometimes a struggle to make my way to the Metropolitan Opera or Carnegie Hall or The Blue Note or The Jazz Gallery, but sixty-six years ago, it was nothing for me to make my way from Troy, New York, to Town Hall in New York City in the middle of the winter, February 28, 1959, to be exact, to sit in the balcony to hear The Thelonious Monk Orchestra in concert. If I'd known Riverside Records was recording the concert and planned to release a record I still would have made the trip.

I remember almost nothing about the trip to New York or my return to the undoubtedly snowed-in and frozen-in Troy, but I do remember bits and pieces of the concert, that the quartet played the first half and the orchestra played the second and I remember the "encore" performance of "Little Rootie Tootie." Someone, possibly even Orrin Keepnews, announced they were repeating the song because of recording difficulties. But I don't remember if I was sitting next to Paul Bacon or even the photographer who took the photograph Paul later used on the album cover. It was taken from the balcony, maybe from about the same place I was sitting.

The old circa 1960 stereo LP of the concert still sits on a shelf at 830 Broadway. I was proud when I bought it because I could say, "I'm on this record!" The CD reissue pales by comparison. It does have the extra "Little Rootie Tootie," but the colors on the booklet are wrong, the cover photograph is out of focus, and both Monk and Pepper Adams are partially or mostly missing. Paul would have been horrified. I often wondered if Paul is also on the record, cheering Monk on and thinking about how he might design the LP jacket. It seems likely that he was there since he'd been a serious Monk fan for over a decade. I've also wondered what happened to the first half of the concert? I can't imagine Orrin passing up a chance to record the quartet in Town Hall.

And then time passed. I lost track of Paul until the mid-1980s. I saw him at The Cajun, we began to see each other for an occasional lunch, and then in 1985 I needed a special design for *The Floating Jazz Festival* and asked Paul to come up with one. He did, and it was so good we decided to not just use it as a logo but to create a poster, a book, and even a special drumhead using Paul's design, a Phil Woods look-alike Merman, playing an alto saxophone.

As years passed, Paul incorporated the little Merman into other posters and designs. Then, beginning in 1989 Paul became our poster designer-in-chief and created posters and programs for *The Floating Jazz Festival* and its offshoots until the last festival in 2002. He also designed all the posters and programs for seven sailings of *The Blues Cruise*, and *Western Swing at Sea*.

Chiaroscuro booklet cover designs

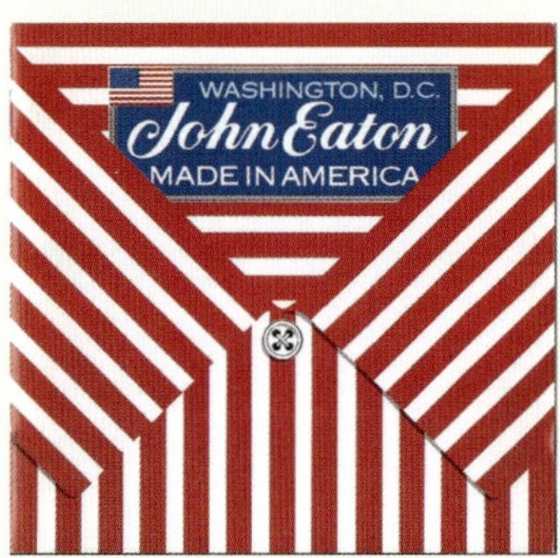

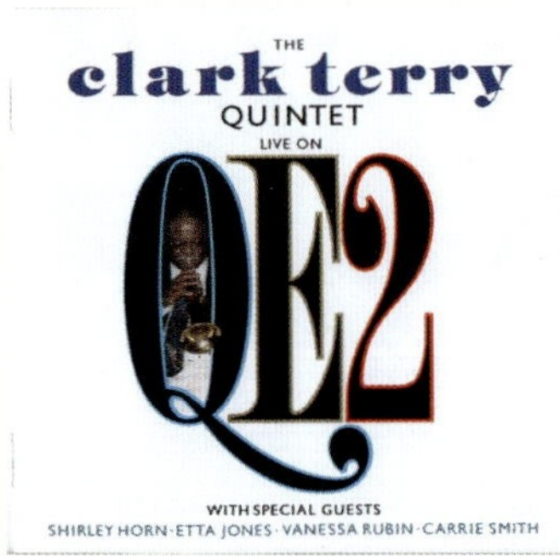

Eight Chiaroscuro CD booklets designed by PB.

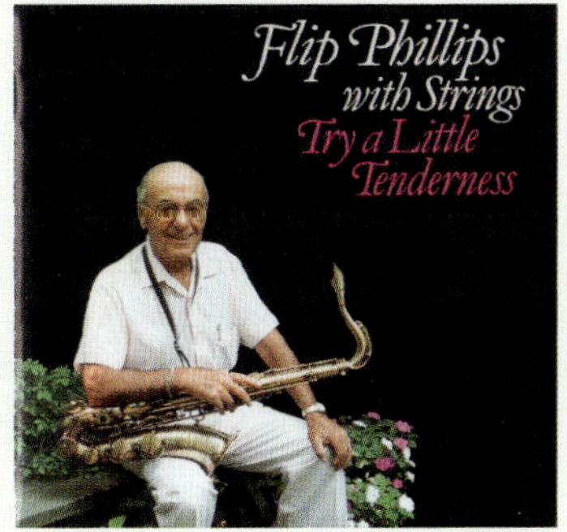

Eight Chiaroscuro CD booklets designed by PB.

Three Floating Jazz Festival posters designed by Paul Bacon. (Author's collection)

The Chiaroscuro reissue. (Author's collection)

Paul Bacon's first CD booklet cover design. (Author's collection)

The Ghosts of Harlem dust jacket by PB. (Author's collection)

When Andy Sordoni and I reacquired Chiaroscuro from AudioFidelity Enterprises in 1987, we knew we could use our old covers from the analog LP era, but we planned many new recordings that would be issued as CDs, and in those days all CDs had booklets that would need covers. Paul did his first for us in 1989, John Eaton's *Indiana on Our Minds,* and over the next twenty years he did thirty-five more. He almost did thirty-six.

In the 1990s Paul recorded seventeen songs with a band led by the pianist Keith Ingham and issued it privately as *Girl Crazy* because each selection on the CD was named after a girl, "Mary," "Ida," "Margie," etc. It was and is a charming recording, but it languished after Paul's death in 2015. Chiaroscuro picked it up and reissued it as CR(D) 379 in 2021, and all those girls immortalized in the songs Paul chose are smiling.

And when not designing posters and programs and CD booklets, Paul designed a spectacular poster and program for *Enter the Guardsman*, Shelley Shier's initial production for her company, Broadway Bound. When it was time to issue my book, *The Ghosts of Harlem*, in an English-language edition, Paul got the call, and this led to another notch on his legends list.

The publisher, Vanderbilt University Press, loved Paul's dust jacket design and after the book was published decided to do a little additional marketing. Their head marketeer called and asked the name of the typeface Paul had used for the cover; they wanted to use it in the marketing campaign. I had to explain it was a unique typeface, one that Paul had designed and created by hand for this dust jacket. He was incredulous.

In 2020, possibly the last Paul Bacon dust jacket appeared. Maybe another will turn up, but I'm not holding my breath because this one was at least twenty-five years old. In the early 1990s I wrote a book based on my teenage correspondence with the legendary baseball player Ty Cobb. The book is called *Sincerely, Ty Cobb,* and Paul designed a terrific dust jacket. But the book wasn't published for any number of reasons, and then in 2020 it was, with Paul's original dust jacket perfectly reproduced from the original artwork. It looked wonderful but probably sold fewer copies than Paul's first, *Chimp on My Shoulder,* from 1949.

Other than Paul Bacon, I have never been privileged to know anyone who had read and understood over seven thousand books. And it is possible the number is many more than seven thousand, because I'm sure Paul read many before he began designing dust jackets in 1949 and after that didn't restrict himself to just Doctorow, Kerouac, and Heller. Just like he didn't restrict his listening to what he'd first heard as scratchy shellac 78rpm records spun by his Newark Hot Club pals in 1940. He was lucky, just as I was lucky.

Before Paul went off to the Pacific and wandered around during World War II, he could hear first generation traditionalists and mainstreamers and the beginnings and evolution of bebop uptown and downtown and did. Just as I was able to hear all kinds of jazz on the first two 12" LPs I owned in 1955, Columbia's *I Like Jazz* which covered ragtime to Rugolo and everything in between and *Jazz of Two Decades* on Emarcy, that presented a sampling of the best of the past twenty years. And we talked about that, and I listened carefully to what he said for about three decades and learned a lot, as did anyone who was lucky enough to be in his presence for a minute or two and pay attention.

Sincerely, Ty Cobb dust jacket by Paul Bacon. (Author's collection)

Americans in Paris

3

Tony Bennett

(August 23, 1926 – July 21, 2023)

Saturday, January 18, 1969

It started over half a century ago. That's a long time no matter who's counting, and it was all because the crooked and soon to be disgraced, resigned, and convicted Spiro Agnew was having a party or a ball or a celebration of some sort at that old armory or field house that was on the other side of the parking lot near the stadium where once upon a time the Washington "formerly Redskins" played their home games for their legions of fans in Washington, DC.

Tricky was due to get inaugurated on the twentieth, that was a Monday, and we'd arrived in Washington on Saturday afternoon. It had already been a long, long weekend. On Friday night I had to take care of a roomful of musicians that included Eddie Condon and Gene Krupa, and the next day I managed to get myself together to drive Eddie, his wife, Phyllis, and my longtime girlfriend, Marilynn Danitz, to 3900 Watson Place NW. The four of us had permission from Squirrel Ashcraft to camp out at his then empty four in one apartment until all of the Inaugural Balls had concluded and we could get it together to return to New York City.

Why were we going to one of Richard Nixon's big parties? Simple. A couple of months earlier Eddie had learned they were going to have a couple of jazz bands for the inaugural celebrations, he wanted to be one of them, dropped a dime (or maybe it was a quarter by then), spoke to Bill Hearst (Patty's daddy) who was arranging the balls for Tricky and he hired Eddie on the spot. I had the key to Squirrel's apartment, knew how to reach him in Spain to get permission, and a car to take us there.

I was ready to give up for the day and looked forward to a soft bed and softer girl, but about 6:30 or 7:00 Eddie wandered in from his wing of Ashcraft Towers, all tuxedoed up and ready to go. He seemed puzzled I wasn't dressed as nicely as he and asked why. I probably said something like, "Why should I dress up to take my clothes off to go to bed, which is where I am heading." He probably replied something like, "Because we're going to Spiro Agnew's ball."

My feeling was I'd rather have an empty bed of thorns than have anything to do with Spiro Agnew. I told Eddie I was exhausted because of not getting any sleep for two days, I had to run a recording session the next day, and so I had to pass on the soon-to-be felon's ball. He should go and have a good time. Eddie was only sixty-four at the time and hadn't slept much himself, but when there was the likelihood of not only a convivial gathering of his pals but that one of the pals had brought a couple of pounds of smoking material to Mr. Law & Order's ball, there was a strong motivation to attend. Eddie said something like, "OK, I'll just go get a cab," and left. I headed to the kitchen to see if Claudine, the most loyal and thoughtful of maids, had left any edible treats in the fridge.

3900 Watson Place NW was and is in a lovely residential neighborhood near the National Cathedral, where Squirrel would have his memorial service a dozen years later. But it is not a neighborhood in which one will be able

OPPOSITE
Tony Bennett in his studio with self-portrait. (Author's collection)

to hail a cab. Eddie came back looking forlorn and said there were no cabs and asked if I would drive him to the ball, that I was also on the list. I agreed but told him I wasn't changing clothes and sticking around. And how would he get home? He wasn't worried about that; he'd found a way for half a century. So we headed to the ballroom next to the football field.

We arrived, and there were plenty of spots to park since the former Redskins weren't playing that night. I walked Eddie over to an entrance where a ramrod-straight secret servicer said we had to go to an entrance around the corner. I was dressed as I had been the day before but my attire, as well as myself, was one day more rumpled. An overused, ill-fitting car coat with pockets filled with gloves and a scarf, some kind of a cap, no jacket or tie, old blue jeans, and so forth. But Eddie looked sharp and was ready for action.

At the next gate the guard looked puzzled but said to go to the next gate a few yards away. We went in the door with Eddie in the lead and were stopped by another ramrod-straight youngish secret servicer who asked Eddie for his name. "Eddie Condon," he said. He may have added, "And this is Hank O'Neal." Then the guard asked Eddie for identification, Eddie paused and thought about it for a moment and then took off his hat and pointed to his name embossed in gold on the inside of his hat. The young secret servicer had never been shown this kind of identification, and he had no idea what to do, other than possibly call in reinforcements and escort us both to the parking lot. But the Central Intelligence Agency saved the day.

It was against all the rules to use CIA credentials for non-governmental purposes but to me this was a governmental purpose: If Spiro's ball wasn't the governmental event of the evening, what was? I grabbed my credential out of my pocket, showed it to the young agent, saying, "Excuse me, sir, this is me and this is Mr. Condon, and he has been invited to this function and would like to attend. And I'd like to be on my way and attend to other business."

Perhaps he thought I was under deep cover when the only other business with which I was concerned was getting under some as soon as I got back to the Towers and under some more inviting warm and cuddly covers. But just as all this was taking place, Bobby Hackett and his band as well as Tony Bennett, whom he was accompanying, walked by. Bobby yelled something like, "Hi Eddie, hi Hank!" Eddie was admitted to the largest smoking room in Washington, and I set a speed record from the parking lot to 3900.

Sunday, January 19, 1969

There were probably twenty telephones in Squirrel's expansive apartment, and one was ringing much too early on Sunday morning. After a dozen rings or so I grabbed it and mumbled something and an immediately recognizable voice on the other end was asking, "Where am I?" It was Eddie and he was unsure where he was; he only knew he had a telephone in his hand, was a bit worse for wear, and could use a drink. I decided to deal with the first question. I said, "Eddie, look at the telephone, does it have a number on it? You're probably in a hotel somewhere, read me all the numbers." I was right; he read me the two numbers. The first one had a 703 prefix. He was in a hotel in Virginia, I had the number and the room in which he was freeloading. I said to hang up and I'd call him right back. He did. I called. It was at the Key Bridge Marriott, the operator rang the room number, Eddie answered and I said, "Don't move, stay where you are," but Eddie said, "Where can I get a drink?" I said, "Eddie, you are in Virginia; Virginia is dry on Sunday. You are out of luck." He then said, "Bring me something from Squirrel's cabinet."

I took a quick shower, gathered up what I needed for the recording session, filled a 7-Up bottle with vodka, corked it with a rubbed stopper, and headed to the Key Bridge Marriott. It was a short drive, then I found a parking spot and headed to the room from which Eddie had called, only to find it empty except for a sound asleep Bobby Hackett. I was glad that when I was in his company he usually was making beautiful sounds with his cornet. I retreated to the hallway, found a chambermaid and asked if she'd seen a well-dressed man wandering aimlessly in the hallway and she pointed to an open door a few steps away. I walked to the open door, peered in, and saw Eddie holding assorted bottles of liquid nourishment and speaking with someone out of view. At some point Eddie slowed down for a minute, noticed me in the doorway, and said, "Get in here, I want to introduce you to someone."

I did as I was told, and the someone was Tony Bennett, wearing very little. And that was my first meeting with Tony, who was gracious and welcoming, despite his lack of formal attire. I seem to recall Eddie was telling some kind of a joke about liberating the bottles he was holding. After we laughed a bit and said nothing for a couple of minutes, we exited with Eddie well-armed to face the day that was just beginning.

The chore for the day was to produce a record featuring Don Ewell as a solo pianist in Manassas, Virginia. I had to pick up Don and then drive to the tiny town where the

With Wayne Wright, Ruby Braff, John Giuffrida, and George Barnes at WARP/Downtown Sound in 1973 (Author's collection)

battles of Bull Run were once fought a hundred or more years earlier, but on that January 19th day, the only thing under attack was to be a perfectly tuned Steinway D resting in the middle of the stage of a high school auditorium. Don was the only soldier, and he was armed with extraordinary talent and a list of a dozen tunes he wanted to put down for posterity.

Eddie had adjourned to the back seat where he could stretch out and enjoy his morning libation. Don was sitting up front, next to me. At some point Don decided he might need a little help and asked Eddie to pass the Scotch he'd liberated from Tony in his direction. Eddie did, and Don took a big gulp. As he passed the bottle back to Eddie, he said how strong it was and he "needed some wash." He spotted the bottle of 7-Up in my pocket, perfect "wash" he instantaneously surmised, grabbed it, and before I could do anything since I was watching the road, took another enormous gulp, this time of vodka. He was surprised and quiet for the rest of the trip. I do not recall if Eddie broke into song.

We arrived at the school and made our way to the backstage area of the auditorium. Don didn't linger, he walked past the piano without so much as a glance, stopped at the edge of the stage, and hurled the Scotch and vodka combo onto the floor in front of him. This was disconcerting to the dozen or so people who had come to the recording session. Fortunately, the recording gear had been set up elsewhere.

Don made his way to the piano, sat down, and rested for a moment. I asked him to play a little so I could test levels and possibly move microphones around. And then he began to play for real and was flawless. Each song was a minor masterpiece, even the Earl Hines medley, where the competition was kind of tough. It turned out to be the first record I'd ever organized that received a five-star

Formal attire in case the cameras rolled. (Author's collection)

Not so formal. (Author's collection)

review in *Downbeat* magazine but it wasn't for my label, because I didn't have one yet. Close but no cigar.

When Don's last notes were fading away, he left the piano smiling, the massive Steinway D had performed perfectly and was probably very pleased with itself. But before I turned off the machines, Eddie said, "Keep it on," and he went to the piano and played a short piece he called "Don't You Realize," a little recorded present for our host in Washington, Squirrel Ashcraft. When he hit the last note he turned around and looked at me and said, "That's the best thing you ever recorded in your whole life!" Maybe, maybe not, but certainly the most unusual.

Throughout July, August, and September 1973

I didn't see Tony for a few years, but then in 1973 our paths began to cross, often in unusual ways, and it was all because a film producer, Elliott Kastner, wanted to make a documentary film to be titled *This Funny World.* I had an inexpensive recording studio that was well-known and approved of by Ruby Braff, whose funny world also included Tony Bennett, the other star of Kastner's documentary, and Ruby brought Tony by, who also felt comfortable in my low-key, low-cost studio. And so they rehearsed and relaxed for the next couple of months.

Tony was working with the Ruby Braff/George Barnes Quartet, perhaps the finest "new" mainstream group to be organized and recorded in the early 1970s. I had actually recorded them in July 1973 for what would become my twenty-first release later that year, and Tony was so impressed with the group he wanted to record with them as well. I took pictures of Tony and the group, and Tony made sketches of them as they played, one of which I used on the back of my record.

Tony also had a concert appearance scheduled later in the year. In fact, everyone was impressed; they had a run at the Rainbow Room and George Wein had presented them at a Newport in New York concert in July. In Tony's own words:

> *My main focus in late 1973 became the brilliant trumpet playing of Ruby Braff. I'd known Ruby since 1951 when I first played Chicago. Ruby heard George Barnes and Bucky Pizzarelli playing at the St. Regis Hotel in New York, and he sat in with the two guitarists. He loved the way that combination sounded and suggested to George that they start a group. They gradually worked out a lineup of two guitars, a trumpet, and a bass. When I heard about this group, I had to check them out. I thought they were great, and Ruby said to me, "Why don't you come and sing a couple of tunes with us, and relax for a while, you know?" I was singing almost exclusively with big bands then, and even with a good sound system I always had to belt it out to be heard above the music.*
>
> *I liked the groove I got into with this intimate group so much that I did two special concerts with them at Alice Tully Hall in New York. Ruby and George played the first half instrumentally, and then I came out in the second half and sang with them—two entire evenings of Rodgers and Hart. Two weeks later I recorded twenty-four Rodgers and Hart songs with Ruby and George, with Frank Laico as engineer. It was later released as* Tony Bennett: The Rodgers and Hart Songbook.

To backtrack a little, in the early 1970s, after Tony had left Columbia, he formed his own record company with a Buffalo-based businessman, Bill Hassett. The label was called Improv, and over the course of four years or so they released some wonderful records. Tony's justly famous collaborations with Bill Evans were highlights, but so were the two he made with the Ruby Braff/George Barnes Quartet.

With Earl Hines at WARP/Downtown Sound.
(Author's collection)

CBS RECORDS RECORDING STUDIOS TAPE DATA SHEET Safety filed under 116785

NOTE: Complete this form. Secure to box containing tape described hereon.

PROJECT NUMBER | STUDIO | JOB NUMBER 228346 | REEL | SPEED 15"

DATE | SHEET NUMBER | PROGRAM Tony Bennett - Rogers + Hart | MONO | 8 TRACK

[x] NEW YORK | CHICAGO | CLIENT Tobill Records | [x] 2 TRACK | 16 TRACK

HOLLYWOOD | SAN FRAN. | PRODUCER | 3 TRACK | DOLBY

NASHVILLE | OTHER | CO. ENG. | RE. ENG. | 4 TRACK | OTHER

TIME	MASTER NUMBER	PROGRAM TITLE	TAKE NO.	CODES	TIME MARK
		Side II		Spiral	
2:40		1. Spring Is Here			
3:18		2. Have You Met Miss Jones			2:40
3:20		3. Isn't It Romantic?			6:01
1:24		4. Wait Till You See Her			9:24
3:09		5. I Could Write A Book			10:51
					Total 14:04
		Scribe IMP 7113 B			

** TIME START AT MARK 000,00 — FILE — HOLD — PICK UP — SHIP

* CODES: V = FALSE START, b = SHORT FALSE START, B = LONG FALSE START, C = COMPLETE TAKE, © = MASTER

CR 724 REV 6/71

One of the master tapes left at WARP/Downtown Sound. (Author's collection)

And so there was a great deal going on at WARP, soon to become Downtown Sound. Tony was rehearsing for upcoming concerts, recording sessions, and documentary filming. I witnessed everything that happened in my studio, attended the concerts in Alice Tully Hall, and took a lot of photographs documenting the rehearsing and relaxing of all the musicians scheduled to perform and a number who just happened to turn up. Like Earl Hines and Ray Nance.

I was told that Elliott Kastner actually filmed Tony and the group on Christopher Street going to the studio, but I never saw any footage. He never filmed anything at my studio. He also allegedly filmed at least one of the Alice Tully Hall concerts, but I never saw that footage and I've never spoken with anyone who has. Though many people far smarter and aggressive than I have searched for it, not a frame of film has been found as far as I know. Presumably, all the footage for this never-to-be-completed documentary is lost. Elliott Kastner was a brilliant if erratic producer and though he completed many fine films the list of those that were incomplete or still-born is long.

All of this activity is thoroughly documented in Thomas Hustad's bio/discography of Ruby Braff, in which he states:

> *Album notes to CR 121 also report a film featuring Tony Bennett with the group "should be in full production" by the release of this album, produced by Elliott Kastner. Portions of this production were filmed at Madison Square Garden (the Honeydreamers Ball in New York), Buffalo, New York (both at a concert and during a two week*

Relaxing during a rehearsal break at WARP/Downtown Sound in 1973. (Author's collection).

engagement at the Buffalo Hilton Hotel) and Alice Tully Hall at Lincoln Center in NYC (September 14 and 15, 1973). Tony Bennett presumably still owns the film, which has never been released. It was originally developed as a potential 90-minute television special . . .

At 3 p.m., the day prior to the upcoming programs at Alice Tully Hall, Tony Bennett held a rehearsal with the Ruby Braff – George Barnes Quartet in a studio on Christopher Street.

The quartet opened a concert at Alice Tully Hall in Lincoln Center to a packed house with one hour of Rodgers and Hart tunes. Tony Bennett joined the quartet to sing 21 Rodgers and Hart tunes . . . the ad indicates "Be in the Movies with Tony Bennett as both performances will be filmed."

One thing that did result from all this activity in the studio is that it led to Improv working out a distribution arrangement with AudioFidelity Enterprises, the company that was distributing Chiaroscuro at the time. They were no more successful with AFE than I was, but I did remain friendly with Bill Hassett long after he left the music business. Because Downtown Sound prepared some of their master tapes for release, they were stored at the studio. I recently came across a master safety of the album he did with Bill Evans. Why it wasn't returned when the Downtown Sound was closed is a mystery. It's an interesting souvenir, but I'm sure the CD reissue sounds better.

1981—1982

In 1981—82, when I was part of Hammond Music Enterprises, there were other opportunities to help one another. HME had a good distribution arrangement with CBS, and we had discussions about matters of mutual interest. CBS and Tony had gone separate ways a decade earlier. It was a big mistake on the part of CBS, but they didn't figure it out for a couple of decades. There were meetings and meetings, but nothing developed, other than Tony and his son Danny attending some HME meet and greet fundraising events. But prior to one of the meetings, I met Tony at his apartment. He was living at 101 West Fifty-Fifth at the corner of Sixth Avenue. This was the first time I visited with him uptown; everything else had been downtown at my old studio or in neutral venues. This visit was when I first became aware he not only sketched but painted as well. He was working on a large painting that depicted a view out his window, looking south. Avenue of the Americas was filled with yellow taxis, a theme he's returned to on many occasions.

January 1992

As the 1980s slid into the 1990s, Tony's career blossomed under the continued sound guidance of his son Danny, and as much as we would have enjoyed having Shelley Shier be part of one of our festivals, he couldn't give up the time. One night maybe, but a week was out of the question. Shelley Shier did engage him for one night in San Francisco for a special event at the Fairmont Hotel's Venetian Room in January 1992, a fancy one-nighter on January 4th. I hadn't seen him for five or six years, but he was still the same, easygoing, traveling light, throw-a-garment-bag-over-his-shoulder-and-go Tony. It was a great show, and less than a week later Shelley and I met up with him for a double date at Rainbow and Stars to hear the McGuire Sisters.

May 12, 2003

In 2003 I decided it might be a good idea to record John Bunch once again, and my idea was to dig into his past and do something a bit unusual. The idea was to record him doing updated nonvocal versions of many of the favorite songs he had done with Tony when he served as his music director in the 1960s and early 1970s. John thought it was a good idea, and we started picking tunes. He picked many of them with Tony, who by them was living just around the corner from NOLA Recording Studio, where we planned to do the recording. We released *Tony's Tunes* a few months later, and a drawing Tony had done of John in 1987 was featured on the cover booklet of the album. This is an excerpt of what I said in my producer notes in the same booklet: "John had called Tony to see if he wanted to drop by and hear what the group was doing to some of his favorite tunes, but when we finished Tony was still a no-show. We hung around for a little while after the session, maybe until 6:30 or 7:00; then we all went our separate ways. Tony showed up about 7:30, had a listen, liked what he heard and later, telephoned John and told him so. He said he'd also be honored to have his drawing of John on the cover of the CD booklet and so it is, making this project even more personal."

The booklet cover drawing by Tony for John Bunch CD. (Author's collection)

Window display for the exhibition of Tony's paintings. (Author's collection)

In discussion with Clint Eastwood at Mission Ranch. (Author's collection)

September 16–18, 2005 (and Beyond)

Then the 1990s slid into the 2000s, and success piled on top of success. While Tony was still Tony, his management often wasn't. In 2005, Tony was featured at the Monterey Jazz Festival and many of his paintings were exhibited at a charming gallery down the road in Carmel. It was a magnificent performance, and along the way, plans were set in motion for Clint Eastwood and Bruce Ricker to produce an American Masters film about Tony, one that I hoped would have a better outcome than Elliott Kastner's *This Funny World*.

The events leading up to the production made for a soap opera of monumental proportions, primarily because of Tony's management, but eventually the film was completed, successfully aired on PBS in September 2007 as *The Music Never Ends,* and released on DVD a few months later. Other than onstage, the film was largely made at Mission Ranch in Carmel and at 830 Broadway in New York City, mostly in 2007, where many of Tony's friends showed up to pay tribute, including Harry Belafonte, Alan and Marilyn Bergman, Mel Brooks, Bill Charlap, Ray Kinstler, Arthur Penn, and Jonathan Schwartz. We did Gay Talese at his home uptown, Martin Scorcese at DGA, and Don Rickles at Warner Bros. I was a fly on the wall behind a camera throughout the production and didn't run out of film.

After the concert in Monterey, during one of the few moments when he wasn't being handled, Tony said something like, "It's been a long time, hasn't it?" I nodded, we spoke for a couple of minutes, and then he was on his way. We got together a month or so after Monterey in October at the Metropolitan Museum of Art. The evening news wanted to film a segment about Tony's painting and where better than at the Met. There were many opportunities to take pictures of an old American master songsmith admiring old masters from centuries past.

We were together at the Newport Jazz Festival that summer and lots of pictures jumped into my camera, on stage and off.

The next time I saw him was in 2007 when the documentary was being finished up, first at his Central Park South apartment and then at his studio next door, where there wasn't a handler in sight. These days I'm pretty sure he's happier to have a paintbrush in his hand than a microphone. At least that's the way it looks in this photograph.

The Music Never Ends was screened at the Ziegfeld Theater on September 10th and premiered on PBS in the American Masters series on September 12th. It was well received, and no one was surprised by that.

Filming a news feature at The Metropolitan Museum of Art.
(Author's collection)

After the news feature at the Met.
(Author's collection)

At work in his home studio on Central Park South.
(Author's collection)

In discussion with George Wein at the Newport Jazz Festival. (Author's collection)

On stage with Lee Musiker at the Newport Jazz Festival. (Author's collection)

At work in his home studio on Central Park South. (Author's collection)

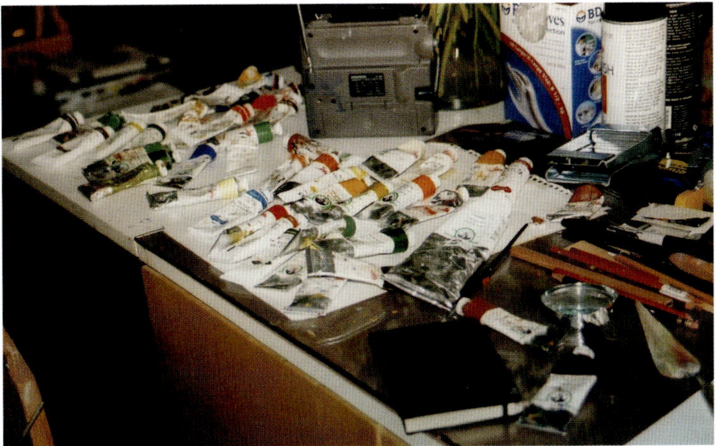
Tubes of paint at the ready. (Author's collection)

4

Eubie Blake

February 7, 1883 (?) – February 12, 1983

IN THE FALL OF 1968, Don Ewell and Willie "The Lion" Smith were holding forth at The Village Gate. I was always short of funds in those years. Normally, I couldn't afford to spend an evening at the Gate, but because Don Ewell was sleeping on my couch at the time and knew how to get the cover charge waived, as well placing my bar bill on his tab, I was able hang out and listen to the two giants go at it on an almost nightly basis.

I don't remember how long the duo performed at the Gate, but I remember a Saturday evening when something out of the ordinary happened. The place was crammed, and an enthusiastic audience urged Willie and Don to go at it well past the customary first set. Willie finally called a halt to the good-natured cutting and announced there was another great pianist in the house. High praise from The Lion. Willie said that Eubie Blake had agreed to play a couple of tunes during intermission and asked Eubie to the bandstand.

There was polite applause, but not much of it, and it's unlikely more than a handful of people in the room had even heard of Eubie. At the time, Eubie was about eighty-five years old, rarely played in public, and not well-known. I knew about him only because I had some of his old records, notably a late 1950s LP entitled *The Marches I Played on the Ragtime Piano*, but I had no idea he was still alive or could play at a serious level. I was in for a surprise.

A frail, stooped, bald, but well-dressed man walked slowly to the piano. He played something, I don't remember the first song, but it was greeted with the same polite applause as when he was announced. Then he spoke to the audience. His remarks were fun and entertaining, and at the end of his comments he said, "Now I want to play something I wrote in 1898." That seemed to get some attention, and Eubie launched into a rollicking version of the "Charleston Rag." He tore it up, and when this seemingly frail old man finished there was sustained applause.

Then he said something like, "Now I want to play something an American President used as his theme song." It was "I'm Just Wild About Harry." By this time, he had everyone's attention. Following "Harry," it was the longish, concert version of "Memories of You." When he finished, everyone was standing and cheering. Willie was off to one side, derby cocked, and beaming. Eubie retreated to his table, and the evening continued at a less emotional level.

One of the reasons I found the experience so interesting was that Eubie Blake was a "pre-jazz" artist. He was living in Baltimore in 1898 when he wrote "Charleston Rag" and didn't have any of the influences associated with New Orleans; Buddy Bolden was only twenty, King Oliver and Jelly Roll Morton were thirteen. Scott Joplin's "Maple Leaf Rag" wasn't published until 1899. Where did this man come from, I thought, and how could he still be playing so well?

OPPOSITE

Eubie Blake at the Top of the Gate, New York City, 1967. (Author's collection)

Nobel Sissle and Eubie at Columbia's
30th Street Studio. (Author's collection)

At the end of the next set, I asked Willie if he could please introduce me to Mr. Blake, which he did. I was very enthusiastic and told Eubie I'd never heard anything like what he'd just done, at least not from a living pianist. After a short conversation, he suggested I should come out and visit him at his home in Brooklyn. A few days later I found myself in front of 284A Stuyvesant Avenue, preparing to walk into another time and another world.

The Eighty Six Years of Eubie Blake LP.
(Author's collection)

I asked Eubie about many things, but the main thing I stressed that day was he should make a recording, maybe even a live recording, in front of a cheering audience. I'll never forget his response. It was something like, "You're the second white boy who's asked me to make a record this week." I asked who the other "white boy" was. He replied, "John Hammond." I said, "Mr. Blake, that's the white boy you should pay attention to." The rest of the time we spent together that first day was figuring out a way for him to sneak a cigarette away from his wife's prying nose. He managed by suggesting we take a walk around the block. Which we did, more than once.

LP jacket and liner photo for *Jazz Piano Masters* release in 1977. (Author's collection)

Once I was back in Manhattan, I telephoned John and told him about my meeting with Eubie. John said it was true. He wanted to record Eubie for Columbia but couldn't because the engineers were on strike, and no one could get any studio time. And he was terrified. Eubie was eighty-five years old, and even though he was playing very well, John was afraid he might die at any moment. I told John he shouldn't worry. I had a fine studio at my disposal, one with two excellent Steinway pianos, and I wasn't on strike. He asked, "Where?" I said, "At Sherman Fairchild's, 17 East Sixty-Fifth Street." John said if I could deliver the studio, he could deliver Eubie.

We both delivered the goods, and in late November everyone assembled at Sherman's home. By everyone I mean, John, Eubie, Noble Sissle, Marian McPartland, and Sherman himself. We recorded for two days and got good takes of seventeen songs, including two vocals with Nobel, his singer/song-writing partner. Then, in December, the striking engineers gave Columbia a Christmas present and returned to work, but there was such a backlog there was still no room for Eubie. Fate intervened when Vladimir Horowitz cancelled a recording scheduled for December 26th. Eubie took the slot and began the process that would eventually lead to *The Eighty-Six Years of Eubie Blake*. The recordings we made at Sherman's remain unissued, but since Sony seems disinclined to put Eubie back into the marketplace perhaps I should dust off the old tapes and get Eubie's other recordings issued.

Of course, to everyone's surprise, except Eubie, he had fourteen years to go, and I was able to work and socialize with him on many occasions. He was a frequent guest at Downtown Sound, and I featured him with Teddy Wilson, Claude Hopkins, and Dill Jones at a New School concert in 1972. Eubie stole the show, and no one was surprised. This was something he did on a regular basis for the better part of a decade. I wound up paying everyone once again in 1977 and releasing the concert as a Chiaroscuro LP in that year.

This is how I described Eubie's performance that night on the LP jacket:

> *And then, before John could even announce him, Eubie Blake, "the wonder of the ages," as John described him later that night, burst upon the stage. It was lucky Eubie went on last or no one else would have had a chance; you can't follow him because anyone following Eubie is anticlimactic and besides, he played twice as long as anyone else. He played joyously, with enthusiasm and vigor and the audience responded in kind. Perhaps it wasn't*

always so much fun for him, but in 1972, the opportunity to play before a few hundred students, whose grandparents weren't even born when he wrote his first song, was worth far more than the money he got for his night's enjoyment.

Earlier that year I recorded Eubie at an Overseas Jazz Club concert on February 7th, 1972. We recorded it because, at the request of the OPC, we were recording all the Overseas Jazz Club concerts at the time. It was a remarkable afternoon of music with Maxine Sullivan, Earl Hines, Billy Taylor, Jo Jones, and a number of others, and it's all on tape. There was an interchange between Earl Hines and Jo Jones that was simply outstanding. There was even a cake for Eubie, and I grabbed a picture of him cutting it.

Birthday bash in 1972 with Billy Taylor and Max Kaminsky in the background. (Author's collection)

Columbia's interest in their octogenarian was short-lived, but Eubie's cause was taken up by Carl Seltzer, a man who was even more enthusiastic about his playing than I. Carl went so far as to establish a record label, Eubie Blake Music, and released a number of fine LPs. I helped him as often as I could and was able to interact with Eubie a good deal. In 1977 I released about half of the New School concert, and then in 1999 the entire concert was released on a Chiaroscuro CD.

The first release on Eubie Blake Records. (Author's collection)

Eubie wasn't the finest pianist I ever heard, far from it, but a case could be made he was the most joyous. In his later years Artur Rubenstein missed a lot of notes, but there was nothing quite like being in his presence. Eubie was much the same. He'd tear into a run and get about 95 percent of it, but it was still wonderful because he was having so much fun getting the 95 percent.

During the 1970s, Eubie was very busy. He was a regular at various incarnations of George Wein's Newport Jazz Festival, either in New York or Newport. One of the most fascinating things involving Eubie was the resurrection and adaptation of *Shuffle Along*, his hit Broadway show from 1921. It was revived in 1978 and created enough positive buzz that an "adaptation" featuring twenty-one of Eubie's songs opened at the Ambassador Theater where it ran for 439 performances. There was a beautiful portrait of Eubie featured in the Playbill, taken by Tom Caravaglia. Two years later, when I moved to 830 Broadway, Tom turned out to be my downstairs neighbor. His portrait of Eubie was taken in his studio.

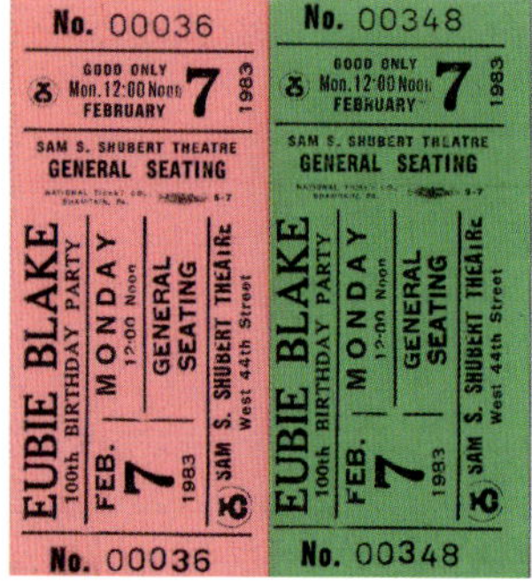

Two tickets to the "100th" birthday party at the Shubert Theater. (Author's collection)

At WARP/Downtown Sound in 1974. (Author's collection)

In 2016 *Shuffle Along* appeared once again, not with its original title, but with one that could have won the Tony for longest Title of a Broadway Musical: *Shuffle Along, or the Making of the Musical Sensation of 1921 and All That Followed.* It was also widely praised, and tickets were hard to find because of the music and the stars who had been assembled to sing the songs, multiple Tony winners Audra McDonald, Brian Stokes-Mitchell, and Billy Porter. But the show only ran for four months because Audra McDonald had to withdraw due to an unexpected pregnancy.

But Eubie wasn't done. In October 1981, he was awarded the Medal of Freedom in a ceremony at the White House and made his last professional appearance in 1982, one week before his ninety-ninth birthday. Then he slowed down a little.

The last time I heard Eubie was in the Shubert Theater on February 7th, 1983. It was allegedly his one-hundredth birthday celebration. Eubie was in ill health; he had a bit of pneumonia he'd picked up during an appearance in Washington, DC, a few weeks earlier, but he was part of the proceedings via a telephone hook-up. He heard everything and made a little speech at one point. A thousand or so of his friends crammed into the theater that day, and one great artist after another performed. Fifteen years earlier I'd seen a frail looking Eubie Blake wipe up Don Ewell and Willie The Lion, at least in terms of audience approval. Had he been at the Shubert, he'd have found a way to wipe up everyone there, and just as Willie stood there beaming at The Village Gate, it would have been all smiles at the Shubert.

There was always a bit of confusion about Willie's birthday; not the day, the year. February 7th was etched in stone; 1883 and 1887 were less solid. But February 12th, 1983, was for real. It should be noted, *The New York Times*, the "paper of record," elected to go with 1883, with the headline:

> ***EUBIE BLAKE, RAGTIME COMPOSER, DIES 5 DAYS AFTER 100TH BIRTHDAY***

And that's good enough for me.

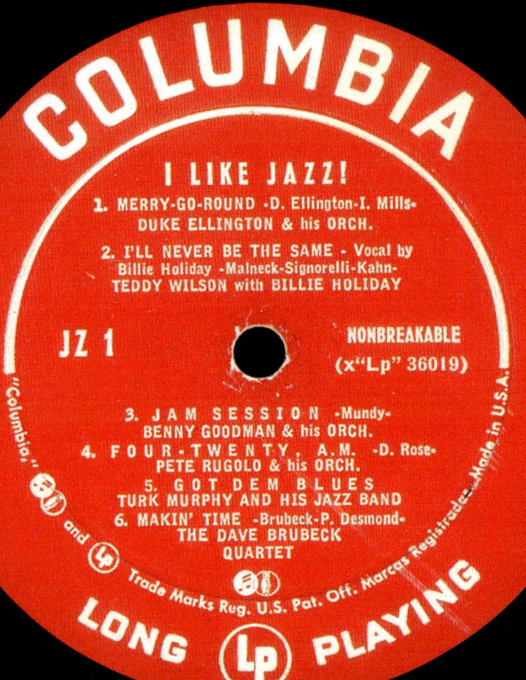
COLUMBIA
I LIKE JAZZ!
1. MERRY-GO-ROUND -D. Ellington-I. Mills-
DUKE ELLINGTON & his ORCH.
2. I'LL NEVER BE THE SAME - Vocal by
Billie Holiday -Malneck-Signorelli-Kahn-
TEDDY WILSON with BILLIE HOLIDAY
JZ 1
NONBREAKABLE
(x"Lp" 36019)
3. JAM SESSION -Mundy-
BENNY GOODMAN & his ORCH.
4. FOUR-TWENTY, A.M. -D. Rose-
PETE RUGOLO & his ORCH.
5. GOT DEM BLUES
TURK MURPHY AND HIS JAZZ BAND
6. MAKIN' TIME -Brubeck-P. Desmond-
THE DAVE BRUBECK
QUARTET
"Columbia," and Lp Trade Marks Reg. U.S. Pat. Off. Marcas Registradas Made in U.S.A.
LONG Lp PLAYING

I LIKE JAZZ!
Lp

5

Dave Brubeck

December 6, 1920 – December 5, 2012

THE FIRST TIME I HEARD Dave Brubeck it cost a dollar, the second time it may have cost twice that much, and the third time it was free. The last time I heard him it was also free; an hour or so ago I played the DVD of the film about Dave I worked on with Clint Eastwood and Bruce Ricker. There were fifty-seven years of good listening and fine times in between, and a decade worth of listening to CDs and LPs and watching DVDs since his death in 2012.

Dave Brubeck was featured on the very first 12" LP I ever owned. He may well have been the first noted jazz artist I ever heard in person, sometime in 1956, but this is a bit unclear since I saw two other concerts that year and I don't remember which was the first. Fifty years later, in the summer of 2006, I heard him on four occasions, and he was just as exciting and musically adventurous. We were in touch frequently at the end of the decade when working on "In His Own Sweet Way," and I heard him a couple of times in 2010, but there were only telephone conversations in 2011 and 2012 until that final visit a few days before his death. From a personal standpoint, I find this remarkable. I began listening to jazz seriously over half a century ago and find myself still listening carefully to Dave Brubeck. This is how it came about.

That first record was a Columbia sampler called *I Like Jazz*, and it cost one dollar, which is why I could afford it. George Avakian's coherent notes discussed various kinds of jazz, ragtime, blues, swing, and progressive; he illustrated each style with one song. The other pianists who turned up were Wally Rose, Teddy Wilson, and Duke Ellington. The "modern" jazz example was *Makin' Time*, and Dave Brubeck was the featured artist. It was recorded in October 1954; the *I Like Jazz LP* came out a little later, in 1955.

In the notes, George said, *Despite his adherence to high standards, he has not been rejected by audiences; on the contrary, he is currently the biggest attraction in the jazz night spots in addition to being the recording industry's No. 1 jazz artist.*

I liked what I heard, but I also enjoyed Wally, Duke, and Teddy. At the time they were just as alive and active as Dave Brubeck. Maybe they weren't "No. 1", but to a novice, they all sounded pretty good. The thing that was nice about George's sampler was he presented all the artists as equals; there was no commentary about one artist being better than another, because one was newer or less old-fashioned. Or that Ellington was legendary and Brubeck was the new kid on the block. They could all play and that was that.

I became hooked on jazz with this sampler LP and a handful of 78s I found in thrift shops. Later in the year, when I saw a Columbia Record Club advertisement that promised three LPs for a few cents in return for buying three or four LPs over the course of a year or two, I took the bait. The three LPs included two more jazz samplers; one featuring music from the 1920s, the other showcased swing performances from the 1930s and 1940s. The third free LP was a commercially issued release, Dave Brubeck's legendary *Jazz Goes to College*. It was and remains a fabulous recording. I played it over and over and while I didn't wear it out, I'm grateful to have a CD reissue.

OPPOSITE

I Like Jazz label, JZ 1 (1954). (Author's collection)

In His Own Sweet Way DVD label. (2010). (Author's collection)

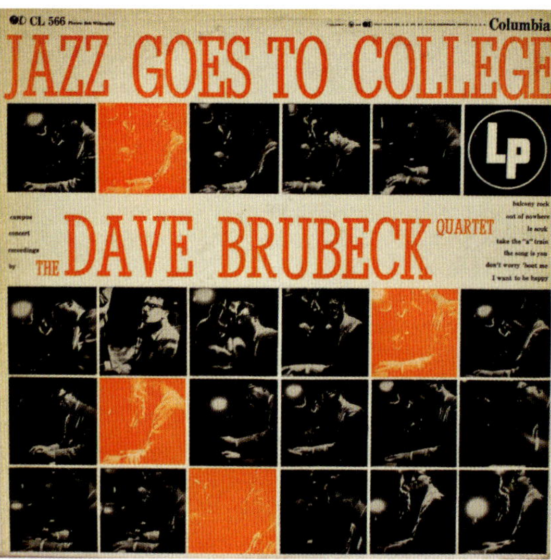

My old well-used copy of *Jazz Goes to College* from 1956. (Author's collection)

Over the next few years, I bought most of the Brubeck records offered by the club. This made Dave the first "modern" player I heard on a regular basis, and these were perfect recordings for a beginner like myself. I didn't understand everything George Avakian wrote in the notes to *Jazz Goes to College*, but I knew I liked what I heard and that was plenty.

The mid-fifties was a time when a jazz artist like Dave could be popular, sell many recordings, play fifty-two weeks a year if he wanted, appear on the cover of *Time Magazine*, and even present a concert in a converted-for-the-night Salina Street movie theater, in a relative backwater like Syracuse, New York. I don't remember the date, but it wasn't the *Jazz Goes to College* quartet; it was after Joe Morello joined the group, which makes it in the fall of 1956. I don't remember much about it except the quartet looked very small from the balcony, and I don't know if the group played "Balcony Rock" or "Le Souk," my two favorites from the first LP.

There came a time when Dave was no longer fashionable; at least he certainly wasn't the "No. 1 jazz artist." He'd never been the favorite of some critics; his records sold too well and he was much too popular for that. I remember all the talk when Paul Desmond left the quartet in 1967 and then a year later, when Columbia decided to drop "old fashioned" artists like Dave Brubeck and Tony Bennett. If Miles Davis hadn't gone electric about the same time, they'd probably have dropped him as well.

The first quartet with Desmond had lasted so long it's not surprising that nothing could easily follow it, at least in terms of stability. Gerry Mulligan joined the group off and on, but he'd been involved with Dave for years and while they made a number of fine recordings together (some as one-offs for Columbia), this wasn't a group destined for longevity. Longevity is what Dave had at the end of his playing days; Bobby Militello held down the saxophone chair since 1988; drummer Randy Jones had been with Dave since 1980.

From the early 1970s, Dave's groups varied considerably, as did his musical output. He had always been interested in music far beyond the boundaries of jazz and set about composing cantatas, oratorios, ballets, and assorted works for large symphonic ensembles. I continued to follow his career with interest and bought his recordings but was disappointed that he never seemed to be performing in live circumstances anytime I was close by. I decided to try and solve this problem by asking him to appear at one of our music festivals at sea in the early 1990s.

I don't know how many times we asked Dave to appear, but he was always busy, always unavailable at the time the Floating Jazz Festival was scheduled. Then there was a break in the action. He was available in June 2000 and would be pleased to sail on *Queen Elizabeth 2* from New York to Southampton. It was Dave's eightieth year, and so, with his permission, we billed our event as a celebration of his eight decades.

His two concerts were like a time machine for me, and they were just as exciting as the concert in Syracuse forty-four years earlier, just as exciting as the records, but this time I wasn't listening on a cheap phonograph or in the last row of the balcony, but backstage, about ten feet away. He hadn't lost a bit of technique, and because it was a trio format, Dave was the only soloist; he pretty much had to carry the burden and did with ease. To me, he was always the member of the quartet that was the hot voice, and he proved it all night long, at each concert on QE2.

With George Wein (2006). (Author's collection)

He didn't retreat to the dressing room after the concerts. He came out and sat with the audience, signing programs, CDs, pictures, whatever was put in front of him. People his age wanted autographs, as did the kids who played in the ship's band, or the children of passengers, who were probably getting signatures for their shy parents. There was, however, no reason to be shy. Dave was just as facile with a pen as he was with a keyboard. He signed everything, posed for pictures, and seemed to genuinely enjoy chatting with his audience. It's rare when an artist can make people as happy after a concert as he has made them during it.

Toward the end of the cruise, I visited Dave in his cabin and was surprised to see he had an electric keyboard set up. He wasn't practicing, he was writing, working on new compositions. I don't know what he writing then, but he was constantly creating new material. I was lucky enough to be able to witness this throughout the summer and early fall in 2006.

Poster for 80th birthday celebration during the Floating Jazz Festival in 2000. (Author's collection)

The Monterey Jazz Festival commissioned Dave to write a new piece to be performed in September 2006. In June of that year, George Wein and Dave got together during a rehearsal for the big band performance scheduled for that year's JVC Jazz Festival. This was the first time I'd ever attended a rehearsal for a group playing Dave's music and was puzzled when Dave wasn't part of it. He was off in a corner talking to George.

Score for *Cannery Row Suite.*
(Author's collection)

At the conclusion of the big band rehearsal, there was a short vocal rehearsal for a new piece, a suite in nine movements, entitled *Cannery Row*, written for eight instruments, two vocal soloists, and an eight-voice chorus. The rehearsal began with remarks by Dave's conductor, Russell Gloyd. This is what he said:

One thing about Dave. He's 85. But that has nothing to do with his inability to read his music. He couldn't do that when he was twenty-five. In 1942, when he was a senior at College of the Pacific, it was discovered that he couldn't read music. This was considered rather embarrassing from a conservatory standpoint. They were going to throw him out, except the entire theory and composition department came to the Dean and said, "If you thrown him out you'll be throwing out the most talented composer we've ever had at the school."

So the Dean said, "We'll give you your degree under two conditions. The first is that you promise never to return and that you promise never to teach music." Dave said, "Deal." Part of that has been fulfilled. Dave doesn't really teach music but he's been back a couple of times. That's where the Dave Brubeck Institute is located, and the Dave Brubeck Archives, so there's a substantial relationship. When Iola (Mrs. Brubeck) got her honorary degree about four years ago, the President said, "What can we do for Dave?" Iola said, "Why don't you give him a pardon and erase his transcript?" They thought that was pretty funny.

Dave in rehearsal, which is why he isn't in rehearsal, will get confused over what he has written and will try to remember what he's supposed to play the next time. So it's easier for him to just not be around for the rehearsal part, but when he gets here and we read it down, it will feel like a performance and that's when it kicks in. It has nothing to do with being eighty-five. It has everything to with "That's Dave." He's always been that way.

The June *Cannery Row* rehearsal was just for Roberta Gambarini and Kurt Elling, the two vocalists, but in early September, all the instrumentalists assembled in Wilton, Connecticut, to run down the entire score. It was a remarkable afternoon of music making. The quartet had performed the previous evening at Tanglewood. They drove from northwestern Massachusetts and arrived in the early afternoon. Dave rested about thirty minutes and then rehearsed for four hours. There were musical moments that were as exciting as anything I'd heard for many years.

Two weeks later, all the instrumentalists and vocalists assembled in a building on the Monterey Fair Grounds and performed the entire suite. There had been revisions since the rehearsal earlier that month, and there were more revisions that afternoon. There were more revisions on the Jimmy Lyons Stage the following day and at one point I spotted Dave sitting at a piano backstage, about thirty minutes before show time, making a few changes on his score, and took a picture, one that Dave likes a lot and is entitled *The Red Pencil*.

The premiere of *Cannery Row* was an unqualified success. The audience even sang along at one point. The following day Dave met with Clint Eastwood and discussed the structure of a documentary film that was being considered, and then he headed south with Iola and Russell for more concerts. His energy and continuing creativity were simply amazing.

A few days later I was asked to write a treatment for the proposed documentary. I couldn't have been happier. I gave the film the title *In His Own Sweet Way*. This is part of what I said:

The Red Pencil, adjusting the score of the *Cannery Row Suite*, Monterey, 2006. (Author's collection)

Duet with Clint Eastwood at Mission Ranch, 2003. (Author's collection)

In the second half of the Twentieth Century there were many artists who shaped the development of jazz, but three young men who emerged in the 1950's, each with a highly original voice, Miles Davis, John Coltrane and Dave Brubeck, not only captured the public's imagination, but in their own unique way determined the evolution of jazz as we know it today.

At the end of the century, Coltrane had been dead for over three decades and Davis for almost two. Today, Coltrane and Davis can only inspire and educate in the abstract. Of this triumvirate of American musical icons, only the oldest of the three, Dave Brubeck remains, a revered and respected elder statesman, but still as vital and innovative as ever, capable of inspiring by example.

Suddenly my teenage years and first love of jazz were coming full circle. I was working with the man who was featured on that first LP, the first of fifty or sixty thousand LPs, cassettes, and CDs that would follow. Since it was now easy to ask such things, I asked Dave if he might be interested in being part of the annual *Christmas Music – The Jazz Feeling*, an NPR radio show I'd hosted for the past two decades. I said I wanted to devote the entire show to his music and performance, as well as Iola's lyrics. He thought that was a fine idea and set about rounding up five decades of performances. We recorded it at his home on November 16th. The show ran on many NPR stations in December 2006. It is one of the most exciting shows in the series and one reason is that it included major portions of a piece Dave and Iola had written some years earlier in 1975, a Christmas cantata, *La fiesta de La Posada*.

We began to work on *In His Own Sweet Way* during the 2006 Monterey Jazz Festival. Bruce Ricker was the director; Clint Eastwood was the executive producer. Early on in the project, Dave and Clint had a bit of a reunion at Clint's Mission Ranch in Carmel, where they'd filmed sequences together for *Piano Blues*, a film that was part of Martin Scorcese's 2003 PBS blues project. Clint enjoys sharing a piano with others and I enjoy taking photographs of him doing it. This is when we structured the documentary.

But back to 1955 for a moment. George Avakian's final paragraph in the *Jazz Goes to College* liner reads as follows: "If the Dave Brubeck Quartet handed down to posterity nothing but the recordings in this group (particularly, I feel, Balcony Rock and Don't Worry 'Bout Me), it would hold a secure and most extraordinary place high in the annals of the history of jazz."

George was right about the record, but wrong about Dave's contribution to the annals of the history of jazz. It is now over sixty-five-plus years later and Dave's contributions to the history of jazz continued to 2012. *In His Own Sweet Way* premiered on TCM on Dave's ninetieth birthday, December 6, 2010, and he was almost silly busy throughout 2011. I received an email on April 6, 2011, from Iola that in part said, "We are on our way to Penn State today. Dave and Ramsey Lewis are splitting a bill there this weekend. I can't believe Dave is still 'at it,' but he has the Blue Note and the Ninety-second Street Y coming up as well as Blues Alley in Washington. Hard to keep a good man down." She forgot to mention he'd also be at the Newport Jazz Festival in August. He headlined the first one in 1954 and has a room named after him at the Viking Hotel in Newport to prove it.

But the clock was ticking and everyone knew it. On November 24, 2012, the telephone rang, and it was George Wein. He said he planned to drive to Wilton the next day to "say goodbye" to Dave and asked if I would like to do the same. The next day we made the trip and spent a quiet afternoon sitting in the kitchen of Dave and Iola's home, sipping tea and eating cookies, mostly chocolate chip cookies. Dave really tore into the cookies, and I promised I'd make him some more on Sunday and send them off on Monday, which I did. They arrived in time, but Dave died on December 5th. A few days later the first Christmas card of the season arrived. It was from Dave and Iola and was postmarked a couple of days earlier.

The way I looked at it, it had been a lifelong celebration full of great music, wonderful adventures, and spreading joy and happiness around the world. This was just a short break in the action, and the music would continue to do the same as long as people had ears with which to hear and the time to listen.

Dave and Iola Brubeck for *Christmas Music the Jazz Feeling*, 2006

A Celebration of the Life
and Music Of
Dave Brubeck

You are cordially invited

Saturday, May 11, 2013
4:00 PM
Cathedral Church of St. John the Divine
1047 Amsterdam Avenue
New York City

Program for memorial service in 2013. (Author's collection)

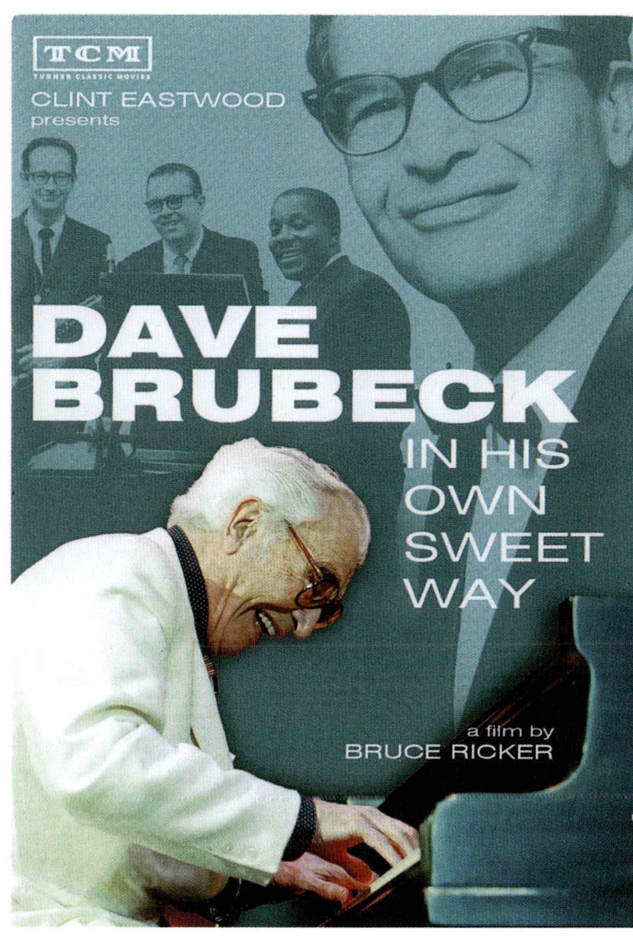

Clint-Eastwood-Filme (37)

DAVE BRUBECK
"IN HIS OWN SWEET WAY" **86½ Min.**

Präsentiert von Clint Eastwood

Mit Dave und Iola Brubeck, Clint Eastwood, Yo-Yo Ma, Jamie Cullum, Ashley Cahn, Sting, George Lucas, George Wein
Autor, Koproducer: Hank O'Neal
Sprecher: Alec Baldwin
Executive Producer: Clint Eastwood
Regisseur, Producer: Bruce Ricker
USA 2010

Originalversion – Deutsche Erstaufführung

Credits at a German film festival. (Author's collection)

6

John Coltrane

September 23, 1926 – July 17, 1967

I SAW JOHN COLTRANE in performance a handful of times in the 1950s when I was a teenager and then never saw him again in person. I arrived in New York City to become a permanent resident on June 5, 1967; he died on July 17th. The first time I was in his presence, he was just a speck, one of four guys on a big stage. That's all I could see from where I was sitting in the next to the last row way up high on the top balcony of Carnegie Hall. He was a miniature figure, a tiny person holding a saxophone that produced a big sound, one that was robust and alive and exciting all at the same time. It was at the very first jazz concert I'd ever heard in New York City, the first time I was in that legendary auditorium. I was seventeen years old, and it cost $2.00, the cheapest seat in the house. Or maybe it was $1.80.

John Coltrane was the horn soloist in the last group that performed on the first show that night, November 29, 1957, and the group he was in had a bunch of tough acts to follow. Coltrane, standing in front but as part of the Thelonious Monk Quartet that also included Ahmed Abdul-Malik (bass) and Shadow Wilson (drums), concluded a concert that began with the New York City concert debut of Ray Charles and a small seven-piece group, Dizzy Gillespie's big band, then Dizzy's band with Billie Holiday, a quartet fronted by Zoot Sims that included Chet Baker and Mose Allison, and the Carnegie Hall debut of Sonny Rollins with Wendell Marshall and Kenny Dennis. It was quite a night, one that went on for another couple of hours with a midnight show featuring the same lineup. It went on without me; I had to be back at the Commodore Hotel by midnight and today, six plus decades later, I have no memory of how I made my way back from 57th and 7th to 42nd and Lexington on what would have been my very first day in New York City.

I also have almost no memory of what songs John Coltrane or anyone else played or sang that night. I can look up the names of some of the songs on the Carnegie Hall website and both of the Monk sets that night were released as a Blue Note CD in 2005, but that's another story that I'll tell a little later before you come to the end of this one.

This was the first time I saw John Coltrane, but it wasn't the most memorable. They say you always remember the first one, but this time I also remember the second. While it might not have been as exciting an overall concert, it was to me the more interesting Coltrane experience, and just because of one song. It was one year and three hundred sixty-four days later, November 28, 1959, in Town Hall instead of Carnegie Hall, and I was still on Thanksgiving break, but this time from Syracuse University instead of Nottingham High School. I remembered the concert, but no one else did. For the longest time it was just a vague memory of something I knew had happened but had no way to verify it.

Then in 2002 I ran into Bob Brookmeyer at the Oslo Jazz Festival. He remembered because he was also there, and he was on the one song I remembered: Count Basie's "One O'Clock Jump." But even though someone sensible had verified it, I was still pretty much all alone. Bob had been there and played in Basie's jam band, but he didn't really elaborate much.

OPPOSITE
John Coltrane as seen by George Wein at his Newport Jazz Festival in 1963. (Author's collection)

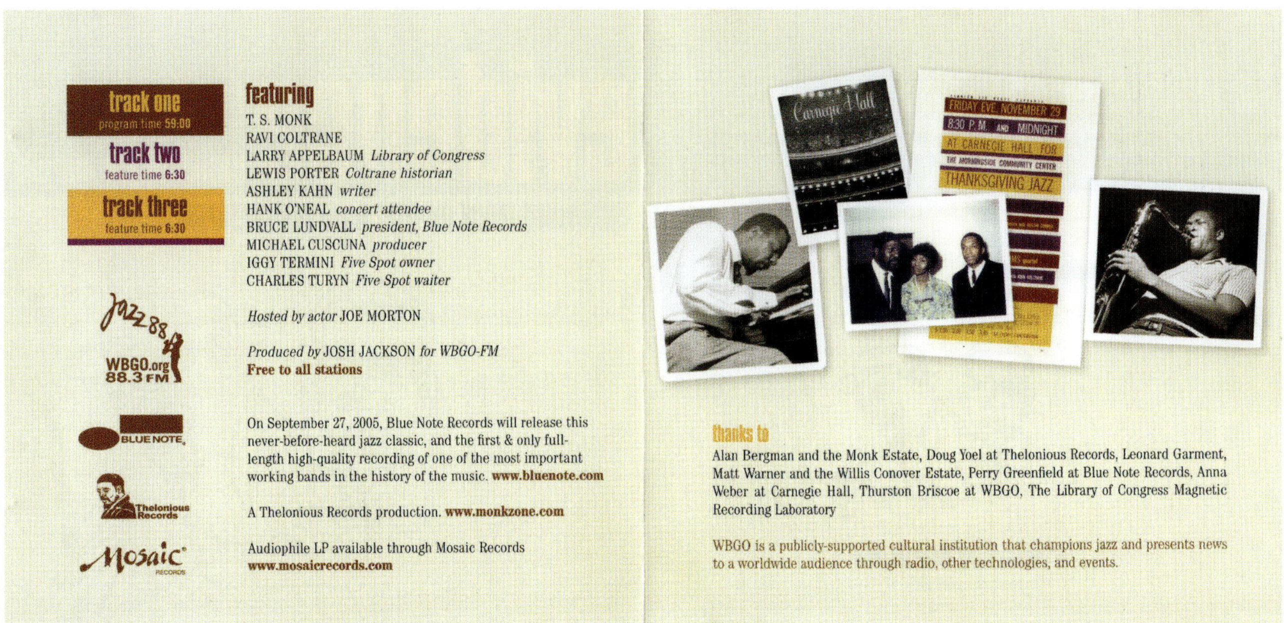

The inlay card for the special Blue Note CD release of the WBGO radio documentary. (Author's collection)

A decade later I purchased a book, *The John Coltrane Reference*, and it has an entry for this concert. Lewis Porter, who compiled this fine survey, wasn't at the performance and he relies on the written commentary by John S. Wilson and Whitney Balliett, who covered it for *The New York Times* and *The New Yorker* respectively, and the memory of one of the participants, the same Bob Brookmeyer I'd spoken with in Oslo in 2002.

Reading Porter's synopsis of the reporting by John and Whitney, the all-star lineup that night was The John Coltrane Quartet, an Ornette Coleman group, the Jazztet with Benny Golson and Art Farmer, a Thelonious Monk group with Elvin Jones, Cecil Taylor, and a Count Basie jam band that closed the concert. John Wilson doesn't mention Coltrane and wrote that the Basie group played "One O'Clock Jump" with Elvin Jones and Milt Hinton in the rhythm section. The other musicians mentioned by the two critics are Lee Konitz, Zoot Sims, Bob Brookmeyer, Scott LaFaro, Ernestine Anderson, Elvin Jones, Pepper Adams, McCoy Tyner, George Duvivier, and Art Taylor. It would seem there was a fair amount of mixing and matching that night, and maybe Whitney covered the 8:00 p.m. show and John did the 11:00.

This is what I remember. I saw the Jazztet with Farmer and Golson. It probably also included McCoy Tyner and Curtis Fuller because they were the guys on the record the group made a couple of months later. I remember the Coltrane Quartet but not the individual musicians. My guess is it was Wynton Kelly, Paul Chambers, and Jimmy Cobb because these three guys recorded with Coltrane for an album ultimately released as *Coltrane Jazz* for Atlantic the week before and after the Town Hall concert.

I have no recollection of Monk with Scott LaFaro and Elvin Jones or Ornette's group; I just don't remember those details from sixty plus years ago. But I do remember Basie and every musician in the band, except I do not remember if it was Milt or George on bass. I do remember it was Art Taylor on drums and I remember the way the guys were set up on stage; Basie, Taylor and bass stage right with Coltrane out front in the curve of the piano and Adams, Brookmeyer and Sims stage left, in a row facing the other four musicians. Even as a nineteen-year-old novice it looked like a white guys versus black guys contest. Maybe it was just the luck of the draw or who was available for the jam band. But what I really remember is that on the last number, Coltrane tore it up; he was a swinger working with Basie and playing with Zoot. It was an exciting way to finish up the concert.

About the same time I saw Coltrane a third time and once again it was in Town Hall, another one of those 8:00 and 11:00 p.m. double headers. My guess is that it was in early 1960 but I can't be sure.

Cecil Taylor, solo, opened the show. He was supposed to play for twenty minutes or so and would be followed by a Dizzy Gillespie group. Cecil played for about forty minutes and when Dizzy finally came out, he walked to the microphone and said, "Well . . . Goodnight." And everyone laughed, except maybe Cecil. The guys who played the early show had to watch the clock because the house had to be turned and ready to go by 11:00 or 11:30. Ornette Coleman's Quintet opened the second half of the show and was followed by the Miles Davis Sextet with Adderley and Coltrane. I don't remember anything more than this. I never saw Coltrane perform live again.

In January 1963 I found myself in Washington, DC, and was not aware of him ever appearing there. I suspect he did but I didn't know about it. In June 1967 I was assigned to the CIA office in New York City. John Coltrane was ill and not active then; he died five weeks later in July. But two years earlier, in 1965, Coltrane's son, Ravi, was born. Thirty-two years later, in 1997, Ravi appeared as a featured soloist during our 15th Annual Floating Jazz Festival, and his performances were praised from one deck to the other.

Fast forward to February 2005. A really smart guy, Larry Applebaum, made the discovery of a lifetime in the archives of the Library of Congress where he was head of the recording lab at that time. The discovery was boxes of Voice of America recordings that contained reels of old acetate tape recordings, identified as simply *Carnegie Hall Jazz*. One box was marked *T. Monk*. Larry played the tape marked *T. Monk* and recognized it was a concert recording of Thelonious Monk with John Coltrane; the concert I'd seen as a teenager on November 29, 1957.

This discovery launched a chain of events that led to issuing the two sets Monk and his quartet played that night as a Blue Note CD. BET produced a television special they called *Discovering Monk & Coltrane—One Night at Carnegie Hall* and radio station WBGO produced *Evidence—Thelonious Monk Quartet with John Coltrane at Carnegie Hall.*

I don't remember all the details of how and why Blue Note, BET, and WBGO made their way to me, but it was probably because of Bruce Lundvall. I am not a Monk or Coltrane expert and I'm not one of the go-to talking head jazz scholars who appear regularly in jazz documentary films. I'm usually on the other side of the camera. But somehow, the producers sought me out, and the reason was pretty simple: except for Sonny Rollins, who made his Carnegie Hall debut that night, I was the only person they could find who still had his wits about him, or was even breathing, who had been in the audience that night. So I was pressed into service with a bunch of other people who were related to the new CD in some manner.

It was a fascinating exercise, and the CD release was successful. I was told about $250,000 in various advances and fees had to be paid for it to be issued, so it had to be a success or someone was in big trouble.

Now we need to fast-forward again to November 2013. The only times I'd seen or heard Ravi Coltrane since the Floating Jazz Festival days was at The Jazz Gallery, a nonprofit jazz venue for young and emerging artists with which I'm affiliated. Or better still at my studio on Broadway where we often have fund raising events for TJG, and at one of them a dozen or so people paid $500 apiece to hear a very private concert featuring Ravi and his pal, Vijay Iyer. These events are kind of modern day rent parties, and just like Fats Waller managed to do in the old days, Ravi and Vijay made sure the joint was jumping.

Another fast-forward and COVID-19 came calling. In March 2020 New York City was locked down, and musicians and clubs and audiences were in trouble. In July of that year there was a brief break in the action, TJG upgraded some of its video and broadcast equipment, and we began a series of live stream video events we called our *Lockdown Sessions*. Suddenly TJG was broadcasting live concerts all over the world, reaching places we'd never been before, while providing employment to the members of one band a week. Sometimes these were groups with celebrated leaders, such as Ravi Coltrane, who volunteered to appear with a great quartet so long as his sidemen had a payday. So we now had a televised rent party, one that worked for all concerned.

And this brings me back to that funny concert in Town Hall in 1959, the one where I heard Benny Golson for the first time. And to the release of the Carnegie Hall concert featuring Thelonious Monk with John Coltrane. I was asked to say a few words about the Carnegie Hall event because I was there. Maybe it would have made sense to ask Benny Golson about the 1959 Town Hall concert when I had the opportunity in 2021 at The Jazz Gallery, but I messed up and didn't. After all, he was there and like me in 2005, he still has all his wits about him in 2021. He was only ninety-two then and made it to ninety-five.

COVID lockdown streaming concert with Ravi Coltrane at The Jazz Gallery, February 2, 2021. (Author's collection)

Ravi Coltrane and Vijay Iyer at 830 Broadway, November 11, 2013. (Author's collection)

Benny Golson announcement from The Jazz Gallery. (Author's collection)

Reggie Workman's Coltrane Ensemble concert at the New School's College of Performing Arts, 2022. (Author's collection)

LP jacket, *Live at The Jazz Gallery 1960*. (Author's collection)

And you know something really nice? Before the COVID-19 pandemic whacked us in 2020, my board at The Jazz Gallery had voted to award our 25th Anniversary Gala Lifetime Achievement Award to none other than Benny Golson. The event took place on November 19, 2021, almost sixty-two years since his debut concert with The Jazztet in Town Hall. Time flies when you're having fun.

And then it was December 7, 2022, sixty-five years and a week since I first heard of John Coltrane in 1957. I was at The New School Jazz Performance Space, listening to the John Coltrane Repertory Ensemble, a group made up of ten exceptional students in the Jazz and Contemporary Music program of the school's College of Performing Arts. The ensemble is organized and mentored yearly by Reggie Workman, who is one of the last living links to the John Coltrane of the 1960s.

I looked around the room to see if there was anyone who looked to be seventeen years old and saw no one who appeared to be that young, but many in the audience and on the bandstand weren't much older than that. I wonder what they will be listening to in sixty-five years and a week from today? And will they still be playing interesting music and going out to concerts to hear "jazz," if there is even any music called "jazz" in 2087?

The music they are making is far more adventuresome than anything I heard in 1957 and possibly far more interesting. The ensemble consisted of tenor and alto saxophones, bass clarinet, piano, guitar, two double basses, two drummers with full kits, and a vocalist. No one played a dull note and certainly not a wrong one as they worked their way through nine Coltrane compositions.

And then I looked around again and it was a Monday night in March 2023 at The Jazz Gallery, not the old original incarnation of The Jazz Gallery at 80 St. Mark's Place, where John Coltrane premiered his first working quartet in April and June 1960, but the new one at Broadway and Twenty-Seventh Street. And it was sixty-three years later, but John Coltrane was still there, in the person of his son, Ravi, and the music he had recorded all those years before, music that was recorded on tape and then pressed into vinyl long playing records, LPs as they were called in those days long ago. This was a retro listening session; only LPs played on a turntable for an eager, sold-out audience.

But there was a slight delay because of a loose wire somewhere, and while delayed I thought about sixty-five years earlier listening to Coltrane first in 1957 with Thelonious Monk in Carnegie Hall, then with Count Basie in Town

LP jacket, *Live at The Half Note. One Down One Up.* (Author's collection)

Hall the following year, and finally with Miles Davis, once again in Town Hall, in 1959, and never again hearing him in person.

The first Jazz Gallery opened in 1959 and was gone by 1962. I never set foot in the place until some years later when it had become the Theater 80 St. Mark's, and that was to see a movie. I'm sure Coltrane played in the Washington, DC, area when I lived in that city in the mid-1960s, but I wasn't aware of it. When I relocated to New York City in June 1967 I rented an apartment two blocks from the Village Vanguard, the scene of many of Coltrane's musical triumphs, but he died within a month of my arrival. And so I turned to LPs, as did everyone else, and then the delivery system changed to CDs. But LPs were always a lot more fun.

I've been associated with The "New" Jazz Gallery since 1996. Over its thirty years it has evolved into an award-winning, successful nonprofit performance venue, and despite funding from many sources that enable us to present three hundred plus concerts a year we are always looking for ways to generate added income. One of the ways that has been very successful is to have vinyl listening sessions where noted jazz artists act as DJs, playing music that influenced them as children and teenagers and led them to a life in jazz. This was The Jazz Gallery's version of a saxophone spectacular, with Ravi Coltrane and Ben Wendel playing the music of their youth, once the loose wire was tightened.

Once tightened, Ben went first. He picked out a Wayne Shorter track, "The Three Marias" from the 1985 release, *Atlantis*. Ravi decided he liked that album so much he wanted to play a track from it as well. Then back to Ben, who picked a track from *Quiet Nights*, the final Miles Davis/Gil Evans collaboration. Then it was back to Ravi and his choice led to a remarkable musical moment. His choice was Coltrane's *Live at the Half Note,* and the choice led not only to a fascinating listening opportunity but to a photographic one as well.

The three selections up to this point had been four to six minutes long, but the track Ravi wanted to play, *One Down, One Up* was 27:40. He said he'd lived with this live performance since he was a child and felt it was the finest performance of his father extant. And he didn't want to play an excerpt. And neither did the audience. And that he had a vinyl copy was very unusual because the "official" release on these two radio broadcasts from *The Half Note* wasn't issued until 2005, a time when almost everything was just released as a CD. But here was a vinyl release complete with an oversized booklet insert that was passed around for all to see.

Then the music began. I'd been taking a few photographs up to this point, but once the music jumped out of the speakers and Ravi and Ben became very animated, I decided to take more than a handful of photographs and document these two remarkable saxophonists listening to both a father and a mentor, enjoying and reacting to every note. I took about sixty pictures and created a little mini movie. I assembled eight of my favorites. Later, I may assemble all sixty to remind me of how powerful the 27:40 track was, just as forceful at the end as it had been at the beginning; the remarkable sequences of notes and rhythms pouring out of Coltrane's horn and Elvin's drums and McCoy's piano and Jimmy's bass. How the time passed so quickly, and the time was perfect, so perfect in fact that it seemed all four men could have continued for another twenty-seven plus minutes.

It was remarkable to me that there were so many overlapping aspects to my relationship with an artist I never met and only saw briefly on three occasions, and that so many of these overlaps only became apparent many years later. The aftermath of the Monk performance in Carnegie Hall when Blue Note issued the concert; witnessing Coltrane with two legendary groups purely by accident, and a third time with Count Basie, a double accident; The Jazz Gallery #1 from 1959–62 and The Jazz Gallery #2 from 1995 still going strong and well into the future; *Live at the Half Note* being selected by his son as his finest performance, played and broadcast from a jazz club located at 289 Hudson Street, directly opposite the location of the first home of The Jazz Gallery #2, at 290 Hudson Street. A lot of serendipity bouncing around, and once the tone arm was lifted and the turntable stopped I grabbed my coat and left. There was no way any other record could compete with what I'd just heard, at least not in such close proximity.

Once upon a time, in the 1960s when the Canterino family ran the Half Note and The Jazz Gallery #1 was struggling on St. Mark's Place, late at night it was pretty lonely at the corner of Hudson and Spring Streets in the West Village. Late nights were pretty lonely in the 1990s and early 2000s as well. But downstairs in 2023, despite the rain, Broadway was bustling at Twenty-Seventh Street, but the subway station at Twenty-Eighth Street was just as lonely as Hudson and Spring after John Coltrane's last notes had faded inside the Half Note or Roy Hargrove's did the same across the street at The Jazz Gallery. And who knows, but maybe on the right night when it is very quiet and nobody is around, quiet little ghost notes may be lingering somewhere in the darkened building near Hudson and Spring, waiting patiently for years and years, waiting to be heard. Silly thoughts, but then the W train roared into the station, and I stopped thinking about such things.

Listening session with Ben Wendel and Ravi Coltrane at The Jazz Gallery. (Author's collection)

7

Eddie Condon

November 16, 1905 – August 4, 1973

ONE DAY IN THE LATE 1960S when Eddie Condon and I were working on one of the many projects we undertook together in the six years from 1967–73, he said something about "a telephone call to the past." I don't recall what preceded the remark or where it went after he made it. But it is now fifty plus years later and I still think about that casual remark, particularly now as I try to remember and reconstruct the events of those years. Facts and dates and meetings and interviews and social gatherings that made their way to recordings and newspapers and magazines have made their ways to the deepest corners of the Internet, but many of the things that happened or didn't, maybe most others, only exist in the personal mental Internets of those who experienced them. Since the only personal Internet I have unfettered access to is my own, I have to use it as best I can, trying to squeeze whatever I can from my eighty-five-year-old memory bank and make the right withdrawal.

The right withdrawal isn't always that easy, and how nice it would be to be able to make a telephone call to the past. Simply dial up Gramercy 7-0846 and remember in real time. One day that will be possible, but not in 2025.

And so with no way to make a telephone call to the past, I tried to remember as best I could. This is what I came up with.

My name had popped up a couple of times on the inside pages of *The New York Times,* but the first time it appeared on the front page was in 1973, over fifty years ago. It has popped up lots of times since then, including a full-page profile in 2003, but never on the front page. Such was Eddie's reach from the late 1920s until whenever, because in some ways it is still reaching.

When I arrived for my permanent stay in New York City on June 5, 1967, the Israeli-Arab Six Day War had just broken out. When I say permanent stay, I had no idea at the time it would become as permanent as it did. The stay is now fifty-eight years long, but who's counting?

I was downtown that day, looking around for a place to rent, but I wasn't having much luck because most of the people I encountered were far more concerned with the new war than a potentially new neighbor. Within a few days I'd found a place to hang my hat and take off my shoes at 15 Charles Street in Greenwich Village, but except for an office full of new faces at 205 East Forty-Second Street, where the Central Intelligence Agency's New York field office was then located, I only knew three people on the Isle of Manhattan: Max Draisner, a used record dealer; Marian McPartland, the wondrous pianist; and Eddie Condon, the celebrated guitarist and man about town.

At the time Eddie Condon lived at 27 Washington Square North, five minutes and five blocks away. I knew him from a quick meet and greet at Squirrel Ashcraft's apartment a year or so earlier. I got to know him pretty well over the next six years.

OPPOSITE

Eddie Condon's telephone number, as rendered by his brother-in-law, Paul Smith. (Author's collection)

With Squirrel Ashcraft in Washington, DC, in 1966.
(Author's collection)

"Part A" — "the Story"

A third child was born to Bismark Herman and Agatha (Hilton) Beiderbecke on March 10, 1903 in Davenport, Iowa. This child was named Leon (for no reason) Bix (which is a nickname for Bismark) Beiderbecke. Bix had one older brother, Charles Burnette, and one older sister, Mary Louise. The translation of the German name "Beiderbecke" means "By The Brook". The background of the family was a mixture of German and Pennsylvania-Dutch.

Clarification should be given on the usage of the name "Bix". As Charles explains it: "In his younger days, our dad was nicknamed "Bix" (being a short for Bismark) by his friends. When I was born, I was called "Little Bix", and dad was "Big Bix". When Leon was born, he was fully named Leon Bix Beiderbecke". The idea of Bismark being Bix's middle name should be completely dismissed. As Mary Louise offers: "Dad would never have named any child of his after his given name of Bismark".

At full growth, Bix possessed the following description. Dark complexion with brown eyes and dark hair (which was straight), and a straight nose. His height was "around 6 feet". His sister feels he was an inch "over" and his brother feels he was an inch "under". His slender build was packed into 180 lbs.

The Beiderbecke home was located at 1934 Grand Avenue, across the street from Tyler School (named for the President) and was a picturesque two story, white wood frame house, characteristic of the homes built at the turn of the Century. This house was built around 1895. The home was a white structure with a porch across the front. The entry had a beautiful gold ceramic tile fireplace flanked by window seats, and it had a large (27 by 14) living room. The kitchen was average sized with a built-in China Closet on the west wall. The master bedroom (containing three bay windows) opened into the nursery which had a window seat across the front of the room. There were also two additional bedrooms upstairs, and topped by an attic that was completely floored.

Bismark Beiderbecke was a member in the firm of the East Davenport Lumber and Coal Company.

Eddie was a couple of minutes past his prime in 1967. He'd been an A-lister since the mid-1930s, with television shows, concerts all over town, a profile in *The New Yorker*, books, a newspaper column, a stream of recordings, and his name on his own nightclub, the justifiably legendary Eddie Condon's at 47 East Third Street. But there hadn't been a concert since the early 1960s, about the same time as his last television special, no new books were on the shelf, the newspaper column was a memory, and he hadn't made a record in three or four years. The new uptown branch of Eddie Condon's was hanging on by a thread and closed permanently a couple of months later in August. It was not the best of times for Eddie.

Squirrel Ashcraft, the guy who enabled my life to begin to blossom in Washington, shut down his jazz life and went into the CIA and world of intelligence gathering and intrigue very voluntarily. A decade or so later it was easy to get him to try his piano once again. After I became his neighbor and got to know Eddie Condon a little better, it was pretty clear his withdrawal wasn't voluntary, and he wasn't opposed to dipping his toe back into circum-

The first page of the proposed
Bix Beiderbecke biography.
(Author's collection)

stances where he could tap it in time with Gene Krupa or Cliff Leeman. I had a lot of energy and ideas and helped Squirrel get back on track with his musical life; I thought it might be possible to do the same with Eddie. It turned out it was, and we had a fine time doing it until he ran out of gas at the end of the summer in 1973. Actually he'd been running on fumes for the better part of a year; he'd been throwing the pills that kept his cancer at bay out the window for a year or so and no one knew.

Life with Eddie began slowly, but by the end of 1968 there was action on four different fronts, sometimes simultaneously. By the fall of 1967 Eddie probably had come to the realization I wasn't a typical idiotic fan who wanted to know who the piano player was on a record he'd made in 1932. When the esteemed writer/journalist George Hoefer died in November, Eddie gave me a call. My guess is that at the time, his favorite musical cohort in all the world was Pee Wee Russell. At the time of his death, George was working with Pee Wee on a biography and legend has it that at least one chapter was complete. Eddie suggested that since I knew how to spell, understood the music a bit, and possibly could learn to understand Pee Wee, he should introduce me to his pal and I could pick up where George had left off.

This sounded like a good idea to me. I had been thinking about trying my hand at writing something other than intelligence reports about Soviet scientific discoveries and assorted bad Arab actors misbehaving in the Levant. Bob Mantler had just given me a one-hundred-thirty-one-page draft of the first version of the book that eventually was published in 1974 as *Bix—Man and Legend.* This first version by Bob and his writing and research partner, Phil Evans, was clearly a work in progress, one still very much in its infancy and crying out for editorial assistance. This was a project that needed a great deal of attention, one that I was certain I could not handle appropriately. I suggested to Bob that another Bob, Bob Greene, who was a full-time writer and sometimes pianist who loved Bix, might be a better choice.

But Pee Wee was another matter. He was alive and depending on the day in question, possibly well and lived in Chelsea, a few blocks away at Twenty-Eighth and Eighth Avenue. I told Eddie to please make the introduction. Of course, it didn't work out. What I didn't know was that Pee Wee's wife, Mary, had died a few months earlier, and in many ways, she was the glue that held Pee Wee together. I had a couple of meetings with him at his apartment, but nothing came of it. For the next forty years Kenny Davern played "Pee Wee's Blues" on one of Pee Wee's clarinets at almost every concert, but Pee Wee played them all day long, every day, for the rest of his life until he died in February 1969. He wasn't in the mood for a book project.

Pee Wee had been declared dead by a doctor at Squirrel Ashcraft's home in 1939. He'd been getting by for a few days on nothing but liquid refreshment, and one morning he couldn't be awakened. A doctor was called, and Squirrel told me the doctor's words were, "I can't do anything for this man. This man is dead." But the doctor was wrong. Another decade plus of a liquid diet put Pee Wee in the charity ward of San Francisco Hospital in 1951, where he almost checked out again. He weighed seventy-three pounds and was dying of acute pancreatitis and malnutrition. But this time the word got out, and many musical and media friends came to Pee Wee's rescue, led by the always resolute Daisy Decker.

A story about Pee Wee's plight appeared in *Life Magazine*, accompanied by an amazing picture of Louis Armstrong and Jack Teagarden hovering over the comatose clarinetist, and then Louis organized a benefit to raise money to get Pee Wee out of the charity ward and onto an operating table. They removed twenty cysts from his liver and discovered a birth defect that had prevented him from metabolizing solid food, which they fixed.

Later in February, Eddie organized a benefit at Town Hall that raised even more money, and the pot swelled further after Art Hodes and Georg Brunis staged yet another benefit in Chicago. Pee Wee was then flown to New York where he became a temporary member of the Condon household, tended to for a month by Phyllis Condon. He recovered and had eighteen more years of music making.

Then it was February 15, 1969. There were a number of traditional and mainstream jazz bands in town that January to play various Inaugural Balls for Richard Nixon; Eddie and his guys were at the Shoreham opposite Doc Severinsen. Pee Wee was with George Wein's Newport All Stars. Eddie and George and Doc went back to New York City as quickly as they could, but Pee Wee stayed behind, remaining at the home of his friend Daisy Decker. As his condition worsened it became clear he needed to be in a hospital bed. One was found in Alexandria, Virginia, and this time he didn't make it.

I was at home on Saturday afternoon when the telephone rang. It was Eddie on the other end weeping. He'd just learned Pee Wee was dead. It was the first time I'd heard him cry. The second time was a few days later at Pee

Wee's funeral in New Jersey. I didn't take any pictures that day, but someone else did and they gave us five pictures to use in *Eddie Condon's Scrapbook of Jazz*.

The scrapbook was part of a well-thought-out plan to get Eddie back in circulation; concerts and festivals, recording projects, old and new, more outside social activity and, of course, completing the scrapbook. The first things to happen were the occasional festivals and concerts where traditional and mainstream artists were welcomed. There were few of them and Eddie knew it. Johnson McRee launched his Manassas Jazz Festival in 1966, and Eddie managed to take part in every one from 1968 to 1971. These were modest events, they were not as prestigious as the festivals in Newport or Monterey, but they were a good excuse to get out of the house, interact with friends, and usually have a good time doing it. By the late 1960s musicians of the traditional and mostly mainstream sort were regarded by most festival promoters or record executives as dinosaurs.

On July 17, 1954, Eddie Condon played the very first concert at the very first Newport Jazz Festival. In 1956 Eddie and his band were featured once again, and the concert was recorded for release on Columbia Records. He never returned to Newport but did take part in the 1972 Newport Jazz Festival – New York, appearing with Lee Wiley and leading an all-star ensemble in Carnegie Hall on July 5th. It was his last time in Carnegie Hall and next to last concert appearance in New York City. During the years 1968–71, when Eddie was performing in a high school auditorium in Manassas, Virginia, during those four years the Newport Jazz Festival presented exactly three traditional or mainstream groups, Alex Welsh, George Wein's own Newport All Stars and the World's Greatest Jazz Band. Promoters, even promoters like George Wein who played and loved traditional and mainstream music, knew they couldn't sell it, so they didn't try. That there were a few hires in 1972 during the Newport Jazz Festival in New York was simply because there was a large enough population base to support all kinds of music.

There were a fair number of low-level events that got Eddie out of the house on a semi-regular basis, festivals like Manassas, occasional concerts in high school auditoriums, private parties, and occasional sponsorships by well-to-do jazz fans like Dick Gibson. Gibson helped underwrite one of the most peculiar bands I've ever seen, one that featured the co-leadership of both Eddie and Roy Eldridge for a couple of months toward the end of 1969 and into 1970 at New York City's renowned Roosevelt Grill. As I recall, Zoot Sims was in the band, as was Kai Winding and possibly Ross Tompkins on piano. Eddie took the Pork Chop to the Roosevelt Grill but some nights the case went unopened. Whenever I was available, I helped Eddie navigate some of the appearances like the Roosevelt and once or twice put a band together for him, such as a concert in Syracuse, New York, in 1971. A concert that someone recorded and was later issued on Arbors Records.

Eddie Condon's Scrapbook of Jazz

The most consequential project Eddie and I undertook together was the scrapbook project. The dust jacket of the book that was issued reads, *Eddie Condon's Scrapbook of Jazz*. The interior title page reads *The Eddie Condon Scrapbook of Jazz*. Same book, two titles. Whoops.

Fifty-plus years after the fact it is hard to remember the exact sequence of events that launched this ambitious project. Perhaps one night it will come to me in a dream, but in 2025 I remain a bit unsure and every one of the players who were involved at the time are no longer around to ask. There were four primary players who helped get the project off the ground: Eddie and Phyllis Condon, Michael Brooks, and Les Pockell. Eddie and Phyllis are obvious, Michael and Les, less so.

Dust jacket, *Eddie Condon's Scrapbook of Jazz*.
(Author's collection)

Michael Brooks was from the UK, extremely bright and passionate about music and movies from the decades of the 1920s–1940s, maybe in some instances into the 1950s. He was also a terrific writer who knew what he was talking about and could arrange the words in such a way as to make sense, tell an interesting story, and keep his reader engaged. He was about five years older than me.

Les Pockell was slightly younger than I and beginning what would be a very distinguished career as an editor and publisher. In 1968–69 he was a junior editor at St. Martin's Press. At some point he made the acquaintance of Michael Brooks.

I can only surmise the sequence of events that led to the beginning of the scrapbook project was simple serendipity. I was probably at 27 Washington Square visiting or discussing some matter of mutual interest and Phyllis came in and mentioned a box of photographs she had come upon and we began talking about them. I learned that Phyllis had saved photographs of all sorts, scraps of paper, newspaper clippings, all the letters Eddie had sent from the road, as well as memorabilia from hundreds of celebrities in and out of the worlds of music. It turned out there were shirt boxes and breadboxes crammed with fascinating items, both written and visual.

As I looked at all this material a dozen light bulbs went off at once and I thought about how much fun it might to be to assemble it all in book form so the many jazz fans I knew would care could also have a look. By this time I'd met Michael Brooks and told him what I'd come across. Michael had met Les somewhere along the line, told him about the treasure at 27 Washington Square and the three of us arranged a meeting at St. Martin's.

St. Martin's was then located in the Flatiron Building, on the eighteenth floor as I recall, which was reached by the slowest elevator system in New York City. The result of the meeting was that Les and I agreed there should be an Eddie Condon book full of pictures and interesting stories and when possible, stories filled with the legendary Condon wit and sarcasm. When I told them, Eddie and Phyllis jumped on board what was to become a slow-moving train, but one that would travel an interesting route. Eddie once wrote a tune he called "Lets Go Down to the Station and Hum One." That's kind of what we did; we got to the station, humming all the way, and it was a lot of fun.

As I recall, there was an advance of about ten cents, but that was more than I expected. Les had never edited a picture book. It was a learning experience for each of us;

With Pee Wee Russell as seen by Charlie Peterson in 1944. (Author's collection)

With Charlie Peterson as seen by me in 1970. (Author's collection)

I'd never written anything (that wasn't classified) any longer than developing a political philosophy based on the writings of Antoine de Saint Exupéry in his posthumous book, *The Wisdom of the Sands*. And that was just a college paper.

Les and I were both newbies from the standpoint of producing a picture book. Later, we would do a little better with *A Vision Shared*, which we later worked on together and published in 1976. But we got started on the scrapbook, and I began to organize visual sections in chronological order based on the photographs that were available. I quickly realized that even though Phyllis had

St. Martin's Press
invites you to celebrate the publication of
THE EDDIE CONDON SCRAPBOOK OF JAZZ
at the New York Jazz Museum
125 West 55th Street
on Wednesday, November 14th, 1973,
from 5:30 to 7:30 P.M.

Live Jazz
6 P.M. Screening of Eddie Condon Film Clips
Beer compliments of The F. & M. Schaefer Brewing Co.

R.S.V.P. (212) 674-5151
or mail enclosed card

The Eddie Condon Scrapbook of Jazz book release invitation. (Author's collection)

boxes full of material, the book might be far more visually appealing if I looked beyond the shirt boxes under her bed and crammed file drawers.

The book wound up containing five hundred sixty photographs, illustrations, newspaper and magazine clippings, and letters; material provided not only by Eddie and Phyllis but by Squirrel Ashcraft, Jeff Atterton, George Avakian, Johnny DeVries, Frank Driggs, John Hammond, Julius' Bar on Tenth Street, Jimmy and Marian McPartland, Genevieve Naylor, Charlie Peterson, Jean Wettling, and for events toward the end of the project, photographs by myself.

The process for putting the book together was not complicated. Eddie and I looked at our raw material, segregated it into sections, made a selection of visuals that seemed reasonably coherent, which told a bit of a story or illustrated something we felt was important or would appeal to a casual reader, and then I'd ask Eddie to tell me about the circumstances behind it. I'd transcribe his remarks, we would both refine them, and that would be the caption for the photograph. There were also a handful of longer written statements that were drawn from letters from John Steinbeck, John DeVries, or others and occasional remarks from George Avakian and myself.

The sheer volume of material we assembled led to problems and we kept uncovering fascinating items as we went along. We wound up with five hundred sixty illustrations. When the captioning and assembling began it was far more complicated than we'd anticipated, and this pushed back the publication date. Another problem was I had a full-time job elsewhere and was not always available, plus I was launching a new record company and trying to engage Eddie in as many concert festival and recording projects as possible. But in early 1972 it appeared as if we were nearing the finish line and then Eddie said something like, "We have to see Genevieve." This turned out to be a fateful remark, one that helped the project immensely and also set the stage to bounce my life in yet another direction.

Genevieve Naylor was an exceptional photographer and a longtime friend of Eddie's. She'd been married for many years to a fine painter, Misha Reznikoff, who had died the previous year. Many musical gatherings featuring Eddie and his friends had occurred at their home, plus she had a good eye for design. A meeting was arranged, and Genevieve came down to Washington Square to inspect what we'd been up to.

Her reaction was that the scrapbook project was a fine idea, she would like to donate some photographs to our endeavor, and that she'd help in any way she could to give the project a more polished and professional look. Genevieve had been the official photographer for *The Eddie Condon Floor Show* television broadcasts, and it turned out she had some remarkable photographs that were not in the shirt boxes under the bed. As she was leaving that day she tossed out a casual remark suggesting she'd be happy to help with the design of the book, but if we wanted her to help we had to hurry because she was going away to spend the summer with her photography teacher in Maine. She added we could reach her by telephone at 207-997-3763. I know that's the number because I wrote it down and wound up calling it for the next thirty years.

Time passed and soon it was the summer of 1972, and the illness that would grab Eddie in August 1973 was kicking in. St. Martin's didn't want an outside designer and wanted to get our handiwork into production, and they did. We turned over all our raw material to Les Pockell and he and his team got to work. I supervised as best I could, and the project moved forward toward a fall 1973 release. It moved just a bit too slowly; Eddie died in August, the book was released on November 14th, two days before his sixty-eighth birthday.

One quick glance and its flaws were obvious, beginning with the title, it read one way on the dust jacket and another on the title page. It was also not paginated, which meant I couldn't even tell a reader the page number where an out-of-focus illustration lived. There was no index, no photo credits, and no acknowledgements. The book was printed on matte paper when semi-gloss would have been preferable.

Despite these obvious shortcomings, the book was favorably reviewed and the flaws were never mentioned in print. There was a wonderful opening night party at the very short-lived New York Jazz Museum. There was live music and movies of Eddie and his pals. I do not recall if the hard drinking crowd was happy, but I note on the invitation beer was supplied by the F & M Schaefer Brewing Company. Eddie and his pals generally viewed beer as a viable option only when more serious drink was unavailable. In February 2025 there are sixty copies of the book available on the combined sites of ABE, Amazon, and eBay, ranging in price from $5.00 to $154.73. It is not a rare book. I have seen very expensive Eddie Condon autographed copies of the book, but buyer beware. I signed a few copies when the book was issued, but Eddie signed none because there were none printed and bound when he died in August 1973.

Making Records

As we were creating *The Eddie Condon Scrapbook of Jazz,* a number of LPs were produced. All of the Eddie Condon LP releases I helped organize or produced during this period were live concert or festival recordings, except for the Columbia two LP reissue set that was produced by Michael Brooks and released in conjunction with the scrapbook and one recording I organized at Sherman Fairchild's home in the summer of 1970. Most of these live recordings were very casual, almost haphazard affairs, as were the events at which they were recorded. The exceptions were the three LPs drawn from Town Hall Concerts in the mid-1940s, a recording of unknown origin from Eddie Condon's (uptown) recorded in the early 1960s, a professionally recorded broadcast from 1964 I licensed from the Tokyo Broadcasting System, and the New School concert I produced in April 1972. All of these releases on Chiaroscuro and Columbia were worked on and approved by Eddie. I did what I could to ensure the releases on Fat Cat's Jazz and Jazzology were as good as possible, but I'll be the first to admit many production elements on these records were not as good as they should have been.

People had bootlegged recordings of Eddie's records for years and he simply looked the other way. Some of the most awful released in the 1960s were bootlegged on a label called Jazum. Eddie took one look at them and was horrified. He had no quarrels with the music, it was often spectacular or even better, but the records' covers appeared to have been designed by a blind man and the commentary on the back written by someone with a learning disability. Of course, no one had been paid. The bandit who produced them had simply gotten his hands on some radio transcriptions, copied them, and issued them as if he was the rightful owner. There was little to do except tell anyone who would listen that the producer, a jazz fan based in Pittsburgh, was a creep.

Three Chiaroscuro Eddie Condon LPs. (Author's collection)

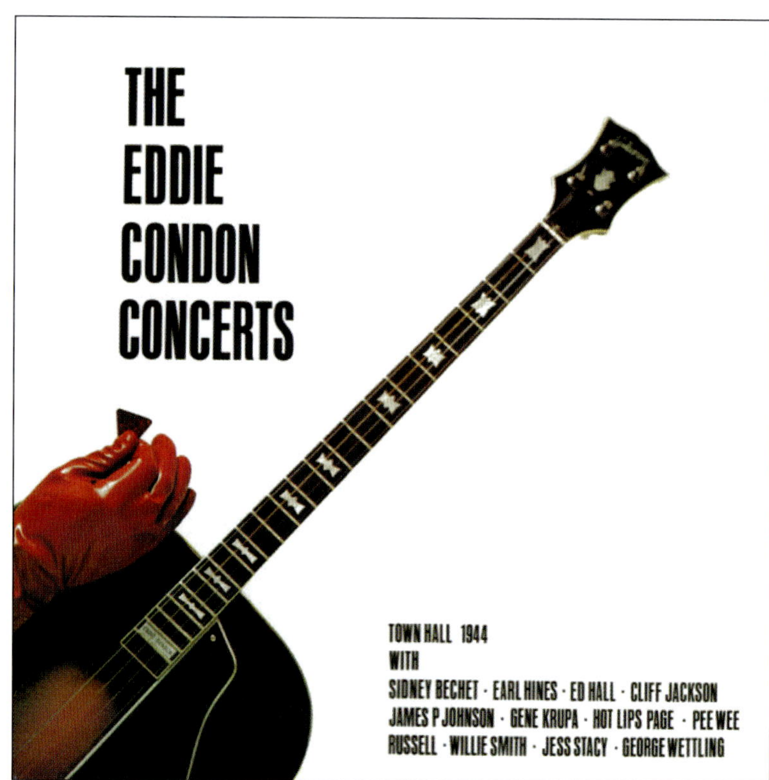

I left a copy of one the records at Washington Square, and one day Eddie asked if there was anything that could be done about the records. I said not really, unless you want to take the "producer" to court. Then I tossed out another idea, which was for Eddie to select some of the broadcasts he felt were special and issue them properly, paying musicians at the going rate, creating decent jacket artwork, good liner commentary, and acting responsibly. He thought that was a good idea, and since Pee Wee Russell was on his mind we decided to create an album from the Town Hall concerts that would focus on the work of Pee Wee.

We enlisted Eddie's favorite designer, John DeVries, to handle the artwork, using one of Charlie Peterson's iconic photographs. We asked Pee Wee's close friend Jeff Atterton to write notes. Eddie selected fourteen tracks he really liked and we had an album. A short while later we organized a second release that featured mostly pianists, sixteen tracks selected by Eddie, and once again Johnny DeVries handled the artwork and design, but we switched annotators; this time going with the esteemed Dan Morgenstern, who was still in charge of *Downbeat* magazine at the time.

The third in the series was to feature a dozen vocals by Lee Wiley, Eddie's favorite vocalist; she was about ten miles ahead of whoever was in second place. It was a very special record; Eddie recorded a dozen new spoken introductions for each selection and John DeVries created what may have been his finest LP cover design and wrote an incredible essay about Lee. He called it "Pokey" because that is what he called her, short for Pocahontas. But the record was never issued.

At some point during the production cycle, Eddie's old publicist, Ernie Anderson, returned to the US from the UK where he'd been living as a tax exile, found out about the record and told Lee that he owned all the rights to Eddie's Town Hall concerts and that if she allowed the record to be issued he'd never speak to her again. Of course, this was utter nonsense; Anderson didn't own the rights to anything other than his tax bills, but he had terrified Lee and rather than have her fret for ten seconds Eddie and I decided to just put the project on hold. And it stayed on hold after both Eddie died in 1973 and Lee in 1975. There has been some discussion of resurrecting it in 2025; all the music and artwork are well-preserved. Stay tuned.

Eddie and I managed to organize two more LPs, neither of which he lived to see issued. One was quite special, drawn from recordings made in 1964 by the Tokyo Broadcasting System during his tour of the Far East. I was able to license this material from TBS. It was an incredible band and possibly the first time and, in some instances, only time Buck Clayton, Vic Dickenson, Pee Wee Russell, Bud Freeman, Dick Cary, Jack Lesburg, Cliff Leeman, and Jimmy Rushing ever visited that country. Once again, Johnny DeVries outdid himself with the design and Dan Morgenstern spelled each word correctly. The second LP was created from a tape recording discovered at 27 Washington Square, a recording or possibly a recording of a broadcast from Condon's uptown club in the early 1960s, featuring Ralph Sutton and Peanuts Hucko. I was thrilled to be able to use George Wettling's painting of the original Eddie Condon's on the cover.

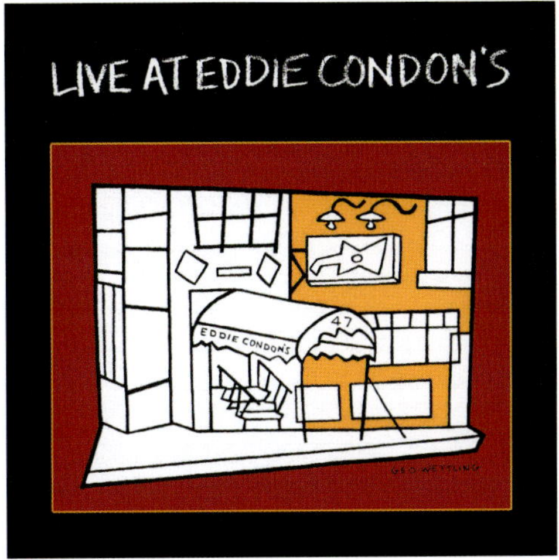

Two later Eddie Condon Chiaroscuro LPs.
(Author's collection)

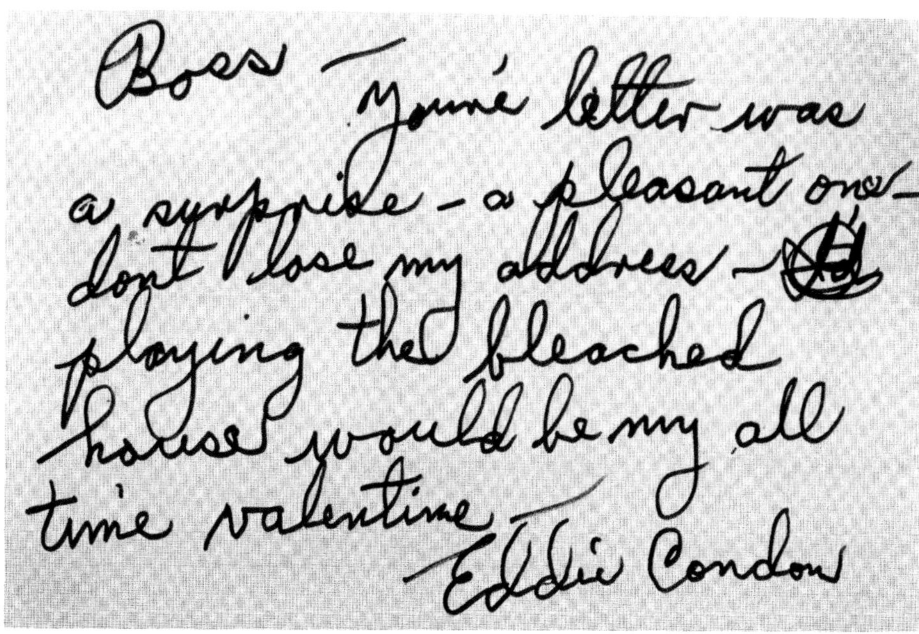

Boss —
Your letter was
a surprise — a pleasant one —
don't lose my address —
playing the bleached
house would be my all
time valentine —
Eddie Condon

Note to President Richard Nixon. (Author's collection)

Concerts, Festivals, and Tours

Then there were the concerts, festivals, and tours that ranged from remarkable to pedestrian and various levels of excellence in between. Almost every note Eddie and his pals played at these concerts was recorded, and some found their way to LP releases.

Eddie hadn't spent much time in the Washington, DC, area since the historic kerfuffle when he wasn't allowed to bring his all-star ensemble into the once sacred lady's powder room known as Constitution Hall in the 1950s. The dumbest Daughters of the American Revolution, the old ladies who ran the hall in those years, knew better than to say Eddie and his guys couldn't perform there because of "colored musicians." The DAR had taken a licking when they prevented Marian Anderson from appearing in at the hall in 1939, which in turn led to Anderson's historic concert at the Lincoln Memorial, so this time the old ladies said Eddie was banned because his music might draw "undesirable" elements. It was a front-page story in the *The Washington Post*, but despite all the favorable publicity, Eddie decided to forget about venues run by ignorant pearl-clutching racists.

But times had changed by early 1968, and Eddie headed south to visit the battlefields of Manassas, Virginia, and the annual jazz festival that had begun in that sleepy little railhead in 1967. He had a good time and went back for the next three years. He also went to Washington, DC, to lead a band that performed at the Inaugural Ball held at the Shoreham Hotel in January 1967. The performance went well and the story behind it has been recounted in the previous Tony Bennett chapter. President Nixon sent Eddie a thank you letter, and Eddie replied in a typically casual fashion as noted above.

The appearances at the Manassas festival were all recorded and were generally acceptable. They appeared on a label called Fat Cat Jazz, FCJ 103 (*Eddie Condon's Augmented Barefoot Mob – 1968*), FCJ 114 (*Eddie Condon's Strolling Reunion Commodores – 1969*), FCJ 124 (*Lou McGarity: Jazz Master – 1970*), and FCJ 130 (*Wallace Davenport: Bourbon Street Parade – 1971*).

The most exciting concert I arranged for Eddie took place on April 3, 1972, at The New School, five blocks north of 27 Washington Square. In late 1971 the university asked if I would produce a series of jazz concerts in the spring that could serve two purposes: to fill up as many seats as possible in their often empty auditorium on an off night and to provide live musicians for my audio engineering class to practice recording. I had a budget of $400 per concert.

The New School had once been a hot bed of jazz and presented good concerts in the 1940s, but there hadn't been jazz in this venue for over twenty years. That was about to change, and the first person I asked to take part was Eddie. I told him I had a budget of $400, or about $75 a man if we had a quintet. The first person he called was Gene Krupa. It would cost Gene more than that just to get his drums delivered, but he didn't care and signed on immediately. Then he called Wild Bill Davison who'd relocated to New York City and he signed on as well. I filled in Dick Wellstood and Kenny Davern. The event was lightly advertised but the concert was not only sold out but people were backed up on Twelfth Street. Eddie Condon and Gene Krupa and Wild Bill Davison together for $10? Plus Kenny and Dick? Who could believe it?

Jazz at the New School LP cover. (Author's collection)

The band was ready for action. Eddie played nicely but most of the excitement was generated by Davern and Krupa. My recording class had a two-track ReVox and four-track Scully trying to capture as much of the music as possible, and they got 99 percent of it plus some commentary. There were encores and at the end someone in the audience screamed, "We ain't leavin,'" but eventually they did. A few months later I was able to find enough money to pay the musicians for a recording date, and we issued most of the concert on an LP. Twenty years later the entire concert was issued as a CD. In the late spring of 1973, *Downbeat* and Dan Morgenstern gave *Jazz at the New School* five stars. Eddie didn't give it a thought, but Gene Krupa was thrilled and wanted to make another recording with Teddy Wilson and Lionel Hampton. It didn't happen but that's another very long story.

Leading an impromptu ensemble in Carnegie Hall in 1972. (Author's collection)

A couple of months later Eddie moved uptown and led the bands at a George Wein-produced Newport in New York concert in Carnegie Hall. There were a few thousand more people at George's event. It was a poignant reunion of Eddie with many of his musical pals, Bobby Hackett, Wild Bill Davison, Max Kaminsky, Georg Brunis, J.C. Higginbotham, Benny Morton, Barney Bigard, and a bunch of others. But the real icing on the cake of his last fling in Carnegie's Hole, as he usually called it, was Lee Wiley, who was on hand to sing the songs. Someone took a picture from the wings and we used it as the end papers for the Scrapbook. You can see part of the Porkchop resting on a folding chair.

In the late summer of 1972, Eddie's last concert tour set sail under the auspices of Columbia Artists Management. The group was called Stars of Jazz and included Art Hodes, Barney Bigard, Wild Bill Davison, Rail Wilson, Jim Beebe, and Hillard Brown. Eddie got top billing, and in late September I escorted him to the group's concert

At Alice Tully Hall, September 1972.
(Author's collection)

Eddie Condon, ace guitarist now with Bud Freeman's Summa Cum Laude orchestra at Nick's Greenwich Village, N. Y., has been signed for a part in Vinton Freedley's adaptation of Dorothy Baker's book, 'Young Man With a Horn.' Yarn revolves around the life of Bix Beiderbecke, looked upon as the great super-soul on cornet. Condon was a pal of Beiderbecke's.

Condon's never been an actor and was written into every scene in the show soon to go into rehearsal. Burgess Meredith plays the Beiderbecke part. Freeman's outfit may play the show from the theatre pit.

Notice in *Variety*, mid-1940s.
(Author's collection)

Eddie Condon, Jazz Leader for 50 Years, Dies at 67

Eddie Condon, the jazz guitarist who performed with most of the outstanding jazz musicians of the last half century, died yesterday at Mount Sinai Hospital at the age of 67. He lived at 27 Washington Square North.

Mr. Condon, considered one of the greatest left-handed jazz guitarists and as handy with a quip as with the guitar, made his final appearance in public at the Newport in New York Jazz Festival in Carnegie Hall on July 5. On that occasion, his concert was devoted to traditional jazz in company with almost a dozen of the musicians with whom he had played. He was hospitalized two days later.

A book of reminiscences, "The Eddie Condon Scrapbook of Jazz," on which he collaborated with Hank O'Neal, is scheduled to be published next month by St. Martin's Press. A

Continued on Page 52, Column 6

The New York Times

Eddie Condon in jazz festival at Carnegie Hall last year

The New York Times, August 1973. (Author's collection)

at Alice Tully Hall in New York City. I was able to sit down in front, smuggled in my Nikon, and took pictures from the fourth or fifth row. Neither Alice's nor the Columbia Artists police threw me out. The group toured all over the East Coast; some of the concerts were recorded and Jazzology issued three LPs drawn from these concerts.

And then time passed and it was 1973, the book had been designed and was in production at St. Martin's Press, but Eddie was slowing down. He was supposed to have done another concert at the New School, but he wasn't feeling up to it and Max Kaminsky subbed for his old friend. By the late spring he was failing, suffering from what was diagnosed as Paget's Disease. There were other problems as well, and in the summer he took up residence at Mount Sinai Hospital uptown. I recall his next-door neighbor was Ed Sullivan, who was also having a rough time.

Eddie had survived a lot of hospitals and there'd been a lot of close calls, but he didn't survive this one. He died on August 4th. The next day his death was announced on the front page of *The New York Times*. The obit had been in the morgue a good long while, there were possibly versions from the early 1940s, but the initial newsworthy aspect of the article had been written in a hurry and not fact checked; the Carnegie Hall performance mentioned had actually taken place in 1972, a year earlier.

A funeral service was planned for a few days later at Campbell's uptown. I was pressed into service to organize a band and some eulogists. Among others, those who spoke were Gene Krupa, Johnny Mercer, and Milt Gabler. The band was made up of Wild Bill Davison, Kenny Davern, Earl Hines, and most importantly, Lee Wiley, who made everyone cry when she sang "Back Home Again in Indiana." The TV crews were on hand; ABC did the best job and ran a segment on the evening news.

When it was all over, friends and family retreated to my recording studio. There was a lot of music and stories and reminiscing. Unhappily, I only took pictures of the musicians who came down, Johnny Windhurst and Kenny Davern plus Eddie's brothers-in-law Sid (on drums) and Paul Smith (on guitar). Later that night I guess we all watched the evening news and then got back to whatever we'd stopped doing earlier in the day.

And life danced along for fifty years. Phyllis Condon and her brothers and sisters are long gone, Eddie's daughter, Liza, died in 1999, but his other daughter, Maggie, survives and still lives in the Washington Square apartment with all the ghosts, real and imagined, that still appear now and then. Maggie has done much to keep the flame alive; in the late 1970s we worked on a screenplay that was based on many of her father's adventures and misadventures. She really wanted it to happen. The movie and Broadway show people had been after him for years, particularly Burgess Meredith.

In the mid-1940s, *Variety* announced that Meredith was planning to make a feature film based on Eddie's life. Jimmy Stewart was slated to play Eddie and John O'Hara was set to write the script. But they picked the wrong Jimmy; it should have Cagney, not Stewart.

The film was never made but one was always in the back of many minds. One night, sometime in 1980, Maggie thrust our finished "screenplay" into the unwilling hands of a young Woody Allen after he'd played a hot set of New Orleans standards at Michael's Pub, then his favorite performance venue. I have no idea if Woody even gave it a glance, but nothing came of it. There were various fits and starts after that, but nothing resulted from them either, other than fits and no starts. But there is always hope there's still a movie out there, another project that might keep the Condon light burning for a minute or two longer. It's a pretty good American story, and we're at a time when a good cheerful American, or as the publicists in the 1940s used to say "Americondon," story might be welcomed.

One possibility could be Maggie's son, Eddie's grandson, Michael Repplier, might get interested. He's a hot young producer at ABC TV and already has a couple of Emmy Awards to prove it. His beat has mostly been true crime, but maybe he could shift a little. Just before the pandemic popped he found all the videotapes of his grandfather's funeral service in the ABC archives and was fascinated by what he saw.

And in 2022, Billy Crystal came into town for another run on Broadway with a new show, *Mr. Saturday Night*. In 2023, I'm sure he remembers the benefits Eddie threw for his father, Jack Crystal, when there was trouble after the Commodore Music Shop failed and funds were scarce and life was shaky. Billy's much too old to play Eddie, but there are a bunch of kids who aren't and there are dozens of young musicians who can create the music. Who knows what might happen if things line up properly.

8

Clint Eastwood

May 31, 1930 –

I'VE ALWAYS WONDERED if Clint Eastwood ever has any down time. Today, at the age of ninety-four, does he ever have any time off, maybe at home, lying down on the couch after a long day, perhaps listening to the evening news or some music he loves? Or is there always a script to be read, a business proposal to consider, an old friend to save from the scrap heap of life? Is there always a new movie that needs editorial input, something that Joel Cox needs to tweak, is there always a new project to worry about with Gary Roach at Malpaso? I haven't seen him for a decade plus, but in the years I did, while he always appeared outwardly relaxed and in control, I never saw him when there wasn't something going on.

I don't mean to infer that Clint Eastwood was or is my best pal or that I even knew/know him very well. He may not even remember my name. I worked on various projects with him beginning in 1996 and for the next fifteen years, but after the Dave Brubeck film was completed in 2010 and Bruce Ricker died in 2011, there was no more contact. I was at his home in Bel-Air a single time to watch a movie, stayed at his guest house twice, met him at screenings in New York City on various occasions, but only had two sit down meals with him in restaurants as opposed to snacks at the Monterey Jazz Festival, used his Mission Ranch in Carmel as a B&B when working on projects of mutual interest in Carmel or Monterey, and have taken a zillion pictures of him while working on these projects. These projects were documentary films, for which I served as the still photographer, writer, older jazz eminence, or various combinations of all three.

The common denominator for all this activity was the late film director Bruce Ricker, who was one of Clint's best pals. I'd known Bruce forever, at least since the mid-1970s when he was first beginning work on his legendary film *The Last of the Blue Devils*, the film that led him to Clint and subsequently led me to Clint as well.

I worked on seven documentary films and one feature with Bruce, and Clint was involved with all those films in various capacities. These projects were:

Eastwood After Hours (1996)

Clint Eastwood: Out of the Shadows (1999)

Piano Blues (2003)

Mystic River (2003, soundtrack only)

Tony Bennett: The Music Never Ends (2007)

The Monterey Jazz Festival (2005-7, unfinished)

Johnny Mercer: The Dream's on Me (2009)

Dave Brubeck: In His Own Sweet Way (2010)

Some of these films led me to make hand-made books of photographs, sometimes with text, and the texts in these books serve as an easy introduction to my relationship with Clint.

OPPOSITE

Clint Eastwood at Symphony Hall, Boston, April 1, 2003. (Author's collection)

With Jon Faddis, Joshua Redman, and Flip Phillips. (Author's collection)

With Gary Smulyan, Lennie Niehaus, Jon Faddis, and James Moody. (Author's collection)

Handmade Book #1. (Author's collection)

Before *Eastwood After Hours* A Few Afternoons of Jazz

The first time I met Clint Eastwood and about ten seconds after saying hello and how are you kind of things, I took a bunch of pictures of him. This was in 1996, October 17th to be exact. He was standing outside Carnegie Hall looking at a poster announcing a show dedicated to him called *Eastwood After Hours*. A couple of seconds later, two New York City policemen jumped on him; just ordinary policemen, not a security detail, just guys who wanted to take pictures and get an autograph. It was a good photo op for me, so I took pictures of the policemen taking the pictures of him and with one another, from which I fashioned a handmade book, which was only appropriate for a guy who played a few policemen in his day. He was, as always, gracious and accommodating, and unlike Albert Popwell's bank robber at the end of *Dirty Harry*, the two cops got very lucky with autographs and posed pictures.

I had signed on to be one of two still photographers for *Eastwood After Hours* and a couple of days earlier in the week had been doing the same at SIR studios where forty or so of the best guys and gals in New York were rehearsing for the Big Show. And it was going to be a big show. Warner Bros./Malpaso was funding it, George Wein was producing, and my pal Bruce Ricker was the director of record. But as I was to learn, when Clint is on set, regardless of where the set may be and who is nominally in charge, he is where the buck stops. But Clint was never on set at SIR, so no one directed Arthur Elgort, another jazz fan/photographer, and myself and we got to wander about and do as we pleased. And later, as is very much his custom, Clint let the rehearsal and performance at Carnegie Hall simply happen, evolve as it should naturally.

Carnegie Hall was as good a place as any for my debut of seeing Clint in action, something I would be fortunate enough to see on multiple occasions over the next fifteen years. *Eastwood After Hours* was structured to be a valentine for Clint, a wonderful concert that featured dozens of his favorite musicians, one that would thrill not only the guest of honor but all those in the sold out house and the many thousands of others who would enjoy the film that was being produced and later released as a DVD, as well as a two-CD set of all the music that was recorded that night.

Clint is serious about his love of jazz; he plays decent amateur-level piano, writes wonderful melodies for soundtracks à la Charlie Chaplin, and whenever it makes

Eastwood After Hours DVD.
(Author's collection)

sense features jazz in the soundtracks of his films. He produced and directed *Bird*, which many consider the finest biographical film dealing with a jazz musician; his music director for three-plus decades was the noted jazz saxophonist Lennie Niehaus; and he was on the Board of Directors of the Monterey Jazz Festival for many years and did all he could to make that festival be the world-renowned event it is today. *Eastwood After Hours*, however, put all his love of music and related accomplishments in perspective.

The rehearsal on the day of performance had been going on for a couple of hours and Arthur Elgort and I had the run of the place, which is rarely the case in the overly structured Carnegie Hall. As the afternoon wore on, other photographers began to wander into the hall, but they didn't seem particularly concerned with what was happening on stage, and the combination of musicians was remarkable, perhaps a once in a lifetime opportunity to photograph this person with that person. No, they seemed content to lounge around and listen to the rehearsal. They didn't really care about Jon Faddis, or Jay McShann, or Barry Harris, or Flip Phillips, or any of the other thirty or so legendary musicians on stage.

Then it came time to rehearse the ending of the concert, when Clint would come on stage, offer a few remarks, retreat to the piano for a moment, play a little, and then turn it over to Jay McShann for a jam session-like finale. The moment he came on stage, all the other photographers who had been lounging like lizards in the sun suddenly sprang to life and pushed and shoved their way to the lip of the stage. Flashes popped nonstop, and power drives ran frame after frame through dozens of cameras. The new digital guys probably filled each and every nook and cranny in their camera's memory cards. People were standing in seats, everyone looking for the best angle. I have no idea if any of them got the good shot they were looking for, but I know it was pretty rough for the few minutes Clint was on stage. I do know they missed a lot of good ones with other musicians. I thought to myself, "I'm glad I don't do that for a living."

Barry Harris. (Author's collection)

Lennie Niehaus and Jon Faddis. (Author's collection)

With Jay McShann and Bruce Ricker. (Author's collection)

The concert itself was inspired, civilized, and beautifully structured. George Wein had been doing that kind of thing since the early 1950s and knew exactly what to do. In addition to all the jazzers, there was a twenty-piece symphonic ensemble to perform Lennie Neihaus's specially commissioned suite based on Clint's themes from various soundtracks of his movies.

There were fifteen musical segments, beginning with "Misty," featuring just Kenny Barron and Barry Harris, and ending with "Lester Leaping In" with everyone on stage. It was occasionally wonderful mayhem, but structured mayhem, because most of the fifteen musical selections were related to one of Clint's films. "Misty" was, obviously, from *Play Misty for Me*, Clint's directorial debut, and there were songs associated with *Bird, The Bridges of Madison County, In the Line of Fire,* and even *Honkytonk Man*.

James Carter, Joshua Redman, Roy Hargrove, and James Moody. (Author's collection)

Arthur had a truckload of cameras and equipment and extra-long lenses and was assigned to shoot the stage from the back of the house. I had a couple of Nikons, one for black-and-white and another for color, and was assigned backstage, dressings rooms, and casual, unexpected encounters. We had a wonderful time. I wound up with about five hundred black-and-white photographs and slightly fewer color images, from which I fashioned this handmade book that documented the film/recording from rehearsal to backstage celebrations in the various dressing rooms.

Out of the Shadows

Sometime in mid-1999, Bruce Ricker told me he was planning to produce a documentary film about Clint Eastwood, that Clint had given his approval for the project to go forward, and that there was every expectation it would in early 2000. I had known Bruce for many years, and knew of his relationship with Eastwood, so I didn't doubt for a moment that he'd produce the film on his own terms.

Later that year, Bruce asked if I'd like to sign on as a still photographer. I'd had so much fun photographing *Eastwood After Hours* in 1996 I was tempted to begin loading my cameras as soon as I got off the telephone. Other than early 2000, the exact timing for the project was unclear. All I knew was that the film would be part of the fall 2000 American Masters series and that as many as twenty-five people would be interviewed on camera, both in New York City and in and around Burbank and Carmel, California.

A few thousand telephone calls later, I was told cameraman Vic Losick was scheduled to turn them on pretty soon and we should be ready to roll sometime in February. Much to my surprise, his camera was scheduled to roll at my 830 Broadway office and a truckload of equipment arrived on February 8 in preparation for the interviews with Nat Hentoff, my old friend and neighbor, and Meryl Streep, who it happens was also my neighbor, I just didn't know it.

Out of the Shadows DVD. (Author's collection)

Handmade Book #2. (Author's collection)

My studio turned out to be the location of choice because it was large enough to accommodate all the equipment, I could determine its availability, and it was an easy walk for both people scheduled for interviews.

Noel Coward once said that everything is a matter of lighting, and within about an hour Vic Losick proved it, turning one of the rooms at 830 into a beautiful set. Nat's interview was set up so that the old Steinway piano from my 1970s recording studio, Downtown Sound, was in the background. This was only appropriate, since Nat had heard a couple of hundred recordings made on that piano, written liner notes for some of them, and published critical essays on even more.

As soon as Nat completed his interview, the camera, lights, and all the furniture were moved around and, suddenly, a new room appeared, ready for the appearance of Meryl Streep. I hadn't seen her in person for about a quarter of a century, since we shared a table at The Ballroom on the opening night of Joe Papp's first (and only?) cabaret appearance in the 1970s. I am sure Meryl didn't remember anything about the evening other than Papp's appearance, which was wonderful, but I recall she looked exquisite all those years ago, and, of course she still did.

Bruce conducted each of the interviews working with nothing other than a yellow pad, which appeared to contain little more than some hastily scribbled notes, but he had a head full of pertinent data and the ability to improvise just the right question when required. The questions were interesting and to the point, and the answers were remarkably illuminating, so much so that on occasion I found myself simply enjoying the conversations and not always catching the right photographic moment.

Two months later, more interviews were scheduled in New York: William Goldman at his home, Eli Wallach at a friend's apartment, Janet Maslin at a Warner Bros. screening room, and Phyllis Huffman at her midtown office. Two additional interviews were scheduled at 830—Rip Torn and Stanley Crouch. Vic and his guys managed to alter the room once again for Rip Torn, but we never got to see the fourth variation; Stanley Crouch simply failed to appear, the only unprofessional episode of the entire project. Perhaps he lost his way walking across Twelfth Street, just as he occasionally lost his way as a jazz and cultural critic in recent years.

A week or so later, the California portion of the project began in earnest. Five members of the New York production team—Bruce, Vic, and myself, along with Karen Bernstein, the project's production manager, and Jesse

Meryl Streep. (Author's collection)

Nat Hentoff. (Author's collection)

Sweet—camped out at the storied Château Marmont on Sunset Boulevard. Other than a copy of Helmut Newton's remarkable oversized book *SUMO* on display in the hotel's lobby, there was no decadence to be seen anywhere. The ghost of John Belushi and other deceased guests never appeared, but Gene Hackman, Lenny Niehaus, and Richard Schickel did. They were thoroughly interviewed, and once again one room was made to look like three. The old Macintosh Power Book on which I kept notes even appeared in the Schickel interview.

Most of the next few days were spent at the Warner Bros. lot in Burbank. Karen Bernstein was concerned because there was nothing in writing that stated we could use the Warner Bros. facilities. Bruce continually assured her that all that was required were the magic words "Clint has signed off on it," but she was hard to convince. We arrived at the studio gate early on the morning of April 18. Bruce said something to the guard, a call was made, the magic words were passed along, and the action was faster than immediate. The gate swung open, and we were off to Soundstage 4. We even had parking passes, which I'm led to believe are sometimes harder to come by than soundstages.

A long line of legendary figures in the movie business then made their way into the cavernous soundstage, took a seat before the camera, and recounted experiences and impressions of working with Clint over the years. Some even sat in the beautiful custom-made leather director's chair we'd pinched from his Malpaso office to use as a prop. Henry Bumstead, James Garner, Jack Green, Joe Hyams, Jeff Lewis, Bill McKinney, and Buddy Van Horn were interviewed over the next few days. We moved across the street to interview Joel Cox in his editing room that is part of the Malpaso complex.

The other Southern California interviews were conducted at different locations: Donald Sutherland, looking very much like the elegant movie star he was, and the noted novelist Walter Mosley at hotels in Santa Monica and Beverly Hills respectively and Barry Reardon in his Encino office. Then we headed north to Carmel to camp out at Mission Ranch and conduct interviews with Ruth Woods, Eastwood's ninety-one-year-old mother; his then wife, the lovely Dina Ruiz Eastwood; and of course the man himself.

At this point, the production team was joined by film critic Dave Kehr, who was to conduct the interview with Clint, and the curator and historian Mary Lee Bandy, who was to interview Ruth Woods. Both were inspired choices. Dave is an expert on Clint's films, as well as the credited writer of *Out of the Shadows*. Mary Lee, the head of the film division of the Museum of Modern Art, was not only

With Karen Bernstein, Dave Kehr, Mary Lee Bandy, Bruce Ricker, Vic Losick, and Anthony Wall. (Author's collection)

Kincaid Photography truck parked at Mission Ranch. (Author's collection)

a longtime supporter of Clint's films but also a protégé of the legendary Willard Van Dyke, who just happened to have been a high school classmate of Ruth Woods.

Helmut Newton's big nudes and the dark shadowy corridors at the Château Marmont were in stark contrast to the bucolic surroundings of Mission Ranch, where an inflatable Easter Bunny stood guard at the ranch's restaurant door. This alone should have told us the interviews would be as relaxed and charming as the location, but if the bunny and jellybeans hadn't been enough, the seemingly permanently parked, fading green Kincaid Photography pickup truck from *The Bridges of Madison County* amplified the point. The truck was a useful backdrop for group photos, as was Edward Weston's legendary location, Point Lobos, which can be seen in the distance across the water in some of the photographs.

If we were treated like princes at Warner Bros., we were treated like kings at Mission Ranch. When all the interviews were complete and most of the hard work was done, Clint and Dina Eastwood delighted everyone with a memorable evening of fine food and conversation at the Stillwater Bar and Grill overlooking Pebble Beach's eighteenth hole. I sat across from Clint who shifted into jazzer mode and quizzed me all night long. The closest thing to a serious conversation that evening was Bruce's offer of $100 to anyone who came up with the best title for the film. No one did, but later Dave Kehr won the prize with his suggestion of *Out of the Shadows*. It is unclear if he collected.

But it wasn't over yet; there was still another trip to California in the works. Lenny Niehaus completed his "Clint Eastwood Suite" and other incidental music for the film. This had to be performed and recorded, as did Morgan Freeman's narration. An interview in *New York* with Martin Scorsese was also in the works.

In mid-July, recording sessions were scheduled for Lenny's ten-movement suite, each movement inspired by one of Clint films. An eighty-piece orchestra was assembled at the Eastwood Scoring Stage on the Warner Bros. lot; Joshua Redman was to be the featured jazz soloist, but there were some other exceptional jazz musicians added to the symphonic ensemble.

The musicianship of Lennie and the large ensemble was remarkable. One section of the suite never advanced past the rehearsal take, and none needed more than one or two takes. Some of the overdubbing took a little longer, but the recording was done in two days. Morgan Freeman's narration was even faster; three or four hours of studio time had been set aside for his narration, but he completed the recording in less than one. He was finished and out of the studio door before the tape was rewound.

The Scorcese interview was on again, off again, but it was finally arranged to be held at his Park Avenue office on July 28. There was already a rough cut of the film, so anything Scorsese may add might mean removing something already selected. It turned out Scorsese had a great deal to say in the eleventh hour, and much of it was used in the film—even though this was probably a nightmare for the editor. Scorcese's interview was very complicated from the photographic standpoint because while the previous subjects had all been very relaxed, this was not the case with Scorsese. There had been very little time with Donald Sutherland; there was half as much with Scorsese. That any light reflected from Scorsese worked its way into my camera that day is remarkable.

I used four cameras on this project: two Nikons, a 2.8 Rolleiflex, and a Deardorff view camera. All of the photographs I included in the handmade book I made for Clint are from the Nikons, except those of Clint that were taken with the Deardorff and another using the Rolleiflex. The lighting came from either the stage lights for the film or a flash, except for those taken outdoors. A flash was used more often than the stage lighting, which tended to be not unlike the atmospheric lighting used for the film *Bird*.

The photographs chosen for the album were simply those I thought were representative of the people interviewed and I found interesting on a photographic level. Whenever possible there is both a black-and-white and a color image of the people I photographed during the interviews. In some instances, I included more images or group shots if they seemed appropriate. One color photo was digitally manipulated, but which one is a secret. I missed three people who were interviewed and filmed by Bruce—I was unable to make the sessions because of personal business obligations and my apologies are offered to Richard Slotkin, Dani Janssen, and Forest Whitaker for not including them in the Festschrift.

The text that accompanied the photographs came from the on-camera interviews. I simply extracted portions that seem to make sense. They are mostly chronological, appearing as the comments that were actually made. In a few instances, a statement from one part of an interview was combined with one from another, but only if the subject matter was the same. The sequence in which the interviews and photographs were presented is the sequence in which they were conducted. Nat Hentoff was the first interview; Martin Scorsese the last.

Outside Symphony Hall. (Author's collection)

Mystic River (April 2003)

In early 2003 I finally managed to clear time to make my way to Boston to see the production of *Mystic River* in action. Principle photography was long completed, but Clint had written many melodies he wanted to be used in the soundtrack. Lennie Niehaus had orchestrated them, and at Clint's insistence Warner Bros. had hired a well-known local band to record the music. The big band, more commonly known as the Boston Symphony, had their own hall and recording was scheduled to begin on April 1. It was quite an adventure.

Clint's music has been recorded frequently over the years and used as soundtracks for his own films and those of others, but this was the first time it had ever been recorded by a symphonic ensemble as prominent as the Boston Symphony Orchestra. All hands were on deck to make certain everything went off without a hitch. Still photographs were hardly the most important matter to be considered, and since there were no questions about jazz to be asked or answered I was able to assume my favorite position as a fly on the wall and take pictures as situations developed, beginning with Clint outside the hall waiting impatiently for things to get underway, followed by Lennie and Clint and recording personnel in the basement of Symphony Hall making certain everything was sounding as it should.

Lennie headed upstairs and assumed his position on the podium and the music began. It was all flawlessly produced and recorded, and the music soon filled the hall, all of which, both the orchestra and chorus, was recorded and in the can by late afternoon. That left plenty of time for casual pictures and hijinks. Clint was given a conducting lesson and soon "conducted" the orchestra. Many of the musicians on stage had put down their violins and

With Dina Eastwood on the podium. (Author's collection)

Conducting the Boston Symphony Orchestra. (Author's collection)

With Lennie Niehaus. (Author's collection)

Symphony Hall and the Boston Symphony Orchestra. (Author's collection)

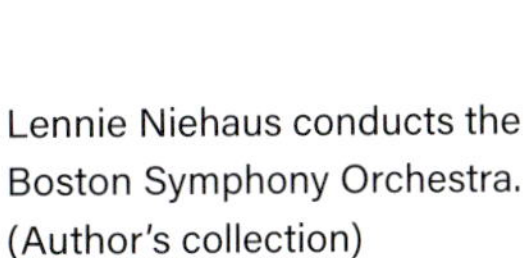

Lennie Niehaus conducts the Boston Symphony Orchestra. (Author's collection)

horns and were busy taking photographs of their guest conduction, and I had a fine time taking pictures of them taking pictures.

At one point Dina Eastwood joined Clint on the podium, and that led to some nice pictures as well. Then finally, when the dust had settled, Clint wandered over to a Steinway D that had been pulled to the side of the stage and relaxed a little, fiddling with some new themes for the next movie. It was a perfect day, no mishaps anywhere along the way. All the music was in the can, and I had a bunch of photos ready to be printed and used. One photo of Clint "conducting" actually turned up in some Warner Bros. publicity. It was a cute picture.

Piano Blues (June–July 2003)

Three months later, there were more pictures to be taken for another project. Martin Scorcese was producing a series of films for PBS concerning the blues. He'd asked Clint to create and direct one of the films that was to be called *Piano Blues* and shooting was scheduled to take place on June 30 and July 1 in Los Angeles and Burbank, California.

Piano Blues DVD. (Author's collection)

This was a very different situation than a couple of months earlier in Boston because this one not only involved multiple musicians, but Clint was both directing and in a couple of instances planned to do some piano four hands, just for fun, notably with Ray Charles at Ray's RPM Studio. Once again, the shooting days went flawlessly and there was not a wasted moment.

Ray arrived on time at RPM and the camera crew had everything set up. I remember when Ray entered the room, he had a cigarette in each hand and both were lit, smoking a bit and ready for action. I guess he wanted to be sure. He chatted with Clint for a moment and then the two of them went to the piano and talked some more. The conversation was all that was captured for the film itself, and it was intercut with excerpts of older filmed performances featuring Albert Ammons, Pete Johnson, Joe Turner, Jay McShann, and two long complete performances by Ray, his band, and four Raylettes.

Playing Ray Charles's Steinway. (Author's collection)

Ray didn't play very much that day and whatever playing he did was not used in the finished film. He was not doing well health-wise, and while highly spirited and enthusiastic, he was having a very hard time breathing, coughed a good deal, and was dead in less than a year. This may well have been one of his last on-camera

With Ray Charles. (Author's collection)

With the entire crew. (Author's collection)

Handmade Book #3. (Author's collection)

Pete Jolly, Dr. John, Henry Gray, and Clint. (Author's collection)

interviews. The next day all the shooting was on a Warner Bros. sound stage and featured Dr. John, Henry Gray, and Pete Jolly.

In 2006 I created the last of three handmade books that featured pictures and text from the films I worked on with Bruce and Clint. This is the introduction to *A Few Pianists*.

In early October 1996 the production of *Eastwood After Hours* was well underway when Bruce Ricker asked if I'd like to join Arthur Elgort and photograph the rehearsals and performance at Carnegie Hall. He didn't have to ask twice. There were many opportunities for interesting photographs during those three days in October, and over the years there have been other equally interesting gatherings of musicians during music festivals, video projects, and recording sessions that involved Clint Eastwood.

The piano remains my favorite musical instrument. I never figured out how to play it, but I've listened to others very seriously. Along the way I've recorded many of the finest jazz pianists. At least half of the releases on Chiaroscuro Records feature groups led by pianists or in solo recital. The same holds true for the concerts and festivals I've produced over the years. I love to present pianists as either the leader of the band or a soloist. All these recordings and performances have afforded access to the finest pianists of the last forty years, and I've usually had my camera close by.

A dozen pianists, either alone or with others, are pictured on the following pages. Kenny Barron, Barry Harris, Jay McShann, and Renee Rosnes were part of *Eastwood After Hours* in 1996; Ray Charles, Dr. John, Henry Gray, and Pete Jolly were prominently featured in *Piano Blues* in 2003; and Dave Brubeck, Hank Jones, and Oscar Peterson headlined the Monterey Jazz Festival in 2006. Clint Eastwood is the common denominator; he's pictured at all these events, as well as at Boston's Symphony Hall during the *Mystic River* recording session in 2003.

There are many stories that can be told about these photographs. Some of my favorites involve Barry Harris in 1996, playing two pianos, saying he "always wanted to try to do this." I have no recollection of how the music turned out. In 2003, Ray Charles entered his studio with not one, but two lit cigarettes, one for each hand. He was rarely without one during the recording. This year, in 2006, a favorite moment was spotting Dave Brubeck backstage, about thirty minutes before show time, making changes to his *Cannery Row Suite*. Then there is the fuzzy picture of Clint Eastwood, who volunteered to take an indisposed Dave Brubeck's place in a piano trio including Oscar Peterson and Hank Jones. I shot it through a hole in the wall with an exposure of about half a second.

Video cameras and audio recording documented all these events with precision and clarity, but sometimes a frozen moment, a picture that doesn't move or make a sound, can convey a sense of time and place with a different kind of feeling. A few of these images manage to do this.

The Last Projects, Finished and Unfinished

All the documentary films Bruce Ricker made with the assistance, collaboration, and support of Clint Eastwood were made with modest budgets, and as I look back over the photographs I took from the years 2005–2010 the overlap of projects becomes obvious. It even extended to projects such as the film *George Wein—A Man for All Festivals* that Bruce worked on for over a decade and was never completed. It is also interesting to me that four of the subjects of these documentaries were artists who are profiled in this book, and I knew a fifth, Johnny Mercer, well enough to correspond with frequently, even though I only met him a single time.

The Monterey Jazz Festival film was never completed, but a DVD of Tony Bennett's performance at Monterey 2005 was included as a bonus with *Tony Bennett: The Music Never Ends*. When Dave Brubeck was at Monterey in 2006, he came down to Mission Ranch and interacted with Clint, and much of this footage was used in *Dave Brubeck: In His Own Sweet Way*. Many of Clint Eastwood's movies were blockbusters, but just as many were only moderately successful. These were some of his artistic favorites. He knew how to be thrifty when he had to, and this rubbed off on the documentary films with which I was associated. And because of the way some of these projects were filmed and later assembled or even left unfinished, there are bits and pieces of extraordinary footage unused and largely forgotten.

George Wein: A Man for All Festivals (2003–2008, Unfinished)

The film about the life and career of the noted impresario, George Wein, will be recounted in another chapter of this book. It was a grand undertaking, but one that didn't work out as it should have for any number of understandable and equally large number of unfathomable reasons.

With Ornette after the metaphysical interview. (Author's collection)

The Monterey Jazz Festival (September 2005–2007, unfinished)

I saw more of Clint at the three Monterey Festivals, culminating with its fiftieth anniversary in 2007, than all the rest of the films combined. This was because he was a jazzer and was always around during the festivals, an MC at certain concerts, conducting interviews, interacting with musicians he enjoyed, and at least in one instance performing as a pianist quite by accident but also as a matter of necessity. Maybe there were other performances, but I only saw one in 2006. The other reason Clint was visible was all the people in charge of production, sound, and cameras were living at Clint's Mission Ranch in Carmel, and he lived just down the road.

The general idea that was being discussed for the film was "fifty years of Monterey," but I don't think there was ever an overall outline as to what Clint, Bruce, and Tim Jackson, the head of the festival, hoped might be a finished film. I think the plan was to film everything that looked good and then see what might be put together when the dust settled, and for three years that's what they did. You can tell Clint was deeply involved with the project; all you have to do is look at the photographs of him conducting interviews with Sonny Rollins, Jim Hall, Ornette Coleman, James Moody, his old friend from *Midnight in the Garden of Good and Evil*, Hank Jones, Dave Brubeck, Tony Bennett, and a host of others, either at the Monterey Fair Grounds or Mission Ranch.

The Ornette interview was perhaps the most interesting. His afternoon concert on the Jimmy Lyons Stage had gone well. I watched from backstage and much to my surprise, Ornette even spoke briefly to the audience. There was plenty of light and I took photographs from the wings. Once the concert was completed, the loose plan was to arrange an interview with Ornette and Clint, excerpts of which could possibly be used in the larger film being made/considered, but it almost didn't happen. The only reason it did was because James Jordan, formerly of the New York Council on the Arts, now full-time manager of his cousin, Ornette, was in favor of the interview. When I asked Ornette if he'd like to do the interview with Clint, he replied, "No," but then added, a pause and a half later and after a stern look from his cousin, added, "But I will."

The interview lasted about half an hour and was not what anyone expected. Clint and Ornette rarely touched on jazz, the Monterey festival, or even anything that related to music. It was all about life, death, assorted metaphysical theories and concepts, as well as a fair amount of hokum. Clint clearly enjoyed himself and kept the conversation moving along until it became too convoluted. There may well be a remarkable small film hiding somewhere in those digital files, but that will take some work.

There were and are many other wonderful memories of musical moments I witnessed during those Monterey weekends. Many of them involved circumstances where Clint interacted with the artists and many when he was not present. A few of those when he was in camera range were remarkable.

In 2006, Oscar Peterson was scheduled to close the festival on the Jimmy Lyons stage. On the same day, but earlier in the evening, at about 7:00, Dave Brubeck presented the world premiere of his *Cannery Row Suite*. After a long intermission, Oscar was to follow Dave with his trio beginning at roughly 9:00. At the other end of the fairgrounds, Hank Jones' Trio was scheduled to perform at Dizzy's Den at 9:00. Roberta Gambarini was his guest, doing double duty, since she'd covered the lead female vocal parts with Dave Brubeck an hour earlier. She'd made it to Dizzy's Den on time thanks to an electric go-cart.

The plan was to close the festival with a piano spectacular, featuring Oscar (eighty-one), Dave (eighty-six), and Hank (eighty-eight), possibly the world's oldest piano trio. This was a great idea but if things didn't go perfectly the possibility of a train wreck loomed large. I had been backstage and on stage since about 4:30 and there was a rehearsal for Dave Brubeck's new composition, *Cannery Row Suite*. It was a staged performance with Roberta Gambarini, Kurt Elling, and Chris Brubeck as loosely costumed performers, a modest set, a narrator, Dave's regular quartet, half a dozen other vocalists, and a second pianist. As I recall, Dave even wore a floppy hat during the performance, one that went off without a hitch. But the rehearsing, new writing, and the performance itself had taken a bit of a toll on Dave, and he went down to the dressings rooms to rest up for the gala conclusion.

On stage for the Piano Trio.
(Author's collection)

At 9:00 Oscar and his trio hit on time, as did Hank over at Dizzy's Den. I can only assume that Hank's performance was as perfect as was his custom. Despite having come down with shingles the day before, he delivered the goods and after his set boarded the electric scooter and was driven to the Jimmy Lyons Stage.

Holding the piano lid for Oscar Peterson.
(Author's collection)

Oscar was finishing up his set and was noticeably tired. He'd just finished a week of performances in San Francisco and there was some speculation he might not make Monterey. Everyone was much relieved when he arrived safely. When he finished his set, he thought he was done for the night and as he saw the stage being rearranged for the piano spectacular, he realized he wasn't. This was reinforced when Clint went on stage and reminded him. He was game and so was Clint. But it was late, getting cold and the eighty-six-year-old Dave Brubeck was exhausted from his earlier performance it was impossible for him to perform. When Clint went out to speak with Oscar, he knew that he was looking at a rough situation; Oscar was out of gas, Hank was available but hurting with the shingles, and Dave had already been taken back to the hotel. This meant their third pianist was Clint, at least for part of the finale.

I don't know what movie it was in but there's a line in one of them when Clint talks about planting your feet and telling the truth. Well, he sat at the piano with a microphone in hand and told the truth. The music got underway, a little differently than everyone had perhaps imagined, but it worked out just fine. A young pianist from College of the Pacific, Glenn Zalski, who'd been part of Dave's performance earlier in the evening, eventually took over for Clint. I found a hole in one of the sets or curtains and took a single picture of Clint at the piano telling the truth. It is about a half second exposure and fuzzy, but it's all there is. Later, when everything had settled down, I grabbed a couple of pictures of Clint helping Oscar sign the piano and then helping him to the elevator that took him down to ground level. It was the last time I saw OP.

With Oscar and Hank Jones. (Author's collection)

Saying goodbye to OP. (Author's collection)

With Kelly and Oscar Peterson, and Bruce Ricker. (Author's collection)

With Diana Krall, Dexter, and Frank (2007). (Author's collection)

With Kelly, Oscar, Bruce, and Tim Jackson. (Author's collection)

Then it was late Saturday afternoon a year later and I was also exhausted. I don't remember why I was so beat up, but I remember my plan was to head to the shaded parking lot where we'd stashed the rental. I planned to rest for an hour or so before another six hours behind a camera. I'd just settled into the back seat when my mobile rang. It was a call from Clint, who asked where I was, and I said I was in the parking lot getting some additional film. He said that was OK, but could I come back as quickly as possible because he needed a photo to be taken right away. So I passed on the rest and made my way to wherever Diana Krall's tour bus had stopped. She had just arrived from somewhere to close the show on the Jimmy Lyons Stage that night. But now she was far more concerned with wrangling her two twin sons, Dexter and Frank. Clint was helping as best as he could and he wanted a posterity picture for his scrapbook, just to prove he can handle good babies as well as bad guys. I don't know if these pictures proved the case, but they were the last baby pictures I ever took.

The fifty years of Monterey film are a distant memory. This year is the sixty-eighth festival, and advertising clips feature Clint from years ago, as well as clips of other great artists presented years ago. There are a zillion musical treasures resting on the shelves at Malpaso in Burbank. At least there were about ten years ago when someone borrowed one to use for a project in Poland. It is unclear how this footage will ever be used.

Tony Bennett: The Music Never Ends (2007)

Of the documentaries that Bruce completed, this was the one with the most complicated history. It took forever to get started, but once it did the process flowed smoothly. After a great deal of back and forth, three loose ends came together in September 2005: an extended face-to-face meeting and filmed interview with Clint at Mission Ranch, an exhibition of Tony's paintings and lithographs at Oliver, Elliott, and Sebastian Fine Art in Carmel, and the cleanup spot on Saturday night at the forty-eighth Annual Monterey Jazz Festival. To my eyes everything went perfectly but it took forever to overcome various hurdles and for the film to become part of the WNET American Masters series. I don't remember all the details and probably wasn't aware of them as they were happening, but all I have to do is look at the stills I took. Between September 2005 and the spring/summer 2007 there was no action, then in the space of a couple of months we filmed interviews with Mel Brooks, Harry Belafonte, Danny Bennett, Stephen Holden, Bill Charlap, Everett Raymond Kinstler, Arthur Penn, and Jonathan Schwartz at 830 Broadway, Gay Talese at his home, Don Rickles in Burbank, Martin Scorcese at DGA, and Tony at his 100 Central Park South studio and his home a few doors west.

With Tony Bennett at Mission Ranch. (Author's collection)

The Music Never Ends DVD. (Author's collection)

There wasn't a dull one in the bunch. Harry spoke about Tony's social activism, Ray was his art teacher, Mel about performing in the early days in the 1940s and '50s, Danny on managing and restructuring his father's career, Bill discussed the great American songbook, and the others covered a host of other topics. It was a history lesson that covered many different parts of the history of popular music in America.

Johnny Mercer: The Dream's on Me (2009)

This was the easiest of the documentary films associated with Bruce and Clint because Johnny Mercer wasn't around to second-guess anything, and for the most part it was filmed away from Burbank or Carmel. It provided me with an opportunity to reconnect with André Previn, who I hadn't interacted with since the Mel Powell Pulitzer Prize adventure in the early 1990s. The diversity of the talking heads, all the way from performances by Michael Feinstein and Dr. John to commentary by George Wein, Tony Bennett, and Stephen Holden, pointed out the universality of Johnny's music. The very personal commentary by Jean Bach was also revealing, particularly regarding Johnny and Judy Garland.

The Dream's on Me DVD. (Author's collection)

André Previn and Qi the Pup at 830 Broadway. (Author's collection)

Jean Bach at home in Washington Mews. (Author's collection)

The back of the Mercer/Condon Mandolin that now lives at the Bix Beiderbecke Museum in Davenport, Iowa. (Author's collection)

Dr. John and Michael Feinstein at Bennett Studio. (Author's collection)

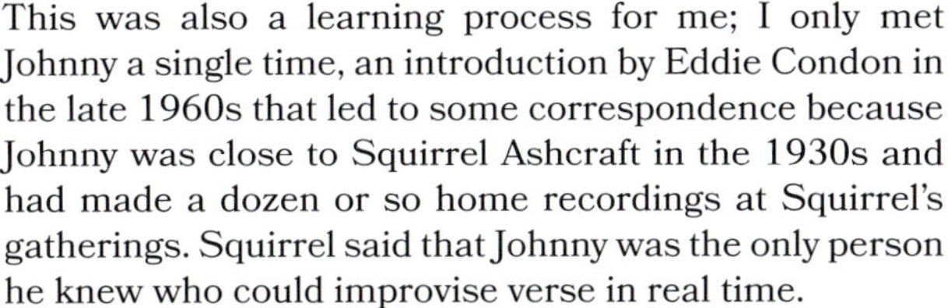

This was also a learning process for me; I only met Johnny a single time, an introduction by Eddie Condon in the late 1960s that led to some correspondence because Johnny was close to Squirrel Ashcraft in the 1930s and had made a dozen or so home recordings at Squirrel's gatherings. Squirrel said that Johnny was the only person he knew who could improvise verse in real time.

But Jean Bach really knew him; her husband Bob Bach had written a wonderful book with Ginger Mercer about Johnny, *Our Huckleberry Friend*. It was a beautiful scrapbook filled with pictures and the lyrics of most of Johnny's most famous songs. That book and Jean's comments filled in a lot of blanks.

A few years earlier, Phyllis Condon had given me the special mandolin Johnny had made for Eddie. It wasn't much of a mandolin because Johnny had the back altered so it could used to smuggle a bottle of whiskey past pesky Ginger and Phyllis. Johnny had the name *Eddie Condon* inlaid on the instrument in Eddie's handwriting. I ultimately donated the instrument to the Bix Beiderbecke Museum in Davenport, Iowa, because Bix also liked whiskey and I had no need to smuggle any.

The back of the Mercer/Condon Mandolin that now lives at the Bix Beiderbecke Museum in Davenport, Iowa.

Dave Brubeck: In His Own Sweet Way (2010)

In His Own Sweet Way was the only film in the series that I served as anything other than still photographer, advisor, and location provider. I actually wrote this one and was credited as a co-producer, but it was also the end of my career of working with Clint in any capacity. Bruce Ricker had been the driving force in getting these various documentaries off the ground since 1996, and he was slowing down because of health issues.

The Dave Brubeck project had its origins in 2003 with the *Piano Blues* documentary. Dave was featured in that film and then four years later in 2007 when Dave's *Cannery Row Suite* was premiered at the fiftieth Annual Monterey Jazz festival and the cameras were running. Clint was and is a long-time Brubeck fan. In an interview with *Jazz Times*' Lee Mergner at the time of the film's release he said:

> *My early love for jazz coincided with Dave Brubeck appearing on the scene in the late 1940s and early 1950s in Northern California where I grew up. As jazz was developing into one of the great American art forms, Dave and his music – seeing him in person – really inspired me in my artistic career. Coming full circle in 2007, I was given the opportunity to make this documentary about Dave, which I readily accepted. Our goal was to have something to celebrate Dave's 90th birthday. Dave Brubeck is an American Legend. He is a bonafide original who not only introduced a whole new generation to the world of jazz, but who continues to make significant contributions to the music today and to explore the international language of music. Hopefully, in Dave Brubeck: In His Own Sweet Way, we've been able to capture Dave, his life and his music for the ages.*

That pretty much sums it up. I was part of that generation Clint was talking about; my first Columbia $1.00 sampler had a track by Dave and *Jazz Goes to College* was the first LP I owned that wasn't a sampler. I managed to see the "classic" quartet live as a teenager in Syracuse and later in many other contexts, all of which are detailed in the previous chapter devoted to Dave.

It was almost a perfect project. The only thing that went wrong is there is no DVD of this film. The film was finished on time and was presented on TCM on Dave's birthday in 2010, and a couple of additional times as well. Then an argument erupted regarding a Warner Bros. DVD release. The legal people representing Dave thought there was a pot of gold with a DVD release. What they didn't realize was that by 2010 the DVD market was just beginning its downward spiral, which has continued to this day. Warner Bros. was willing to release a DVD just as a favor to Clint and when the legal folks started making demands, the game was over and the result was no DVD. They made a few handmade copies and that was that. Bruce Ricker died in May 2011; Dave died in December 2012, one day before his ninety-second birthday. Clint is ninety-four and will be looking at ninety-five in May. I haven't been in touch with him since the Dave Brubeck film and the last sequences that were done at Mission Ranch in 2007. There is every possibility he doesn't even remember my name, but I suspect that if the circumstances were correct or maybe if he spotted one of the handmade books of photographs, he would.

CLINT EASTWOOD
PRESENTS

Cover Photographs By

DAVE BRUBECK: IN HIS OWN SWEET WAY
A DOCUMENTARY

In His Own Sweet Way BBC promotional flyers.

CLINT EASTWOOD PRESENTS
DAVE BRUBECK: IN HIS OWN SWEET WAY

Directed and Produced by **Bruce Ricker**
Executive Producer, **Clint Eastwood**
Co-Producer, **Patti McCarthy**
Professor of Film, University of the Pacific
Co-Producer, Writer **Hank O'Neal**
A Rhapsody Productions, Inc. Documentary
For The Brubeck Institute at the University Of The Pacific,
Steve Anderson, Director
In conjunction with BBC Arena
Co-Producer-Anthoı

Paul Desmond, Dave Brubeck & Leonard Bernstien, 1960 by Don Hunstein

From The Creative Team that brought you:

Johnny Mercer: This Time The Dream's On Me
Tony Bennett: The Music Never Ends
Piano Blues
Eastwood After Hours
Straight, No Chaser
The Last of The Blue Devils

c

9

Sherman M. Fairchild

April 7, 1896 – March 28, 1971

MOST PEOPLE don't get accidentally killed in hospitals they've helped build. I don't mean die, I mean accidentally killed. The odds of this happening are pretty slim. A baby born in 1895 in upstate New York? What would be the odds that the baby would live a glamorous, exciting life and then be killed in a hospital in New York City seventy-six years later? Pretty slim. But that's exactly what happened to Sherman M. Fairchild.

These days, if I stopped people wandering down Broadway and asked them if they knew anything about someone named Sherman M. Fairchild, I'd probably have to stop about one hundred thousand people before anyone would recognize his name. He's been dead for over fifty years and wasn't a household name when he died in 1971, and that was just fine with him. I only knew Sherman for four years, from late 1967 until his death in March 1971, but they were very interesting years. We spent a good deal of time together and the impact he and his friendship made on my life was both considerable and long-lasting. In fact, it still is impacting me today, fifty plus years later. Who was Sherman and why was he interesting? This is the short version:

Around the turn of the century, Sherman's father, George, took control of a modest time clock company, the International Time Recording Company. A few years later this company became known as the Computing Tabulating Recording Company (CTR), with Fairchild as its chairman. He wasn't a hands-on chairman because at the time he was a member of the US House of Representatives, from 1907 to1919, representing New York's thirty-fourth Congressional District. In 1914, Thomas Watson, on the run from the law and the National Cash Register Company, became part of Fairchild's company but maintained a low profile. In 1924 CTR changed its name to International Business Machines with Fairchild as chairman of the board. When he died a few months later, Watson took over and everyone knows what happened after that.

A few years earlier the elder Fairchild had assisted his son with a business venture involving aerial cameras, one of Sherman's first business ventures, and then upon his father's death, Sherman inherited stock in the newly named IBM company worth about two million 1924 dollars. At the age of twenty-eight, he joined the board of IBM and was the largest single stockholder in the company. When he died in 1971, he was still on the board and largest single stockholder. Sherman sold some of his stock to launch other business ventures, and some people say if he hadn't sold any of the stock to start these companies he'd have been even wealthier, but he certainly wouldn't have had as good a time.

When I began my New York City CIA tour in 1967, I knew of Fairchild through my friend Marian McPartland. "Oh, you have to meet Sherman," she'd say, "he loves jazz pianists." I met Sherman, but under other circumstances; I needed to ask a question of someone at one of his companies. Fairchild Aerial Surveys was now Fairchild Camera and Instruments and built sophisticated cameras, some of which were installed in satellites and high-flying airplanes like the U-2. There was something someone

OPPOSITE

Sherman M. Fairchild aerial photographer. (Author's collection)

NAMES & FACES

Fairchild's ever-expanding universe

One of world's richest, most inventive septuagenarians, Sherman Fairchild keeps pioneering technological frontiers. He is forever creating new products and new companies

Sherman, 1930 and 1970. (Author's collection)

in Washington needed to know and I was charged with gathering the information. In late 1967 or early 1968 I met Sherman at 17 East Sixty-Fifth Street, his home in New York City.

It was unlike any home I'd ever visited in New York. It had once been an ordinary old-fashioned town house, but Sherman had gutted it and built a very modern residence. The various levels were reached not by stairs, but by ramps so that his elderly Aunt May Fairchild, who also lived there, wouldn't have to navigate stairs. There was an enclosed interior courtyard, there was a lot of glass, and the expansive living room, slightly below street level, boasted two perfectly matched Steinway L pianos. Sherman had removed the legs from the pianos and mounted each on a marble base. This annoyed the people at Steinway and they refused to service them.

My first meeting with Sherman was in his dining room, overlooking the music/living room and courtyard below. I asked him about who I should speak with at his facility in Syosset, he gave me a name and said he'd make sure I got a good reception. He also said he'd heard about me from Marian and he wanted to give me a tour of his unusual home. This is when he told me about the Steinway L pianos and Steinway's annoyance, but he also took me

The inner workings of a Fairchild Compressor.
(Author's collection)

to the back of the living room, around a corner, down a short hall, and pointed to a small door. "Have a look," he said. I opened the door and found a narrow staircase that wound up into a small room, maybe four by eight feet, that overlooked the two pianos in the living room. This modest room was a compact, state of the art, two-track recording studio, crammed with the best equipment money could buy. Some of it, I was to learn later, was manufactured by the owner of 17 East Sixty-Fifth Street.

Did I forget to say that in 1931 Sherman had founded a company called Fairchild Recording Equipment Company? Or that in the late 1940s the Fairchild tape recorders were far superior to those made by Ampex, but they were too good and too expensive, so just like VHS beat Beta, Ampex beat Fairchild? Or that at the time Fairchild Limiters and Compressors were still the industry standard and in 2025 are still regarded as the best ever made and will set you back about $30,000 if anyone is willing to sell one, which happens very rarely?

Or that, working in conjunction with the legendary Bob Fine and Lawrence Scully, he helped to develop the variable pitch system that allowed LP records to be produced with fat grooves for loud passages and low frequencies and thinner grooves for quiet passages and high frequencies? Or that he wired his living room for sound; crammed the room full of outstanding microphones and suggested if I ever wanted to record something just to let him know? Or that he'd outfitted the living room so that if a flashbulb went off it would set off electronic slaves that would flash from dozens of other sources? There were never any nasty flash shadows at 17 East Sixty-Fifth, and if someone played well, they could be recorded perfectly.

He took me to the basement where there was an office complex. The lady in charge was Patricia Reybold, the daughter of his close friend Malcolm Reybold. He told me if I needed to track him down, I should ask Patricia to do the tracking, which she did with efficiency and enthusiasm for the next four adventurous years. Then he sent me on my way but emphasized that if I wanted to bring musicians by to record, just to let Patricia know.

I don't remember the first recording session, but I know they started very soon, continued until early 1971, and there were many of them. Classical, jazz, blues, even a little pop, with artists as diverse as old timers like Joe

Venuti, Cliff Jackson, and Eubie Blake; blues artists such as Blind Gary Davis and John Paul Hammond, Benny Goodman's vocalist, Jane Harvey, and a classical duo, Phillips and Renzulli.

I taught myself audio engineering in the small room on 65th Street; it was on-the-job training but with world-class musicians making real records that would be released into the real world. I fouled up a few times but usually found a way to cover it and make it right. And those now over half a century old LPs, now reissued as CDs, still sound pretty good. Just a few days ago someone told me how much they love the sound on a Dick Wellstood record I did at Sherman's in 1969, when I was just winging it and trying not to let anyone down.

1969 was also the year that the first steps were taken to launch the record company that eventually morphed into Chiaroscuro and the year that Sherman started to be helpful with advice on what kinds of film to use for my first ventures into taking something other than snapshots. In fact, he arranged for RGB, a company based in Hollywood, to send a batch of color film for me to use and when I'd used it he sent it off for processing. If the bill for the processing was $19.75 and I gave him a twenty, he'd give me back a quarter. This is the way he was and it worked out just fine.

He was just as precise when it came to ordering reprints. He knew the man on one line was better than the guy on the other. The memo below was written a couple of months before he went into the hospital for the final time. I kept using that processing company for over a decade after his death, and it is still in business at the same address on Highland Avenue.

The record company that evolved into Chiaroscuro in late 1971 began as Halcyon Records in 1969. Halcyon was Marian McPartland's name, and it had but one release on its own before Sherman, Marian, and I formed our partnership. The one record was a duo album entitled *Interplay* and featured Marian accompanied by Linc Milliman on bass. Marian had started the recording project at another studio but finished it up at 17 East Sixty-Fifth. It was issued as HAL 100 and was quickly folded into the "new" Halcyon Records, a company run by the most unlikely trio to ever produce records.

Some of the recordings made at 17 East 65th Street. (Author's collection)

3 x 3.60	10.80
3 x 3	3.00
Air mail ref 60	1.80
Mailing from here	30
	15.90

letter-liminator II FORM NO. 1101/3 ▪ Another Time-Saving System by Regent Standard Forms, Inc., 15th & Wallace, Phila., Pa. 19130

SHERMAN FAIRCHILD
17 EAST 65th STREET
NEW YORK, N. Y. 10021, U.S.A.

message

TO Hank O'Neal

DATE 1/13/71

Here's an order envelope, card to be mailed back that they have received the order and mailing box for the film, in case you want any prints made. For some reason or other, I find the 5 x 7 prints at 80¢ each and the 11 x 14 for $3 are better than the 8 x 10. Apparently the people on those two lines who set the color balance do a better job than the fellow on the 8 x 10 line. Note that you have to add $1.50 for shipping and mailing irrespective of the size of the order.

SIGNED SMF

reply

DATE

SIGNED

SENDER: Snap out Yellow copy only. Send White & Pink with carbons in tact.

RECEIVER: Write reply, keep White original, return Pink copy to sender.

Sherman's photographic advice and the first order from RGB. (Author's collection)

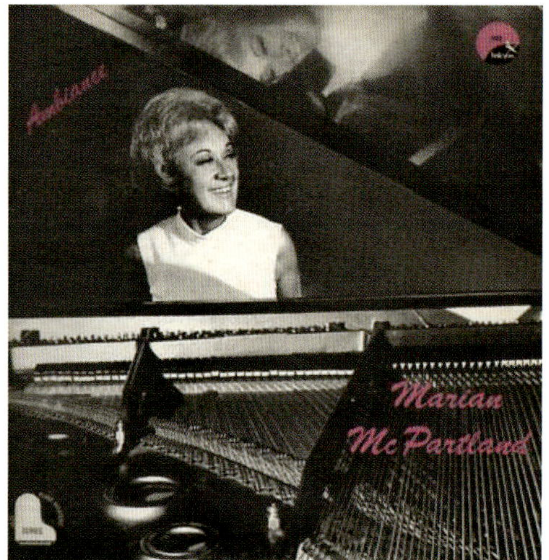

The first three Halcyon releases. (Author's collection)

Willie The Lion Smith at 17 East 65th Street.
(Author's collection)

Sherman, Marian, and I became partners in the record company in late 1969 or early 1970. This story is outlined elsewhere, but this company and its evolution put me in touch with a number of Sherman's other friends, including Walter Burke, his power of attorney, Ed Everett, who ran Fairchild Recording Products and helped me with all kinds of electronic equipment that I still use forty years later, and Jack Andersson, a wonderful photographer, who showed me some tricks and took fine photographs for our earliest recording projects. The association with these people set the stage for the development of the next phase of my life.

The first four records we produced and released were by Earl Hines, Bobby Henderson, and Marian in a trio setting and finally, in mid-1970, Willie "The Lion" Smith, a project with which Sherman was deeply involved.

He even wrote wonderful liner notes for the album.

> *I met Willie The Lion longer ago than either of us care to remember. Gene Austin, with whom I was in the music publishing business to me to hear him at a smoky, one-room speakeasy called Pod's and Jerry's on 133rd Street. I used to go there on many a night and Willie was always ready to play my favorites, Sneakaway, Echoes of Spring and Rippling Waters. Later I remember hearing him play duets with James P. Johnson, at the Pied Piper in Greenwich Village and I continued to be fascinated with his marvelous technique and rich harmonic innovation. My being such a fan of Willie's started a friendship that has gone on through the years.*
>
> *Willie played at my home many times. I recall one memorable New Year's Eve party in the thirties when he and Fats Waller joined their talents at the two grand piano is, and Fred Astaire got into the act as well, playing piano-accordion. We didn't have the convenience of tape or even adequate disc recording then, or we would have put down a never-to-be-repeated jam session for posterity.*
>
> *Willie has been to my house more frequently in recent years, and now I have mikes in the piano and a tape recorder running even before he comes through the door, so that not a note will be lost. This record grew out of these informal sessions, and the result – made live at Blues Alley in Washington, D.C – is Willie The Lion at his best, exuberant and in his element in this spontaneous setting. After forty years of listening to Willie play, I'm extremely happy to continue to be a part of it.*

The obvious question is why didn't we simply record Willie The Lion at 17 East Sixty-Fifth Street? Why embark on a live recording at Blues Alley? The answer is equally simple. We did record The Lion at Sixty-Fifth Street but the results were not as good as anyone wanted or expected. Willie The Lion was nervous. We'd do four or five takes of a tune and there would be something wrong with each one, we undertook four recording sessions but there was nothing that was first rate. Sherman and I became very frustrated, as did Willie.

At one point Willie told me he had a week at Blues Alley in Washington coming up in June and I thought "why not try a live recording" where Willie would be playing for a live audience instead of a dead tape recorder. I called Squirrel Ashcraft and booked myself into Ashcraft Towers. I took enough of Sherman's gear to Washington to do the job, recorded for two nights and got all we needed, or so I thought. It turned out that while the music was wonderful, the recording was a little shaky. It was out of phase, but a little device Bob Fine had built with Sherman's assistance, the Fairchild Compatibilizer, solved the problem and a fine LP was the result.

Live at Blues Alley was issued in late 1970 and proved to be the final release of the short-lived partnership. By this time Halcyon began to fray; Marian's primary interest was in recording herself, and Sherman and I were interested in other pianists as well. This led to disagreements but Sherman cleared up this problem by returning to Marian the name Halcyon Records, two completed records and one as yet unreleased master, Marian's duets with Teddy Wilson, as well as her initial financial investment in the partnership. She went her way with Halcyon, which remained active for about a decade and released almost twenty LPs. Sherman and I went on alone and Chiaroscuro was chosen as the label name.

As time passed, I got to know Sherman's closest friends, including Diahn Williams, the number one girl friend, and Connie Sharpe, hot on her heels at number two. Diahn must have been living at Eastfair at least part time because that's one of three numbers I have in an old telephone book. I wonder if it still rings if I were to dial it. Connie had an eastside New York number, as of course, did Patricia Reybold, his administrative assistant who managed everything perfectly. Happily, she also liked jazz bands a bit and even accompanied me one year when I traveled south to record the Manassas Jazz Festival in the early 1970s.

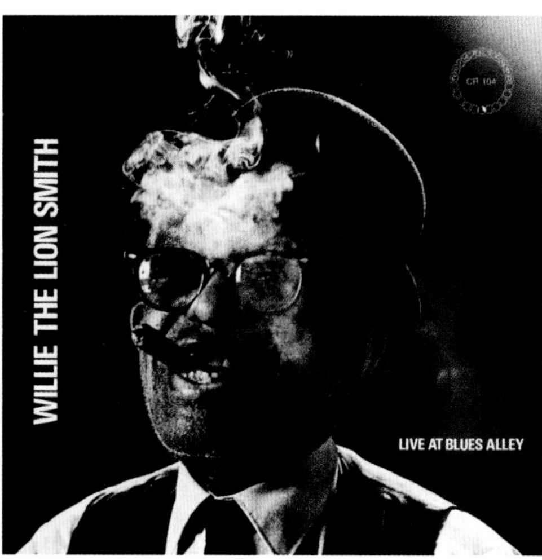

The final recording for Halcyon featuring Willie The Lion Smith. (Author's collection)

Both Diahn and Connie were lovely actresses, and each had modest success in movies and television. After Sherman's death, the two girls had a jolly time throwing one another's possessions out the windows of Eastfair, Sherman's Normandy-style chateau that sat on sixty-six acres in Lloyd's Neck, Long Island. I was told Sherman's will stipulated that Diahn receive 1 percent of his estate and Connie receive about a quarter of a million dollars plus a bunch of artwork, but only artwork on a specific floor. The gossip was that there was an enormous squabble over a tapestry that hung between two floors. But both wound up winners and lived happily ever after. Diahn acquired Eastfair, married the noted lawyer Thomas McGrath, and they still live at this wonderful castle. Connie was cast as Al Pacino's wife in *Serpico* and later married the producer of the film, Marty Bregman.

Eastfair was a remarkable place. It looked as though it had been transplanted from France, stone by stone, and looked that way because it was modeled on an old castle. Maybe all the stones were imported from a kingdom with castles. Besides Jerome Kern's piano, the main thing I remember about it were the tables in the long entrance hall on which were displayed many photographs of very lovely women in elegant silver frames, girlfriends and friends who were girls from the 1920s until the present. I remember admiring a radiant portrait of Gloria Swanson.

The house wasn't on the water, but the property was and there was so much of it, Sherman had sold off a few pieces, at least one lot(s) to Malcolm Reybold. When I told him my father was looking for a place close to New York

SIDE ONE

1. Relaxing (Theme)
2. Music On My Mind
3. Sweet Georgia Brown
4. Honeysuckle Rose/ Squeeze Me
5. Contrary Motion
6. Conversation on Park Avenue
7. Take Me Out To The Ball Game
8. Relaxing

Produced By: Hank O'Neal & Sherman M. Fairchild

Cover & Liner Photographs: Jack Andersson

Recording & Album Layout: Hank O'Neal

Mastering: Fine Recording, Inc.

Previous Halcyon Releases in the Jazz Piano Masters Series

HAL 100—Interplay
Marian McPartland Duo

HAL 101—Quintessential Recording Session—
Early Hines, solo piano

HAL 102—A Home in the Clouds
Bobby Henderson, solo piano

HAL 103—Ambiance
Marian McPartland Trio

City to build a retirement cottage he offered to sell him two acres on the water for $10,000. I wish my father had written the check. I'll bet I could find Eastfair on Google Maps if I looked hard enough.

Everything came to a crashing halt in February 1971. I went over to 17 East Sixty-Fifth on a Monday afternoon and asked Patricia if everything was set to go see Oscar Peterson the following night at the small club that was once located in the basement of the Plaza Hotel. By this time, Sherman and I were completely on our own; Marian had pulled back from the partnership and wanted to do her projects by herself, which her talent allowed her to do with grace and skill for many years. Sherman knew Oscar was no longer signed to MPS and this was two years before Norman Granz launched his last recording company, Pablo. Sherman wanted to snatch Oscar and had the resources to do it.

Patricia looked at me and said, "Don't you know?" All I knew was that Sherman was scheduled to have a physical the previous week. And this is what happened, as best as I can remember. The doctors found a couple of polyps in Sherman's intestine. This was probably more serious for him than it would be for a younger person in better health. He was seventy-six and had undergone a colostomy some years earlier. They'd checked him into Roosevelt Hospital and operated to remove the polyps. This should have been the end of it, but it wasn't. And he didn't seem to be recovering properly.

There was a second operation to see if they'd twisted an intestine that was causing a blockage, but they couldn't find anything. There was a third operation to see if they'd left a sponge inside. They hadn't. Meanwhile, Sherman was in rotten shape with various problems; raging fevers were the most prominent. His three primary visitors were Walter Burke to keep a lid on things, Jack Andersson to talk about pictures, and myself to play cassette tapes and talk about music to take his mind off pain and other annoyances. His artist of choice for about a month was Ralph Sutton.

After the third operation the problems continued and there was also a problem with his breathing. It didn't look good, but he hung on. I went by one day to play a tape for him, and he looked at me and said, "Hank, I'm not going to die." I agreed with him but was worried.

A day or so later, Walter Burke was standing outside Sherman's room reading the *Wall Street Journal*. A short article caught his eye. It said an impure batch of Abbott Laboratories intravenous glucose had been discovered. It had sickened hundreds and killed a handful of people. Burke looked in at Sherman and saw the bottle of glucose dripping into Sherman's arm. He also saw the name Abbott Laboratories. He alerted the doctors. Tests were done and it was determined Sherman was dying of blood poisoning. Steps were taken to reduce this, but it didn't work. Though it did manage to stop his heart. They got it back going but finally all the stress from the three surgeries and the poisoning and the heart stoppage and the fevers were just too much, and the hemorrhaging began. He died on March 28.

I was told that in addition to Diahn and Connie, he'd left his closest staff seven years' salary and remembered the Salvation Army, which he once told me was the best charity he could think of, and many other charities as well. It was a substantial estate; at the time of his death he was still the largest stockholder in IBM and IBM was the bluest of the blue chips in 1971. One day when Patricia and I were playing in the basement we calculated that at the time he was taking in about $15,000 a day in dividends.

A few weeks after his death I was summoned by his lawyers. They told me the small record company we had founded was Sherman's last venture with which he was personally involved, but his last will predated its formation. They added that because of the complexities and size of his estate and because everything would be scrutinized very carefully, all the rules had to be followed as precisely as possible. They added they knew Sherman would have wanted me to continue the company and I should have his share, but because no mention of this was made formally, I would have to purchase Sherman's share from the estate if I wanted it.

My voice was probably shaking, and I asked how much that might be. With a smile, one said, "We feel Sherman's initial investment would be appropriate." Sherman, Marian, and I had each put up $500 to start the company. I was able to buy the company, all the masters, the bank account, and the stock for $500; this was the beginning of more adventures in music, photography, and hundreds of exciting new friends and associates that continue to this day.

But there was still one more project to finish; one Sherman and I had planned in January, to record Mary Lou Williams. This is how I described it in the liner notes of Chiaroscuro 103:

> *In January 1971, when Sherman Fairchild and I decided to continue the Jazz Piano Master series as it was originally conceived, we put our heads together to decide upon an artist to record. Shortly thereafter, I asked John Hammond about his ideas*

for a choice. Without hesitation he said, "The single most important person to record in New York City right now is Mary Lou Williams." Mr. Fairchild agreed and the project was underway. Within a week, however, Mr. Fairchild entered the hospital with an illness that would prove fatal, and, because of this and other factors, the production schedule was delayed. In June, recording was finally completed and this release is Mary Lou's first solo record since 1946. It is a magnificent record, and I'm certain Mr. Fairchild, as co-producer, in spirit, if not in fact would be very proud.

I somehow managed to scrape together $540, union scale for a solo piano record in 1971. Mary was happy to have it and I was thrilled to be able to give it to her. It may not seem like much but that was just about my monthly take home pay with the CIA and in 2025 dollars it is over $4,000. This was the first recording I'd funded on my own and when the check came back I saved it. I didn't have the fancy Bank of New York account in my own name yet so I used my old personal account. It even had my "official" name, the same one that was on my CIA credential. My signature is awful; I was probably terrified.

I still have the bank account. In 1971 it was a very fancy account at the Bank of New York, with personal bankers. A few hundred million can ensure such things. Some years ago, The Bank of New York sold most of its more modest accounts to JPMorgan Chase. I still have the old account number at Chase but not the fancy service.

In 2025 Wikipedia noted:

Sherman Mills Fairchild (b. April 7, 1896 – March 28, 1971) was an American businessman and investor. He founded over 70 companies, including Fairchild Aircraft (Fairchild Aviation Corporation), Fairchild Stratos, Fairchild Hiller, Fairchild Recording, Fairchild Industries, now Fairchild Corporation and Fairchild Camera and Instrument. Fairchild made significant contributions to the aviation industry and was inducted into the National Aviation Hall of Fame in 1979. His Fairchild Semiconductor Company played a defining role in the development of Silicon Valley and its business culture. He held over 30 patents for products ranging from silicon semi-conductors to the 8mm home sound motion picture camera. Fairchild is also responsible for inventing the first synchronized camera shutter and flash as well as developing new technologies for aerial cameras that were later used on the Apollo Missions.

He was also a cofounder of Pan American Airlines and American Airlines and was the original developer of Republic Airport.

And they should have noted but didn't that he was not just an investor but also an inventor; was once in the music publishing business; partnered with Gene Austin, the noted vocalist; thought Art Tatum, Fats Waller, and Willie "the Lion" Smith were as interesting and important as Howard Hughes, who was his frequent house guest; built more different types of airplanes than anyone else in the country; was a fine photographer and a decent pianist; ran the company that both funded and developed the first integrated circuit at Fairchild Semiconductor, the first real Silicon Valley company where he both encouraged, funded, and employed Gordon Moore (of Moore's Law and Intel fame); and on occasion made substantial donations to many arts organizations and charities, including museums and hospitals, in one of which he just happened to be killed by a bad batch of glucose. No action was taken against Roosevelt Hospital or Abbott Laboratories.

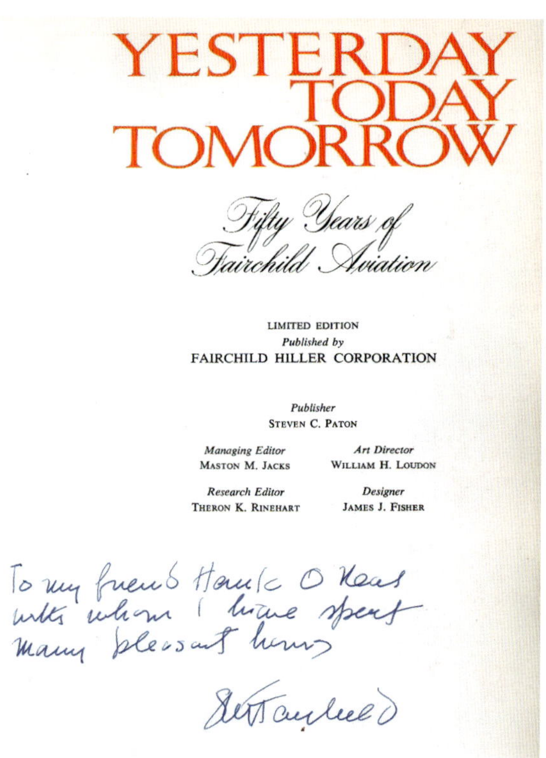

YESTERDAY TODAY TOMORROW

Fifty Years of Fairchild Aviation

LIMITED EDITION
Published by
FAIRCHILD HILLER CORPORATION

Publisher
STEVEN C. PATON

Managing Editor
MASTON M. JACKS

Art Director
WILLIAM H. LOUDON

Research Editor
THERON K. RINEHART

Designer
JAMES J. FISHER

To my friend Hank O'Neal with whom I have spent many pleasant hours

Inscribed *Yesterday, Today and Tomorrow.* (Author's collection)

The original LP release of CR 103. (Author's collection)

The expanded CR(D) 103. (Author's collection)

The Bank of New York account. (Author's collection)

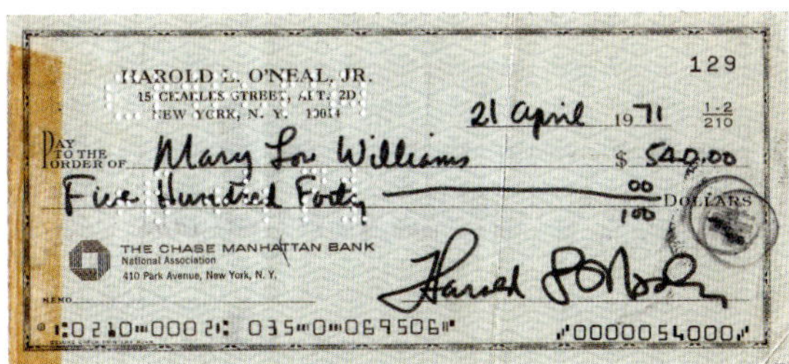

Payment to Mary Lou Williams, 1971. (Author's collection)

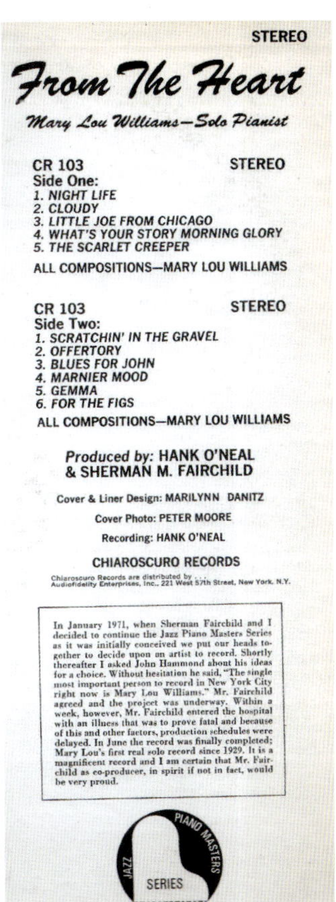

STEREO

From The Heart

Mary Lou Williams—Solo Pianist

CR 103 STEREO
Side One:
1. NIGHT LIFE
2. CLOUDY
3. LITTLE JOE FROM CHICAGO
4. WHAT'S YOUR STORY MORNING GLORY
5. THE SCARLET CREEPER

ALL COMPOSITIONS—MARY LOU WILLIAMS

CR 103 STEREO
Side Two:
1. SCRATCHIN' IN THE GRAVEL
2. OFFERTORY
3. BLUES FOR JOHN
4. MARNIER MOOD
5. GEMMA
6. FOR THE FIGS

ALL COMPOSITIONS—MARY LOU WILLIAMS

Produced by: HANK O'NEAL
& SHERMAN M. FAIRCHILD

Cover & Liner Design: MARILYNN DANITZ

Cover Photo: PETER MOORE

Recording: HANK O'NEAL

CHIAROSCURO RECORDS

Chiaroscuro Records are distributed by . . .
Audiofidelity Enterprises, Inc., 221 West 57th Street, New York, N.Y.

In January 1971, when Sherman Fairchild and I decided to continue the Jazz Piano Masters Series as it was initially conceived we put our heads together to decide upon an artist to record. Shortly thereafter I asked John Hammond about his ideas for a choice. Without hesitation he said, "The single most important person to record in New York City right now is Mary Lou Williams." Mr. Fairchild agreed and the project was underway. Within a week, however, Mr. Fairchild entered the hospital with an illness that was to prove fatal and because of this and other factors, production schedules were delayed. In June the record was finally completed; Mary Lou's first real solo record since 1929. It is a magnificent record and I am certain that Mr. Fairchild as co-producer, in spirit if not in fact, would be very proud.

JAZZ PIANO MASTERS SERIES

10

Astrud Gilberto

March 29, 1940 – June 5, 2023

I DON'T THINK Astrud ever planned on becoming or being "The Girl from Ipanema." But she sang the song on March 18, 1963, at a recording session that featured Stan Getz and her then-husband Joao Gilberto and soon there was no turning back. The recording was released a year later, in March 1964; it won the Grammy for Record of the Year in 1965 and she was forever linked with it.

She told me any number of times it was a surprise to her that she was asked to be on the record, and there is a fair amount of misinformation floating around about how and why things went the way they did, but she was very clear about what happened. It was also clear that during the late 1970s and early 1980s it was much more than the music for the two of us.

Astrud and Joao were married in 1959, and by 1963 things weren't as rosy as they were at the beginning. They divorced in 1964. Her birthday was coming up on March 29, and she intimated to me that being on the record was a birthday present of sorts. Of course, it was a present that a commercially minded recording producer like Creed Taylor would have welcomed, if not insisted on, because he wanted someone to sing the English lyrics to the song, which Joao was unable to do. Astrud's father was a linguist, and she was fluent in half a dozen languages and could sing in even more. She was paid less than one hundred dollars for her efforts and Stan Getz even tried to keep that from happening.

Norman Granz sold the Verve label to MGM in 1960 and the 1963 recording date was for a Verve release, but it would seem the people in control of the label at the time didn't know what to do with "The Girl from Ipanema" as a single or *Getz Gilberto* as an album. They held the record for a full year, finally releasing the album in March 1964 and the single three months later when the album began to make some noise.

The edited version of "Ipanema" only contained Astrud's vocals; Joao had been edited out and the record was a hit, reaching #5 on the Billboard charts. It became the first jazz-oriented record to win a Grammy for Record of the Year. Astrud told me she walked around for a year playing a demo disc of the record, trying get someone to pay attention to it and virtually no one did, but once it was released the public noticed what Verve and the others had not. Suddenly Astrud was something and was prominently featured on a Stan Getz recording in May 1964, *Getz au Go Go*, and a live album from Carnegie Hall with the Getz quintet in October. She was signed to Verve without Getz and recorded the first selections for her own album the same month, and also appeared in a lackluster MGM musical movie, *Get Yourself a College Girl*, in which she sang "The Girl from Ipanema" once more, this time for more than thirty-five dollars. There was also a single release of "The Girl from Ipanema" on the MGM Label. And a career was launched.

OPPOSITE
Astrud Gilberto, 1978.
(Author's collection)

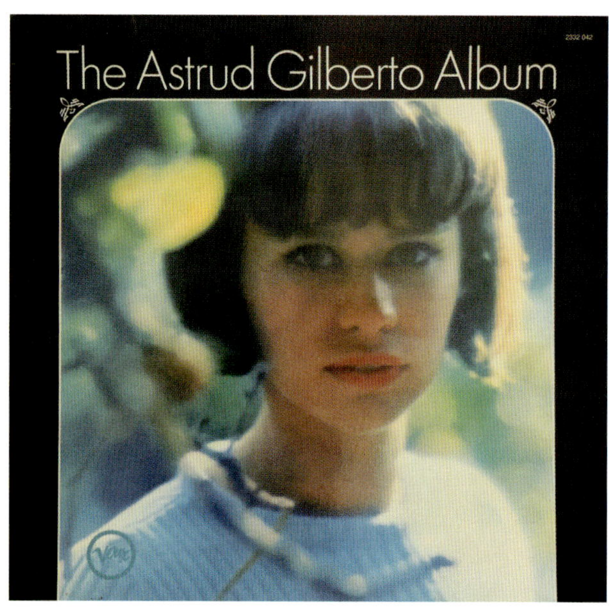

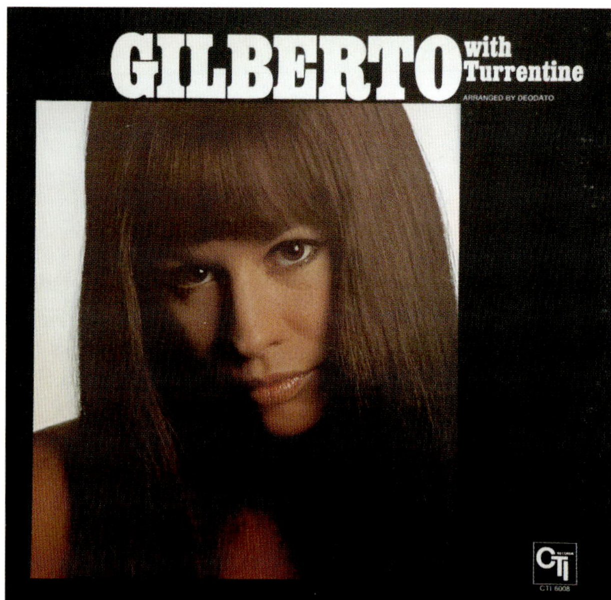

This led to a series of eight well-produced, well-performed releases on Verve between the years 1965 and 1969. Creed Taylor teamed her with Stanley Turrentine in 1971 for a CTI release, and in 1972 she released *Astrud Gilberto Now* on the Perception label. Then she more or less retired from public performance.

In 1976 the noted entertainment executive Bill Gallagher decided he wanted to dip his toe back into the record business and jumped from movies and video at Gulf and Western to resurrecting the struggling Audio-Fidelity Enterprises, the company that was distributing my Chiaroscuro records at the time. By early 1977 he'd found some new methods for financing recording, and it was going well. One day he called and asked that the next time I was uptown to pop in for a visit, which I did a day or so later.

Bill asked me what I knew about Astrud Gilberto, and I said very little other than "The Girl from Ipanema" and a couple of other songs with which she was associated. I said Bobby Hackett loved to play some of those bossa nova hits from the 1960s because he thought they were beautiful. That was about the extent of it. He then said he thought the time was right for a well-produced and financed recording by Astrud, that he was pretty sure he could raise the money, and he had indications she was ready to consider returning to recording and performance. He added, "Would you be interested in handling this kind of project and producing a record with her?"

Astrud Gilberto LPs, 1965–71. (Author's collection)

That Girl from Ipanema LP liner, 1978. (Author's collection)

I was more experienced with instrumental recordings, but he made it sound as though it might be a great musical adventure and was so certain he could raise enough money to finance it I agreed and suggested he should arrange a meeting with Astrud to discuss a possible project.

Everything fell into place, Astrud was eager to get back to work and make a new record, and Bill secured the necessary funds. I then headed down to the Colony Record Shop and bought every one of her out-of-print records, and we met at Downtown Sound on August 4, 1977, to discuss the project. We all got along well at the first meeting and then there were more meetings that month and into October.

Ultimately, we used about forty of the best musicians in New York City, with special arrangements by Don Sebesky (3), Vince Montana (3), who was very hot in those days), Al Gorgini (3), and Ben Aronov (1), who was Astrud's music director. The contracting for the various recording sessions was done by the arrangers and some of those chosen were artists who appeared on Chiaroscuro releases over the years, Gene Bertoncini, Jack Wilkins, George Young, Urbie Green, and Jimmy Knepper. Chet Baker was a guest artist on one selection, "Far Away," and not only played soulful trumpet but sang with Astrud as well. This was a dream come true for her; she had modeled much of her vocal style on his lyrical trumpet and vocal style; she loved his lack of vibrato. It was the

With Chet Baker and Don Sebesky at Downtown Sound, 1977. (Author's collection)

first and only time she would record with him, and this was the final track recorded for the project.

The record was incredibly complex, requiring hundreds of hours of recording and mixing, in a variety of studios. Fortunately, we had unlimited access to Downtown Sound and in some instances cancelled recordings sessions in order to accommodate Astrud's needs. Vince Montana's tracks were all mixed at Sigma Sound in Philadelphia so Astrud could stay close to home.

In addition to overseeing this and balancing a number of strong artistic temperaments, I also had to worry about a suitable cover for the album. I don't know how many photographs I took of Astrud, many hundreds, but none of them were acceptable for reasons that had nothing to do with whether they were any good or not. Ultimately, the photograph chosen by Astrud was taken by a close friend; she insisted on using it, and the cover was not the best she'd ever had.

The music, however, was spectacular, and once the record was released in 1978 began making its way up the charts and even nudged the BeeGees out of the top slot in a couple of markets. But then there was a problem. Bill Gallagher may have been the president of AudioFidelity Enterprises, but Herman Gimbel was the owner, and he panicked at the promotions' costs associated with moving the album up the charts and cut the promotion budget. The record stalled and in about a month, a year of hard work and seventy thousand dollars' worth of production fees were down the drain. This was a great disappointment, but in one way the record served to convince Astrud she should return to singing in public. This helped revitalize her career for the better part of two decades.

The newly resurrected career was also a struggle because Astrud was not enthusiastic about public performance. She was very shy; the fame from "The Girl from

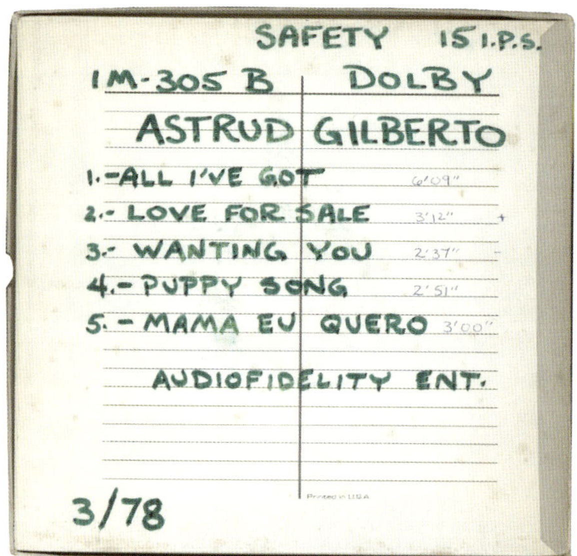

The Master Safety Tapes for *That Girl from Ipanema.* (Author's collection)

Ipanema" had come as a surprise, and she was far more comfortable away from public view. After the release of the new record, she took her first club date at Fat Tuesday's in New York City, and it was such an event a TV crew came in to film an interview and a bit of a performance and broadcast it. When the word got out that she was accepting occasional bookings, she found herself once again in great demand. Despite her reluctance but with a bit of encouragement, if the venue was appropriate, she took more and more engagements. I followed this closely for nearly five years and was always astounded at her professionalism and uncanny knack for surrounding herself with outstanding musicians, notably in the years when Ben Aronov or Gil Goldstein were her music directors. I never heard a bad performance, and I heard a lot of them, from Japan to Switzerland and many places in between.

If you're smart, you don't date your secretary or other girls in the office, or if you are in the theater or a movie set, your leading lady. Or if you're producing an LP, the artist you are producing. But sometimes, on happy occasions, the artist or producer might have other ideas and in this case Astrud did, as did I.

It was complicated in 1979 and 1980. Downtown Sound was on its last legs and not long for this or any other world because even though the owner of the building at 173 Christopher Street had promised to extend the lease, he was having second thoughts. Pegasus Records, the project George Avakian, Gerry Mulligan, and I were hoping to get off the ground was more or less grounded because of the lack of a distribution deal and George was becoming increasingly disillusioned. But at the same time an opportunity emerged that might solve that problem.

Meanwhile, in late 1979, the same year she first performed at Fat Tuesday, Astrud relocated from her nice Main Line home in Philadelphia to The Galaxy, a luxury apartment building in New Jersey on the Hudson overlooking Manhattan. This meant she no longer had to commute to New York City for work or pleasure.

But as 1980 drew to a close, the doors were closing at Downtown Sound and I was looking at transferring everything from thirteen rooms on Christopher Street to a three-thousand-square-foot, largely open space at 830 Broadway, a loft-like space filled with multiple dumpsters' worth of rubbish abandoned by the previous occupants, with marginal plumbing, erratic electricity, an ancient elevator, leaky windows, and a balloon mortgage I had to find a way to pop within eighteen months.

On tour in Japan with Ben Aronov, 1980.
(Author's collection)

But before embarking on that adventure, there was one that was somewhat better. Astrud had always been very popular in Japan and when the word got out she was once again appearing in concert, her former Japanese promoter Tom Nomura wasted no time and organized a month-long series of concerts in all the major and a few minor cities in that country. I had never been to Japan, but Astrud had and even knew enough words to sing a song or two in Japanese.

We left from Philadelphia on June 12, overnighted in San Francisco and headed east. Ben Aranov, Astrud's music director, left from New York and for the next four days Astrud and Ben rehearsed with a group of fine Japanese musicians, Pedro and Capricious. The musicians who made up this group were very popular in Japan, performing Latin and samba classics with Japanese vocalists. They were terrific and worked well with Astrud and Ben. They put together a fine show that premiered in Matsuyama City on June 18. This was followed with concerts in Hiroshima, Kyoto, Okayama, Shizuoka, Osaka, Nagoya, Fukashima, Yamagata, Tokyo, and Sendai. We were back in the United States on July 6.

A dozen concerts in sixteen days and Astrud, Ben, and Pedro et al. performed at 100 percent night after night. There were no complaints and the concerts, almost all of which began at 7:00, were filled with enthusiastic fans. Astrud was gracious and accommodating to everyone involved and enjoyed herself both on stage and off. There were only twelve scheduled concerts, and we were in Japan for twenty-three days so there was plenty of time for travel, sightseeing, and being tourists.

The Japanese tour, 1980.
(Author's collection)

And then, when the notes faded from the last song from the last concert, we got some sleep and the next day headed back to the US and reality on July 6. It was quite an adventure and a wonderful opportunity to not only be with Astrud but to witness firsthand what a celebrated artist endures when on tour.

Once back in New York City it was time to do everything possible to make a success of Hammond Music Enterprises, and one of those things was to interact with people in the record business, either executives or noted artists. Astrud was a noted artist, and she was a welcome presence at many of the gatherings we organized.

There were many other trips and concerts and adventures, all the way from Moosehead Lake, Maine (just a holiday), to St. Moritz to Lisbon to the Caribbean to Manassas, Virginia, to Sand Lake, New York, once again just for holidays. But perhaps the most remarkable engagement undertaken by Astrud in those years was one in which she didn't make an appearance. This is what happened.

Astrud had returned to perform in New York City at Fat Tuesday, but she quickly moved up to a considerably better venue, Marty's. This club was uptown, not in a basement, and, most importantly for someone who didn't drive, they provided Astrud with a limo service to and from each night. And the food was terrific.

Someone from Las Vegas noticed Astrud was doing good business at Marty's, and she was asked to perform at The Sands in that city. After a bit of negotiation, terms were set, a date was selected, and Astrud assembled her accompanying musicians. Gil Goldstein, piano and music director, Arnie Lawrence, alto saxophone, Paul Socolow, bass, Raphael Cruz, percussion, and Peter Grant, drums. But I was unable to make the trip because of problems at Hammond Music. Too bad, because I missed Astrud at her best.

With Tony Bennett at a Hammond Music event, 1982.
(Author's collection)

gran concierto de bossa & jazz

TEATRO NACIONAL
30 y 31 DE ENERO

organizado por el
CIRCULO DE
BIBLIOFILAS, INC.

Program, Dominican Republic concert. (Author's collection)

Wintertime holiday. (Author's collection)

She and the band were surprised when they arrived at the Sands because the showroom in which they were to appear was in disarray. It's unclear if she was to perform in the Brazilian-themed Copa Room, but given her background and her music, that would have made sense.

A renovation/reconstruction project was underway and nothing but a couple of layers of floor to ceiling plastic sheeting separated the show room from a large and noisy casino filled with slot machines and all the dreary games of chance featured in Las Vegas venues.

By the time Astrud and her Ipanemers arrived at the Sands in 1981, most of the mobsters who had gotten the casino/hotels off the ground in the early days, the Frank Costellos and Meyer Lanskys, were long dead or soon would be. Mobsters didn't take an active hand in running the place day to day, but their ghosts were still around and the people who did the day to day weren't exactly choirboys.

It took Astrud about a nanosecond to make up her mind that she would not be performing in a showroom where nothing but Saran Wrap separated the stage on which she would perform from a noisy casino. She made her feelings known to the management, who was not pleased. They ganged up on her, but she held firm and made the Sandies a deal. She agreed to leave her band behind, which would perform the requisite number of shows each night for the run of the engagement. Management would treat them as star entertainers with all appropriate

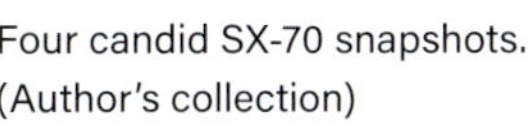
Four candid SX-70 snapshots. (Author's collection)

Jungle CD release. (Author's collection)

The *Chiaroscuro* pre-release sample. (Author's collection)

privileges, she would return to New York, and they would pay for it. The guys in the band were happy to have the work and privileges, and Astrud was happy to be rid of the sand in her shoes and slot machines in her ears.

Now everyone is rid of the Sands. Howard Hughes had it for a minute or two, and the last owner was Sheldon Adelson, who had it blown up. The Venetian now sits on its old footprint in the sand. But there's more to the story and it's pretty wonderful. The band did their three shows a night, essentially playing instrumental versions of what they would have played in back of Astrud. But the irrepressible Gil Goldstein wanted to give the audience a special treat. Each night for the final set, all the musicians traded instruments. Gil played drums, Arnie played piano, some of them sang, some played more than one instrument. No one in the audience seemed to notice, there were no complaints, and management was happy with how well the engagement went without Astrud.

There were tumultuous, complicated fun-filled days in the early 1980s with Astrud. Then things shifted a little in early 1981; Astrud moved from The Galaxy into New York City. And not just any place in New York City, but across the street from 830 Broadway at 49 East Twelfth Street, ostensibly to eliminate commuting time but also for her to keep her eye on me, not that I was straying. The timing of all this is a little fuzzy, but there's a picture of Astrud amid the rubble at 830 Broadway and I distinctly remember pulling myself together from a state of exhaustion at 49 East and making my way to Electric Lady in December 1981 where Allen Ginsberg wanted me to be when he did his guest vocal on *Combat Rock*, the Clash's last commercial recording.

And then a few weeks later we headed to Switzerland where she was scheduled to entertain the swells at Badrutt's Palace Hotel in St. Moritz, the kind of place where exiled royalty lived in luxury and then sat in the corner during the day and watched the world go by. The Corviglia Ski Club, possibly the most elitist private club in the world, sent her an invitation to join them for a special event and she didn't even consider it; Palace management begged her to invite her friend Ivo Pitanguy, the noted Brazilian plastic surgeon who had a chalet in Gstaad, to come to The Palace and lift a few royal faces or tuck some famous tummies. She ignored this as well. Astrud was not impressed with fancy.

We switched our tickets around and instead of returning to New York, went to Lisbon instead where Astrud had a girlfriend who she hadn't seen in years. We spent a week in her marble palace from 1540 or so and then made our way back to our humble quarters at Broadway and Twelfth Street. And then later in 1982 we began to drift apart but remained good friends and neighbors. In 1983, when the first Floating Jazz Festival set sail in September, Astrud and her band was on board the *S/S Norway* and not only thrilled the passengers but even took her group into Charlotte Amalie and gave an impromptu performance in St. Thomas.

And then two creeps made a mess of things. In 2001 Astrud made what was to be her final CD. It was wonderful, full of good songs and fine performances. She wanted me to distribute it on my modest Chiaroscuro label. I was, of course, happy to do so. She was very proud of the recording and had even designed a cover for the CD that included an oil painting she had created herself. This caused a problem.

I got the CD ready for production, alerted our distributor that a new Astrud Gilberto CD was on the way, and they were thrilled up until they saw the cover. They hated it and told me they wouldn't distribute the CD with that booklet illustration, and there was a big fight, with Astrud as firm as she had been at The Sands. She wanted that illustration and there was no negotiation. She ultimately issued the CD herself, and *Jungle* was only available on her website.

Then the other shoe dropped. When we were trying to come up with a cover illustration for "That Girl from Ipanema" in the late 1970s I took hundreds of photographs of Astrud, including a series of her wearing a lovely fur coat. One of my favorites showed nothing but her smiling face, the coat, and her bare legs. She liked it and so did others, but ultimately it wasn't used.

In the early 1980s when my photo website was created, this was one of a thousand plus pictures that were used on the site. At some point a creep hacked the site or got a copy of the picture from somewhere and began selling them on eBay for twenty-five dollars and Astrud was outraged. I didn't even know this was happening until she told me about it and I suddenly became the devil. The picture was fine in 1979 but was not in the early 2000s because in the intervening years Astrud had become an animal rights activist and disavowed furs coats and anything else made from once living animals. I knew she was helping cats and dogs with adoption, but I didn't know it was to that degree. First the record messed up and then the picture and we were never close again, which was was a pity. I remained in touch with her son Marcelo but that was about it.

I was shocked when I learned of her death from an Internet post. There was a lengthy two-thirds-page obituary in *The New York Times* and on various news broadcasts the next day. I had no details from anyone and none were in the paper. Then I had a note from Gil Goldstein. He told me he'd heard from Marcelo she had been feeling a little poorly one day and died the next of a heart attack, sitting alone on her porch. I later read in an obituary that she died of lung cancer. I never knew or saw her smoke anything. She'd turned eighty-three on March 29, and I turned eighty-three on the day she died, June 5, 2023.

11

Dizzy Gillespie

October 21, 1917 – January 6, 1993

IN 1958 I wrote a two-page essay, complete with an illustration cut from a long-forgotten magazine. I entitled the short piece "Ol' Diz." It was for my high school English class and my teacher, Miss Borah, probably thought I'd lost my mind, but she gave me an A- (actually 29/30) just to be nice.

It was my senior year in high school and even though I wrote like a bumbling idiot, I was forming some ideas about the music I enjoyed so much and had actually been fortunate enough to see my two favorite living jazz musicians in person a few months earlier, Dizzy Gillespie and Thelonious Monk.

On November 29, 1957, I was at a gala concert in Carnegie Hall to benefit Harlem's Morningside Community Center. It was billed as Thanksgiving Jazz at Carnegie Hall, and I've been giving thanks for the past sixty-eight years that I was there, in the two dollar seats in the top rows of the balcony. This is who was there that night: Ray Charles opened, Dizzy's big band came next, then Billie Holiday with Dizzy's band. There was an intermission, after which was Chet Baker and Zoot Sims's group, the Carnegie Hall debut of Sonny Rollins, and finally, to wrap things up, Thelonious Monk with John Coltrane. I was but seventeen and sat in the next to last row in the balcony but was smart enough to know that Gods were in the house. But I was mainly there because of Dizzy Gillespie, my favorite jazz musician. Monk was a bonus. It was all being recorded for the Voice of America, but I didn't know it.

But back to my infantile essay. This is what I wrote:

John Birks "Dizzy" Gillespie came out of the hills around Cheraw, South Carolina around 1935. Whether he wore dark glasses and a stylish goatee is a mystery, but nevertheless he carried his trumpet in a paper bag. From the hills to Philadelphia was quite a jump, but ol' Diz made it and he became fairly well known but not really famous until after 1945.

For ten years ol' Diz had been influenced by many different people, and although the change had been steadily progressing, it became natural in 1945. Ol' Diz had now launched into bop and he was truly a pioneer. With already unparalled instrumental technique ol' Diz set out to play faster and better than anybody. He certainly succeeded. Not being satisfied in just being a part of organizations, ol' Diz formed his own band. Of course he still played with Charlie Parker and the Jazz At The Philharmonic; he liked his big band a lot. This band, or herd, is capable of, man for man, making more noise than any other group in the business, and it usually does, producing a sound that put terror in the heart of the bravest man.

OPPOSITE
Dizzy Gillespie at home, Englewood, NJ, March 19, 1991. (Author's collection)

Much to the relief of many people, ol' Diz went to Europe in 1948. He really made those Europeans go wild, with his solos that sounded like a scream in the night. Of course ol' Diz really went for this popularity and is second only to Louis Armstrong in the number of friends abroad.

Ol' Diz is really a happy fellow, so happy he got the name "Dizzy." He was politely removed from one band because of throwing spitballs. He is so happy he is funny, for ol' Diz has appeared at concert in everything from a miner's hat with a light to a turban, to pointed shoes. The things he does are just hilarious.

All kidding aside however, ol' Diz is really an excellent musician, and at the present time he is completely unrivaled from a standpoint of technical ability. Even though ol' Diz is a bit eccentric, you will always get enjoyment out of his concerts or records, for you cannot help but admire his splendid artistry and his "humorous" personality.

"Ol' Diz," 1957. (Author's collection)

Page from "Ol' Diz," 1957. (Author's collection)

I read this "essay" now and cringe. My body was seventeen, but my brain seems to have been about five. I actually showed it to Dizzy, and he was amused but I was wise enough to not let him read it. But time passed and I listened and looked and paid attention and became a bit wiser. And then it was early 1984. The first of what would become twenty years of presenting the Floating Jazz Festival aboard either the *S/S Norway* or *Queen Elizabeth 2* had just taken place in September 1983. The first festival was such a success the owners of the *S/S Norway* had asked us to come back on board in 1984 to present two weeks of music; this time with a budget and lead time to get the best of the best. And to me the number one person I wanted to have on board was Dizzy Gillespie.

Carnegie Hall concert featuring Dizzy Gillespie, 1957. (Author's collection)

I look back at the 1984 program. In addition to Mel Torme and Joe Williams and George Shearing and Benny Carter, our lineup on trumpets were Ruby Braff, Wild Bill Davison, Jonah Jones, Hannibal Peterson, Clark Terry, Warren Vache, and, of course, Dizzy Gillespie, who was onboard for both weeks of the festival. And he returned to the ship for the next four years, skipped a couple, and made his final appearance in 1991. I didn't know it would be his last appearance.

After his first appearance in 1984, it was always the same. As soon as the dates for the FJF were firm I'd pick up the telephone and dial 201-569-4875. If I managed to get him on the other end of the line I would say, "Wanna go on a boat ride at birthday time?" His birthday was October 21, and we were usually at sea around that time.

With James Moody boarding the S/S *Norway* in 1986.
(Author's collection)

This gave us a really good excuse for a birthday party on stage. I'd usually add, "Same as last year." Which meant he'd have fancy air, great accommodations, and a wad of cash. He'd look at his book and never said no unless he was already booked.

In 1986 we planned a big birthday celebration with many of his oldest and dearest friends onboard, including James Moody. That year Dizzy had to fly into St. Thomas via San Juan, and I planned to go to the airport and meet him. I mentioned this to Moody, who insisted on going along and I'm ever so glad he did. I have a funny picture of him running down a walkway to greet Dizzy as he came through a gate. We made our way to the taxi stand and grabbed a ride to the pier in Charlotte Amalie, boarded the tender and headed out toward the *S/S Norway*, at anchor in the bay. The ship's draft was about thirty-six feet, which was too much to dock at the pier. The tender bumped its way through the waves to the side of the ship, a gangway was put in place, and I grabbed a picture of Dizzy and Moody heading up it into the ship, a lucky shot of a perfect moment. Ira Sabin put it on the cover of the next issue of *Jazz Times*.

The following year, in 1987, there was a transportation problem. Dizzy had to pick up the *S/S Norway* midweek in St. Thomas. He flew from Newark to San Juan where he transferred to a smaller plane for the flight to St. Thomas. He arrived on time in both cities but because the plane from San Juan was crowded, his luggage was left behind

At home, Englewood, NJ, March 19, 1991.
(Author's collection)

and was scheduled to arrive on the next flight, an hour or so later. The problem was the ship was due to sail about the time his luggage was to arrive. I called the ship and asked if they could hold it for half an hour, and the reply was they could if I'd pay for the extra fuel that would be used to get to the next port of call on time. This was about twenty thousand dollars. It was somewhat cheaper to buy Dizzy new clothes on board, which he was happy to have. He spent the next few days dressed in what can best be described as beach wear and enjoyed every minute of it. The airline sent the bags along to our next port of call and retrieving them was another unplanned adventure.

The last time Dizzy appear at a Floating Jazz Festival was in October–November 1991. In March of that year, I visited him at his home in Englewood, New Jersey. I had two things in mind to do and wound up with three. The first took about five minutes, a discussion of the Floating Jazz Festival in the fall, and the second, an interview for my soon-to-be-published book *The Ghosts of Harlem* and a formal portrait as well, took about three hours. The third was fixing one of his Rolleiflex cameras that was jammed, and that was also pretty quick.

I took the portrait for *The Ghosts of Harlem* with my large format, old wooden Deardorff camera. Dizzy loved the look of it and gave me a lot that day. It may well be the best portrait in the book, and it has been reproduced countless times. We also discussed my idea of using the picture of Moody and himself boarding the ship in 1986 as the poster for the upcoming festival and the cover of the handout program as well. He thought this was a good idea. I also told him there would be a lot of his trumpet playing pals on board and he thought this was also a good idea.

All went as planned. We had a special birthday concert on board on October 21 and added Arturo Sandoval to his quartet, made up of Ron Holloway, Ed Cherry, John Lee, and Ignacio Berroa. Later in the week we teamed him up with Dorothy Donegan and recorded their version of "Sweet Lorraine," which appeared the following year as a Chiaroscuro release. He then had to write his name over and over again on the posters and programs that showed him boarding the ship with Moody a few years earlier.

1991 Floating Jazz festival program.
(Author's collection)

I had no idea at the time this would be the last time he'd appear at the FJF, he was playing well and was full of good spirits, but I later learned he was being treated for a serious cancer by oncologist Dr. Frank Forte and his team at Englewood Hospital. I didn't know this when I received a telephone call from an old friend in Sweden in the spring of 1992. The friend was Anders Ōhman, a man of many talents. He was an amateur clarinet player and loved jazz in general and Benny Goodman in particular. He also owned a small record company, Phontastic, which issued jazz and classical recordings that were exceptional. I had actually recorded a few for him at Downtown Sound.

But when he wasn't tending to his musical passions, Anders was one of the most prominent lawyers in Sweden, and if that wasn't enough, at the time he was also the Chairman of the Royal Swedish Academy of Music. He told me the Academy had awarded the first, soon-to-be-annual Polar Prize the previous year to one classical and one non-classical musician, and that in 1993 they wanted to award the non-classical prize to Dizzy Gillespie and the classical prize to the Polish Composer Witold Lutoslawski. The first non-classical prize in 1992 had gone to Paul McCartney. The only hitch was no one at the Academy knew Dizzy, and the Academy wanted to know if he would accept the prize before they made an announcement. The question posed to me was would I ask him if he would be willing to accept the prize and come to Sweden for the ceremony.

I was on the telephone in a nanosecond and told Dizzy about the award, one that would be given to him by King Gustav in June 1993. I told Dizzy he didn't have to perform, he just had to show up and collect the prize. I added that the prize also consisted of an award of one million Swedish Krona, at the time about one hundred fifty thousand US Dollars. He was ready to leave the next day, but, of course, that was not to be. He played a few engagements earlier that year, I remember talking to him when he was on the West Coast somewhere, Seattle, I think, but he was not well, just trying to hold on. He lasted until January 1993, six months before prize time.

The story does not end there. The Royal Academy treated Dizzy royally and gave him the prize anyway. Lorraine Gillespie, who was notoriously agoraphobic, made the trip to Stockholm and accepted the prize on Dizzy's behalf. Only four other musicians with jazz credentials have been awarded the prize: Quincy Jones, Keith Jarrett, Sonny Rollins, and Wayne Shorter. But the story did not end there, and it still has not.

Dizzy was very fond of his oncologist at Englewood Hospital, the previously mentioned Dr. Frank Forte. One of Dizzy's last requests of Dr. Forte was that he should promise to never turn away a jazz musician in need of medical care and Dr. Forte agreed. But Frank went a bit beyond this initial agreement and a minute or two later he joined the board of the then-fledgling Jazz Foundation of America, as did others from Englewood Hospital. Since that time the hospital has provided many millions of dollars of medical care to jazz and blues musicians in need and made a significant difference in the many lives they have touched. All thanks to a promise made to 'ol Diz when he could no longer play faster or higher or better than anyone.

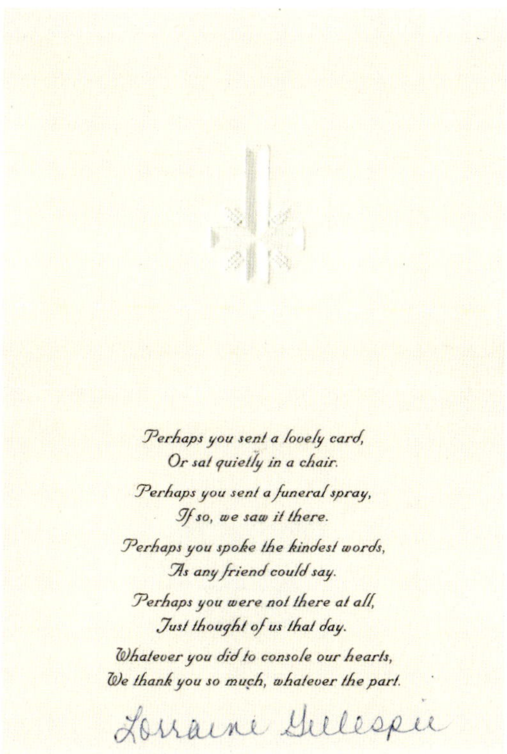
Perhaps you sent a lovely card,
Or sat quietly in a chair.
Perhaps you sent a funeral spray,
If so, we saw it there.
Perhaps you spoke the kindest words,
As any friend could say.
Perhaps you were not there at all,
Just thought of us that day.
Whatever you did to console our hearts,
We thank you so much, whatever the part.
Lorraine Gillespie

Poem from Lorraine Gillespie.
(Author's collection)

12

Allen Ginsberg

June 3, 1926 – April 5, 1997

HAMMOND MUSIC ENTERPRISES opened for business at 311 West Fifty-Seventh Street in an office above Media Sound in January 1981. A month or two after we'd gotten settled in, John Hammond asked me to step into his office and as I did he suggested I close the door. It turned out he wanted to hand off one of his projects from the 1970s to me and didn't want anyone to know he was doing so because he wasn't sure I'd be interested. We could have left the door open and broadcast it to the office and beyond because I was in, and it began a wonderful sixteen-year adventure that was musically exciting, led to remarkable photographic opportunities and numerous new friendships.

John was always a vigorous social activist, and he was keenly interested in musical artists who used their words and music to support causes in which he believed. When he first played me the Bruce Springsteen reel-to-reel demo tapes, he told me how much he liked the words. The music was fine but the words really moved him. And the same thing was true of the artist he sprang on me a minute or two after we began our conversation.

The artist was Allen Ginsberg. John had started a project with Allen a few years earlier, but Allen was hardly a conventional musical artist. Of course, he was a celebrated poet but as a musical commodity he was a bit shaky, and the words of his poetic songs were often somewhat controversial. All of this meant that despite John's reputation and track record with Bob Dylan and George Benson and Bruce Springsteen, Columbia Records was not interested in issuing an Allen Ginsberg album.

But now John had his own label with his name on it. He could do whatever he wanted if there were sufficient funds to get it done. He told me that Allen was coming in the next day to discuss the project and he wanted me at the meeting to make the handoff and assure Allen I wasn't an idiot. We met the next day, I passed the test, and Allen and I worked on music and photography and book projects until his untimely death in 1997.

The first order of business was to get to know Allen and gain an understanding of the recording project, what had happened in the 1970s, what Allen wanted to happen in the 1980s, and what he envisioned as a finished product. It was not very complicated; he had enough well-recorded material to fill up two LPs and he wanted to call the record *First Blues*, a shortened version of *First Blues – Rags, Ballads, and Harmonium Songs 1971–74*, the title of a book published by Full Court Press in 1975 that contained the words and music for many of the songs already recorded. He gave me a copy of the book so I could read it in a bit.

Allen also wanted a special and informative LP jacket, in this case a four-panel gatefold album, plus a special booklet that would include the lyrics to all the twenty-four selections plus extensive written commentary he would create for the album. There was also talk about reproducing

OPPOSITE
Allen Ginsberg video shoot at 830 Broadway.
(Author's collection)

a dozen or more photographs. John gave me the exalted title of executive producer, and we were off and running. My first chore was to convince others in the office that the project made any sense at all, which I did, after which Allen I conferred and figured out the best way to move the project forward.

One of the first things we discussed was the album jacket. I wanted something special but appropriate to the music Allen had recorded. He suggested that we ask Robert Frank to create something unique for the album. At the time, Robert was almost as famous as he is today and very reclusive. I also knew he'd only worked on one record cover, the Rolling Stones' *Exile on Main Street*. I thought it was a long shot, but Allen had known Robert forever, had been a featured player in his first film, *Pull My Daisy*, and had been close to him ever since. He said he'd ask him and Robert signed on immediately and took photographs for the project in June.

I was away on record business, but when I returned Allen said he'd arrange a meeting. It was a Sunday afternoon in July or August when Allen called and said to meet him at Robert's home at 7 Bleecker Street. Peter Orlovsky was standing in the doorway waiting for me. The building was and is old, a bit run down, and fifty years earlier had probably had a commercial facility of some sort on the main floor. Peter said to follow him upstairs. It had the same green façade it does in 2025.

I walked up a narrow stairway and at the top of the first landing was a small dark room where a couple of people seemed to have crashed and were sleeping it off. Up a little further and there was an old-fashioned kitchen. Peter pointed into a kitchen that had a George Booth cartoon quality to it. The refrigerator wasn't plugged into the ceiling light, but it had that feel to it. Peter said, "That's the studio, where we took the pictures." I thought he was joking but he wasn't. We climbed up to the next level and walked down a hallway into a large room facing Bleecker Street and it seemed as though I'd been transported back in time to the 1950s and 1960s, when Allen wrote *Howl* or Robert filmed *Pull My Daisy*.

The room was crammed with stuff, piles of film cans, old movie editing machines, four or five people, including Robert and Allen, at least one girl, a mattress on the floor. Lots of disorganized stuff, and in the background a tape was playing, a guy singing the blues like he really meant it. I felt like I was an outsider, "the man" if you will, because I more or less had a job with an office and a desk, even though I probably hadn't been paid in a month and was flat broke.

Skip James at Edgewood Recording Studio, Falls Church, Virginia, 1964. (Author's collection)

It was a mild summer afternoon, Allen looked very serious in a jacket and tie, and I was second in the GQ standing because I had on reasonably clean jeans and a shirt with a collar. Everyone else was more or less disheveled. It was an awkward moment; nobody seemed to know just what to say until Robert, trying to be friendly, said, "Do you like the music?" I replied something like, "Sure I like it, I was there when it was recorded. It was an incredible session and the first time I took photographs during a recording session. It was in Falls Church, Virginia, in 1964. The guy singing is Skip James, singing 'Sickbed Blues.' I got to know him pretty well, visited him in the hospital a couple of times. He wrote that song because he had cancer and was in and out of the hospital."

Everybody got real quiet, the music filled the room, and then Robert said, "You actually knew Skip James?" I said I sure did and told them a little story. When Skip left Washington and moved to Philadelphia he gave me

With John Hammond at his HME office. (Author's collection)

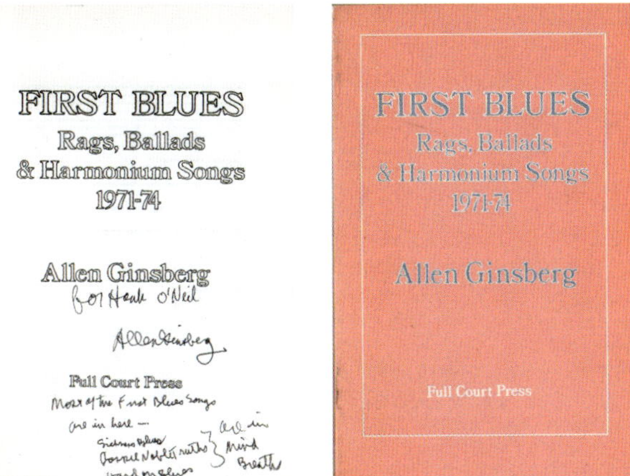

First Blues (Author's collection)

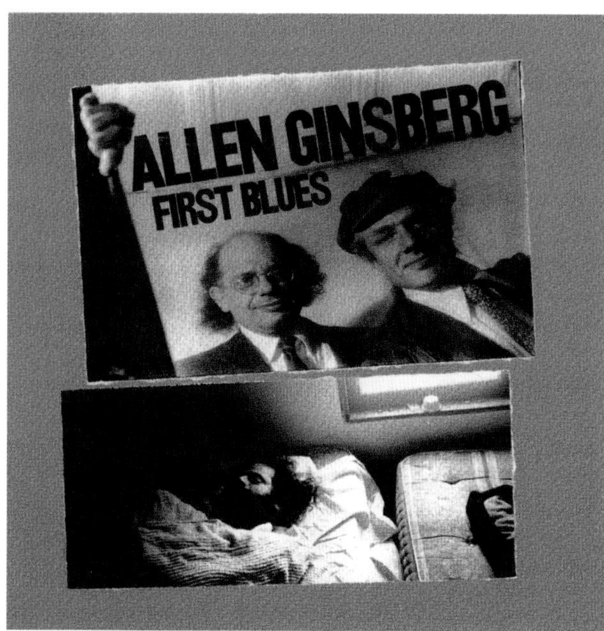

First Blues album jacket. (Author's collection)

The Ginsberg Gallimaufry

CW2X 37673

Boulder, Colorado — Spring Edition 1983

Naropa Institute

Rags, Ballads & Harmonium Songs, Chanteys, Come-All-Ye's, Aborigine Song Sticks, Gospel, Improvisations, Renaissance Lyrics, Blake Hymns, Bluegrass, Hillbilly Riffs, Country & Western, 50's R&B, Dirty Dozens and New Wave.

"Allen Ginsberg is not only one of the world's best poets but one of its finest citizens as well. Long impressed with his musical abilities I recorded Allen in 1976 but CBS refused to issue the results, considering the songs obscene and disrespectful. I am thrilled to finally be able to present Allen on my own label; not only the 1976 sessions but those from 1971 and 1981 as well. I will present "disrespectful" music like this as often as possible."

—John Hammond

The Ginsberg Gallimaufry newspaper album insert. (Author's collection)

his old piano. I moved it to my apartment in Virginia and even though it was beat up and sounded like it came from a haunted house and I never tuned it, I was glad I had it. When I moved to New York City in 1967, I gave it away to a friend who also liked Skippy, and yes, I called him Skippy, as did a number of others.

Robert and I got on well after that, but we bonded over Skip James, not anything to do with photography. He did a terrific album cover. He used two new pictures and one old one from the 1950s for the front and back. The inside of the double fold album was to feature strips from some of his films, primarily *Me and My Brother*. I asked him how he wanted these arranged and he replied, "You seem to know what you're doing so just do it." Nobody complained.

Robert's idea for a jacket precluded using any of it for notes, written commentary, or photographs other than his own. This meant coming up with an insert that could accompany the two LPs. We decided on creating a ten page insert that would include all the lyrics to the twenty-four songs, all the photographs he wanted included, both current and historic, a statement by John Hammond, lengthy descriptive notes by Allen, and production credits, all under the heading of *The Ginsberg Gallimaufry*. John DeVries designed the tabloid newspaper-like publication, the cover of which featured an oversized pen and ink portrait of Allen, accompanied by Allen's catch-all list of the types of music included: *Rags, Ballads & Harmonium Songs, Chanteys, Come-All-Ye's, Aborigine Song Sticks, Gospel, Improvisations, Renaissance Lyrics, Blake Hymns, Bluegrass, Hillbilly Riffs, Country & Western, 50's R&B, Dirty Dozens, and New Wave.*

In early 1982, everything was set for the right time to release the album; everything was done and in place, the mastering, test pressings, a completed cover and special insert. And then we waited because Hammond Music Enterprises was broke.We often didn't have money to pay the telephone bill or meet our modest payroll, let alone issue a two LP set that featured a singing poet who was guaranteed to get no radio play. Then something unexpected happened.

No one at Hammond Music, with the possible exception of John Hammond, realized that Allen Ginsberg was not just a poet who occasionally sang a song, he was not only a unique American personality, but he was also a natural publicity magnet. He was someone who could just as easily be a counterculture icon as someone who could wander into the mainstream and be accepted. On April 14, 1982, he did just that, appearing both in performance and a lengthy chat on *The David Letterman Show*. He

With David Letterman, NBC Studios, March 14, 1982.

didn't sing "You are My Dildo" that night, and frankly I forget which song he did sing, but it proved to my colleagues at HME that maybe we could sell more than a copy or two of *First Blues*. We began to scramble to find the money to get the record into the marketplace.

When the album came out in early 1983, everyone was pleased. It looked good, sounded good, and there were a couple of tunes that could possibly get some radio play if we could get them to the right people and give them a buck or two to push ours ahead of whoever else was trying to do the same.

I took all the raw materials back to Robert Frank. He gave me the two cover photographs and wrote nice things on the back. He also signed my Japanese edition of *Lines of My Hand*. He wrote *Wednesday Afternoon, Happy New Year*. It was December 9, a little early, but Robert's always been a bit ahead of the curve.

All the while these events surrounding *First Blues* were bubbling about, many other things were as well. Allen was like that, a dozen balls in the air, juggling all at the same time. He was fascinated with his life on the edges of the record business and took an interest in a young man named Marc Edmunds, who, as one of the earliest rap artists, was known as J. Walter Negro. Marc showed up at Hammond Music one night when Allen and Peter

With Peter Orlovsky and J. Walter Negro (aka Marc Edmunds). (Author's collection)

were assembling the liner notes for *First Blues* and disrupted things so thoroughly we had to put things together another day.

There was also The Clash, possibly the foremost punk group in 1981. They wanted Allen to appear on a record they were creating and recording at Electric Lady Land in Greenwich Village. The album, *Combat Rock*, turned out to be their final recording and Allen appeared on one selection, "Ghetto Defendant." One day in December 1981, Allen and I wandered over to the studio to meet with Joe Strummer and Mick Jones and watch Joe try to do a vocal overdub. I took a series of photographs of the three guys surrounded by containers of Chinese carryout, and something from one of those containers got ahold of Joe and he spent a few hours trying to do his overdub with a very upset belly. Allen had a tune he called the "Vomit Express"; Joe did it for real at Electric Lady that night. Less than a year later, The Clash came back to the US to tour and support *Combat Rock* and appeared at a concert on one of the piers in New York. Allen and I went, and I took a few pictures backstage, including one of Allen taking a picture of me taking a picture. I have no idea if his came out or not.

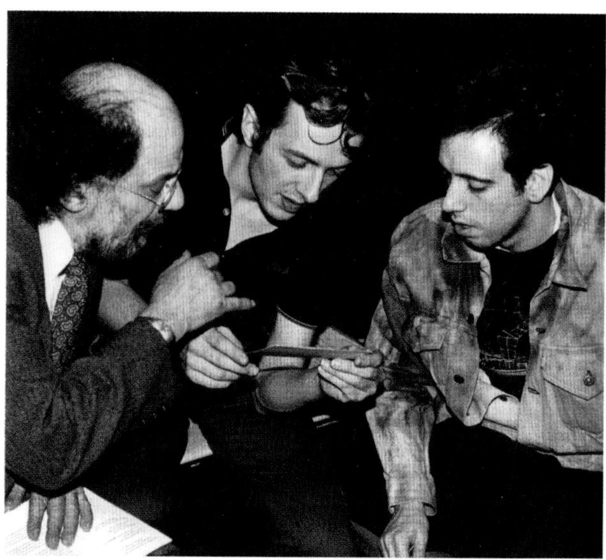

With Joe Strummer and Mick Jones at Combat Rock recording session. (Author's collection)

Allen's association with Robert and my relationship with Berenice Abbott stimulated Allen's interest in photography. He had always taken photographs of his friends but now he began taking them more seriously and devised a wonderful means of presenting them, leaving room at the bottom of 11"x14" prints to write an extended caption or personalized greeting. He also wanted to look at my photographs, both mine and those by others on the walls at 830 Broadway. He really liked Berenice's work and a couple of her photographs from *Changing New York* even stimulated him to write poems that appeared in *White Shroud*, a book of his poetry published in 1986. He also took an interest in photographs I'd taken during the annual Christopher Street gay parade in the 1970s. Allen called the parade Gay Day, and later that became the title of a book that featured 120 of these photographs. This is how the book came about.

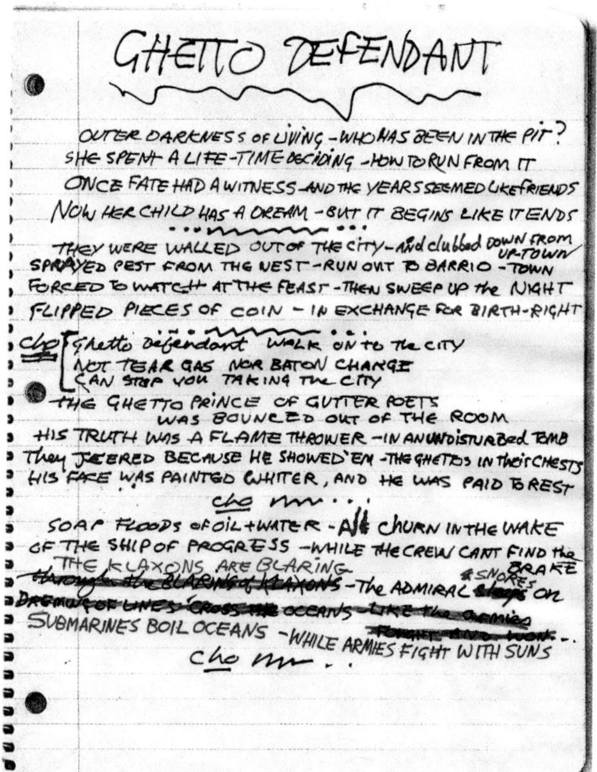

Reworked lyrics by Joe Strummer for *Combat Rock* Clash LP.

One day in 1982, Allen was going through boxes of photographs I'd accumulated over the years, and he came up with a group of small 8"x10" prints from various gay parades from the 1970s. He asked about them, and I explained that in the 1970s I lived above my recording studio at the very far west end of Christopher Street and the annual parade usually formed up in my front yard. It was an incredibly spirited celebration, and good photographs could be found with very little effort. And the more we talked about these photographs the more we both gravitated toward the idea that they should be published. As we talked Allen separated out the pictures he liked best and eventually he selected 120 he felt were the best or might be pictures he'd like to write something about.

We hit on the idea of creating a book of 120 pictures, arranged by year, and Allen would provide captions for each picture, long, short, or in between. He employed his long-proven concept of "first thought, best thought," and got to work. The process was simple. He'd look at a picture, think for a minute, and then turn the picture over and write his first thought on the back. He did this for

With Joe Strummer backstage, New York City, 1982. (Author's collection)

With Robert Creeley in Maine, 1983. (Author's collection)

Singing on the shores of Lake Hebron. (Author's collection)

about 110 pictures; there were about ten he didn't caption, photographs I took in June 1983, a year after he had done the captioning in two or three marathon sessions.

A short time later there was a wild and very hurried trip to Maine to visit Berenice Abbott on her home turf. Allen was scheduled to be at a William Carlos Williams conference in Orono in late August and thought it might be fun to visit Berenice on his way to that event. The plan was to pick up Allen outside Portland, where he was staying with Robert Creeley. All went according to plan. Shelley and I drove to Portland, picked out a cute cat at the local ASPCA to replace Berenice's recently departed Butch, then picked up a nattily attired Allen and a young traveling companion at Robert Creeley's home, and then headed north to Berenice's home on Lake Hebron.

We arrived around noon on a Saturday, and all seemed well from outward appearances, but at one point Berenice pulled me aside and said, "What is Allen doing with that young boy?" I replied, "You know exactly what he's doing with that young boy." And she replied, "Well, I don't like it." We all sat about for the next hour or so and at some point Berenice said, "Well, I guess it's time for lunch. We can go into Monson and the Appalachian Station."

With John Cage, Nam June Paik, and Merce Cunningham at the French Embassy. (Author's collection)

Page from handmade book about William S. Burroughs in residence at 830 Broadway in 1984. (Author's collection)

IN JANUARY 1984 ALLEN GINSBERG TOLD ME HIS OLD FRIEND, WILLIAM S. BURROUGHS, WAS PLANNING TO BE IN NEW YORK CITY FOR A WEEK IN EARLY FEBRUARY, TO CELEBRATE HIS 70TH BIRTHDAY. HE SAID WILLIAM HAD TOLD HIM HE WAS LOOKING FOR AN INEXPENSIVE PLACE TO STAY, THAT HE WASN'T EXACTLY FLUSH. APPARENTLY THE BUNKER ON BOWERY WAS ALREADY FULL AND WILLIAM NEEDED MORE ROOM THAN ALLEN OR ANY OF HIS OTHER FRIENDS COULD OFFER. AT THAT TIME, SHELLEY STILL HAD POSSESSION OF HER EAST 84TH STREET APARTMENT; IT WAS EASY FOR US TO STAY THERE, SO I SPOKE WITH JAMES GRAUERHOLZ, AND VOLUNTEERED THE USE OF OUR SPACE AT 830 BROADWAY. HE WAS HAPPY TO ACCEPT.

WILLIAM, JAMES AND A FEW FRIENDS ARRIVED LATE IN THE AFTERNOON ON SATURDAY, 4 FEBRUARY; THEY REMAINED UNTIL THE FOLLOWING SATURDAY. SHELLEY AND I WERE AT 830 PART OF EACH DAY, AS WERE MANY OTHER PEOPLE WHO ARE PICTURED ON THE FOLLOWING PAGES. I TOOK MANY PHOTOGRAPHS AT 830, AS WELL AS AT LIMELIGHT (6 FEBRUARY) AND DANCETERIA (8 FEBRUARY). MANY OF THE SAME PEOPLE TURN UP IN THESE PHOTOGRAPHS, AS WOULD BE EXPECTED. THERE WERE OCCASIONAL INTERLOPERS, SUCH AS THE INSUFFERABLE VICTOR BOCKRIS, BUT THESE BORES WERE AT THE PUBLIC GATHERINGS. THE PEOPLE AT 830 WERE WILLIAM'S OLDEST FRIENDS AND THE CIRCUMSTANCES WERE VERY RELAXED. ONE DAY THERE WAS TARGET PRACTICE; ON ANOTHER DAY FORMAL PORTRAITS. I CAME IN ONE AFTERNOON AND FOUND WILLIAM SITTING BY A BOOKCASE SIGNING ALL HIS BOOKS, OFTEN WRITING FUNNY INSCRIPTIONS IN MANY OF THEM. IT WAS A VERY INTERESTING WEEK.

WHEN SHELLEY AND I RECLAIMED 830 WE FOUND A NOTE FROM JAMES WHICH READ, *WELL, I MUST ADMIST I'VE FAILED - THAT IS, TO COME UP WITH THE GESTURE THAT WOULD ADEQUATELY EXPRESS OUR GRATITUDE FOR YOUR GENEROUS HOSPITALITY. OH SURE, I'VE CLEANED UP A BIT - AND DRAFTED THE GOOD EFFORTS OF LEFFERTS - BUT THE RUSH OF EVENTS, ETC ..... SO, IT ONLY FOLLOWS THAT I'LL TURN MY MIND TO THAT DANGLING MATTER ON MY RETURN TO BASE IN KANSAS. UNTIL THEN, KNOW THAT YOUR KINDNESS AND FRIENDSHIP ARE WRITTEN ON THE EMULSION OF OUR SOULS - THIS MOMENTOUS WEEK COULD NOT HAVE HAPPENED WITHOUT THE SPACE THAT YOU HAVE CREATED FOR US: WILLIAM, IRA AND I THANK YOU. LET LOVE PRESERVE WHAT FINITE TIME CANNOT - YOURS EVER A FRIEND, JAMES* WILLIAM THEN ADDED *I CAN ONLY ECHO JAMES'S WORD. THANKS A TRILLION. SI AMIGO WILLIAM.*

The Appalachian Station was the only place that served food in Monson if you discount the places that had wieners in a box spinning around light bulbs, but the best you could do at this place was mashed potatoes, white bread, and a piece of pie from the A&P. My heart was already burning when Allen's young friend volunteered, "Oh no, Miss Abbott, just lead me to your refrigerator and I'm sure I can put something together that will please everyone." Berenice was so befuddled by the offer that she did as was suggested and the young man delivered the goods, much to everyone's amazement. Berenice was so taken with his culinary skills she suggested he remain with her for a few weeks, and he said he would if she would take a portrait of him, nude, but that was a bridge or portrait too far. As the dust was settling after our fine improvised lunch, Allen borrowed Berenice's phone and got in touch with the people at the Orono conference and managed to reunite Berenice with her old Clemenceau Cottage roommate, the literary theorist Kenneth Burke, who was also attending the conference. It was a lovely moment.

That night Allen gave Berenice and the rest of us a private reading of *Howl* and she was as befuddled as she had been earlier in the day with the "what's in your refrigerator" offer. Allen and his young friend spent the night at Jolly Roger, Berenice's guest cottage; Shelley and I camped out at Blanchard and the next day we all reassembled at Lake Hebron. Allen was dressed as he would appear at the William Carlos Williams conference, so I took advantage of this and took black-and-white and color pictures of him on the shores of the lake, nicely attired, while vocalizing with his harmonium. This was an also lovely, utterly unique moment. I can't remember how I achieved the perspective. Maybe I was in Berenice's boat.

A few months later there was "Good Morning Mr. Orwell," an event that was the brainchild of the Korean/American video artist Nam June Paik, one that would create a video link that would allow artists in New York City and Paris to interact with one another and give a Bronx cheer to George Orwell's dystopian vision of the year 1984. The video event/installation was to be broadcast live at noon on January 1, 1984. It was also beamed to South Korea and Germany.

The actual broadcast/performance/installation in New York City took place at the studios of WNET, and Allen was one of a number of cultural icons slated to appear, in addition to Nam June, Merce Cunningham, John Cage, Laurie Anderson, Peter Gabriel, Phillip Glass, Joseph Beuys, as well as the Thompson Twins and Oingo Boingo plus the sometimes naked cellist Charlotte Moorman, now fully clothed and playing a cello made of three televisions, all with the assistance of George Plimpton, who hosted the presentation. A few excerpts are still bouncing around on YouTube, notably Laurie Anderson, Peter Orlovksy and his banjo blues yodeling, and Charlotte Moorman.

But prior to the New Year's Day event, there was a reception at the French Embassy on December 19 where everyone gathered and discussed what was going to take place. Allen suggested to me that Shelley and I might enjoy this pre-January 1 event and I should bring my camera along and document what was going on. He didn't have to ask me twice.

A few weeks later there was another birthday, this time for William S. Burroughs. It was a weeklong celebration and a short while after it was over I made a small handmade book that detailed the adventure of that week in February 1984. Rather than try and remember, it is easier to reproduce the short introduction I wrote at the time:

There were many adventures that week at 830 and many led to interesting photographic opportunities. You don't normally have many opportunities to engage in a shooting contest with anyone in New York City, let alone in your own home, especially with an opponent as worthy as William. I happened to have a high-powered pellet gun on hand and a bunch of extra copies of a 12" single by a punk band that was very hot at the time, *Three Teens Kill Four*. The record made an excellent target. William won. There is a video tape of this contest somewhere.

The portrait of Allen and William together is one of my favorites. There was no coaxing involved, no one suggested they hold hands; it was just a spontaneous tender moment for two old friends.

The next year there was the Andy Warhol shoot for Jerry Aronson's documentary film that would be released as *The Life and Times of Allen Ginsberg* and a few months later, the big wedding. The Warhol shoot took place in January. This is how it came about.

In late 1984 Allen Ginsberg told me a man named Jerry Aronson was in the process of making a documentary film about his life and times. Not surprisingly, the film was called *The Life and Times of Allen Ginsberg*. In January 1985, Jerry was scheduled to conduct an interview with Andy Warhol about his relationship with Allen and to offer any pertinent observations he might care to make about the noted poet. Allen asked if I could take a portrait of Andy Warhol that might be used as a still in the film. A few weeks later Jerry called and asked as well.

I take aim at 830 Broadway. (Author's collection)

William does the same. (Author's collection)

The interview was scheduled for January 15, 1985, at Andy Warhol's last and final factory, at 22 East Thirty-Third Street, the studio where he created most of his artwork. I arrived with the crew, and we set up in one of the rooms that made up Andy's studio complex. There were pictures and works in progress scattered about on the floor and people were working on them.

Andy finally appeared, wearing a black turtleneck sweater, ordinary pants, his silver fright wig, and a baseball cap. He sat down in a straight-back chair, the lights came on, the cameras rolled, Jerry asked his questions, and Andy answered them. Or at least he kind of answered them. I took pictures from various angles, close-ups, medium shots and a couple of interiors. At the end of the shoot, he held still for a couple of really ordinary portraits.

I developed my film and had a number of photographs from which to choose, but the more I looked at them the more I was unimpressed with the almost expressionless portraits. Later, when I looked at the finished film Andy was much better and far more animated. But my pictures were dull and bland, Andy wasn't giving anything to a still camera; maybe he'd given all he had to give to the movie camera. But one never knows where things will go and I certainly didn't with these pictures of Andy.

The more I looked at them the more I thought maybe there was a way to take advantage of the blah blah portraits, something that might even appeal to Warhol. I knew I wanted to play with them, so I did. I chose the three or four that seemed the most bland and began to color them with transparent watercolors, red, yellow, and blue. I mixed up the colors and mixed up the pictures. I must have printed about 120 small 4" x 4" square photographs.

I then assembled the photographs by hand and mounted them as a ten-by-ten square grid on an illustration board. I was essentially doing what Andy had been doing for so many years, but I was doing it with his face, in the primary colors he used with such success. Later I made some double and triple and quadruple exposures of my favorite portrait, but only in black-and-white. Then I began to play with them in other ways.

In 2005 I began to rethink these photographs for an exhibition in New York City. Computer technology made the difference, and I was able to refine the images. I could make the pictures any size I wanted. Later I experimented with prints on canvas, smaller at first, and then as large as 52" x 52".

The colorful Andys lived a life of their own; in the summer of 2015, Shelley Shier arranged for forty-two large prints to be installed and become a permanent installation on the second level of the Remington Contemporary Art Gallery, a three level public art exhibition space that has become the artistic and visual cornerstone of Downtown Markham, a new cultural center in the greater Toronto area. In addition to the forty-two large prints on vinyl, an oversized 52" x 52" Double Andy on canvas was displayed in the same location.

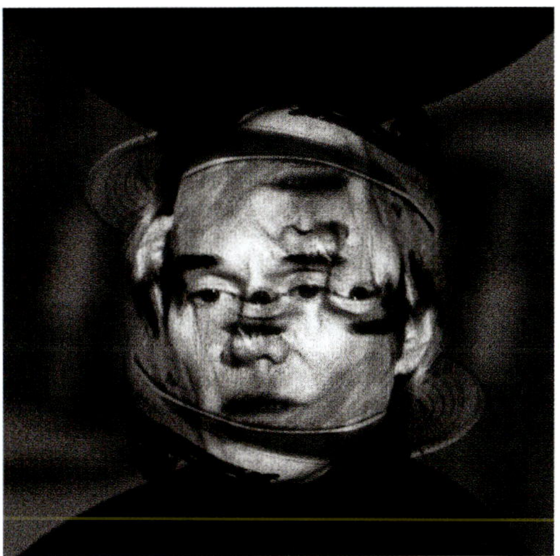

Double Andy. (Author's collection)

36 Andys. (Author's collection)

Then, in 2021 I was approached by a group that wanted to undertake a project to create and market an NFT that would incorporate not just my colored portraits of Andy but also incorporate all kinds of proprietary technology that would do tricky things with the images. It was launched in 2024 and was a failure.

But let's return to the mid-1980s when there was an unending stream of adventures. For example, there was the wedding. I can also date this event precisely because it is on the marriage license, April 14, 1985. It was an unusual ceremony, one that had a spur of the moment feeling but had been thought about for at least a minute or two.

Shelley and I had been living together for almost two years, were getting along fine, and building a successful business together. But one thing that was troubling her was her status as a legal resident and her green card. Our mid-March wedding was not a green card wedding, but I wanted to make sure it didn't have that kind of appearance, as did she. We also had no interest in announcing it to the world. This was easy for me; I had no family. It was not so easy for Shelley, who had an extended family, some of whom regarded me as the Village Idiot, so she elected not to tell anyone, especially north of the border.

We set a date. April 14. We got a marriage license. We chose a maid of honor, Berenice Abbott; two official officiators, Rabbi Nathan Borenstein for Shelley and Father Peter O'Brien, S.J. for me (even though I am not a Catholic, he was the only semi-holy man I knew); and Allen Ginsberg as official wedding photographer, possibly the only time he'd been put in that position. I also arranged to have a real witness, Robert Anderson, the once-upon-a-time Secretary of the Treasury and that was it. And it stayed that way until the morning of. This is what happened.

The ceremony of sorts was to happen around noon, and maybe around 10:00, Allen called and said simply, "Would you like another priest?" I asked what he had in mind, and he said he was with Ernesto Cardenal, who, when not massing in the church, was stirring up the masses as the Nicaraguan Sandinista's minister of culture. I told Allen to bring him along, thinking to myself I could perhaps introduce him to Robert Anderson, a moderate Texas-born Republican and possibly find a sensible back channel into Reagan's ultracons and put some sense into their heads.

But it was not to be. Cardenal got hijacked by someone and Robert Anderson was run over in the street by a pre-COVID-19 bicycle messenger and suffered a broken arm. And so, Allen not only had to serve as wedding photographer, but as a witness as well. He signed the license, along with Berenice Abbott, and this is possibly the only time their signatures appear together on anything. Allen was thrilled to be there because I'd told him his wedding photographer fee would be a discussion with Berenice about his own photography, even though I knew she viewed his picture taking with suspicion. Allen did take some pictures that day, but the results were not his finest work, and, to my knowledge, no one else ever asked him to photograph a wedding.

The only other people in attendance were Rabbi Borenstein's wife and Susan Blatchford, Berenice's close friend and ultimate caregiver. At one point Berenice pulled me aside and asked, "Why are all the people here gay?" I said Shelley and I weren't and although I wasn't sure, neither was the rabbi and his wife. And that was that. It is now forty years later and everyone at the ceremony is dead except for Shelley and myself and the photograph Allen gave us as a wedding present, possibly his most famous image, Jack Kerouac on his fire escape. It is still alive and well on my darkroom wall.

And things bounced along. All the captions for the book that would one day be called *Gay Day* were completed and William wrote a short introduction, but still no one cared—especially publishers. Hammond Music Enterprises, now just called HME, officially failed in the summer of 1985 and no one cared, except possibly the Internal Revenue Service. I was no longer officially associated with the company in an executive leadership position or on the board and thank goodness, but I still had a key to the office.

I had been in Maine for a couple of weeks and when I returned went by to see how things were going at HME and was surprised to find the door locked. I let myself in and discovered disarray and pandemonium. About the only thing that hadn't been ransacked was the closet where master tapes were stored. I grabbed the four reels that were used to create *First Blues*, along with some others I felt to be important, and made my getaway. I turned the tapes over to Allen for safekeeping and future use, of which it turned out there was plenty.

About the same time as I was rescuing the *First Blues* tapes, Allen called and said he was meeting with the Russian poet Andre Vosnesensky in a few days and it would be nice if I'd come by and say hello and take a few pictures. I did, and while there it occurred to me that I'd never taken a portrait of Allen at his apartment; so I put it on my to do list, but it took almost a year to work it out.

With Berenice Abbott at 830 Broadway. (Author's collection)

Holding a portrait of his dying uncle. (Author's collection)

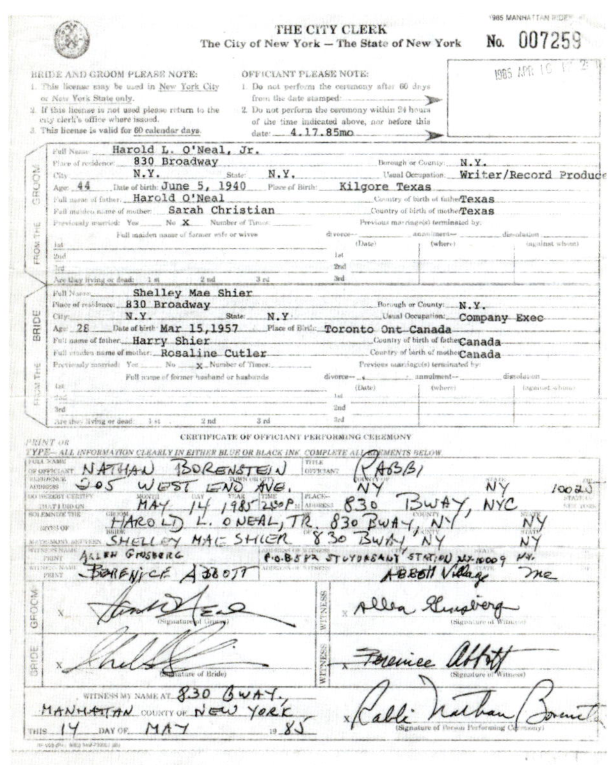

THE CITY CLERK
The City of New York — The State of New York

No. 007259

1985 APR 16

BRIDE AND GROOM PLEASE NOTE:
1. This license may be used in New York City or New York State only.
2. If this license is not used please return to the city clerk's office where issued.
3. This license is valid for 60 calendar days.

OFFICIANT PLEASE NOTE:
1. Do not perform the ceremony after 60 days from the date stamped:
2. Do not perform the ceremony within 24 hours of the time indicated above, nor before this date: 4.17.85mo

FROM THE GROOM
Full Name: Harold L. O'Neal, Jr.
Place of residence: 830 Broadway — Borough or County: N.Y.
City: N.Y. — State: N.Y. — Usual Occupation: Writer/Record Produce
Age: 44 — Date of birth: June 5, 1940 — Place of Birth: Kilgore Texas
Full name of father: Harold O'Neal — Country of birth of father: Texas
Full maiden name of mother: Sarah Christian — Country of birth of mother: Texas
Previously married: Yes ___ No X — Number of Times: ___ — Previous marriage(s) terminated by:
Full maiden name of former wife or wives — divorce — annulment — dissolution
1st / 2nd / 3rd — (Date) (where) (against whom)
Are they living or dead: 1st 2nd 3rd

FROM THE BRIDE
Full Name: Shelley Mae Shier
Place of residence: 830 Broadway — Borough or County: N.Y.
City: N.Y. — State: N.Y — Usual Occupation: Company Exec
Age: 28 — Date of birth: Mar 15,1957 — Place of Birth: Toronto Ont Canada
Full name of father: Harry Shier — Country of birth of father: Canada
Full maiden name of mother: Rosaline Cutler — Country of birth of mother: Canada
Previously married: Yes ___ No x — Number of Times: ___ — Previous marriage(s) terminated by:
Full name of former husband or husbands — divorce — annulment — dissolution
1st / 2nd / 3rd — (Date) (where) (against whom)
Are they living or dead: 1st 2nd 3rd

CERTIFICATE OF OFFICIANT PERFORMING CEREMONY

PRINT OR TYPE— ALL INFORMATION CLEARLY IN EITHER BLUE OR BLACK INK. COMPLETE ALL ELEMENTS BELOW.

FULL NAME OF OFFICIANT: NATHAN BORENSTEIN — TITLE OFFICIANT: RABBI
RESIDENCE ADDRESS: 305 WEST END AVE. — TOWN OR CITY — COUNTY OF: NY — STATE: NY — ZIP: 10025
DO HEREBY CERTIFY THAT I DID ON: MONTH MAY DAY 14 YEAR 1985 TIME 2:30 P.M. — PLACE-ADDRESS: 830 BWAY, NYC
SOLEMNIZE THE RITES OF MATRIMONY BETWEEN:
GROOM: HAROLD L. ONEAL, JR. 830 BWAY, NY — STATE: NY
BRIDE: SHELLEY MAE SHIER 830 BWAY, NY — STATE: NY
WITNESS NAME PRINT: ALLEN GINSBERG — ADDRESS OF WITNESS: P.O.B. 582 STUYVESANT STATION NY 10009 NY.
WITNESS NAME PRINT: BERENICE ABBOTT — ADDRESS OF WITNESS: ABBOTT Village Me

GROOM: x (Signature of Groom) — WITNESS: x Allen Ginsberg (Signature of Witness)
BRIDE: x (Signature of Bride) — WITNESS: x Berenice Abbott (Signature of Witness)

WITNESS MY NAME AT 830 BWAY, MANHATTAN COUNTY OF NEW YORK, THIS 14 DAY OF MAY 19 85
x Rabbi Nathan Borenstein (Signature of Person Performing Ceremony)

Marriage license. (Author's collection)

With Gregory Corso at Allen's 12th Street apartment. (Author's collection)

But the results were pretty good, black-and-white and color and, as luck would have it, Allen had invited Gregory Corso to come by that day, and a few nice portraits of Gregory jumped into my Deardorff. That was one of the wonders of Allen. You just never knew who would turn up and what he might be setting up to look like it just turned up. He was remarkably generous that way; he wanted to make things happen and see how they might turn out, and as often as not they turned out well. And as I recall it was one of the few, if not only, times I had to climb five flights with all my equipment and take off my shoes when I got there. I'd have a hard time managing that today.

The BEAUTY *of* PHYSICS

BERENICE ABBOTT

The Beauty of Physics booklet.
(Author's collection)

There were more adventures in 1987; the ones I can document with photographs are the opening of Berenice Abbott's *Beauty of Physics* show at the New York Academy of Sciences in January and then some months later video and photographic recording of Allen reading and more or less performing his epic poem, "September in Jessore Road." Later that year, I had arranged for him to do the reading at the downstairs studio of my neighbor and fellow photographer Tom Caravaglia, the video of which would be incorporated into a dance choreographed by another longtime friend, collaborator, and one time fiancée, Marilynn Danitz. Allen was at his performing best and gave a dramatic reading. I was a fly on the wall and got some good photographs. In fact, one black-and-white profile shot with a 35mm camera is perhaps my favorite picture of Allen.

And then suddenly there were no more pictures. Allen continued to stop in for visits; we'd meet here and there and exchange books and records and even photographs, but somehow my camera was never at the ready or perhaps I didn't think a picture was necessary. I didn't even take a camera to the opening of his photo shows, of which there were many, or readings at St. Mark's Church in-the-Bowery, and shame on me because I missed many opportunities for possibly unique photographs.

The last time I can officially document he came by was September 30, 1994, the day he presented Shelley and me with a copy of his new book, *Cosmopolitan Greetings*. And only because he dated the inscription. He made a great drawing that covered an entire page and on the other wrote: *TYGER! For Shelley and Hank 9/30/94 830 Broadway Allen Ginsberg*. By this time, he'd sold his archive and decided to use some of the proceeds to buy a living space that was more comfortable than his East Twelfth Street walkup. We discussed the possibility that a floor in 830 might be for sale, but it didn't become available in time and he bought a place on East Fourteenth Street.

I was in Sydney, Australia, when I learned of his death in April 1997. We were there working on a jazz festival project and Allen's passing was all over the news in that faraway land. I was saddened and shocked, but not at all surprised. He was always as energetic as he was caring, eager to pursue all manner of intellectual or social matters, to help an unknown poet or a noted personality, and usually always turning up on the right side of important issues. When he messed up, as we all do, he admitted it and moved on, but in later years he seemed increasingly frail. I found it amazing he could accomplish so much with so many people wanting a piece of him, pulling him this way and that, but somehow he seemed to be able to find time for almost everyone. Perhaps his secret was that he didn't waste any of the time he had.

Reading *September on Jessore Road* at 830 Broadway. (Author's collection)

First Blues, a handmade, limited edition book.
(Author's collection)

Gay Day, an unlimited edition book published in 2006.
(Author's collection)

The Last Word on First Blues CD.
(Author's collection)

The Last Word on First Blues page from CD booklet.
(Author's collection)

Of course, things didn't stop in 1997. I produced *First Blues, Allen Ginsberg 1981–1987* in 1999. This limited-edition book was issued in conjunction with a retrospective of my photographic work up to that time at the Witkin Gallery. The small edition with twenty-six silver prints and an essay sold out during the run of the show. Then, in late 2005, *Gay Day* was picked up by Abrams and in May 2006 was issued as *Gay Day: The Golden Age of the Christopher Street Parade 1974–1983*. When the book was issued there were exhibitions of special prints that included facsimiles of Allen's handwritten captions in New York City, Toronto, Philadelphia, Washington, DC, San Francisco, and Los Angeles.

The Gay Day Archive catalog.
(Author's collection)

In February 2007, *First Blues* was reissued as a CD, and a few months later *The Life and Times of Allen Ginsberg* appeared as a DVD and at various film festivals. In 2009, eleven photographs from the Gay Day parade were blown up to enormous proportions: mural-size prints, five and six feet long, mounted on aluminum and installed at Tender Greens, a restaurant in West Hollywood, California. Allen's captions were embedded in these photo-murals, and sixteen years later they are still on display.

In 2017 an elaborate CD package entitled *The Last Word on First Blues* was released. It contained all the recordings on the two LPs we released in 1983 and added a dozen previously unissued performances. In 2019, Swann Auctions presented the first auction of LGBTQ material, the Pride Sale, and offered what was referred to as the Gay Day Archive and featured my photograph of Marsha Johnson at the 1977 parade with Allen's poetic caption on the cover of the handsome catalog.

June 3, 2026, would have been Allen's one-hundreth birthday, and plans are already being made to have both literary and photographic celebrations. I don't know about any of the literary events that are being considered, but there is keen interest at a major museum in New York City for a major photographic exhibition that year. Hope I see it here and not with Allen somewhere else.

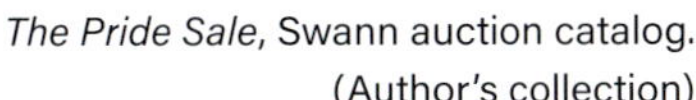

The Pride Sale, Swann auction catalog.
(Author's collection)

13

John Hammond and George Avakian

December 15, 1910 – July 10, 1987 and March 15, 1919 – November 22, 2017

I ARRIVED in New York City on June 5, 1967, and had a list of people Squirrel Ashcraft thought I should contact. Two of the names on the list were John Hammond and George Avakian. I did as I was told and made the calls. John was 475-3994 or 832-1433; George was easier, 787-7778. 1967 was so long ago there were no area codes.

I was a big fan of both of these guys. They'd been making records since the 1930s, and many of those records were among my favorites. I'd read about both of them and had read thousands of words they had written, on the backs of the records they produced or in magazines and other publications. It seemed that I was on the same musical and social page as each of them. But by social I don't mean the Social Register or their circle of friends, but more like social justice issues. John was, after all, a Vanderbilt, and George had run a big division of CBS and had helped organize Warner Bros. Records and the Recording Academy.

I met with John first, a nice lunch downstairs from his Columbia Records office in the restaurant that was once upon a time on the ground floor of 51 West Fifty-Second Street, then as now CBS headquarters. I met with George sometime later, not in his office but at his place of official employment, in the showroom of Avakian Brothers, then, as it had been for many years, one of the finest purveyors of oriental carpets in the city. We met there because George was in exile at the time; he'd left his position at RCA, and while he was still dabbling with Charles Lloyd and Keith Jarrett, he'd become a full-time carpet merchant. As I recall, Avakian Brothers was somewhere on Thirty-Third Street, close to the Empire State Building.

Both guys were cordial, welcoming, and encouraging. Squirrel Ashcraft had told them I wasn't an idiot; they believed it and took a meeting. It was clear to me from the outset that there would be many more with each, and there were, twenty years' worth with John until 1987 and fifty years' worth with George until his death in 2017. Each man was highly intelligent, fiercely opinionated, produced great recordings, and a bit eccentric. John was more eccentric than George, and whereas John could sometimes be a bit naïve, George had a mean, reality-sandwich streak that occasionally surfaced. And each had a secret, one that I didn't discover until it was too late: they each had a grudge against one another.

OPPOSITE

Hank O'Neal (Budd Johnson) John Hammond, and George Avakian. (Author's collection)

Initially I saw more of John since his office was just a few blocks away from mine; he was at Fifty-Second and Avenue of the Americas and I was at Fifty-First and Lexington Avenue. It was also at the time I was beginning to have full reign at Sherman Fairchild's recording studio in the home at 17 East Sixty-Fifth Street.

CBS headquarters was more or less wide open in those days; if I visited with Bob Altshuler to catch up and fill a few bags with the latest Columbia and Epic recordings, it was easy to wander over to John's office, chat for a minute with Liz Gilbert, his assistant, and peek in John's modest office and see if he was in, and, if so, talk about this and that. If he wasn't in and Liz said he was coming back soon, I'd wait for a minute or two, and often there were others waiting as well. One day it was Big Mama Thornton, who, though she passed in 1984, was and remains a highly respected singer/songwriter. She even turned up a few years ago as a character featured in Baz Luhrmann's movie *Elvis*.

That day Big Mama had a new record she wanted to play for John, and since he wasn't there, she played it for me. It wasn't "Hound Dog," but it was quite terrific and far more elaborate, a big orchestra, fancy arrangements, and all the rest. I said, "Miz Thornton, that was wonderful. Who were the people on the record with you?" She looked at me and said, "I don't know. It was just me and a piano player when I did it." I don't remember if John showed up that day, but I'll never forget Big Mama. She was no longer very big; in fact, she looked as if she could have used another piece of pie.

Bobby Henderson LP jacket.
(Author's collection)

The first time John and I worked on anything together was in the fall of 1968, and it involved Eubie Blake. That story is recounted elsewhere but, suffice to say, John was impressed with how things were handled at Sherman Fairchild's private recording studio. He even asked if it would be possible for his son, John Paul, to put down some tracks, and that wasn't a problem. It was the first time I heard him live, and it was the first blues date I recorded at 17 East Sixty-Fifth Street. He was wonderful but not yet as famous as he was to become.

A couple of months later we embarked on another project, one that was ultimately far more successful: making the last recordings of someone John had known since the 1930s but hadn't recorded since the mid-1950s, the legendary pianist Bobby Henderson. The story of that recording and the drama that surrounded it is also told elsewhere, but when that project was successfully completed and the record was issued, we were both relieved and I was convinced John realized for good I wasn't an overly enthusiastic village idiot.

And we stayed in touch, talked a lot, and got to know one another better and better. In those days John had mini-incidents, like mini-strokes and mini-heart attacks, with some frequency, and one day in the Spring of 1971 I was visiting with him at Lenox Hill Hospital and asked him if he could jump out of his hospital bed and record anyone in New York City at that very moment, who would that person be? He didn't hesitate for a moment and said, "Mary Lou Williams." I didn't hesitate either, tracked down Mary Lou and with the help of her spiritual advisor, Fr. Peter O'Brien S.J., we made the record that was released as *From the Heart* in June of 1971. It was her first solo record since the late 1940s. Mary even wrote a special song and dedicated it to John. It is unclear if Fr. O'Brien lit a candle or not, but John lasted another sixteen years, pushing aside as many of those mini-incidents as he could for as long as possible.

Ever since I'd met Buck Clayton in June 1973, I'd wanted to attempt a recreation of the famous *Buck Clayton Jam Sessions* George Avakian had produced throughout the 1950s. I loved the freewheeling jam sessions Norman Granz produced during the same years, but I felt Buck's more structured jam sessions were equally exciting and more likely to be possible and within my modest budgets. It worked out, and in March 1974 eleven great musicians assembled at my studio, the largest ensemble I'd ever put together, and both John Hammond and George Avakian were on site to give me a hand if one was needed. So was Stanley Dance, who was looking after Earl Hines. This was the first time I'd ever seen John and George together; there were no fireworks, and I had no reason to suspect there would be.

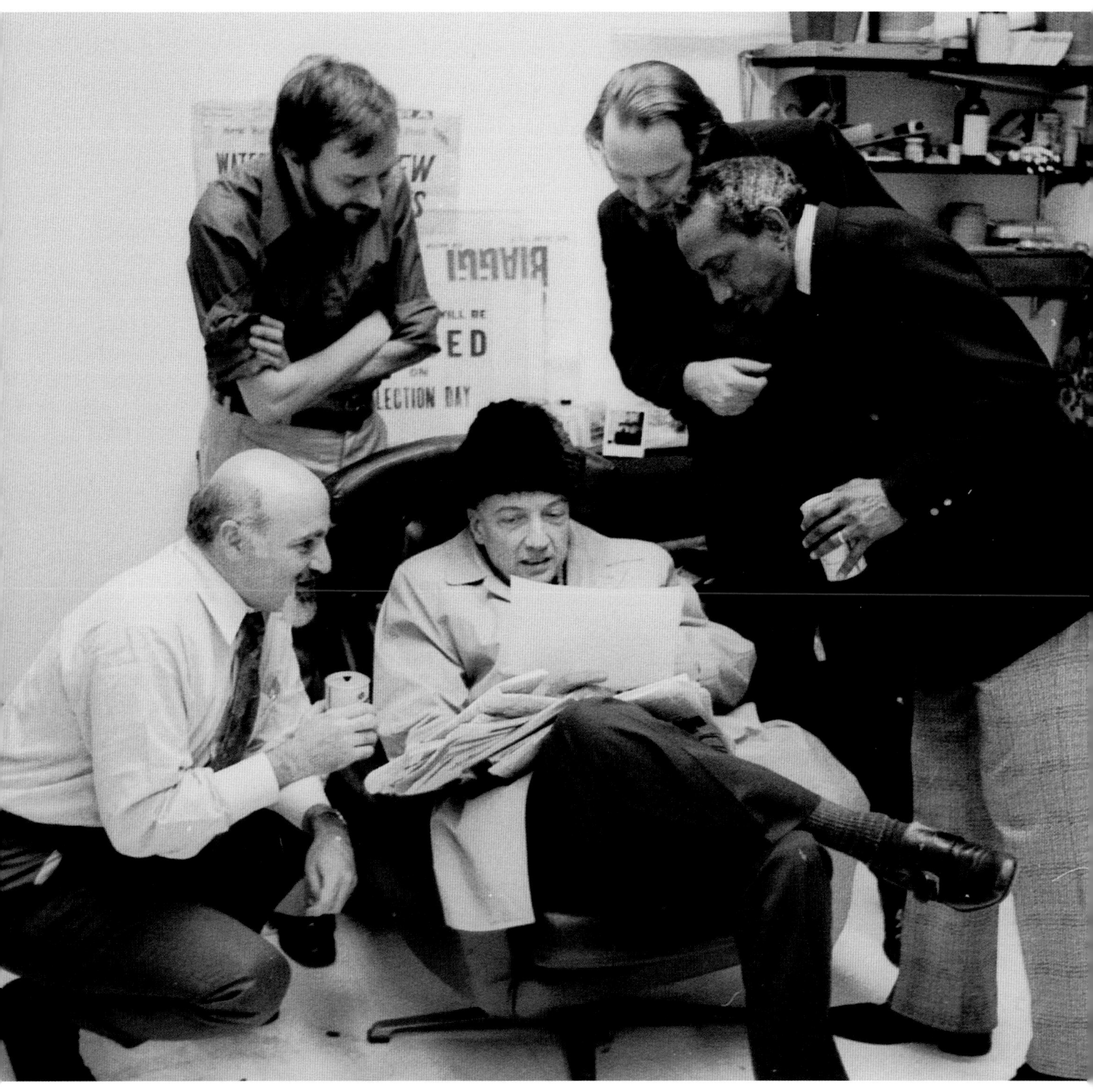

George Avakian, Michael Brooks, John Hammond, Dan Morgenster, and Joe Newman. (Author's collection)

Buck Clayton Jam Session LP jacket.
(Author's collection)

This wasn't the first time George had been to the studio. In the summer or 1972, he called one day and said he thought I should consider making a recording with Ruby Braff, that Ruby hadn't made a commercially released record under his own name in the US since 1961 and that was a travesty. I agreed and a few days or weeks later the three of us met at Jim and Andy's on West Forty-Eighth Street and talked about a possible recording project. I was eager to proceed; I just had to organize my bank account. We recorded in September and October, and the results were worth a bunch of stars in *Downbeat*.

There was one peculiar incident at the session that occurred accidentally. It was an odd twist of fate that I had a houseguest at the time of the recording: Bert Stern. He had experienced assorted difficulties and was the full-time resident of a spare bedroom at 173 Christopher. On one of the days Ruby recorded, I asked Bert to take a portrait of Ruby that might be used as an album cover. He did and we used it.

To back up a couple of years to 1958, when Bert and the pre-rug Avakian Brothers, George and Aram, made *Jazz on a Summer's Day* at that year's Newport Jazz Festival, there were some incidents that didn't endear Bert to the brothers Avakian. I had no idea about any of this at the time of the recording, but no one threw anything at one another, the picture got taken, Bert didn't hang out at the session, and it went off without a hitch. There was an awful lot I didn't know about Ruby, but one thing I learned very quickly was that he was a handful. He also told me that he had so much fun making the recording he wanted to do another immediately.

I asked Ruby what he had in mind, and it turned out to be a reunion with another handful, Ellis Larkins, with whom he'd recorded extensively in the 1950s. John Hammond had been in charge of producing those legendary sessions for Vanguard Records, and I had enough in the bank to afford two musicians, so we undertook this recording a little later in October. It turned out the recording was scheduled for the same day in October that the initial, now long out of print recordings, had been made in 1955, so John was pleased before a note was played by either Ruby or Ellis. He was sure it would be a magical afternoon, and he was at the studio to keep things in order if his old eccentric friends got out of hand. Bert was still in residence and took pictures of Ruby and Ellis together. The pictures were just fine, but the cover turned out awful and when we reissued the LP on CD, I asked Richard Merkin to create a new one and it's terrific. Two other things about the CD reissue: There were four unused tracks, so we used them, and we were able to use six of Bert's pictures in the CD booklet. We had only been able to use one on the LP.

Now John and George and I had Ruby Braff in common. A great deal more would be coming, none of which I could anticipate. And I don't remember exactly how the joint venture record company George and I began to structure was first considered, but it was, and this is what happened.

George liked Downtown Sound and was at the studio frequently. He also liked the way the Chiaroscuro Records was evolving and branching into fusion and the avant-garde. Then, in 1977, I sold Chiaroscuro to AudioFidelity Enterprises. My plan was to develop a new record company using Downtown Sound as a base and continue making similar recordings. After a year of discussions with George, we decided to launch a new recording company project, perhaps bring in one or two additional people and call the company New York Records. George owned the rights to that label name, and we issued an LP using that name featuring a recent recording I'd made with the pianist Joe Turner. We called the album *As Time Goes By* and we began planning our next steps. All the while this was going on I got to know George's wife, the noted violinist Anahid Ajemian, and two of their children, Gregory and Mara.

The next step was for George to bring his extensive archive of "extra" material from his many years at Columbia, Warner Bros., and RCA to Downtown Sound to evaluate. There were many remarkable unissued recordings in his archive, featuring the music of Benny Goodman, Louis Armstrong, Erroll Garner, Dave Brubeck, Gene Krupa, Sonny Rollins, Mahalia Jackson, and many others. We invited Gerry Mulligan to join our fledgling enterprise and he brought in material that was programmed into four LPs, and we began a new recording project with a revitalized Concert Jazz Band. In addition to this recording project with Gerry, we produced other new recordings with Woody Herman and Ruby Braff, the Russian

Ruby Braff and Ellis Larkins LP jackets.
(Author's collection)

saxophonist Roman Kunsman, and an exciting trumpet artist from Texas, Marvin "Hannibal" Peterson. We also purchased a completed master from Lee Konitz that he'd recently made with Martial Solal, and continued recording and rehearsing a number of younger, less well-known artists like James Mason, T. M. Stevens, Phil Clendeninn, and Mike Santiago, all of whom had been on fusion albums released by Chiaroscuro.

As we pursued this venture, George funded the artist fees for the recordings, Gerry funded his Concert Jazz Band recording, and I kept the studio running to do the recording, remixing, and mastering and contributed seven or eight completed masters that I'd not issued on Chiaroscuro. It was all going well, and I still have a copy of the small booklet we released in late 1979 entitled *Pegasus Records 1980, produced by George Avakian and Hank O'Neal.* George had been advised by his lawyer to tread carefully in using the name New York Records, there was a dispute somewhere, so we switched the name to Pegasus. The name was Astrud Gilberto's idea, and she gave me a little white Pegasus doll for good luck.

This is what the booklet said about the new company and George:

> *Pegasus Records was founded in June 1979 by George Avakian and Hank O'Neal. Avakian's credits in record production go back to 1939, when he produced the very first jazz album, Chicago Jazz for Decca. Since then he has been the head of International and Pop Albums at Columbia for ten years, helped found Warner Bros. records in 1959 and was the head of the Popular Music Division of RCA for three years. He was responsible for the success of such jazz artists as Dave Brubeck, Miles Davis, Erroll Garner, and Sonny Rollins and has produced classic albums by Benny Goodman, Louis Armstrong, and Duke Ellington. He was equally active in pop and classical music, producing the first albums of such diverse artists as Johnny Mathis, Ravi Shankar, John Cage, Bob Newhart, and Tony Bennett. Most recently he helped launch the career of Keith Jarrett. After an absence from the record scene for some years (he was in charge of his family's oriental rug business) he has returned to his first love with a flourish and is hard at work with his new independent label.*

George was very enthusiastic, as he had been from the beginning. He was certain he would be able to line up a distribution agreement with a major record company, CBS, RCA, or Atlantic, where just a few years earlier he'd had such great success with Charles Lloyd and Keith Jarrett. But it didn't work out. Despite his past successes, none of the people he approached had any interest in distributing a newly formed, modestly capitalized independent record company and we both became very discouraged.

In the spring of 1980, I tried my best to convince Fred Hayeen at Polydor to take us on. It was kind of our last chance, but after a dozen meetings it didn't work out. By then George had given up and his archive and all our ideas for the future were put on the shelf. Maybe we were forty-five years too early. In 2023, the archivist Matt Snyder announced, via the Jazz Research Group, that he'd finally completed the cataloging of the George and Anahid Avakian papers in the Music Division of the New York Public Library. The NYPL website notes there are one hundred forty-nine boxes and miscellaneous folders that take up 56.72 linear feet of space. It also notes there are in excess of one thousand audio tapes and that it may be possible to listen to some of them in the future.

It is possible that in 1980 or even 2025 no one needs another record by Sonny Rollins or Dave Brubeck or Mahalia Jackson or Benny Goodman or Erroll Garner or Louis Armstrong or any other of the artists in George's recorded archive, but how nice it might have been if he'd had the chance to make some decisions on the best way to present the music he produced rather than leave it to someone fifty years in the future.

But just as George was giving up, something peculiar happened. A year or so earlier, a man named John Moore had booked some time at Downtown Sound to make a recording he hoped to use as a prank. I don't recall the subject, but he paid for his time and that was that. But then in early April, he got in touch with the studio again to undertake another project and this time I was around. We had a discussion about the music business and his possible desire to become involved in it. We agreed to meet a week or so later and in late April John Chandler Moore III and I met at 100 Central Park South, his base of operations in New York City.

I explained to John what George Avakian and I had attempted to accomplish, how we had failed, how George had withdrawn, and how I wanted to find a way to move forward. George had the rug company and a bank account to fall back on; I didn't and had a few more active years. John was intrigued; we sketched out a rough plan that would incorporate what George and I had tried to do with Pegasus but would be better financed and considerably more adventurous. We met half a dozen more times before I hit on the idea that ultimately made our rough plan become a reality.

John with Count Basie. (Author's collection)

At the time, my friend John Hammond was festering, doing nothing in a small office he'd been given by a friend at the Richmond Organization, a publishing company with offices on Columbus Circle. He had been forced into mandatory retirement at CBS and was at a loose end. I suggested to John Moore that if we could convince John Hammond to become part of what we had in mind, that might be all it would take. He agreed. The only problem was that I was to be in Japan for an entire month on tour with Astrud Gilberto.

Sometime in 1979 John had given me a copy of his autobiography, *John Hammond on Record*. On the flyleaf he had written: *To Hank. You're making the kind of music I ought to be doing. All the best, John.* I planned to meet with John when I returned from Japan, tell him what John Moore and I had in mind, which, simply put, was to raise sufficient money so that he could begin making the kinds of records he wanted to and his name would be on the label. We were going to form Hammond Music Enterprises, and he would be the chairman of the company. When I returned from Japan, I made my way to Columbus Circle, met with John on July 22, pitched the idea, and he was interested. One week later I introduced him to John Moore, and we were off and running.

Hammond Music Enterprises, aka HME, aka Hammond Records, and for a minute or two, aka Zoo York Recordz, was a terrific company with a good business plan that almost made it and would have except for a couple of things that went wrong, one of our own doing and another over which we had no control.

The initial business plan was simple. John Moore had a remarkable talent for raising funds in various ways, and John Hammond was certain he could convince the people at CBS to distribute whatever we produced. It didn't hurt that John Moore was able to bring a third John into the mix, his old friend and classmate, the noted attorney John Eastman. It also didn't hurt that John Eastman had just negotiated the arrangement with CBS to distribute his brother-in-law's records, one ex-Beatle named Paul McCartney. John Moore raised $250,000 via a private placement, John Hammond used his good will at CBS and obtained a pressing and distribution arrangement, and John Eastman used his clout at CBS because of his relationship with Paul McCartney to secure the best possible terms for the P&D deal. All three Johns delivered the goods.

There were six of us, John Hammond and his longtime assistant Mikie Harris, John Moore and his assistant Nina Yablon, and myself and Jon Bates. We rented two rooms from Media Sound at 311 West Fifty-Seventh, bought used office furniture on Twenty-Third Street, got a telephone number, the three principals granted themselves a salary of $500 a week, and everyone got to work developing the company.

We had no plans to record anything or release a record. Our goal was to develop a business plan that would lead to a public offering in June 1981; an offering that would raise a couple of million dollars so we could begin acting like a real record company. The word was out, we had money, John Hammond was bursting with enthusiasm and in his office every day, plus we had the same deal as Paul McCartney's at CBS, which was as good a deal as it was possible to get, and we were filling every inch of space in our offices with ideas. We were excited and to prove it we brought on another employee, Chuck Gregory, an old hand at CBS, who was particularly adept at marketing and promotion. I interacted with John Hammond as much as possible; it was fun seeing him every day.

For the first few months we stuck to our plan, and everything was on schedule to do something in June. Our financials, such as they were, were on their way to being certified by the firm of Satin, Tennenbaum, Eichler & Zimmerman, John Moore was working to secure an underwriter and was making good progress, and while our belts were tight, none of us were starving. We assembled a strong board of directors, with all three of the principals bringing in impressive individuals. John Hammond brought in his old friend, George Wein, and this is when I first got to know this legendary figure. George Avakian agreed to be on the board, as did my old friends from CIA days, Juliette Moran from GAF and Mike Uretsky from New York University. The buzz was terrific, the telephone was ringing, and people were interested in the new company. There was a sense of anticipation. After all, John Hammond was the guy responsible for discovering Bruce Springsteen, Bob Dylan, George Benson, Aretha Franklin, and a number of other major artists like Billie Holiday and Count Basie. Who would be the next one? The word was out that he had his eye on some great young talent. Unfortunately, while the talent was young and in a couple of instances were pretty good, we later discovered none were really superstars.

It was at this point that we messed up and didn't stick to the game plan. Our accountants, Satin, Tennenbaum, et al. were really taken with the prospects for the company. So taken in fact, that they wanted to make a $50,000 investment in our company. We all weighed the pros and cons. The main pro was that the $50,000 could be used to make a few records and John Hammond was getting increasingly itchy about not being in the studio. This would stop the itch. The con was that we'd have to hire a new accounting firm to do the financials and this would set back the public offering for a month or two, from June to August, or possibly the fall. We agreed to accept the $50,000 and to celebrate we decided to use some of the money for a Hammond Music announcement party at Sardi's. It was a memorable gathering of close friends, musicians we wanted to record, and people within the record industry. John had a smile on his face all night long.

We had all agreed to take the money and cure John's itch, and though we didn't know it at the time, this probably meant the company would never succeed. John Hammond was able to go into the studio and make a trio record with Polish/Czech jazz pianist Adam Makowicz. He wanted to do yet another solo record with Adam, but I convinced him to do a trio and he was excited when I delivered George Mraz and Jack DeJohnette. It turned out to be his last studio recording.

I undertook a major project with Gerry Mulligan and Dave Grusin. Gerry wrote a number of wonderful originals, many of which required varying personnel. I was simultaneously worrying about a new alternative band called J. Walter Negro and the Loose Jointz and handholding one of John's new discoveries, Al Peterson, and traveling with him to both Detroit and Nashville to discuss his potential with various producers.

One day John told me to make sure I was in the office the next morning because he wanted to introduce me to his old friend, the noted poet Allen Ginsberg. John had undertaken a recording project with Ginsberg in the early 1970s, but CBS balked and refused to issue it. He said he wanted to hand the project off to me for completion because he now had his own label and could issue anything he wanted. The evolution of the record that was produced, *First Blues*, is outlined elsewhere.

John with Barney Josephson of Café Society fame.
(Author's collection)

John with John Moore and
John Brademus (NYU president).
(Author's collection)

John with Michael Moriarty. (Author's collection)

J. Walter Negro and the Loose Jointz.
(Author's collection)

Everything came to a crashing halt in June and into the summer. The federal funds rate hit 20 percent by June and IPOs began to dry up, and the next two years were a financial disaster, both from the company level and on a personal level as well.

Shoot the Pump 12" Zoo York release.
(Author's collection)

By the end of the summer, the $500 a week stipend that allowed for McDonald's and little more was eliminated. I had bought my space at 830 Broadway for $95,000, had managed to pay off $45,000 of it, but was faced with a $50,000 balloon mortgage payment that was due by June 1982. A conventional mortgage was out of the question. Not only were rates about 25 percent, but even if I could have afforded such a rate, nothing was available for me because 830 Broadway didn't have a Certificate of Occupancy and wouldn't until 1992. I had to find a way to pay off $50,000, eat a couple of meals a day, and make thirty-five-hundred square feet reasonably habitable. All this with no salary, no trust fund, no bank account, no relatives to fall back on, and no immediate prospects that anything would be forthcoming in the immediate future.

The company's salvation was completely in the hands of John Moore, who was remarkably resilient. He came up with a variety of ways to keep things running and the telephones from being cut off. He had the idea that he could probably find a way to finance individual records, but we didn't develop that program until 1981.

One of the more interesting episodes in the second half of 1981 was the saga of J. Walter Negro, an adventure that began in excitement and enthusiasm but ended a decade or so later in a tragic manner. It involved "Shoot the Pump," a 12" dance single featuring Marc Edmunds, aka J. Walter Negro, and his band of ruffians, The Loose Jointz. I was simply the executive producer for the record; my friend Fred Miller supervised it and brought it to me. Both Johns at Hammond Music loved it, 3:30 of early hip hop, funk, Latin, and social protest all rolled into one. It was a bust in the United States, the CBS bureaucracy saw to that, but it became a breakaway hit in the UK, thanks to the BBC, and almost became the company's salvation.

One a personal level this was an exciting time. I was usually flat broke but surrounded by the most exciting people in town, and I often had my camera with me to document what was going on. One day I spent the night at an ICP gala sandwiched between Berenice Abbott and Jacqueline Onassis at Windows on the World and all I had was a subway token to get home. But all the while I was hanging out with Allen Ginsberg, The Clash, Robert Frank, Les Paul, Jacqueline Onassis, dozens of great musicians, recording and mixing others, traveling to London with the master tape for "Shoot the Pump," getting the Berenice Abbott book ready for publication, and then, at the end of the year, flying to Switzerland, courtesy of Badrutt's Palace Hotel, to meet up with Astrud Gilberto, who was scheduled to do a very special holiday performance. When I finally arrived in St. Moritz, I was met at the train, put in a sleigh, and transported to the hotel, my first and last time over the river and through the dell.

Astrud sang her heart out at the hotel's gala and annoyed her hosts to no end because she wouldn't personally invite her friend Ivo Pitanguy, possibly the world's most famous plastic surgeon, to come over from Gstaad for the performance and check out the many faces that needed lifting in the Palace Hotel. Still, they gave her a big bag of cash and instead of returning to New York we decided to return via Lisbon, visit an old girlfriend of hers who married a count and who'd promised us a wild New Year's Eve at a resort high above the city. It was all that had been promised, and the return to New York City was a bit of a letdown because I had to start looking for subway tokens and keeping the credit cards from being cancelled.

The fortunes at Hammond were no better than when I left. They were probably worse. There were a couple of investors on the horizon, but they were more or less bottom feeders with suspicious backgrounds. I was dispatched to London, paying for everything with my American Express card. It was strictly Hail Mary. My job was to convince Island Records to license our entire catalog for a couple hundred thousand dollars. I worked on it for three weeks and it didn't work out. The only thing they really wanted was J. Walter Negro and they already had that. When I returned to New York in mid-February, I was beaten up pretty good and was beaten further in the weeks after I arrived.

It was lights out time while I was gone and to keep the lights on a little longer and the telephone ringing, the decision had been made to sell an enormous amount of stock to a couple of outside investors and Chuck Gregory. This meant that the outside investors and Chuck had as much or more stock than John Hammond and myself, and this was essentially the end of any decisions being made on strictly musical merits and substantially shifted the focus of the company.

The musical decisions that were made after this point were also Hail Marys and none of them worked. For the next eighteen months we scuffled and were primarily in the twelve-inch R&B single and pay for play business. Chuck Gregory knew the R&B twelve-inch business; he virtually invented it, and John Moore created a series of sophisticated investment opportunities for various limited partners who were interested in supporting a specific album.

This was a good business plan if the musical acts had the goods, but most of them did not. There was a guy named Lowell Simon who had a record called "The Love Massage." We put it out and it charted for a minute but not high enough to offset the costs. Randy Jones, the cowboy with The Village People, went solo for a single outing and Lenny Seeley and some of the Loose Jointz started a band called Heritage and released "Feel It," which, unfortunately, no one did. J. Walter and his guys recorded a follow up to "Shoot the Pump," entitled "Times Square," but it was never released because the band basically fell apart in England and never fully recovered.

I was more or less in charge of longer-range projects when John Moore was able to find financing. There was Allen Ginsberg's *First Blues*, a great album by Marion Williams, and the reissue of Michael Frank's first album, a fine album that suffered from underexposure because Faberge released it—yes, the cologne and aftershave folks. These albums made their money back and turned a profit, but not a very big one. They were, however, good records and despite their shaky beginnings, they are still available today as CDs on other labels. The other recordings we had available for release in 1982 and 1983 either never saw the light of day or were released and never heard from again. In general, it can be said that all the non-jazz/gospel records that were released may have had a shot at being sold, but didn't, and proved the axiom that there's nothing deader than a dead pop record. The only

Michael Franks LP jacket.
(Author's collection)

Marian Williams LP jacket.
(Author's collection)

exception is J. Walter, who in 2025 still has an amazing Internet and underground presence.

The record company continued to be personally disastrous for me, but there was a bright spot in April 1982 that made a difference that continues to this day. There was still no regular salary, and I was flattened, sometimes even worse than that. All you have to do is look at my earnings for Social Security purposes for the Hammond Music years. From 1981–84 the total amount is $13,999, or about $3,500 a year.

One morning John Moore and I were discussing how we were going to eat for the next few weeks, and he knew I was in a pickle in general but very specifically regarding the balloon mortgage floating above 830 Broadway. Always practical, he said, "Why don't you sell your stock in Hammond?" I probably said something like, "Who'd want it?" and John said, "The two guys who bought stock in February, they want more. They believe in the company and will probably pay you a nickel a share."

Since I didn't have a nickel, the prospect of 230,000 of them sounded pretty good, and it worked out. The stock sale plus the sale of my father's cabin at Round Pond poked a hole in the balloon and surprised Steve Green (now the fancy and highly successful S. L. Green), who was probably counting on me to default so he could grab 830 Broadway and sell it again for twice as much as I'd paid the year before. Of course, this meant I was no longer a stockholder in the company, but I really didn't care. I was still there, hoping for the best, but I wasn't optimistic. I was almost certain John Hammond was going to bail pretty soon because he wasn't having any fun, something he told me on a regular basis. He wasn't in the studio making records, there was no salary, and he was counting his loose change to take the bus from 311 West to 444 East Fifty-Seventh Street.

Then something happened. An unsolicited cassette tape turned up at 311. The tape had been sent to Chuck Gregory by a musical horseman, Chesley Millikin. Chuck didn't want to bother with it and tossed it in my direction suggesting I have a listen. He said he'd never heard of the artist, and I knew even less. At least he'd heard of the manager who'd sent the tape but hadn't been in contact with him for years.

A day or so later I was driving across Ninth Street on my way out of town, and I popped the cassette into my tape deck. An announcer said something like "Live from Steamboat 1874 it's Stevie Ray Vaughan and Double Trouble." It took about fifteen seconds to recognize that this was real deal, maybe even better than that.

With Stevie Ray Vaughan at HME offices, 1982.
(Author's collection)

With Jimmy and Stevie Ray Vaughan at the Power Station, 1982.
(Author's collection)

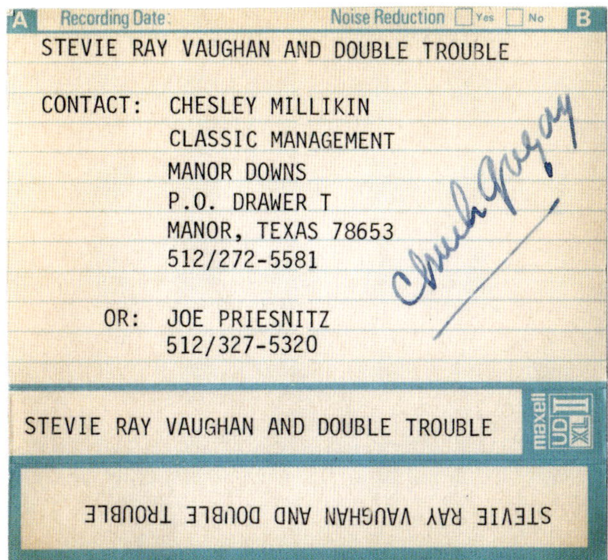

Stevie Ray Vaughan demo cassette.
(Author's collection)

The next morning, I returned to the office and told anyone who'd listen that we should bet the ranch on a young kid from Texas named Vaughan. No one listened very hard; John Hammond, who I thought would back me, wasn't very enthusiastic. I was shocked. This was the most remarkable young (he was twenty-six) guitarist I'd ever heard, and I was met with yawns. There are a bunch of versions of what happened next, mostly true, but some are a bit distorted.

I kept nagging anyone at HME who'd listen that the ranch was still available, but the company was struggling and without the resources to go after an unknown guitar player. Then Stevie played the Montreux Jazz Festival in the summer of 1982. The crowd didn't like him much, but David Bowie and Jackson Browne did. Stevie recorded with Bowie and almost toured with him and later in the year got some studio time through the good efforts of Jackson Browne. These tapes became the basis for what was released in 1983 as *Texas Flood*, but Stevie still didn't have a record deal, and HME was as broke as ever.

In late 1982 I had a chat with Chesley Millikin, who told me they had some new material they'd like to play for John Hammond. I said I'd set it up, but the presentation had to play on John's ego: If they were sufficiently humble, asked John to take charge, ask his advice, give him the respect he should have, they might have a chance.

The meeting was held in John's little office in Media Sound and it worked. I took photographs of some smiling guys who looked ready to move on to the next stage, which they did. HME didn't get the record; John took it to Epic and a minute later took himself along with it. HME wasn't doing well, John was itchy, and Stevie was just the ticket to get back into a nice office at CBS in a consulting capacity, which he continued for the next few years. I don't know when the deal went down, but I have photographs of John with Stevie and the band, plus Jimmy Vaughan, at the Power Station and they're dated January 12, 1983. Strangely enough, Chesley Millikin wasn't at this session.

Some months later the record was released and it did very well. Someone at CBS told me they were spending $1.00 a record in terms of promotion, at least for the first 250,000. It ultimately went gold and was the beginning of a career that burned very brightly until the helicopter crash in August 1990.

Others referred to Stevie as John's last great discovery. Of course, this wasn't the case. I never heard John say he'd "discovered" him, but Stevie was the last artist he backed who had great commercial success after a long run that had begun in the mid-1930s. The people he'd championed at HME, while talented, were not big-ticket artists and had modest careers. It was nice that he was able to go out with a winner.

Long after John had died and two years after Stevie's death, the master tapes from the demo I'd heard in 1981 were remastered and a CD entitled *In the Beginning* was released because Epic had run out of unissued material and Stevie was still a very viable artist. In my mind, these early recordings are still the best, raw, exciting, and without any rock pretense. Ten years after that, in the early 2000s, *Rolling Stone Magazine* voted Stevie the seventh greatest guitarist of all time. He sure sounded that way in 1981 when I first heard the demo tape. I didn't buy the *In the Beginning* CD until 2022, just to scan the cover to use as an illustration; I didn't have to, I still had the demo tape, which I was pretty sure had a better sound, a more gritty feel, than did the cleaned up and remastered CD. In May 2023, Heritage Auctions sold Stevie's acoustic Guild F-412 guitar for $225,000. He was the real deal, just not at HME Records. Life dances on.

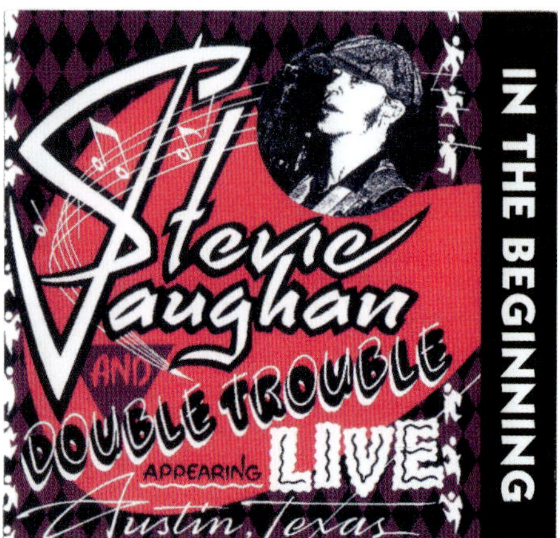

In the Beginning CD booklet cover.
(Author's collection)

Just as John Hammond became less involved with the company that bore his name and eventually left for good, I also spent less time at my desk since I had to bills to pay and the record company was still not in a position to provide a regular salary. In 1983 we moved from 311 West Fifty-Seventh Street to better offices, a block east, at 250 West Fifty-Seventh. Hammond didn't make the move, but I did and maintained an office even though I was pursuing other opportunities, including the sale and licensing of masters I controlled, a relationship with the Internal Revenue Service, and an opportunity that grew out of the earlier meeting I'd had with Peter Martin. The relationship with Martin ultimately led to the formation of HOSS, Inc. and the end of my relationship with Hammond Music, but John Hammond and I remained close.

I kept my office at 250 West Fifty-Seventh and continued to be as helpful as possible, but funding was not forthcoming for any of the projects in which I was either involved or interested and by late 1983 or early 1984, all parties felt it would be better if I no longer had an executive-level position. I was still a vice president, but in name only. I continued to work with John Moore and John Hammond independently on special projects, but few of these projects were related to HME, with the exception of doing whatever I could to help the company in its quest to become a public entity.

The public offering was finally made on August 8, 1984. The underwriter was A. T. Brod and Company, and the issue was sufficiently subscribed to be successful. I was told that a couple of the stockholders with the most to gain had bags of cash on hand just to make sure the offering was successful. I never saw the cash, but it wasn't needed, and after the offering I wasn't either. This lack of need meant I was in the office less and less but was still serving in an advisory status. It turned out this was much to my advantage.

Despite a busy schedule in his new advisory capacity at CBS and the successful public offering by HME, it was clear to me that the long-term prognosis for John and the company that bore his name was not good. It was just a matter of time for each of them. John Hammond lasted longer. I don't remember the exact day, and it isn't noted in any of my records, but HME failed in the late summer of 1985. The last HME entry in my diary is a meeting on July 16th.

I was out of town much of the summer, either in London, Maine working with Berenice Abbott, or in the Caribbean planning for the most ambitious series of jazz cruises anyone had ever undertaken. After one of the trips, I decided to drop in at the HME offices. When I arrived the door was locked. This puzzled me but it was not a problem; I still had keys. I went in and discovered an empty, largely looted office. It looked like the evacuation had been fairly rapid and everything that was electronic or personal was gone. About all that was left was the furniture and basic office supplies. But the people who were so eager to get their stereo out had left behind the most valuable items; there was still a shelf of master tapes. I liberated tapes I thought were valuable, those by Allen Ginsberg, Adam Makowicz, and a few others. Later, I came back and moved out my father's old office furniture, which I'd left in what was once my office. The liberated tapes eventually became CDs, and the office furniture was first used at 830 and then was transferred to our country home, Glenside, in Thornhurst, Pennsylvania. I have no idea what happened to all the rest.

Despite all the excitement surrounding Stevie Ray Vaughan, John Hammond was slowing down. George Wein presented a wonderful concert in his honor at the 1985 Kool Jazz Festival in Avery Fisher Hall, but his health failed shortly thereafter, and he had a series of debilitating strokes. Esmé Hammond died in May 1986, and it wasn't too much later that John took a bad fall at The Century and was bed-ridden from that point on. It was then that I began to see him more often. If I was in town, I tried to call on John on Friday or Saturday afternoon, to just talk, listen to Billie Holiday records, or simply read him the paper. There came a time when the guy who always had a bag full of papers at the ready could no longer read one, so he was grateful for someone who could fill in the gaps. His full-time nurses usually had soaps on the small television in his bedroom.

The last visit entry in my diary is for June 27, 1987; he died on July 10, when I was on my way to Maine for Berenice Abbott's birthday celebration. I remember talking to a *Rolling Stone* reporter from Berenice's cabin on Lake Hebron, but I don't remember what I said or anything about what the magazine might have written about John.

Roman Kunsman CD booklet cover, 1979–2003. (Author's collection)

I knew him pretty well, maybe better than most, because we'd worked on so many things together for two decades, and the main thing I knew was that everybody bought the act. Sure, John was a Vanderbilt and, sure, he lived a couple of inches from Sutton Place, and he had a house in the country, and the press said he'd discovered everything except the light bulb.

I also knew that there were a lot of times he couldn't pay his credit card bills, that he didn't own the apartment that was an inch away from Sutton Place, that he took the bus home because he could afford it, that he'd sold all his old records to Bob Altshuler because he was broke, and at the end, despite all the accolades and success and flamboyant reputation, the only things he actually owned were his clothing, some books, and his bedroom furniture. He also knew what he had done and what he hadn't. A lot of things were claimed in his name that he didn't claim. Could he be a horse's ass? You bet. Was he often arrogant? Of course. Was he sometimes a bit hypocritical? Yes. But did he know he was all these things? Of course he did.

One day in the early 1980s, I bought a paperback that contained many of the writings of Otis Ferguson, possibly the finest jazz critic of the time. In a *New Republic* article entitled simply "John Hammond" from 1938, he called John on the carpet for a few dozen reasons. I told John about the anthology and how the article had given him

One Step to Chicago CD booklet cover, 1992-2021. (Author's collection)

George Avakian at 830 Broadway, 2007. (Author's collection)

the business. I asked him what he thought of it. John said, "It was an accurate portrait of me at the time." He added that he shared my opinion of Ferguson's skill. In other words, John recognized the warts and knew full well what he was and what he wasn't.

He was a remarkable talent scout, the most enthusiastic enabler the jazz and pop business has ever seen, and a casual producer. He knew he didn't "discover" Stevie Ray Vaughan or even recognize his unique abilities early on. It took a little nagging for him to come around. Sure, he signed Aretha Franklin, but he didn't know exactly what to do with her, and Jerry Wexler did. The same for Bob Dylan; I wonder if anyone knows that stride pianist Dick Wellstood is on one of the Dylan records John produced?

And on it goes, but there is no one in the business who ever enabled such a broad group of extraordinary musicians to make their way into a recording studio and into the marketplace. In July 2022, the United States Postal Service issued a beautiful stamp featuring the folksinger/social activist Pete Seeger. In the 1960s and 1970s, Pete was virtually banned because it was alleged he was a card-carrying communist. The same was said of John Hammond in the 1930s and 1940s. Of course, it wasn't true, but John had the courage to record Pete and arrange for the records to released on Columbia.

He had a good fifty-year run, and John Moore and I had the hope that we could tap into the ears, energy, and enthusiasm and somehow cap his career with a few new successes and in the process launch a record company. We gave it a shot, but we missed the mark by a couple of months. Meanwhile, George Avakian was to remain active and a presence in the world of music until 2017; he outlasted John by thirty years. And in those thirty years I never heard George say anything hateful about John, but I know there was a good deal of anger on both sides. While Hammond Music was struggling to keep the lights on George resigned from the board and sued the company and all the officers of the company because of leftovers from the stillborn Pegasus Records venture. All of this went away after HME failed in 1985 and after 1987 George and I worked together to release some of these masters. The Roman Kunsman project was released on Chiaroscuro's Downtown Sound label in 2003.

There was a memorial service for George in the Bruno Walter Auditorium on March 27, 2018. The family asked that I be one of the eulogists. This is what I said, recounting some of out adventures and his oversized importance in world of music and the arts in general:

"All people's lives are filled with people who made a difference to them. George was one of those who made a difference in mine. This is how.

When I was a teenager in 1955 discovering I liked jazz, George was producing some of the best records of that decade and one was called *I Like Jazz*. It cost a dollar and was the first 12" LP I owned. It turned out to have been the perfect way to start. I noticed a guy named Avakian had written the following on the back of the album:

> *This long playing record is a capsule story of the development of jazz, in performances by key jazz musicians who have created the history of their music. Each example represents a different aspect of jazz. For details – see your Columbia dealer.*

I didn't see the dealer but a few months later the Columbia Record Club offered three records for another dollar. One was called *Jazz Goes to College*; the others were samplers. George produced them all. And once again this guy named Avakian had written the notes on the back of the Brubeck album. I still have those LPs and they still sound just as good.

A few months later I saw his name on the front of a book at the library. It was called *New Hot Discography*. It listed all the old jazz records that I would soon be searching for.

Fast forward a dozen years. It was 1967 and I'd just landed in New York courtesy of the CIA. I had a short list of names, people Squirrel Ashcraft had contacted and suggested they be nice to me. I found John Hammond at CBS and Neshui and Ahmet at their Atlantic offices near Columbus Circle but found George at Avakian Brothers downtown in the thirties. I wondered why he was surrounded by beautiful carpets instead of making jazz records. He had his reasons and we stayed in touch.

In the early 1970s, when I had started my own modest label George called one day and said he wanted to introduce me to someone who needed to be recorded. I met George and Ruby Braff at a place midtown. Ruby hadn't made a record in the US for a decade and George wanted to remedy that and so we did. It was the first of many projects we did together in the 1970s and early 1980s. We even started a joint venture that didn't go very far but resulted in some good records.

George also introduced me to Anahid and his children. Anahid led to music in other directions and Gregory even became a presence at Downtown Sound, my recording studio. Along the way George continued to work with me on projects. One thing I learned early on was that if a project made sense, he didn't say no. Interview Merce Cunningham about improvising with Baby Dodds? He set it up. Ask Lotte Lenya to write liner notes? Not a problem. He was always encouraging and if possible a willing participant. If I was short and needed a thousand to make the budget he didn't say no, he was always helpful. He only said no to one thing. I nagged him for years to write everything down, a memoir, an autobiography, rough notes, talk into a recorder, anything. He had the history of jazz and much of modern music in American in his head. Just like that *I Like Jazz* LP was a capsule story of the development of jazz, George had the same thing in his head. But there was always an excuse. I'm hoping that he did in secret and one day an archivist here at the library will be going through George's papers and will come up it. We'll see.

In April 2017 I visited with George at the Esplanade. I had taken a young writer, Aiden Levy, to meet him. He was about the age I was when I'd first met George, fifty years earlier. Aiden was working on a book about Sonny Rollins and wanted to hear about *The Bridge* and the other records George had done with Sonny. About the only thing George didn't remember was the name of an assistant engineer on one of the dates. At one point we were discussing another record, an old record from the twenties or thirties. I said one thing, George said another. I spotted a copy of *New Hot Discography* on a shelf, grabbed it and gave it to George. He quickly found the listing and he was right. I wasn't surprised

A few years later, in 2021, a wonderful musician, Dan Levinson, asked if I'd help with the release of a recording George had undertaken in 1992 but hadn't been able to release, *One Step to Chicago – The Legacy of Frank Teschemacher*. It was released in August 2022; my contribution was just to write some liner notes, included as a foreword to the wonderful eighty-page book that accompanies the CD. It is an elaborate production, maybe one of the last unissued recording that will be issued of a George Avakian production. It was a nice way to go out; a full circle project, one that celebrates the first jazz album he or anyone else ever produced: *Chicago Jazz*, issued by Decca in 1939. It was fun to be associated with it, even in just a minor capacity.

14

Hugh Hefner

April 9, 1926 – September 27, 2017

Meet Me Tonight in Dreamland

Legend has it that back in 1956, a couple of years after Hugh Hefner founded *Playboy*, Frankie Trumbauer's last words to his wife where something like, "It was just as much a surprise to me as it is to you." Not so surprising perhaps, except these last words came as a very long-distance telephone call from Frankie to his wife, Mitzi, and records indicate he'd already been dead for a few hours when the call came in. In later years, this was always a puzzle to her. Now stick with me, this all makes sense.

Frankie was a big-time jazz guy in the 1920s and 1930s. His closest pal was Bix Beiderbecke, the incendiary young man with a horn who roared through the twenties and died at twenty-eight, becoming the most romanticized musical figure of those legendary days. His friend Eddie Condon described his pure, bell-like tone as just like a girl saying yes. Such was his fame that among certain people, just the mention of his name can cause emotional outbursts that encourage disparate souls to bond instantly, and to possibly use this as super glue, I had created a handmade CD of various artists performing Beiderbecke compositions, one that I knew would intrigue Hugh Hefner.

It was just as much a surprise to me as it was to the widow Mitzi when the telephone rang in January 2004, this time from the very alive Jimmy Shier, suggesting I should drop everything and hop on the first available flight to Los Angeles. And make sure that I packed all my cameras; rumor had it I could take decent pictures under pressure and write a word or two about the process and any interesting sidelights that might develop. Jimmy said my subject was another legendary, equally romanticized, but fortunately much longer-lived figure: Hugh Hefner. Hefner, he said, was a jazz fan, probably owned some records I'd produced, and he felt we might hit it off in a photo interview situation.

It sounded like a challenge and a possible adventure; my travel agent had the flights, hotel, and car arranged in half an hour, and a couple of days later, I was in the air wondering what would happen at the storied Playboy Mansion and how I would handle taking suitable pictures and interviewing the legendary Hugh Hefner for *Toro Magazine*. Hefner was, after all, a master of the interview and a guy who knew a little bit about what kind of pictures should go in a magazine.

I'd almost grown up with *Playboy*; I was thirteen when the first issue came out. A year or so later my father subscribed, or maybe he just bought single copies. I don't really know where they came from, but I know the magazine was always around the house, until there was no longer a house for them to be around. For a kid in a backwater town, looking at that magazine was the stuff of dreams and a continuing source of inspiration and perspiration. Of course, I also liked the cartoons, serious articles, and the jazz polls. Doesn't everyone say that? But I meant it and continued to until the magazine shut down a few years ago, particularly when it came to the cartoons.

OPPOSITE

Hugh Hefner, Playboy Mansion, Bel-Air, California, 2004. (Author's collection)

And so, it was fifty years later as the big limo slowly rolled down the driveway of the Beverly Hills Hotel headed to Playboy Mansion. Inside were Michael Bratty and Jimmy Shier representing *Toro Magazine*, and *Playboy*'s long-time Toronto rep, Gino Emprey, who'd set up the meeting. They were in charge of making sure I didn't fold under pressure and to ask questions themselves if I did; I had a list of questions, and my cameras and film holders were loaded, ready for whatever might occur. Someone asked the driver if he knew his way to the Playboy Mansion; the reply was the same as if you'd asked a taxi driver in Manhattan about the Empire State Building.

It was about a five-minute ride west on Sunset Boulevard, left turn onto a small street, up a hill, stop at an enormous iron gate, words spoken into an intercom, the right words, and the gate swung open. The first thing I saw was a street sign, but instead of saying, "STOP" or "NO LEFT TURN" it said, "PLAYMATES AT PLAY." I didn't see one crossing, but imagined there might be one hiding in the verdant foliage. We proceeded up the hill slowly, just in case, and turned a corner, and while it wasn't quite as remarkable as Joan Fontaine's first view of Mandeley in *Rebecca*, it was a grand old English mansion with the same feel, and this one was real, not a set.

Bill Farley, an executive with Playboy Enterprises who handles marketing and special events, met us with a smile. I didn't know if we were the day's only special event, but he made us feel that way. He'd scheduled a tour of the grounds, part of the house, and lunch. He asked me about pictures, and I suggested it would be terrific to take a portrait outside with my large format view camera. He said this was unlikely, that Hef (yes, he did say Hef) preferred to be photographed inside the house.

Then the tour began. The guest cottage and game room were filled with posters, neon signs, pinball and slot machines where everyone was a winner, and a 1940s jukebox loaded with big band classics—a nickel a play, but who carries nickels these days? Back outside, onto the manicured grounds. It was all perfect; flowering shrubs, orange trees, hundreds of blossoms on the walks, a star from the Hollywood Boulevard Walk of Fame, a wishing well, and an array of extra-large satellite dishes possibly strong enough to not only find any television station in the world but probably bring in the Mars Rover as well.

Then we had a peek inside the famous grotto and other outbuildings. The gymnasium was off limits; perhaps the Playmates were down there instead of in the bushes. Back outside to view the wildlife; there was an aquarium, colorful parrots on perches, preening peacocks, down-soft ducks on the loose, and a cage full of monkeys that once ran wild until they began stealing golf balls from a nearby course and were caged as punishment. Then back to the mansion, up a sloping hill overlooked by two imposing statues of lions at rest. When we reached the top, we paused to look around. All this on six acres in the middle of Beverly Hills, landscaped and situated in such a way that there was not another house in view. At most, we were a couple of hundred yards from Sunset Boulevard, but just as no uninvited eyes looked on Norma Desmond, none looked on those sleeping lions as they guarded the mansion.

The interview and photo session were scheduled for after lunch. Bill Farley had worked some magic and said it might just be possible for me to set up the big view camera outside and do a portrait in the doorway. And so I set it up; a 5"x7" Deardorff on a tripod for the black-and-white, a 2.8 Rolleiflex for the color, and two 35mm Nikons with 28-200mm zoom lens, one for color and the other for black-and-white. I knew I would have little time. I preset the focus for both cameras on tripods. Then Bill came back and dropped a bomb. No pictures outside. I started to rethink the picture, whether there were any possibilities inside, and began taking the cameras down.

Then a window flew open, and Hugh Hefner himself stuck his head out and yelled something like, "Let's try it outside." So I put the cameras back together and got things focused just as my subject came out the door and said, "Let's get this over with quickly." And I did; two pictures with the Deardorff, four with the Rolleiflex, and about a dozen with each of the Nikon cameras. It took about three or four minutes, and then it was into the house for the interview. I only had a second to break down the cameras and left them outside, except for the 35mm Nikons, which I knew I'd need during the interview.

The interview was going along nicely, and when someone else popped a question, I grabbed a picture when I could. The official Playboy photographer, Elayne Lodge, took a few herself, documenting the interview. I asked questions, took pictures, and listened carefully, preparing for the next question. I was impressed with Hefner's answers, his easy, charming manner, and obvious candor. This is part of what he said that afternoon:

"I started *Playboy* as a response to all the hypocrisy that resulted from puritanical repression. It was also a response to my own typically Methodist, very Puritan upbringing. After college, and before I started *Playboy*, I did a post-graduate paper comparing the sex laws of the then forty-eight states. The results of the Kinsey Report

Outside the Playboy Mansion.
(Author's collection)

on sexual behavior were out, pointing out the majority of adult men engaged in almost all forms of sex. It was clear to me that almost all men would probably be in jail if the laws were enforced, and these laws, so-called sodomy laws, varied a lot from state to state. The greatest sexual offences in English Common Law were reserved for abominable and detestable crimes against nature, and this usually meant any kind of sex that wasn't solely for the purpose of procreation.

"About that time, I wrote a paper outlining how in some states you could get serious jail time for violating these sodomy laws. Sodomy included any form of non-intercourse, which meant oral sex, anal sex, heterosexual or homosexual, inside or outside of marriage, and I made a case against these laws in my paper.

"In the beginning, in the 1950s, *Playboy* was really a lifestyle magazine that devoted most of its attention to fun and games, food and drink, fashion, and beautiful ladies. In the early 1960s, 1962 actually, that changed when I began writing the 'Playboy Philosophy' and including interviews of subjects of importance in *Playboy*. Many of these interviews and much in the 'Playboy Philosophy' dealt with these repressive sex laws and in the middle 1960s we formed the Playboy Foundation and literally tried to change a lot of these laws with a fair amount of success. The Supreme Court finally declared that sodomy laws were illegal and had them struck down.

"I thought much of the war had been won by the later part of the 1960s, and it surprised me that when we got to the 1980s there was a backlash and things became conservative again. In the 1970s, I thought marijuana would become legal and, surprisingly, there are still problems with that and many drug laws are even more prohibitive today, particularly in terms of recreational drugs that are not so harmful.

"In some ways there are several things that have been troublesome, but on the other hand, the pleasant surprise is that some things have come as far as they have. One example is that these days people wait longer to get married. There was a piece in *USA Today* yesterday about how not too long ago most people got married in their late teens or early twenties, but now the average marriage age is middle to late twenties, and that's a good thing. When I was growing up, when I was in college, my relationship with the girl I would eventually marry was two and a half years of foreplay. You eventually wound up sleeping with the girl you were going to marry, but the notion that a good Methodist girl or boy, or a Catholic or a Jew could live with someone other than their wife or

The first interview.
(Author's collection)

husband was unthinkable back then. I made a point in the 'Playboy Philosophy' that you need to wait and find out who you are before you can pick out a mate. I think the changes we see today are a good thing. It was those kinds of prohibitions that forced people into marriages that didn't work.

"The magazine has evolved over the years. There's a lot of difference between Marilyn Monroe in the 1950s and the 50th Anniversary Playmate. Women are healthier now, a little thinner, a little taller, and I think some of that has to do with *Playboy*. When the magazine began there were really two concepts of what made a woman beautiful and both were about the same. In fashion and women's magazines the models looked like they were somebody's older sister and fashions were very conservative. The Christian Dior 'New Look' was in, but skirts were halfway down to the ankle and young women wore girdles and bullet bras. *Playboy* stressed a more natural, girl-next-door look. At the same time, men's magazines were essentially outdoor adventure books. The whole notion of *Playboy* was to live your life with a bit of style. It was the first magazine to really put the emphasis on a readership that was essentially single, young, urban and urbane, and interested in indoor activities.

"*Playboy* wasn't just about sex and nudity, then or now. If it was, we'd be bankrupt like *Penthouse*. We've always tried to give sex a good name, to see it as a natural part of the fabric of life. Nudity doesn't have the impact it once did, but *Playboy* has always been a lifestyle magazine that incorporates sex as part of a total package. Just like a woman, some men may be more drawn to a face, or breasts, or legs. There are many variations of the female, but it's the total package that makes it all worthwhile. In publishing you look for variations on a theme, and a nude can be very erotic. It can be more erotic if a single garment of some sort enhances a nude. A nude is certainly sexier if she wears a pair of high heels.

"Just like Marilyn Monroe and Colleen Shannon are very different, times and my focus are also different. I bought the Chicago Playboy Mansion in December 1959 and it was much larger than this house, which I bought in 1971. The Chicago house had seventy rooms and no grounds. It had an indoor pool, underwater bar, and a bowling alley. This was a time when I was working around the clock creating the empire so to say, and there was a wonderful mystique about that house. You didn't know if it was day or night, and I worked and played much of the time throughout the night. The bunnies worked the clubs and had dormitory rooms in the mansion. Parties would begin at midnight and go until dawn.

"It was a lot like Las Vegas. If you think about the Rat Pack, Sinatra, Martin, Sammy Davis, that's what the Chicago Mansion was like. It had a real James Bond quality to it. It was filled with gadgets, and Ian Fleming drew inspiration from the Mansion in both the books and the movies. When Dean Martin did the Matt Helm series and his television show, he lifted ideas from the Mansion. We were running pictorials on James Bond and publishing Ian Fleming stories, so there were a lot of connections. In *Diamonds Are Forever*, Bond is identified as a member of the Playboy Club and in another, *On Her Majesty's Secret Service*, while he's cracking a safe, he's going through a magazine, and when he leaves the office he takes the centerfold with him. Ian Fleming said that if James Bond had been a real person, he'd be a *Playboy* reader and a member of the Playboy Club.

"For awhile I split my time between Chicago and Los Angeles, even before I began the television show *Playboy After Dark*, I was flying back and forth in a private plane, a DC9 I'd painted black. It was indoors in Chicago, outdoors in Los Angeles. We're just a block from Sunset Boulevard, but you don't feel like you're in Los Angeles here. You feel like it's England, or in the country. The California Mansion is much more of a home for me, and living here has been the most satisfying time of my life.

"Then as now, my interests have been more indoor-oriented, they've always been much more romantic than pursuing hunting and fishing. The common connection with my male friends these days is the same; an inner circle of friends that meet on Monday nights, and it's not about outdoor sports, it's about a love of movies and the music of our childhood. We usually have a buffet and then pick out a movie from the 1930s or 1940s, the kind of film we used to watch when we were kids on Saturday afternoon: crime films, westerns, musicals, or serials like *Flash Gordon*. It's really about a reconnection with my childhood and much of my life is spent holding on to the kid I was when I was young.

"The influence of my repressive home was tremendous, but the other major influences were music and the movies, which to me were very romantic. I've suggested before that my life has been a quest for a world where the words of the songs are true, the impossible dreams, the happy endings, the kind of things you only find in the movies and songs by Gershwin and Rodgers and Hart. That's what my life is about today.

Playboy Mansion interior. (Author's collection)

"I was born in 1926 and reached adolescence during the big band era, and I was very much influenced by the music of my early teens. My first favorite was Tommy Dorsey, then Frank Sinatra, and Harry James in my senior year. I also liked Glenn Miller and Duke Ellington, but in that time I also discovered Bix Beiderbecke, the great white cornet player who lived prior to the big band era, a guy who influenced me very much. His life was tragic; he died of alcoholism in his late twenties. He also came from a repressive German home in the Midwest.

"This love of jazz has stayed with me. We had the first Playboy Jazz Festival in August 1959. It was called the greatest single weekend in the history of jazz. We had Louis Armstrong, one of my idols; we had Ella Fitzgerald. She flew in from Monaco where she had just performed for Prince Ranier. We not only had the Duke Ellington Orchestra, but the bands of Count Basie, Jack Teagarden, Miles Davis, Dizzy Gillespie, Dave Brubeck, and Cannonball Adderley. When it was over I was asked if I'd do it again the next year and of course I did, and then in the following months I started hosting *Playboy Penthouse*, a syndicated show that looked like a party. Then I bought the Mansion and in February 1960 we opened the first Playboy Club in Chicago. Those three events changed everything for me in a short span of time. I got to meet my idols, the people who'd influenced me when I was a kid. I hired them for the festivals, the television shows, and the clubs. The festival is now forty-five years old. You can see the music is very important.

"I love old movies just as much. The people who came by on Mondays for the movies were Mel Torme, until he died; my brother, Keith; Don Addams from *Get Smart;* Robert Culp; Mark Canton, who has a great jazz film collection; and a few others. We act like a bunch of young kids when we get together, or like a bunch of guys who hold onto memories of childhood. Robert Culp has a complete collection of Big Little Books, and Mel had all kinds of things like that. I have stuff in my room upstairs that duplicates the masks of Frankenstein and The Mummy, and last April, one of my friends gave me an exact duplicate of the Maltese Falcon for my birthday. He wrapped it up in a Chinese newspaper and tied it up with string, exactly like they had in the movie.

"I feel it's difficult to explain to people who don't understand that my life is much better now. People think I'm the luckiest guy on the planet because I've lived out what turned out to be not only my fantasies but also a lot of other guys' fantasies. And the honest truth about that is that it's even better than it seems and the reason it's even better is because of the childhood connection and my friends. The fact that I remain relatively untouched by my success and have remained a true romantic and remained close, on a friendship basis, to most of the women I've been romantically involved with throughout the years. The friendships and the connection with my childhood are really what it's all about for me, and I can't even begin to explain it. It's the stuff dreams are made of.

"The movies are very different today; some things are better, and some are not. I grew up in a time when there was a Production Code, where married couples couldn't even be in the same bed together. You never see a toilet in a movie made in the 1930s or 1940s. A complete rejection of nature. It was certainly a rejection of sexuality, and I was aware of that when I was very young. They even took Betty Boop's garter away and I objected to that. I remember Tarzan when I was a kid and the second Johnny Weismuller film, *Tarzan and His Mate,* that came out in 1934, before the code. It had some very sexy underwater nude scenes, then the code got very, very tough, and in the next film she was covered up. I was about eight years old, but I knew there was something going on that was not right.

"The old classics are probably better than the new ones. The reality is they make wonderful movies today but they also make a lot of crap. I guess they did back then too, but there really was a golden age when they created incredible films. About ten years ago, to celebrate the fiftieth anniversary of *Casablanca*, we rented the film and showed it on a Friday night. The following week we showed *The Maltese Falcon*, followed by a Bogart and Lauren Bacall classic, *To Have and Have Not*. By then we were hooked on those old classics, and we called ourselves the Casablanca Club. We tried on both Friday and Sunday nights, but Friday turned out much better and we still run the old classics. There are still some things I'd love to see, films that have been lost forever. There are four Charlie Chan films that have simply vanished. I pay back by supporting the film preservation archive at UCLA and Eastman House. I've also funded a class in film censorship at USC, and more recently endowed a chair and a school for studying film at that university.

"We run new films on Sunday nights. A couple of weeks ago we saw *Something's Gotta Give* with Jack Nicholson, and last Sunday we ran *Cold Mountain*, and I liked that very much. I liked *Mystic River* a lot and wrote Clint a note and told him so. The new *Matrix* movie was disappointing, but I enjoyed *The Lord of the Rings* trilogy. The special effects are really extraordinary, but while the films may be technically better, they're not always as good in terms of storytelling. You can make fine movies with special effects; one of my favorites is *King Kong*, and I hear there's going to be a remake, with the director who made *The Lord of the Rings*. He says he plans to stick close to the original, set back in the 1930s.

"Speaking of new movies, there are plans underway for a film about my life. Scott Silver, who wrote *8 Mile*, is working on the screenplay. Brian Grazer is the producer. We don't know who'll play me but there's been some talk about Hugh Jackman. We were in New York for the fiftieth Anniversary of *Playboy* and I took the girls to see *The Boy from Oz*. I was a huge fan of Peter Allen and Jackman does a terrific job. In the middle of the first act he stopped the show, breaks the fourth wall, talks to the audience and introduces me. It was very nice; he did a fantastic job. And I understand he's marvelous in *Oklahoma*. I had no idea he could sing until I saw *The Boy from Oz*.

"*Playboy* is both a public enterprise and a family business. I've always had mixed emotions when it became public because it is such a personal operation. We did that so we could expand, because for the first twenty years we really could do whatever we wanted to and what mattered to me was producing a very good magazine. That was my priority. My daughter runs the business now; she has a board of directors and stockholders, but I still control a majority of the voting shares and serve both masters.

"I don't approve every picture, just a little tweaking now and then, but I approve the cover and the Playmates. I approve who's going to become a Playmate, but it's part of a process, with test shooting and input by the photo department. It's remarkable, but over the last fifty years, most of the major sex stars have appeared in the magazine and we'll continue to pursue those who we think our readers would like to see. The ones they might like to see today are Britney Spears and Catherine Zeta-Jones.

Playboy Mansion interior. (Author's collection)

"Of course, I always tend to fall in love with and prefer girls who look like the platinum blondes of the 1930s, or Dale in *Flash Gordon*. It was the best serial ever made and had a major influence on me. Music, movies, and romance are the great equalizers, and they run my life. I love it here, and couldn't imagine being anywhere else."

The interview was over, but the conversation continued. We talked about music and the cartoons in *Playboy*. I said I'd brought along a handmade Bix Beiderbecke CD that featured fourteen different interpretations of "In a Mist," one of Beiderbecke's most famous compositions. In looking back at the transcript of the interview, it reads HH: "Oh, wonderful!" and someone has written in the word, "excited." This isn't surprising. About half an hour earlier, when we began talking about music and the movies, the tone of the interview changed remarkably, becoming less an interview and more of an introspective conversation, and it continued this way after the last official question was asked.

Toward the end of the interview, I'd brought the justly famous cartoonist, Jack Cole, into the conversation. The transcript reads: HH: "I have an original Jack Cole hanging on the wall right outside my door. Come up and have a look at it when we're finished." As I suspected, it was Cole's most famous and widely reproduced watercolor, the one of a voluptuous, but clearly vulnerable, little lounge singer, clinging to a microphone, with the words, "I ain't got no bod-eee. . ." written underneath.

We talked about censorship and how it played a part in Jack Cole's untimely death, and then, since the interview really was over, I asked Hefner if he was serious about going upstairs to see the painting. He looked at me and asked, "Were you serious about that Bix Beiderbecke CD?" I said it was waiting for him in the next room, along with a handful of other samples from my Chiaroscuro jazz catalog. Seventy years after his death, the young man with a horn could still work his magic.

A word or two about the Playboy Mansion, at least the three or four rooms I saw: It looks and feels like someone's home, probably because it is. It feels comfortable and lived in. The couches, chairs, in fact all the furnishings and pictures, ooze comfort. It is also tasteful, with nothing out of place. The only thing that was not perfectly in place was a little ball, clearly the property of a dog that had the run of the house, and clearly that ball's place was anywhere the dog wanted it to be. Later, I was introduced to Panda the Pomeranian, an adorable little black-and-white critter marked just like a panda.

I'd left the CDs on a table in the large reception room/theater that was next to the library where we'd conducted the interview. Hefner was happy to have the "In a Mist" variations in his hand but was equally pleased when I told him that because Chiaroscuro's *Last of the Whorehouse Piano Players* CD had been featured prominently in *Playboy*, it had become the best-selling recording in our catalog. Then he led us out to the foyer and up the stairs to the second floor.

As I said, the house was immaculate, but when we turned the corner and headed up a second flight of stairs, everything began to look different. Jack Cole's little singer was staring down at us from the second floor, and when we reached that level, a long hall stretched off to the left, filled with paintings, posters, and photographs, some in frames, some not, all casually leaning against the wall. There were piles of CDs, an empty box that once held a mechanical Ray Charles doll, and books of all sorts.

Panda the Pup. (Author's collection)

I asked Hefner if I could take a picture of him with the Jack Cole watercolor. He thought that was a fine idea and it's probably the best one I took that day, in black-and-white or color. Then he said, "Well, as long as you're here, come on in," and he opened the door to his bedroom. And like the Maltese Falcon I spotted on a mantelpiece, appearing very sinister perching next to a LeRoy Neiman Femlin statue, this spacious, comfortable room was what dreams were made of, and everything in the room was evocative of the reality that Hefner's dream had come true, and these vestiges of the dream were all there in their proper place, to make sure it endured.

There were walls of pictures, three video screens at the foot of the bed, piles of video tapes and DVDs, books, posters, CDs, records, gadgets, toys, movie memorabilia, in fact, memorabilia of all sorts. Everything in the room could be used to conjure up a wonderful memory from the past, the immediate past and the distant past. How I wanted to take a few pictures, but I thought it would be inappropriate even to ask. The room was so rich with detail and the emotion that went into creating the detail was so apparent, it would have been wonderful to set up the big camera, get everything in focus, and document it for posterity. There aren't many places like that in the world.

Hefner walked us around the room; it lasted no more than five minutes, maybe less, and then, as suddenly as he'd appeared in the window before I took the pictures outside, Hefner said good-bye, and, clutching his handful of CDs and a Diet Pepsi, vanished into his time machine masquerading as a bedroom. As we walked back down the stairs, Bill Farley said, "I don't know how you managed that. It took me ten years to get into the bedroom." I wasn't surprised at all. What would be a better entrée than talking with Hugh Hefner about a guy who made music that sounded like a girl saying yes?

With Madame X, Gerald Wilson, and Herbie Hancock.
(Author's collection)

My first visit with Hugh Hefner was on January 6, 2004. *Meet Me Tonight in Dreamland* was the result of that visit. Two months later, in early March, I was back in Los Angeles, doing double duty, first at the Playboy Mansion, for the press release party announcing that year's edition of the Playboy Jazz Festival, but also to work with Bruce Ricker on a planned documentary film about George Wein.

Hef launched the Playboy Jazz Festival in 1960 and forty-six years later it was still growing strong and still is, except now it is held at the Hollywood Bowl and, as of 2025, is known as the Hollywood Bowl Jazz Festival. It remains a two-day event and features many of today's biggest names in jazz. Interestingly enough, one of the biggest names at the 2004 festival was Herbie Hancock. He was back on stage once again in 2023.

Hef was always a jazz fan and proved it in many ways. Every year there was a Playboy jazz poll. It eventually morphed into a "jazz and pop" poll but in the early years it was a serious undertaking and in the late 1950s there were even LPs issued to coincide with the winner of the poll. I was probably the only person in Syracuse who looked at the poll results before I turned to the centerfold.

Playboy Jazz Festival launch, 2004.
(Author's collection)

In 1969–70 he produced fifty-two episodes of *Playboy After Dark*, a forty-five-minute television show that featured assorted celebrities in a party-like setting. The primary jazz-oriented performers were often vocalists, Tony Bennett, Mel Torme, Lou Rawls, Buddy Greco, Joe Williams, Sammy Davis Jr. and O. C. Smith, but Dave Brubeck with Paul Desmond and the quartet, Buddy Rich and the Modern Jazz Quartet were also prominently featured.

And so I interacted with Hef on exactly two days, many days less than anyone else chronicled in this book. But Hef was such an outsized figure in the cultural firmament of the United States, I thought it would be more than appropriate to include him simply because maybe it may inform the unsuspecting that he was a good guy who was very good for jazz and the men and women who make it. From the musical standpoint and many others he was a positive force.

This is also an excuse to publish a handful of photographs that, except for the portrait in the doorway, have never appeared in print. I didn't know Hef well; how can you after a few hours on a couple of days? I took a bunch of photographs, swapped a CD filled with Bix Beiderbecke tunes for some good stories, and that was that, but I was very glad to have had the opportunity.

VRS • 8508

DOWN BEAT

A NIGHT AT COUNT BASIE'S

with MARLOWE MORRIS, organ • EMMETT BERRY, trumpet

VIC DICKENSON, trombone • BOBBY HENDERSON, piano

BOBBY DONALDSON, drums • AARON BELL, bass

15

Bobby Henderson / Jody Bolden

April 16, 1910 – December 9, 1969

WHOEVER HAD HEARD of Bobby Henderson in 1969? Or 2025? Almost no one, and the people who had heard of the person whose birth name was Bobby Henderson knew him by another: Jody Bolden.

In the late 1960s, the Vanderbilts, Rockefellers, and Sherman Fairchild coalesced as an unlikely trio around the equally unlikely personage of a sixty-year-old virtually unknown pianist, a man with two names, an invisible man so ravaged by lung cancer he could barely speak above a whisper, who could still play the piano but only for four or five minutes at a time before becoming utterly exhausted. Why and how did this happen? This is the story.

I knew Bobby Henderson for less than a year, barely long enough to get a recording done. I never took a picture of him. Somehow there was never time, or I didn't have a camera close at hand. There was always a reason, but never a good one. This was one of my earliest recording/production projects, one that began in John Hammond's office in mid-February 1969 and evolved haphazardly. I'd gone by for a visit, and when I arrived, John, as usual, was bubbling with enthusiasm. He couldn't wait for me to sit down so he could play me his latest "discovery."

He had a reel-to-reel tape in his hand and was fumbling with his tape recorder. He said something like, "You'll have no idea who this is." He got the recorder going and within about five seconds I said, "That's Bobby Henderson." He demanded to know how I recognized his "new" discovery so quickly. I told him it was simple, because in the late 1950s, purely by accident, I'd been given a record he'd produced as a happy birthday present. The record was called *A Night at Count Basie's*, and Bobby was the featured pianist. I said, "Bobby Henderson is very distinctive," and John was astounded. Then he got serious.

John said he'd "found" Bobby once again, after having lost track of him for many years. He was living in Albany, dying of lung cancer, short on funds, and John was determined to make one last recording of his old friend. His associates at CBS had no interest in Henderson, and he didn't know where to turn. I told him not to worry, that I had an idea; we'd record Bobby at the same place we'd recorded Eubie Blake a few months earlier, Sherman Fairchild's studio at 17 East Sixty-Fifth Street. Except this time, I'd ask Sherman to fund the operation. John said to give it a try.

I telephoned Sherman, told him about Bobby, adding that he was a great pianist (I lied and said he was a cross between Art Tatum and Fats Waller, Sherman's two favorites), and the project was set in motion in about five minutes. John then began making arrangements for Bobby to come to New York, which turned out to be more

OPPOSITE
A Night at Count Basie's album jacket. (Author's collection)

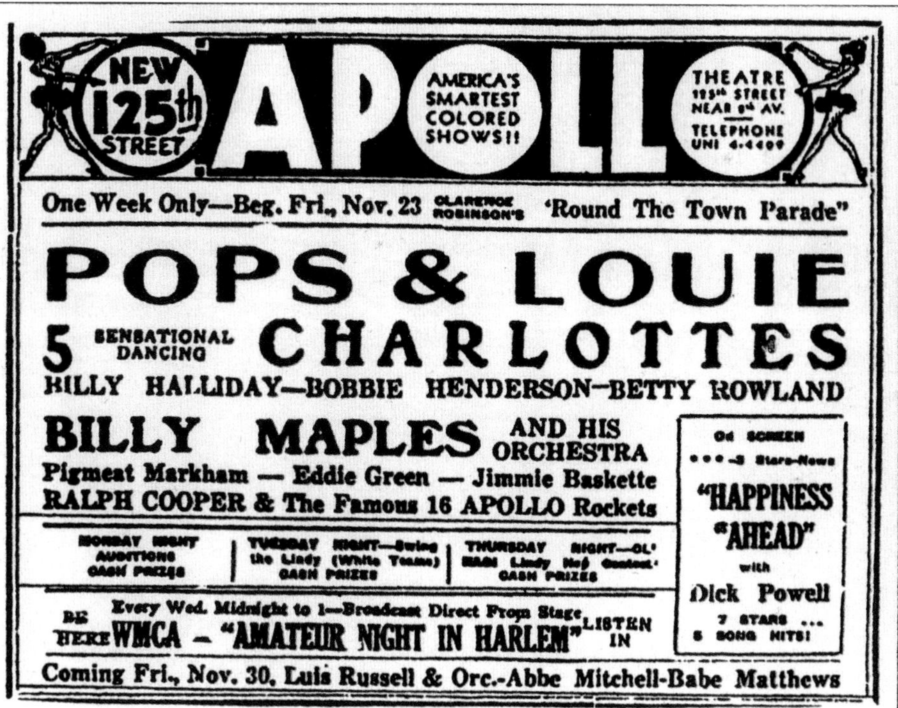

Apollo advertisement, 1934.
(Author's collection)

complicated than expected. John covered the transportation costs; I provided my couch on Charles Street to save on hotel bills. John's apartment was closer to Sherman's home, and somewhat larger, but 444 East 57th wasn't much of a crash pad, and John was afraid his wife might complain. Maybe, maybe not; the former Esme O'Brien Sarnoff wasn't exactly a quiet behind-the-scenes kind of person, and she was a confirmed jazzer.

A word or two about Bobby Henderson, a man remembered by almost no one, except maybe older citizens of Albany, New York, and aficionados of exceptional, though obscure, pianists and William Kennedy, who not only writes eloquently about rascals in Albany but wrote about Bobby and was his friend as well.

Bobby Henderson came on the Harlem music scene in the early 1930s. He was a remarkable player but never recorded in the early days of his career, other than an unissued test pressing in 1932, accompanying Martha Raye of all people. It has never turned up, nor has an aluminum record John Hammond cut in the mid-1930s. Hammond remembered Henderson as a phenomenal pianist, one not unlike my description to Sherman Fairchild. He was Billie Holiday's boyfriend, accompanist, and advisor in those years; in fact, there was an announcement in *The Amsterdam News* they were to be married, but it didn't work out. There is also an ad for November 23, 1934, announcing Billy Halliday [*sic*] and Bobbie Henderson [*sic*], third billing at the Apollo, after Pops & Louie and 5 Sensational Dancing Charlottes, so I know the stories about Billie and Bobby working together are true.

Bobby did get married, but not to Billie, and the story I was told is that before he was divorced from whomever he did marry, he also married someone else. Somehow, he managed to get out of town, and for the next thirty years or so maintained two families and two names, living a low-profile life in Albany, New York, from the mid-1940s onward. The deception continued until his death; Jody Bolden in Albany, Bobby Henderson everywhere else. I'm told both families were at his funeral, but I don't know this for sure.

Bobby Henderson 1950s recordings. (Author's collection)

Bobby Henderson, 1940s. (Author's collection)

John came upon Bobby by accident in 1956. He'd stopped in Albany for the night, checked into a hotel, and, always the talent scout, couldn't stand to remain in his room when there might be an undiscovered artist somewhere out there in the night. He didn't have to look very far. There was a joint across the street called the Kerry Blue; a picture in the window identified the resident pianist, a man named Jody Bolden. Bolden looked familiar, and no wonder; he was Bobby Henderson from all those years ago.

John brought Bobby/Jody to New York and recorded him for Vanguard. Three LPs were the result: the previously mentioned *A Night at Count Basie's* (1956), a Fat's Waller tribute, *Handful of Keys* (1956), and an album that was probably a mistake, *Call House Piano* (1957) on a tack-hammer piano. John also convinced George Wein to give Henderson a shot at Newport in 1957, and this resulted in half an LP on Verve. And that was it.

No one paid much attention to the records, and this isn't surprising; the recordings were well-played, and on some selections masterfully, but in 1956 the way Bobby played the piano was considered as old-fashioned as the Original Dixieland Jazz Band. This is a pity because the live recording at Count Basie's is truly exceptional, maybe the best record ever made at a bar in Harlem, except possibly the Charlie Christian sides from Minton's. Bobby went back to Albany, continued his existence as Jody Bolden, earned a living, and was never heard from until John "rediscovered" him once again in 1969.

When Bobby arrived in New York City in mid-April, he seemed so frail I was surprised he could stand up, let alone play the piano. He was still a very handsome, almost courtly gentleman, but it was clear he was seriously ill. He was charming to talk with, but I never heard him speak louder than a whisper. This wasn't an act. He couldn't because the lung cancer was so advanced. When we reached Sherman Fairchild's studio a day or so after his arrival, I didn't know what to expect.

There are no up-tempo selections, or even extended medium-tempo selections, on the album later released as *A Home in the Clouds*, simply because he didn't have the energy to play fast or for very long. There are some stately, somewhat longer slower songs, but I remember these required a monumental effort. I also remember long rest periods between each song he attempted. Bobby would play "Blue Prelude" or "A Home in the Clouds" (his composition) and then he'd adjourn to the couch and rest for a while or perhaps visit Sherman's well-stocked bar.

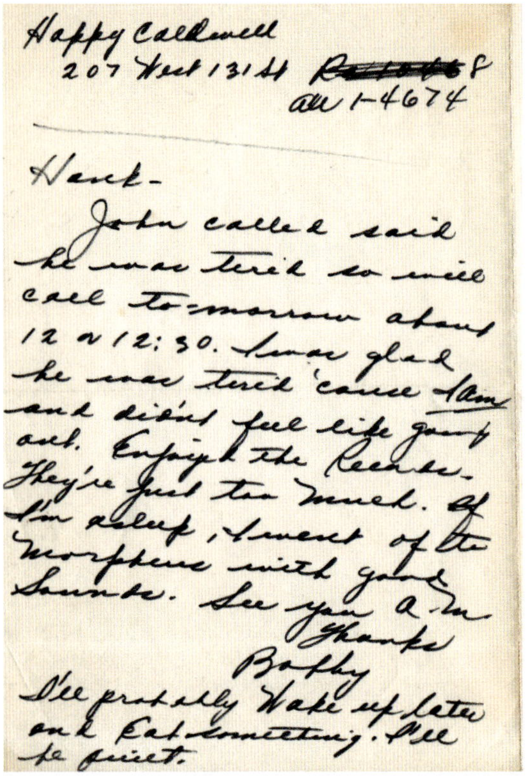
Happy Caldwell
207 West 131 St ~~[struck out]~~ 8
AU 1-4674

Hank-
John called said he was tired so will call to-morrow about 12 or 12:30. I was glad he was tired 'cause I am and didn't feel like going out. Enjoyed the Records. They're just too much. If I'm asleep, I went off to Morpheus with good sounds. See you A.M.
Thanks
Bobby
I'll probably Wake up later and Eat something. I'll be quiet.

Bobby Henderson aka Jody Bolden.
(Author's collection)

This sounds like a depressing scenario, but it wasn't, because what Bobby did play was so marvelous and virtually flawless. He played solo piano with the same kind of feeling that Billie Holiday evidenced on her first recordings in the 1930s; he sounded like Billie transformed into a piano solo, particularly on selections Billie had also recorded, songs like "Lover Man" and "I Wished on the Moon." I wondered who had influenced whom. I wish I'd thought to ask or that we had more time. Bobby's time at the piano was nothing short of perfection, but we all knew he didn't have much of it left.

It was slow going, but ultimately there was enough material for two LPs, with no multiple takes of anything except "A Home in the Clouds." As I said, he took his time, but the playing was flawless. Five decades later, I wouldn't change a note. It probably helped that there was a small audience. John Hammond's cheery enthusiasm was always helpful; Sherman Fairchild ducked in and out, Marian McPartland was there most of the time, as was Bobby's friend from Albany, JoAnne, better known as Pug, Horton.

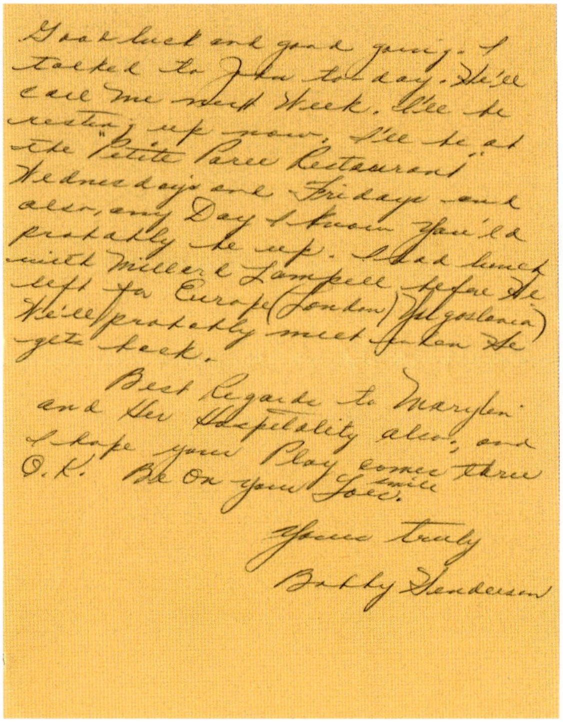
Good luck and good going. I talked to John to day. He'll call me next Week. I'll be resting up now. I'll be at the "Petite Paree Restaurant" Wednesdays and Fridays and also, any Day I know you'll probably be up. I had lunch with Millard Lampell before he left for Europe (London) (Yugoslavia) We'll probably meet when he gets back.

Best Regards to Marylin and Her Hospitality also, and I hope your Play comes thru O.K. Be On your Toes. (smile)

Yours truly
Bobby Henderson

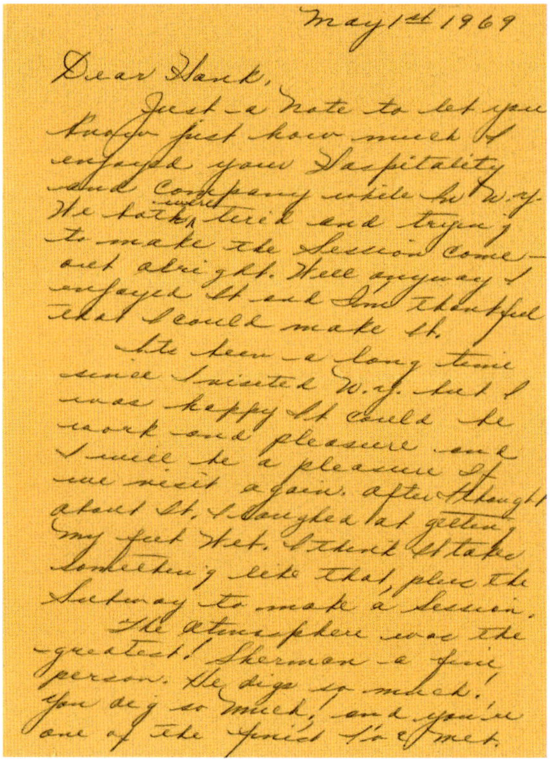
May 1st 1969

Dear Hank,
Just a note to let you know just how much I enjoyed your Hospitality and Company while in N.Y. We both were tired and trying to make the Session come-out alright. Well anyway I enjoyed it and I'm thankful that I could make it.
Its been a long time since I visited N.Y. but I was happy it could be work and pleasure and it will be a pleasure if we visit again. after thought about it, I laughed at getting my feet Wet. I think it takes something like that, plus the Subway to make a Session.
The atmosphere was the greatest! Sherman a fine person. He digs so much! You dig so much, and you're one of the finest I've met.

Letters after the recording sessions.
(Author's collection)

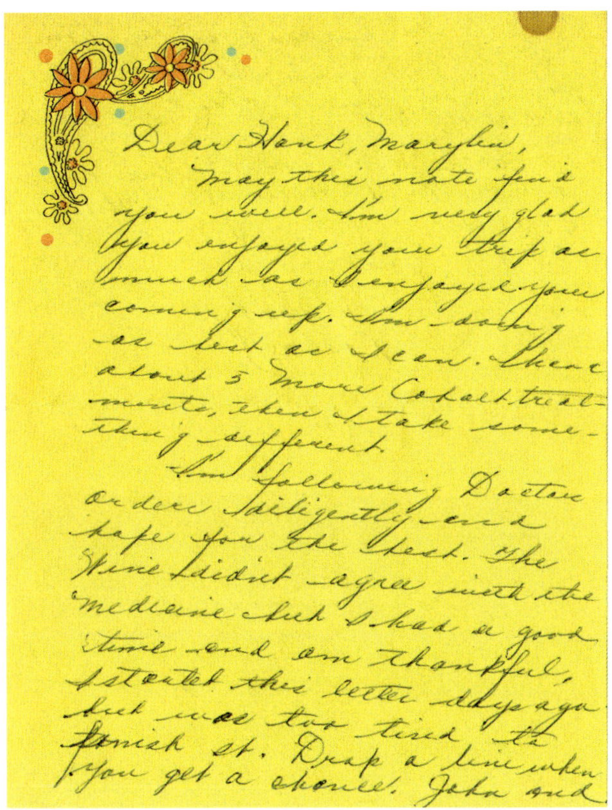

Dear Hank, Marylin,
May this note find you well. I'm very glad you enjoyed your trip as much as I enjoyed your coming up. I'm doing as best as I can. There about 5 more Cobalt treatments, then I take something different.
I'm following Doctors orders diligently and hope for the best. The Wine I didn't agree with the medicine but I had a good time and am thankful. I started this letter days ago but was too tired to finish it. Drop a line when you get a chance. John and

Letter after visit with Bobby at the Albany Medical Center. (Author's collection)

Peg are in England on Vacation with their youngest [illegible]. I guess you must have received a card.
Well write when you can and keep New York under control.
Your friend
Bobby
(Rascal)

Envelope for letter after visit to the Albany Medical Center. (Author's collection)

Everyone present was thrilled by the playing and deeply moved by his courageous performance. In retrospect, what he did on those two afternoons reminded me of Dinu Lipatti's final recital at Besancon in 1950. Lipatti's leukemia was so advanced he could barely sit at the piano, but his Chopin waltzes and Schubert impromptus were transcendent. He was to be dead in less than three months, but somehow he managed at that last recital. Bobby lasted a few months longer and managed just as well.

I began to work on the LP and remained in touch with Bobby. He wrote friendly, gentle letters and on the telephone expressed hope he might go into remission as he underwent more aggressive treatment for his advancing cancer. I made plans to visit Bobby in Albany when the tapes were edited and sequenced and managed to do this on August 17, 1969. The only reason I know this is because of a date written on a box of tape.

While the big-time music event that weekend was taking place down the road at Woodstock, mine was considerably lower key. By this time Bobby was in the Albany Medical Center under the personal care of its resident cancer specialist, Dr. John Horton. Bobby was pleased with what he heard and suggested we take the recording gear downstairs to the hospital recreation room, where there was an old piano. He said he wanted to make some new recordings. I did as I was asked, once again, not knowing what to expect.

I set up the tape recorder and a couple of microphones, and Bobby made a valiant effort. I remember he was wearing a flimsy, hospital-issued, thin blue-and-white robe. He sat proudly at the old out-of-tune upright and tried very hard, but by this time his fingers were so thin they were almost falling between the keys. He had no sense of where his fingers were on the piano, but he still managed to play half a dozen songs and reminisce a little bit about his days in Harlem in the 1930s. I haven't heard the tapes for thirty-five years, but I still remember the excruciatingly poignant performance. I was just a kid, less than thirty, and *A Home in the Clouds* was only the second record I'd ever produced from start to finish, and the artist, an exceptional artist in every way, was dying in front of me.

I knew there was no way we could manufacture the record in the few weeks or months Bobby might have left to live. Leo Meiersdorff had delivered a wonderful cover illustration, but there was no time to have it turned into an album jacket. The next best thing was to get a test pressing, which was arranged. Then I pulled in a favor from someone Marian had introduced to me, a wonderful lady named Mary Packard, who was close to the Rockefeller family. Mary had always said if I ever needed to get something to the governor, she would see to it. This was the time.

I delivered a tape of Bobby's music to Mary in late September, she passed it to Governor Rockefeller, and the governor wrote Bobby a short letter filled with praise, adding he was looking forward to hearing the finished record. A month or so later, some of Bobby's friends in Albany, primarily Bill Kennedy, better known to the literary crowd as Pulitzer Prize–winning novelist William Kennedy, pushed the right buttons and the front page of the arts section of the *Albany Times-Leader* was devoted to his career and the forthcoming record. It didn't hurt that Bill wrote the article. Bobby died a few days later on December 9.

The record was issued in early 1970, and though I went on to make many solo piano recordings with other far more celebrated pianists, *A Home in the Clouds* remains my favorite. Five decades later Bobby Henderson is largely forgotten, a footnote at best. He rates a paragraph in the new *Biographical Encyclopedia of Jazz* only because Ira Gitler was old enough to remember; Bobby didn't make the *Grove Encyclopedia of Jazz* because Barry Kernfield isn't. Most of his Vanguard recordings are available on CD; *A Home in the Clouds* isn't, but that's a tale to be told another day.

There's a mysterious postscript to this sad story. In April 1970, a year after the recording sessions in New York City, I'd gone on a day trip with Maggie Condon to check on my father's summer cottage on Round Pond, near Sand Lake, New York. The cottage is about twenty miles from Albany, and some of that city's residents have summer homes on the small lake. It was early in the season and none of the cottages were inhabited, or so I assumed.

After we checked the cottage and did a few things to prepare it for turning on the water in May, we decided to put a canoe in Round Pond and take advantage of a peaceful spring day. We paddled around for a few minutes and then drifted to the opposite side of the small lake. It was very quiet. The lake was still, barely a ripple. Then we heard the music. Someone was playing a piano, very softly. Maggie didn't recognize it, but I did. It sounded like Bobby Henderson. I recognized him in John Hammond's office, and I recognized him on the lake. It was one of the tunes from the record, just not played as well, but with his phrasing; sort of like the way he'd played in the hospital when his thin fingers seemed to be falling in between the keys.

The music was coming from Dick William's cottage. Dick was a lawyer who'd handled some of Bobby's affairs; his wife, Jean, was a good amateur pianist. Bobby had spent many happy hours at their summer home and frequently played their piano. The music continued as we drifted toward the shore. We beached the canoe, got out, and walked through the bushes to the house. By this time the music had stopped and there were no other sounds. We reached the house and knocked on the door, but there was no response. We peered in the windows. There was no one there, but we could see the big piano was open for anyone who wanted to play it. The house was deserted. There was no car or anyone anywhere in sight. But we'd both heard the music. There was no easy explanation, and to this day I still don't have one.

"A Home In The Clouds"
We'll live up in a castle that's built upon a cloud,
a private little castle with no one else allowed,
That's my Dream of a Home In the clouds with you.
We'll have no need for sandals the sky will be our floor,
We'll use the stars for candles they'll twinkle at our door,
That's my dream of a Home in the Clouds with you.
While the man in the man in the moon, Scatters Silver over the sky,
We can hum any tune, make each song a sweet Lullaby,
Among our prize possessions we'll have a Radio, to broadcast our impressions to folks on earth below
That's my Dream of a Home In the clouds with you.
Words By: Kaye Parker
Music By: Bobby Henderson and Benny Carter 1927-1929
To "Hank" Sincerely Bobby Henderson

A Home In the Clouds by Bobby Henderson. (Author's collection)

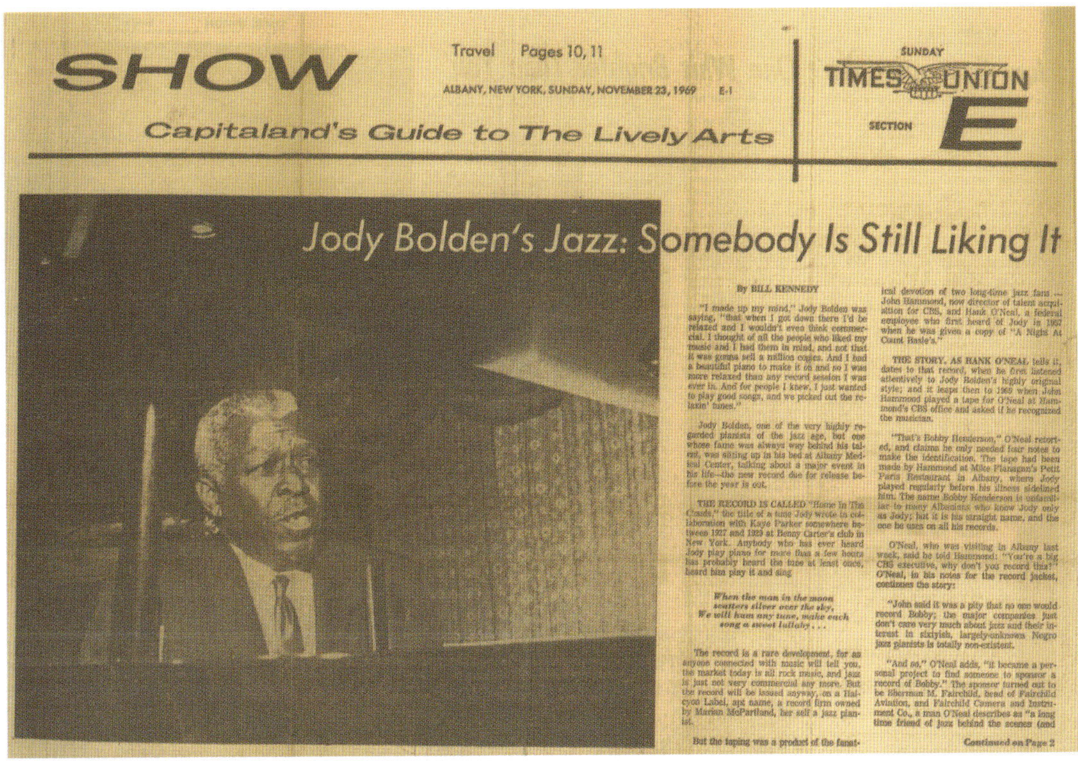

SHOW

Travel Pages 10, 11

ALBANY, NEW YORK, SUNDAY, NOVEMBER 23, 1969 E-1

Capitaland's Guide to The Lively Arts

SUNDAY TIMES UNION SECTION E

Jody Bolden's Jazz: Somebody Is Still Liking It

By BILL KENNEDY

"I made up my mind," Jody Bolden was saying, "that when I got down there I'd be relaxed and I wouldn't even think commercial. I thought of all the people who liked my music and I had them in mind, and not that it was gonna sell a million copies. And I had a beautiful piano to make it on and so I was more relaxed than any record session I was ever in. And for people I knew. I just wanted to play good songs, and we picked out the relaxin' tunes."

Jody Bolden, one of the very highly regarded pianists of the jazz age, but one whose fame was always way behind his talent, was sitting up in his bed at Albany Medical Center, talking about a major event in his life—the new record due for release before the year is out.

THE RECORD IS CALLED "Home In The Clouds," the title of a tune Jody wrote in collaboration with Kaye Parker somewhere between 1927 and 1929 at Benny Carter's club in New York. Anybody who has ever heard Jody play piano for more than a few hours has probably heard the tune at least once, heard him play it and sing

When the man in the moon
scatters silver over the sky,
We will hum any tune, make each
song a sweet lullaby . . .

The record is a rare development, for as anyone connected with music will tell you, the market today is all rock music, and jazz is just not very commercial any more. But the record will be issued anyway, on a Halcyon Label, apt name, a record firm owned by Marian McPartland, her self a jazz pianist.

But the taping was a product of the fanatical devotion of two long-time jazz fans — John Hammond, now director of talent acquisition for CBS, and Hank O'Neal, a federal employee who first heard of Jody in 1967 when he was given a copy of "A Night At Count Basie's."

THE STORY, AS HANK O'NEAL tells it, dates to that record, when he first listened attentively to Jody Bolden's highly original style; and it leaps then to 1969 when John Hammond played a tape for O'Neal at Hammond's CBS office and asked if he recognized the musician.

"That's Bobby Henderson," O'Neal retorted, and claims he only needed four notes to make the identification. The tape had been made by Hammond at Mike Flanagan's Petit Paris Restaurant in Albany, where Jody played regularly before his illness sidelined him. The name Bobby Henderson is unfamiliar to many Albanians who know Jody only as Jody; but it is his straight name, and the one he uses on all his records.

O'Neal, who was visiting in Albany last week, said he told Hammond: "You're a big CBS executive, why don't you record this?" O'Neal, in his notes for the record jacket, continues the story:

"John said it was a pity that no one would record Bobby; the major companies just don't care very much about jazz and their interest in sixtyish, largely-unknown Negro jazz pianists is totally non-existent.

"And so," O'Neal adds, "it became a personal project to find someone to sponsor a record of Bobby." The sponsor turned out to be Sherman M. Fairchild, head of Fairchild Aviation, and Fairchild Camera and Instrument Co., a man O'Neal describes as "a long time friend of jazz behind the scenes (and

Continued on Page 2

Times Union article, November 29, 1969.
(Author's collection)

A Home in the Clouds LP jacket and liner.
(Author's collection)

16

Earl Hines

December 28, 1903 – April 22, 1983

I NEVER ENCOUNTERED a musician who never made any mistakes other than Earl Hines. I met him on March 15, 1970, in Sherman Fairchild's living room, a room that also served as a recording studio. The plan was to make a very special record, and the record we made was number one—not on the charts, just in chronology, CR 101, *Earl Hines, Quintessential Recording Session*. And he didn't make any mistakes that day.

Perhaps he made mistakes all the time when I wasn't around, a regular Knuckles O'Toole, or was all thumbs on the days I wasn't in his presence. But if the tape recorder's reels were spinning around and tape was passing quietly past the recording heads, magically embedding music on the zillion particles of ferrite oxide on the tape, and I made sure they were spinning every time I heard him, he never made a mistake. I made a dozen LPs with Earl Hines in the decade of the 1970s, and, except for a weeklong live engagement, there is not a single alternate take or breakdown in the Chiaroscuro archive.

In the early 1940s, Charlie Parker was in the saxophone section of an Earl Hines big band. There is scarcely a more important and revered instrumentalist in jazz. But listen to Parker's legendary "Ko Ko" recording session from 1945. The complete, unedited results reveal many false starts, incomplete takes, and various versions of most of the selections. "Ko Ko" is a remarkable, justly famous recording. Yet, in retrospect, in the history and development of jazz and all that came before it or after it, "Ko Ko" is no more important for alto saxophonists who followed in the footsteps of Charlie Parker than the eight solo recordings Earl Hines made for the QRS company in 1928 were for pianists or even John Coltrane's *A Love Supreme* was for saxophonists in 1965. But Earl is so long ago his importance has been pushed aside for the new, but at sixty years old, *A Love Supreme* is many years older than Earl's QRS solos were when I first heard them in the 1950s.

Because most of our encounters were at recording sessions and concerts, I can date most of them precisely.

Quintessential Recordings Session #1
March 15, 1970 (CR 101)

Back on the Street
March 22, 1972 (CR 118)

Live at Dinkler's Motor Inn
October 24–28, 1972 (3) (CR 116/180)

Live at the New School
March 27, 1973 (CR 157)

This Is Marva Josie
1973 Thimble TLP 4

OPPOSITE
Earl Hines, Downtown Sound, 1974.
(Author's collection)

Quintessential Recording Session #2
November 1973 (CR 120)

A Buck Clayton Jam Session
March 25, 1974 (CR 132)

Quintessential Recording Session #3
March 26, 1974 (CR 131

Live at the New School
April 15, 1974 (CR 160)

Hot Sonatas with Joe Venuti
October 22, 1975 (CR 145)

In New Orleans
November 3–7, 1977 (CR 200)

There were only three times when I was with him for an extended period beyond a concert or recording date; the recordings in Syracuse in 1972 and New Orleans in 1977 and the time he and Marva came up for a weekend at my summer cottage at Round Pond in upstate New York. The idea was to take album cover photographs for Marva in a woodland setting; some of these photographs turned out very nicely, but she wound up going with one taken in New York City's Central Park. But all you have to do is to count the days; I was with him on less than a month's worth in eight years.

This personal interaction is interesting, but Earl's aversion to repeating himself and never making a mistake at the keyboard and suggesting a need for a second take is far more so. He just would not repeat anything. He played a song, played it well, and that was it. He never began a song then stopped and began again. It was all in his mind before he played the first note. The few alternate takes in the file are from sessions where he was part of a group, such as a Buck Clayton jam session, or with Jonah Jones or Joe Venuti, but if there was a need to do something over, it was never because of Earl.

The simple truth is, I never heard him make a mistake. He often worked himself into some pretty tight places, but he never failed to astound everyone as he emerged musically victorious. My guess is it was a combination of phenomenal technique, a flawless ear, a sense of bravado, and total confidence in his ability to do anything he wanted at the keyboard. Maybe I was just lucky, or perhaps I just caught Earl during an eight-year run when he was supremely confident, and his solo technique was in top form. The first time I met him in March 1970 is a perfect example.

At Sherman Fairchild's home/studio for first "QRS" session, 1970. (Author's collection)

In early 1970, I hit on the idea of asking Earl to recreate the eight legendary piano solos he'd fashioned for the QRS piano roll company in 1928. QRS had decided to branch out into phonograph records, and Earl was chosen to record eight selections. The people who compile lists claim the eight sides were recorded in Long Island City on December 8; the same people also claim he recorded two of the same songs for the Okeh company the following day in Chicago. Maybe such a feat would have been possible, but I tend to doubt it. Someone has the dates wrong.

Nonetheless, eight original compositions were recorded in New York, and two selections were repeated a few days later in Chicago. The music survived, but as time passed, the eight original selections on QRS became almost impossible to find. Yet, thanks to copies and bootlegs, these eight selections were as important in the evolution of solo jazz piano as any recordings up to that time, and their importance has not diminished over time.

At Sherman Fairchild's home/studio for the first "QRS" session, 1970. (Author's collection)

QRS 7037. (Author's collection)

I didn't know Earl in 1970, but I did know his close friend Stanley Dance, who also served as his business manager and biographer. I telephoned Stanley and he liked my idea. He said he'd pass it along to Earl, who was not very busy in recording studios in 1970, and recommend he undertake the project. I ran the idea by my musical partners, Marian McPartland and Sherman Fairchild, and both were enthusiastic. We made an offer of $500 and Earl accepted. A date was set to record: Sunday, March 15, 1970. We hoped we could begin around noon.

Sherman, Marian, and I got to 17 East Sixty-Fifth Street early; Stanley arrived with Earl a little later. He'd flown in from Toronto, where the evening before he'd played an engagement at the Colonial Tavern until about 2:00 AM, rested a little, caught an early morning flight to New York, and came directly from the airport. He looked impeccable. Suit pressed, not a hair out of place, or should I say, all his hair was in place. He gave the impression he hadn't given much thought to the project at hand.

I anticipated Earl might not have spent much time wondering about what he might do with these eight bits of musical history and had brought along a Milestone LP reissue of the eight QRS selections, just in case he might want to hear one for old time's sake. By 1970, only one of those early compositions, "My Monday Date," ever turned up in his performances. It was unlikely he'd played any of the other seven, except possibly "Blues in Thirds," for many years, or even thought about them.

I don't remember the first song Earl recorded that day, but it was the same for each song. I told him I had a recording of all the songs if he wanted to hear one to refresh his memory, and he thought that was a good idea. I'd play the LP; he'd listen carefully to his 1928 performances, usually sitting on the piano bench with his back to the piano. Then he'd turn around and run his hands over the keys, apparently working everything out in his head, and would finally announce he was ready to try one. I'd retreat to the recording booth, Earl would play the song, and that was it. This routine was repeated seven times. No second takes of any selections. The album was completed in less than an hour and a half.

Each of the eight selections was a masterpiece of structured improvisation. He didn't just throw them off. Two selections were short; "Panther Rag" and "Chimes in Blues" were about the same length as they were in 1928, but the other six were five to seven minutes long. The next year, the *Quintessential Recording Session* made its way to the final five in the Grammy competition for Outstanding Jazz Soloist. It didn't win, old-time guys on little labels with only three releases in the marketplace didn't win in those years any more than they win today, but it was nice to know a few people had taken notice.

Every studio date I did with Earl over the next few years was just the same. He'd just arrive and do it. We did two more quintessential recordings of original compositions and then a special recording in New Orleans that became the one-hundredth Chiaroscuro. In between there were solo, duo, sextet, and jam session dates; some live, some in the studio. The most amazing display of his facility I ever witnessed, however, occurred at an out-of-the-way motel in Syracuse, New York, in October 1972.

A month or two earlier, Stanley Dance tipped me off that Earl was going to be doing something unusual. Instead of his normal quartet, he was going to work for a couple of weeks with the legendary guitarist Tiny Grimes. Earl usually had a saxophone in his quartet, but for this short period Tiny would be in the group instead. Stanley suggested this might make for an interesting recording opportunity.

I jumped at the idea, but then learned the closest the quartet would be to New York City was Syracuse, at a place called Dinkler's Motor Inn. I bit my lip and agreed to do a remote. I didn't know anything about Dinkler's, but I knew about Syracuse. I spent my high school and college years in that town. And so, I filled my car with remote recording gear and headed north, unaware that this modest motel in upstate New York was going to be the scene of one of the most remarkable bits of musicianship I'd ever witness.

Quintessential Record Session LP jacket.
(Author's collection)

An Evening with Earl Hines LP jacket.
(Author's collection)

On stage with Hank Young and Bert Dahlander, Dinkler's Motor Inn, 1973. (Author's collection)

Earl was set to perform five days, Tuesday through Saturday. Two sets a night for the first three days, three sets on the last two. Tuesday was just used to set up the gear, run levels, and do some general testing. Earl played his regular show that night. *The Louis Armstrong Medley, The West Side Story Medley, The Canadian Sunset/Eddie Heywood Medley*: the kinds of things people would like to hear in the lounge of a motel in Syracuse. Nothing very remarkable made its way into the ReVox recorder. At the end of the evening, I gave Earl the list of tunes Stanley and I had selected. He'd never recorded any of them, or at least this is what Stanley had told me, and I had no reason to doubt it.

All the equipment was set for recording on Wednesday night. I thought Earl might try one or two of the new tunes. No such luck. He played the show twice. Now I had two takes of everything. The same thing happened on Thursday. He played the show twice. Three takes of everything. On Friday morning I casually suggested it might make sense to try some of the songs that night. Earl was having none of it. He played the show three times.

It was now the last day, and I was beginning to get nervous. I visited with Earl Saturday morning, and said we had to try and get some things down that night. I knew better than to suggest too strenuously. He just gave me the "don't worry" look and suggested I take Marva Josie, his vocalist, to the football game that afternoon. Syracuse was playing Pitt at old Archbold Stadium. I went to the game with Marva, Syracuse won, and I hoped I would later that night at Dinkler's. Marva said I shouldn't worry about the recording, but I did.

Earl played the show the first set on Saturday night and repeated it on the second set. I had just about given up. He sat down at the piano to begin the third set at about 11:30 p.m. He reached inside his coat pocket and took out the piece of paper that listed the songs we wanted for the recording. He then proceeded to play each song on the very long list, coaching his band and cueing them along the way. It was about a two-hour set. When he finished the list, he played "Its a Pity to Say Goodnight" and that was that. He picked up the piece of paper, said goodnight, and went back to his room. There was enough exceptional material for two LPs, which I was only too happy to pay for.

It was an astonishing display. Stanley and I had picked tunes he never played, things like "Lester Leaps In," "All of Me," and the old chestnut from the 1930s, "Who?" Each was perfectly executed, flawlessly constructed, and either exciting, beautiful, or both. The only tunes on the album that didn't come from that long last set were Marva's vocals, some of which had turned out better on other evenings. I don't know if he'd been sitting in his room thinking about those tunes for four days, but I doubt it. He was probably just exercising his hands and watching a ball game on television. It was simply phenomenal musicianship.

Quintessential Continued and *Quintessential 1974* LP Jackets. (Author's collection)

We made another quintessential solo LP in 1973 and yet another in 1974, but an incident in March 1974 during my first *Buck Clayton Jam Session* points out how his peers reacted to Earl. It was a great twelve-piece band playing original arrangements by Buck. As we were working out the solo order for the first tune, it became clear no one wanted to follow Earl on the first tune, "Boss Blues." The only guy who was game was Zoot Sims. It went very well. A rehearsal and then a good take.

With Joe Venuti, 1975.
(Author's collection)

Hot Sonatas LP jacket, 1975.
(Author's collection)

Marva Josie LP jacket, 1975.
(Author's collection)

Buck had structured all the arrangements so they'd last about twelve to fifteen minutes. He had four originals, which would easily fill an LP, but it didn't work out that way. The structure of "Lazy Blues," the third tune on the date, was an introduction and then various soloists in a selected order. The soloist would play a long chorus with rhythm and then a second chorus accompanied by the entire ensemble. It worked just perfectly until about ten minutes into the song, when Earl launched into his solo. He played the first chorus and everyone in the ensemble was so fascinated by what he was doing that no one came in on the second chorus. Earl just kept playing and it got better and better. Finally, Buck got his attention, the rest of the ensemble woke up, and everything worked out fine. But it was a twenty-six minute take. I wasn't complaining, but it meant I never issued all the material from that session until the CD era.

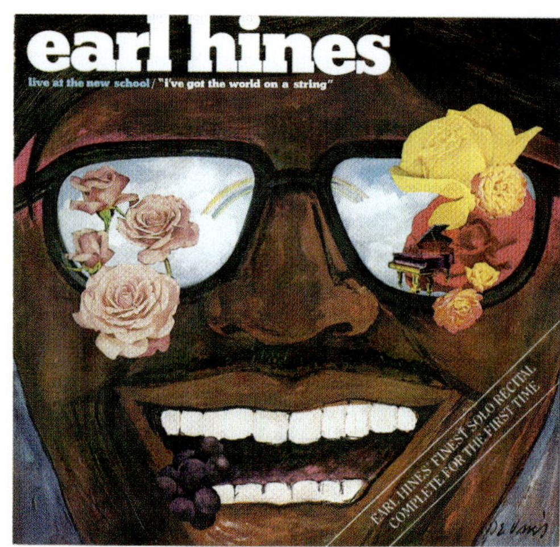

Live at the New School, 1973 LP jacket.
(Author's collection)

I kept in touch with Earl throughout the early and mid-1970s. There were two concerts at The New School, an incredible duet recording with Joe Venuti, *Hot Sonatas*, the only time these two legendary figures ever recorded together, assorted Christmas songs, and a wonderful eclectic date that featured Marva Josie. This is how eclectic: There were two trumpets on the date, Joe Newman and Jerry Schwartz, more commonly known in later years as Gerard and longtime conductor of the Seattle Symphony and one of the most recorded and honored US-born conductors of the twentieth and twenty-first centuries.

Then there was "White Christmas." In 1973, I began a tradition of asking artists to record a Christmas tune that I'd produce as a 45 single and send out as a Christmas card. Everyone I asked was eager to make a recording because I'd give each of them five hundred copies for their own use. Earl and Marva were no exceptions. I'd sent my 1973 record to each, and Marva decided she wanted to make a record for Christmas 1974. Earl was at the studio to record *Quintessential 1974* and when he'd completed the four new tunes he'd written for the record, Marva suggested they make a Christmas record. Earl asked what she had in mind, and she said, "White Christmas." Much to my surprise, Earl said, "How does it go?" Marva sang it through a single time, Earl listened carefully, fiddled a little, and then they did it. One take in March; one thousand singles in December, each cluttering many mailboxes around the land.

Then it was November 1977, and we made our final recording together. It was the one hundredth Chiaroscuro, and I'd long planned to have number one hundred be with Earl; a fitting bookend because he'd made the first, eight years earlier. This is how I described the record fifty-five years ago, when my memories of our five days in New Orleans were fresher than they are today. The routine was not much different from the way it had been five years earlier in Syracuse at Dinkler's Motor Inn, except the surroundings were a bit more interesting, and I didn't have to worry about running a tape recorder:

The New Orleans Hyatt Regency is a bright new hotel; an architectural wonder of glass, steel, and brick, a twenty-four-story courtyard and silent, whizzing transparent elevators that move in rapid fire order from floor to floor, transporting a gaggle of conventioneers from here to there, in this case, the Automobile Dismantlers of America, the kind of folks who generally convene in and inhabit hotels like the Hyatt Regency in a city such as New Orleans.

In addition to the mandatory bars, restaurants, meeting rooms and novelty shops, there is also a nightspot in the hotel called Le Club. It is the latter that is responsible for my being in the Hyatt Regency, the type of hotel I usually don't enjoy very much, and certainly not the kind I would normally pick in a city like New Orleans. But here I am, pacing back and forth in front of Le Club, much in the same way I used to lurk about in front of the old Metropole twenty years earlier, when they wouldn't let me in because I was only sixteen. In this case, however, I don't want to go in unless I have an ally.

About 9:30 the ally appears; he bounds off the elevator, nattily attired in a dark blazer and cream-colored pants, and strides briskly towards Le Club. I intercept him before he can enter; I don't want to miss my chance and Earl Hines smiles a smile at least a foot wide, happy to see a familiar face. He says quickly, I'm late, let's talk after the first set. He then takes me by the hand and leads me through the assembled dismantlers to his table by the bandstand. Thank Goodness. There's not another seat in the place.

I settle in and remember I'm in New Orleans to make a record with Earl; Chiaroscuro number one hundred.

Christmas recordings, 1974 and 1975. (Author's collection)

Earl made number one and I want to reach the centennial mark with him. I've also always wanted to make a record in New Orleans and, given the state of the jazz scene in that city, I know it might be necessary to import someone to get anything special. The timing, and Earl's engagement in the city, makes it all very easy.

Le Club is very much a surprise, I normally hate jazz rooms in hotel chains; for the most part they have little class, force artists like Earl Hines to play on rotten pianos through poor amplification systems, and do not pay any of the performers enough. They are also smoky. La Club is smoky, but the piano is good, the kids who run sound and lights are very good and, judging by Earl's accommodations at the hotel, he is well paid. To make matters even better, Le Club is decorated with a dozen massive paintings by my friend, Leo Meiersdorff. Leo has been responsible for many cover paintings for Chiaroscuro; in fact he was in charge of the cover for my very first record, the one previously mentioned. He did that one for free; I was too poor to pay him, but he was eager and had been camped out on my couch for a month or so. Life is now better for both of us and, happily, Leo will be paid for this album. It is, however, a charming coincidence to see his paintings all around the room.

The first set boils to a close; I pay $8.00 for my orange juice, Earl grabs me and we quickly find ourselves in the twenty-four-story courtyard talking about old times and the record we will make a few days later. His marvelous vocalist and frequent companion, Marva Josie, joins us as soon as she gets away from the fans in Le Club, and then it is really like old times. Earl doesn't much want to talk about the record; he says he has it in his mind and the only thing he really wants is a good piano. I tell him he has a nine-foot Baldwin and he smiles. He's heard it before. We make a date to go over songs the next day, but I'm pretty sure that the exercise will not be particularly fruitful. Earl just doesn't like to scheme about record dates too far ahead. By far ahead, I mean anything much in advance of walking through the studio door.

The next afternoon I call Earl on schedule. He's slumming it in a six-room suite the hotel has provided; my little room costs $55. I hate to think what the suite costs. In any event, Earl is relaxing, watching Alabama thump LSU. We go over some of the music I've brought along and listen to a few tapes. I have enough possibilities to cover about a dozen records. We narrow the selections down to a manageable number, but I'm certain Earl will still change things once he gets into the studio. We chat a while longer and then I go out to pester Leo Meiersdorff, to see if he has finished all the cover paintings I've asked him to do.

Leo lives in New Orleans on a permanent basis now and is something of a celebrity. In the French Quarter it's hard to pass by a souvenir store or poster gallery that does not feature his lithographs and in a number of the finer art galleries his original paintings command stiff prices. As I expect, Leo has outdone himself; his studio floor is covered with massive watercolors of Earl, Bobby Hackett, and Lee Konitz. He has half a dozen portraits of Earl and has picked out the two he feels are the best to be used for the album. He asks that I give one of the others to Earl and have him autograph yet another for his own collection of paintings. Everything is working out perfectly.

Monday is the day to record. Jill Cook is scheduled to arrive at 6:30 in the morning. She's a game girl, flying all that way to help mind things in the studio and have a bit of a holiday in New Orleans. An understudy will handle her dancing chores for a couple of days. She's taken the Delta redeye roach coach, and this after two shows on Saturday and another on Sunday. No airplanes are anywhere in sight; there's enough fog that morning to ground the ground. The plane finally makes it a couple of hours late; we fetch Earl at the hotel and then dash to Alan Toussaint's Sea Saint recording studio.

Sea Saint is a good hall. The Baldwin is in fine shape; the action loose and quiet. Earl is all smiles. An easy set up with two U-87s in the piano, a quick level check and we are ready to go. In the next three-and-a-half hours Earl completes fourteen songs. All are at least wonderful; the seven on this album are exceptional. Jill makes certain she watches Earl carefully after he completes each song; an extra broad smile from Earl rates a star on the take sheet. All the songs on this album had that big smile; a couple were even super wide. The infectious playing catches on and at one time or another various people working at the studio stick their heads in to see what is happening and why Jill and Roberta Grace, our engineer, are bouncing in their chairs.

We wrap the date after "Blue Skies" and Earl and I start talking about nothing in particular; Guy Lombardo's death was in the papers a couple of days earlier and we talk about his passing. Earl mentions how fond he was of Guy, in fact, how most all the jazz artists in the early days were and that Guy liked jazz. He even wants to put one of Lombardo's tunes in one of his medleys. He then starts playing "I've Got a Right to Sing the Blues," a tune he does for Jack Teagarden. We hurriedly turn on the machines and get in another song. Thank goodness.

Earl Hines In New Orleans LP jacket, 1977. (Author's collection)

Back to the hotel. I show Earl the cover paintings; he roars with appreciation. He couldn't be happier. He keeps one for himself, signs one for Leo, Jill, and myself, and then we realize we should quickly vanish. On the way back from the studio, Earl bought a bag of Popeye's fried chicken about two feet tall. He's dog tired after the recording and wants to do nothing except relax and dig into that chicken, maybe watch the ball game, and he doesn't need any help or company. It's time to let him relax. Jill and I hop in a cab and scoot over to the Royal Sonesta where Leo and his wife, Diana, have something cooked up. Leo knows the head chef at the Sonesta, he decorated some of the rooms there as well, and he has promised to arrange a feast.

As we speed through the night and finally wind up on Bourbon Street, a pest hole in every sense of the word, I can't help but think of Earl, back at the hotel, watching the ball game and eating his chicken, while up and down that street there are a bunch of groups that pass themselves off as jazz bands, but if you were to take the aggregate talent of everyone playing on Bourbon Street that night, you might come up with about 10 percent of what Earl can do even when he's tired. During the recording he said he was tired, he kept telling me, "It's the middle of the night for me," and more than once he said this was his last solo album. Fat chance. I'll bet we start scheming about another one when he gets back to New York. There's talk about a Morton project, and he has been glancing at an Erroll Garner folio. And who knows, maybe he'll put together some new songs of his own, which to me will be much better than anyone else's songbook. I'll wait for next time with as much eagerness as I waited for the first one and all the others along the way.

None of these projects ever worked out. Earl was in New York City less and less and then, in the early 1980s, he had some health problems but was still performing regularly and recording for other companies, but never for a major. His last recording seems to have been on a Brazilian label in 1981.

A couple of years later in mid-April, 1983, we launched The Floating Jazz Festival and began to line up the talent for our new venture. My first call was to Earl Hines. He said he'd be happy to be part of it. He died a week later, before we even had a chance to write a contract.

Earl Hines was not only the most remarkable pianist I ever worked with, he was perhaps the most remarkable musician. He was the consummate professional, a man who not only had perfect musical time but was always on time, every time, always did the job well, even if it was just to play the show, was impeccably dressed, courteous, good natured to a fault, was giving to others, and never made a musical error. He loved a musical challenge and probably other kinds of challenges as well.

Here is an example. In 1973, I asked another of my favorite pianists, Dick Wellstood, to write the liner notes for one of Earl's quintessential solo dates. Wellstood wrote as well as he played piano, and his notes for the Hines album were nothing short of amazing.

One day in March 1974, a few weeks after the LP had been released, Earl came down to the studio to discuss another solo album. He asked to see the new release and was pleased. He then asked me to read him Wellstood's notes. This is what I read:

Behold Earl Hines, spinner of yarns, big-handed virtuoso of the black dance, con man extraordinaire, purveyor of hot sauce.

Behold Earl Hines, Jive King, boss of the sloppy run, the dragged thumb, the uneven tremolo, Minstrel of The Unworthy Emotion, King of Freedom.

Democratic Transcendent, his twitchy, spitting style uses every cheesy trick in the piano-bar catalog to create moving cathedrals, masterpieces of change, great trains of tension and relaxation, multi-dimensional solos that often seem to be about themselves or about other solos—"See, here I might have played some boogie-woogie, or put this accent there, or this run here, that chord there . . . or maybe a little stride for you beautiful people in the audience . . . " Earl Hines, Your Musical Host, serving up the hot sauce.

For all the complexity in his playing, Hines exercises fairly simple harmonic vocabulary, and in any event his peculiar stuttering rhythmic sense gives his phrasing such force as to make harmonic analysis almost meaningless. The dissonances he uses are more that result of his fascination with the overtone of the piano than of any concern with elaborate harmony substitutions. Accented single notes making the upper strings ring, or open fifths or octaves sounded a tone or semi-tone apart (either will do) at opposite ends of the keyboard are to him among the most beautiful of sounds.

His is the music of Change, based on the rhythms of the body in a graceful way unique to the older Jazz players. This may be why he is more successful as a soloist than as a trio pianist. The trio's oscarine petercision, a crutch for many, is a cage for Hines. It's need for relentless accuracy and predictable responses only betrays in the tiny imperfections of freedom in his playing; when he is playing alone, these imperfections meld into a sweet flexible instrument of expression.

Hines is not a "stride" pianist. His rhythm is too straight four-four, too free. He does not possess the magisterial dignity of James P. Johnson, the aristocratic detachment of Art Tatum, the patience of Donald Lambert, the phlegmatic unflappability necessary to maintain the momentum of stride. Hines needs silence in the bass, room to let the flowers grow, space to unroll his showers of broken runs containing (miraculously) the melody within, his grace-noted octaves ("That's the way we make the piano sing!",—Eubie Blake), and his wandering, Irish endings.

His is Freedom in discipline, infinite choice in a limited sphere, the tension of Will vs. Material—his is human creativity. Behold Earl Hines, King of Beasts!

After I finished, he nodded and suggested we go out for dinner. As we were walking along Christopher Street, he said something like, "If you every make a record with that Wellstood boy, let me write some notes about him." I didn't ask Earl, but I should have. And I'll bet he'd have worked Dick over pretty good.

As I said previously, I was never with Earl anywhere but a performance venue, hotel room, restaurant, walking along streets here and there, or recording studio, and no, I didn't know him well. The closest thing to a non-professional venture was when he and Marva came upstate for that photo shoot, and while I was in the woods taking pictures of her, he was back at the cottage watching a ball game on a tiny black-and-white television screen. I was probably with him on no more than twenty-five plus days, but my goodness they were exciting days, and all the moments were special and filled with remarkable music.

Mona Hinton, President
OL8-8975

New York Jazz Musician's Fund, Inc.
311 West 74th Street
N.Y., N.Y. 10023
873-0733

Tavia Konitz, Secretary
787-5522

FINANCIAL STATEMENT

DECEMBER 31, 1988

Balance in Checking Account	$ 645.83
Balance in Day-to-Day Savings Account	9,851.92
Balance in C.D. #1	23,598.69
Balance in C.D. #2	13,593.67
TOTAL	$47,690.11

Balance in Outstanding Loans Due $13,347.86

	AMT.DUE	PD.TO DATE	OWING
CURTIS FULLER	350.00	50.00	300.00
N. MONK	2,500.00	-0-	2,500.00
CECIL PAYNE	300.00	50.00	250.00
JO JONES	2,717.86	-0-	2,717.86
FRED WAITES	700.00	-0-	700.00
PATTI BOWN	500.00	-0-	500.00
LAUREN DRAPER	500.00	150.00	350.00
KIT MC CLURE	500.00	425.00	75.00
F. GANT	300.00	-0-	300.00
ALBERT DAILEY	700.00	-0-	700.00
OLIVER JACKSON	3,500.00	1,000.001	2,500.00
AL GREY	1,150.00	300.00	850.00
LEE KONITZ	750.00	750.00	-0-
PEPPER ADAMS	1,000.00	-0-	1,000.00
HOWARD MC GHEE	105.00	-0-	105.00
ED PHYFE	500.00	-0-	500.00
			$13,347.86

17

Milt and Mona Hinton

June 24, 1919 – December 19, 2000 and April 24, 1919 – May 3, 2008

THE OTHER DAY I came upon a document/letter dated December 31, 1988. It was on the letterhead of the New York Jazz Musician's Fund, Inc. and was the organization's financial statement for that year. Mona Hinton was listed as president; Tavia Konitz was secretary. It also noted the sixteen musicians to whom the organization had loaned money in 1988. The sixteen were: Curtis Fuller, N. Monk, Cecil Payne, Jo Jones (D), Fred Waites, Patti Bown, Lauren Draper, Kit McClure, F. Gant (Frank), Albert Dailey (D), Oliver Jackson, Al Grey, Lee Konitz, Pepper Adams (D), Howard McGhee (D), and Ed Phyfe. The small "D" in pencil next to a name meant deceased.

Only one musician on the list had paid back their loan (Lee Konitz, probably because his wife got after him) and nine had paid back nothing at all, including the four who were deceased. This was the JFA before the Jazz Foundation of America was organized in Herb Storfer's living room the following year. That the organization had any money to disperse was largely because it had been launched and funded by George Wein, who had given all the proceeds from certain concerts he produced over the years to the fledgling fund.

The importance of the founding of the JFA can't be overstated. In 1988, sixteen men and women were assisted by the New York Jazz Musician's Fund. This organization's mission was ultimately assumed by the newly formed JFA and existing funds from NYJMF were transferred to the new organization. To put it in perspective, in 2024, the last year where records are complete, JFA assisted over seventeen hundred individuals and handled over eight thousand cases. So JFA today can be traced back to Milt Hinton teaming up with Mona Clayton in 1939 and Mona's work with NYJMF and George's support of it.

I don't remember when I first met Milt Hinton. It was either when he subbed for Jack Lesberg one night at the Roosevelt Grill when I was recording Bobby Hackett in April/May 1970 or the "lost" Joe Venuti date at Sherman Fairchild's home/studio in the same year. But it is safe to say I met him in 1970, now fifty-five years ago, and at the time, old man time was only a sprightly sixty. I met Mona Hinton a few years later, at their cozy home in St. Albans, Queens.

If someone asked me to sum up Milt in one word, it would be "generous" or possibly "thoughtful." If they allowed two words they might be "superb musician." Mona Hinton was equally generous and thoughtful, but if given two words to define her, the two words would be "business woman" because she took care of the business so Milt could spend his time being a superb musician, just as she looked after all those guys in Cab Calloway's band in the 1940s and the people on the New York Jazz Musician's Fund list.

OPPOSITE

Jazz Musicians Fund list.
(Author's collection)

Milt Hinton and Mary Lou Williams, 1973.
(Author's collection)

With Bobby Rosengarden and Hank Jones, 1976.
(Author's collection)

I didn't get around to using Milt on one of my records until 1973 for one simple reason: I was usually too poor to hire enough musicians to form a trio, but as soon as I was able to do so Milt was my first call and remained my first call for the rest of the decade. The first recording was in 1973; Milt was Ruby Braff's first call when he made his Chiaroscuro debut that year, and that's just the way it went. When I managed to get enough money together to ask someone to assemble a band for a recording, usually mainstream guys like Buddy Tate or Buck Clayton or Joe Venuti, they had free reign to choose who made up their ensemble and Milt was always there. It wasn't that he was my first choice, which he would have been, but he was also the musician's first choice, so I never had to make the call.

The Trio LP jacket, 1976.
Author's collection)

Between the years 1970 and 2011, I produced roughly two hundred records and/or CDs. Milt Hinton was the featured bassist on dozens of them. Between the years 1983 and 2002, our production company, HOSS, Inc., produced twenty years' worth of Floating Jazz Festivals. Milt was featured at each festival, from 1987 to 1995. The only reason he wasn't on them after 1995 was because he was then eighty-five, and it was becoming hard for him to travel. He could still play just fine, but navigating the airports and transportation was increasingly difficult. When I assisted Hans Zurbrügg in compiling his legendary *Jazz & Blues Art Box* that contained DVDs of the 237 concerts presented at the Internationale JazzFestival Bern between the years 1983 and 2002, Milt was featured on many of the DVDs, either on bass, leader, Master of Ceremonies, or sometimes all three.

In the recording studio Milt was usually not the leader, but the leaders and stars sought his guidance, and I grabbed some examples of this in photographs. When there was a problem with something on the *Buddy Tate and His Buddies* date, Milt and Mary Lou Williams can be seen sorting it out. When Hank Jones was in an accident and couldn't make the second Buck Clayton jam session and Tommy Flanagan took over, he looked to Milt for guidance. But there was one 1970s Chiaroscuro date where Milt was at least a co-leader, and I explained some of it in the now forty-five-year-old producer's notes:

I was sitting at my desk in the studio one afternoon and the telephone rang; Bobby Rosengarden was calling from Florida. He was working a job with Hank Jones and Milt Hinton and said the three of them had improvised their way into an exciting groove, and some fine music was being made. He added it was one of the best trios he had ever been part of and should be recorded. It struck me as a sound idea and I suggested we try and record it a few weeks later when they all got back to New York; naturally there were delays, Hank and Bobby had a gang of dates all over the country (par for the course for these great musicians) and Milt was going to London with Bing Crosby. We set a date in October; later it had to be postponed a week, but finally we had a Monday date when all could assemble.

Milt arrived first; he was understandably blue because of Bing's death but had some wonderful stories to tell about the trip that somehow helped to cheer things up. Hank then bounded in as precise and natty as ever, and finally Bobby arrived with seventeen porters carrying what must be the heaviest trap case in the world. That's the only thing wrong with using Bobby on a date: the trap case! Invariably I get stuck with carrying that case up to my second-floor studio and I know someday I'm going to collapse with it.

The three guys set up in the studio; Fred Miller had everything in order very quickly. Sessions like this are a piece of cake for Fred, and for those who find interest in such matters, this was a two-track date. A good engineer can do it and do it well. You can still use eight microphones on the drums and not have to have them on separate tracks if you are a good engineer (and if the drummer is any good).

We romped through the songs because everyone came prepared; they knew where they were going and what they wanted to do. The only spur of the moment choice was Hank's solo version of "Oh, What a Beautiful Morning" (Bobby and Milt yelled at him and made him do it). There were multiple takes on all the tunes, but only because the guys were trying to make a great take even better, and in a couple of instances there were inserts, usually for cleaner endings.

It was a remarkable recording. It featured four standards, three originals credited to "The Trio" and Milt's composition, "Mona's Feeling Lonely," which probably was a regular occurrence because Milt was always so busy and constantly on the go. And it was a real trio of leaders; not the Hank Jones Trio. All were equals, and the LP was well received, with one noted critic calling it the best piano trio recording of the decade. It took twenty-six years to release it as a CD, and by then all the alternate takes had been misplaced. The only alternates were extra photographs to fill up the CD booklet.

In addition to the recordings and concerts, there were many extracurricular adventures with Milt; one of the earliest had to do with a book. In June 1986, I signed a contract with Doubleday to create a book of text and photographs to be called *The Ghosts of Harlem*. The premise of the book was to interview and photograph forty to fifty musicians who'd been active in Harlem when the uptown music scene was exciting, vital, and at its creative peak; let them tell their stories and then explain when and why the scene collapsed. One of the first people I met with was Milt Hinton in his basement playroom, workroom, practice room, storeroom, darkroom, at his home in St. Albans, Queens, on January 27, 1987. I was lucky that I started at the top.

Milt was smart, erudite, forthcoming, and helpful in every way imaginable. He looked at my list of names, the people I hoped to interview and photograph with my big wooden Deardorff. He gave me advice on who I should avoid, and who might be what he called "white shy" and said if anyone in that category avoided me, he suggested I should just ask them to call him, and he'd tell them

I was "OK." And he told stories about gangsters like Al Capone in Chicago, who saved his finger, Ann Robinson in Harlem, who saved him when he was struggling, working with Eddie South and, of course, his years with Cab Calloway throughout the 1930s and 1940s.

He said many wise things that day. Here are a couple of excerpts:

> *I've been very lucky. I just wish I could pass more along to students and to young black kids who should know more about their heritage, there's just so many things people ought to know. I was just thinking about one the other day, the Gaiety Building. It was one of those buildings up at 46 and Broadway they were tearing down to make way for that new hotel. There was all kinds of talk about tearing down those buildings, but they mainly just talked about the theater. Everybody raising hell about the theaters but not one person says anything about the Gaiety, where all the great black entertainers had their offices, all the black stars like Bill Robinson and Sissle and Blake. Not a word. There were so many black entertainers in that building that George M. Cohan used to call the building Uncle Tom's Cabin. I guess all the young black folks don't know anything about it, but this was the place where a lot of black music was first organized. Why does a white guy like you have to write this book about Harlem? Aren't there any young black writers who care? In my classes I try to talk about things like this. It's a very sad thing with us. I can go down to a little college with young kids and I can say to the young black kids, look if you'll come out to my house, man, I think I can help you and I get so very few of them to come by. I don't just offer it to black kids; I offer it to anyone in my class.*

At the end of the interview, I asked him one last question:

> **Hank:** *Do you remember the last time you played in Harlem?*
> **Milt:** *I do and it's very sad. I was playing for a woman up at City College who was very interested in black creative dancing. She was working with a lot of kids but many of them were misbehaving, but she kept on trying. She finally got all these kids together to put on a concert. She knew I'd worked at the Cotton Club, so she asked me to get the music together. I put a good band together, Eddie Barefield, Eddie Bert, Jimmy Nottingham, good people like that. Just seven pieces. We rehearsed all afternoon, and it was going to be a good show. After rehearsal Mona and I went out to dinner, and we found out Martin Luther King had been shot. We stayed at the bar trying to get some details but then went back to the school and everybody there was going crazy. Everything was in a turmoil, so there was no concert. We just packed up our instruments and left. That's the last time I played in Harlem and you know how long ago that was.*

Then I took a black-and-white portrait for the book and a color portrait for me and then talked about photography for the rest of the afternoon. Milt was a remarkable photographer and had great access to take them. In his lifetime he took roughly seventy thousand black-and-white photographs and seven thousand color chromes. He processed his own B&W film and printed in his basement darkroom. When *The Ghosts of Harlem* was scheduled to be published, he took a picture of me in his darkroom and that was the photograph the publishers used on the book's dust jacket flap. This massive archive has been organized and is maintained by David G. Berger and Holly Maxson. Three books featuring Milt's jazz-oriented photographs have been published: *Bass Line* (1988), *Overtime* (1992), and *Playing the Changes* (2008).

Chiaroscuro was revitalized in the same year and Milt and I began discussing a recording project that would take until 1990 to bring to fruition; a project that would be perhaps the most ambitious Chiaroscuro recording to date, one in which Milt would be the leader and pick all the musicians with whom he wanted to record with at this stage of his career.

Milt picked out twenty-three musicians and they were assembled into various groups. Many of the artists chosen were well-known "leaders," men like Dizzy Gillespie, Lionel Hampton, Joe Williams, Flip Phillips, Cab Calloway, Clark Terry, and Buck Clayton. Milt had known some since the 1920s and had been in their bands, but now he was the leader. The record was to be called *Old Man Time*. It was mostly recorded at Rudy Van Gelder's studio in Englewood Cliffs, New Jersey, but a few tracks were done on the *S/S Norway* and the Lionel Hampton session was at RCA Studios in New York City. It was an afternoon filled with great music and terrific conversation, because Milt and Hampton had been in high school together in Chicago and there was nonstop conversation about those days. Milt promised he'd make certain his sometimes unruly and unreliable classmate behaved, and he did.

Perhaps the most interesting group was one he assembled that was called "The Survivors." Everyone in the band had to be at least seventy-five years old and, to use one of Milt's lines, "older than dirt." In addition to Milt, the group included Doc Cheatham, Eddie Barefield, Bud-

Portrait for *The Ghosts of Harlem*, 1987. (Author's collection)

In Milt's darkroom, 1987. (Author's collection)

dy Tate, Red Richards, Al Casey, and Gus Johnson. Buck Clayton wrote two originals, and this time Cab Calloway worked for Milt and sang "Good Time Charlie" with The Survivors. But part of this group also made a recording that day on which no one played a note. They just talked. It was very special.

I thought it would be fun to take the three guys who'd been with Cab for many years and put them all together in a room with Cab and let them just talk about what it was like in the 1930s and 1940s. It worked better than I could have imagined. After a minute or two, they forgot about the recording and just talked, and for 13:09 it was 1939 or some year close to that. In retrospect, this may be the most important recording on the CD, other than Milt's 43:00 "Jazzspeak" that closes the second CD.

But this was just part of *Old Man Time*. Working with David Berger and Holly Maxson, we picked out the fifty-eight most prominent then active jazz-oriented bass artists and asked each to write a tribute to Milt to be included in the booklet that accompanied *Old Man Time*. The twenty-four-page booklet, Chiaroscuro's largest, contains fifty-seven tributes, statements that ranged from thirteen words from Ron Carter, *Milt is the standard that all of us try to measure up to*, to a ninety-line poem from Jay Leonhart, and everything in between.

But there was more to come with Milt in 1990. In May, Chiaroscuro recorded with a new version of an old band, Soprano Summit, now called Summit Reunion because Kenny Davern had ceased playing his soprano saxophone and turned it into a lamp, or was it a doorstop? There is always some level of friction when six all-star musicians assemble on stage or in a recording studio, but this was especially true when Kenny Davern and Bob Wilber, temperamental polar opposites, got together in a recording studio. And of course, it fell to Milt to be the peacemaker, which he accomplished with typical aplomb, and the result was one of the finest Chiaroscuro CDs of the 1990s. There was even time toward the end of the recording session for an unusual, special recording, which Milt would both play on and then later in the year introduce on National Public Radio.

In the mid-1980s, Andrew Sordoni, my partner at Chiaroscuro, produced the first edition of *Christmas Music: The Jazz Feeling*, a show that would become a long running series of Christmas radio broadcasts for National Public Radio. The program became an NPR fixture for a quarter of a century and utilized the facilities of NPR station WVIA, located in northeastern Pennsylvania. Andy wrote and produced the show, and I was the on-air

Old Man Time, CD. (Author's collection)

Old Man Time CD booklet cover. (Author's collection)

At the Glenside waterfall, 1990. (Author's collection)

Christmas Music: The Jazz Feeling, 1990. (Author's collection)

The Trio 1994 CD booklet cover. (Author's collection)

host, working in conjunction with a noted jazz personality. WVIA uploaded the show to the NPR satellite, and it was picked up by many NPR affiliates all over the country. In 1990, the on-air personality was Milt Hinton, who traveled to Pennsylvania to record the show that fall. We stopped at Glenside, my then-home in rural Pennsylvania, I took a picture of him standing on my spillway with his camera ready to get a picture, and we recorded the show later that day at WVIA.

We played and discussed jazzy Christmas-oriented recordings by pianists Fats Waller, Ramsey Lewis, Ed Higgins, Ray Charles, Bobby Timmons, and groups led by Lockjaw Davis, Gene Ammons, Glenn Zottola, and Bob Barnard as well as the Manhattan Jazz Quintet. But as far as I was concerned, I was happiest with specially recorded performances that premiered on this show, "Hark the Herald Angels Sing" with The Survivors and "It Came Upon a Midnight Clear" with Summit Reunion, both of which featured Milt.

1990 was Milt's eightieth year. He not only had *Old Man Time*, a bunch of other recordings, concerts all over the world, two weeks aboard the *S/S Norway* as part of our Floating Jazz Festival and *Christmas Music: The Jazz Feeling*, but in June, George Wein threw him an eightieth birthday celebration in Town Hall. I was lucky enough to be there with a camera in hand. It was both a Who's Who and a mishmash. I heard it all but only managed to catch parts of it on film, notably Doc Cheatham and Wynton Marsalis together as well as Milt himself, wedged in between Ray Brown and John Clayton.

And Milt was there throughout the 1990s. He played his last festivals at sea in 1995, when he was eighty-five. That was the year we produced *The Ultimate Caribbean Jazz Spectacular* in May/June aboard the *Majesty of the Seas* and the *Floating Jazz Festival* aboard the *S/S Norway* in October/November. Milt was part of the new version of The Trio, with Derek Smith replacing Hank Jones and then four months later with Kenny Davern and Flip Phillips on the *S/S Norway*, a group that made a Chiaroscuro CD. It was also Milt's last live recording for the label.

With Red Callender on the S/S *Norway*, 1990.
(Author's collection)

On the M/S *Seaward*, 1989.
(Author's collection)

Suddenly it was 2000 and time for a nintieth birthday celebration, a spectacular event that was part of George Wein's 2000 JVC Jazz Festival in New York City. The concert was produced by David G. Berger and Bruce Ricker and featured thirty all-stars, including the best of the basses, Ron Carter, Bill Crow, Richard Davis, Kyle Eastwood, Jay Leonhart, Jack Lesberg, and Christian McBride. With such an abundance of basses, Milt just had to sit still and supervise. In the program notes Berger wrote, *Milt's seventy years in music span a large part of the history of jazz. His expertise and versatility as a bassist made him the consummate sideman who was called upon to perform with a roster of the Century's jazz greats, from Keppard, Armstrong, and Ellington to Tatum, Gillespie, and Coltrane.*

Of course, there was no one else alive for which that could be said, after all, the stretch from Freddie Keppard (1890–1933) to John Coltrane (1926–1967) is quite a long one, but one Milt could cover and did. And despite

Milt Hinton 1910–2000

"Music involves more than just playing
an instrument, it's really about cohesiveness
and sharing. I believe you don't truly
know something yourself until you can
take it from your mind and put it
into someone else's.

Passing on what I've learned and
experienced in my lifetime is an obligation
I take very seriously."

Milt Hinton

A new CD "The Judge at his Best,"
a selection of Milt Hinton recordings
on Chiaroscuro Records, has just
been released. Proceeds benefit the
Milton J. Hinton Scholarship Fund

Cover photo © Chuck Stewart
Design by Robert Appleton
Produced by David G. Berger and Bruce Ricker
Special thanks to Holly Maxson,
Rufus Reid and Festival Productions

Memorial service program, 2000.
(Author's collection)

everything else he had going on, Milt didn't make it to his ninety-first; he died in December 2000, but the day after what would have been his ninety-first birthday, June 24, there was a memorial service for the ages in New York City's Riverside Church. The printed program lists over eighty musicians, and that's probably an undercount. I can still remember the sound of Jon Faddis's trumpet soaring through the massive cathedral. He was out of sight, somewhere way up high toward the top of the church. It was a remarkable moment. It was also remarkable to see so many bass players in one location. There were so many instruments and similar looking soft cases they had to be labeled.

At about the same time of the service, with the help of David G. Berger, we released a special CD entitled *The Judge at His Best – 1973–1995*, drawn for the Chiaroscuro archive of seventeen different LPs and CDs on which he'd appeared. Proceeds from the sale of the CD benefited the Milton J. Hinton Scholarship Fund. And to cover all the bases, no pun intended, we slipped in a card suggesting a donation to the Jazz Foundation of America in Milt's name.

In 2003, there was another Chiaroscuro release, this time of unknown recorded material, featuring Milt leading all-star ensembles. The record was titled *The Basement Tapes* and was compiled from four all-star sessions David G. Berger had produced in 1989. Milt reprises his vocal on "Old Man Time" and his friend, Sylvia Sims, makes her only Chiaroscuro appearance.

Though he was gone, Milt remained a part of my life beyond the records and CDs and festivals. In 2005, Hans Zurbrügg invited Maggie Condon and myself to be present at a special ceremony at that year's Internationale JazzFestival Bern. Hans had produced this outstanding festival since the mid 1970s and also owns a very special hotel in that city, the Innere Enge. It is also known as the Jazz Hotel because it not only houses one of the finest jazz clubs in Europe, Marians Jazz Room, but most of the rooms in the hotel are dedicated to noted jazz musicians.

In 2005, not one but two rooms were being dedicated to Eddie Condon and filled with original memorabilia celebrating Maggie's father and my friend. We were thrilled to be there and, as it turned out, I was assigned to Room thirty-two, a room Hans and Marianne Gauer had dedicated to Milt Hinton shortly after they opened the hotel in 1992. I've returned to Bern dozens of times since then, and I've been assigned the same room so often it is almost like a home away from home.

And so, after fifty plus years, it has been impossible get away from working with and living with memories of Milt and Mona, his music and her savvy and everything else that was generous, thoughtful, and ever so wonderful about them. And why would anyone want to?

Contact sheet, 2000 memorial service. (Author's collection)

The Judge at His Best CD booklet cover. (Author's collection)

The Basement Tapes, CD booklet cover. (Author's collection)

18

Jimmy and Marian McPartland

(1907–91) & (1918–2013)

JIMMY MCPARTLAND was the first noted jazz musician I ever met. I met his wife Marian McPartland a few minutes later, really a few weeks later, but since it was so long ago it seems as if it were only minutes. It was 1965 and they were still married but pretty much leading separate lives and careers, except possibly when they met up at Squirrel Ashcraft's house. Jimmy and Marian were the first married jazz artists I'd ever known well until Bill Charlap and Renee Rosnes got together forty years later, but that's another story, and who's counting.

Despite their separate career paths, the first time I ever heard either perform they were very much together in Squirrel's living room at or near the wonderful old antique Steinway that had been specially tuned for the occasion, the occasion being the resurrection of the Informal Sessions at Squirrel's, the legendary Monday night jam sessions at his home in Evanston that began in the early 1930s and continued for about twenty years, with a short break for World War II.

The horrors of World War II disrupted and changed many lives, but one very positive result of the war was it allowed James Dougal McPartland and Margaret Marian Turner to find one another in Belgium during a USO sponsored concert in October 1944. There was a whirlwind after their initial meeting, they saw one another frequently and married in February 1945. The first time I encountered them together, it looked like this photograph.

Marian was one of two pianists who appeared that night, and as it turned out, the music she and Jimmy made were the best parts of the first record I ever "produced." It was May 1, 1966, a casual dinner party followed by an informal jam session at Squirrel Ashcraft's spacious apartment in Washington, DC. This was the first "informal session" at Squirrel's since he'd relocated to the nation's capital, and the first to be recorded since John Steiner's last effort in July 1953. Of course, Squirrel was the other pianist, but it was Marian who carried the day and performed on most of the selections that were later issued as a private recording.

The next time I set microphones in front of Jimmy and Marian was about three weeks later under very different circumstances. It was May 28 and the second day of the First Annual Manassas Jazz Festival. The festival had been organized by a prominent citizen of Manassas, who was also a rabid jazz fan, Johnson "Fat Cat" McRee. He was an exceptional CPA with a booming practice but just a modestly talented vocalist with a booming voice. He enjoyed singing with professional jazz bands and launched his own festival to do just that. I was involved because I both had access to and knew how to operate Squirrel's

OPPOSITE

Jimmy McPartland, Dick Barrett, Marian McPartland, and Squirrel Ashcraft, 1966. (Author's collection)

Ampex tape recorder and was willing to record the festival in exchange for Johnson doing my taxes.

The Saturday and Sunday afternoon concerts were to be held in the auditorium of Osbourn High School. The auditorium could seat maybe five hundred people, there was a good stage, a Steinway that could be tuned, and plenty of room and rooms backstage. But it was nearly sixty years ago and maybe I've forgotten a few of the details. I can verify some because the material I recorded on the old Ampex Fine Line F-44 quarter track tape recorder led to two releases on Jazzology Records, *On Stage* that featured Jimmy McPartland and his group and *Manassas Jazz Festival* that featured Maxine Sullivan, Doc Souchon, Cliff Jackson, and Fat Cat McRee.

The records are adequately recorded, and the performances are at least acceptable and occasionally very good. The artists on the record were all major players; in addition to Jimmy and Marian, Jake Hanna was on drums, playing hooky from Woody Herman; Ella must have been off that week because Keter Betts is on bass; Blues Alley was closed in the afternoon so Tommy Gwaltney and Steve Jordan were available; and whoever ran the paint store where he worked had given Walter "Slide" Harris the afternoon off. I wrote the liner notes for *On Stage,* and they aren't very good, but this was probably the first example of anything I'd ever written appearing in anything other than a classified CIA publication.

The other things I remember from those two days were the backstage hijinks, some of which I caught on camera. My favorite was Jake Hanna leering at Marian's ample bosom she was thrusting into his face.

But the most remarkable thing that happened that weekend, something that taught me a lesson, was to be prepared for the unexpected and when the unexpected happens, move quickly. The unexpected occurrence involved Bobby Hackett, arguably the most prominent musician at the first gathering of jazzers in Manassas.

Bobby and his group were scheduled to open the festival on Saturday. Bobby was also a fragile diabetic who had to be very careful with what he ingested, particularly in the alcohol department. On Friday night, with the encouragement of someone, he fell off the wagon and wound up under it. When he showed up on Saturday afternoon, well-dressed and looking sharp, nobody was aware of this. Everything looked OK; he had a great quartet, Marian, Keter Betts, and Jake Hanna. The Ampex was fired up, my headphones covered my ears, I pushed the record button, the musicians walked on stage, Marian played an intro to a long-forgotten song, Keter and Jake joined in, and it sounded wonderful. Then Bobby came in and it sounded awful; I looked up from the recorder and saw he looked as if he was struggling to get any kind of a sound out of his cornet. Then I saw him take a step or two back and lean against the piano, as if he were having difficulty remaining upright.

Bobby was having a diabetic attack/seizure of some sort on stage. Many of the musicians were backstage hoping to hear a great set with Bobby at his melodic best, but that's not what they heard. It was just gurgling coming out of the bell of the cornet. Jimmy was backstage and I yelled at him to go out and cover for Bobby. He grabbed his trumpet, jumped on stage and picked up the tune. I began asking if anyone had any food; a sandwich or a candy bar. No one did. At some point in the chaos I grabbed a quick picture from the wings and then left the auditorium in search of something other than alcohol that might be used to stabilize Bobby.

School was done for the year, and it was Saturday. There were no food dispensing machines in schools in those days, and when I found the cafeteria it was locked. In best true crime fashion, I broke a window, reached in and opened the door, but because school was out there wasn't a potato chip or can of beans in sight. I opened cabinets and drawers and finally got lucky; there were two large pull opens for bulk supplies. One was full of flour but the other had sugar. I filled up a coffee cup with sugar and ran back to the auditorium.

By this time, they'd gotten Bobby off stage, and he was on his back in the wings. Doc Souchon was looking after him, but Doc, though he was a medical doctor and had delivered four thousand babies in his long career, was somewhat less experienced in the diabetes department; he didn't know if Bobby was over or under. I suggested it was probably alcohol related, and Doc mixed some of the sugar with water, got it into Bobby, and disaster was averted.

Meanwhile, Jimmy had been joined onstage by the musicians he was scheduled to work with a little later, the previously mentioned Tommy Gwaltney, Slide Harris, and Steve Jordan, and they were into their set. The Ampex had been left unattended, but the reels were still spinning, and the music being made was recorded. I managed to put on a fresh reel at some point and probably only missed one or two songs. The music was eventually released on *Jazzology J-16.* I was credited as Recording Engineer: Harold O'Neal.

Jake Hanna and Marian McPartland backstage hijinks.

The *Manassas Jazz Festival* LP jacket.
(Author's collection)

On Stage LP jacket.
(Author's collection)

With Charlie Butler, Keter Betts, and Steve Jordan at Blues Alley. (Author's collection)

While Jimmy and Marian and their pals were playing a great, extended set, Bobby was carefully removed to the Downtowner Motor Inn and put to bed, where he remained for the rest of the day and managed to recover as completely as possible. He played a terrific set on Sunday. It was not recorded, but four years later, in April and May 1970, I got to record him ten nights in a row at the Roosevelt Grill, and he was magnificent. Every night. Every note.

Then it was October, and Jimmy was the featured artist for a week at Blues Alley. It was perfect timing because Squirrel Ashcraft was retiring after his many years with the CIA, and an elaborate farewell party was planned at the Ft. Myer's Officer's Club. It was set for October 17, and I was determined there should be good music. The house band at Blues Alley was wonderful: Tommy Gwaltney, Charlie Butler, John Phillips, Steve Jordan, Keter Betts, and Bertell Knox.

Jimmy was thrilled to assemble a group to celebrate Squirrel's retirement, maybe even hoping his old friend might have time to become more musically active. He managed to get most of his Blues Alley cohorts for the party, but Billy Taylor Jr. was on bass, Eddie Phyfe behind the drums, and Bill Potts held down the piano chair. Squirrel brought himself, but I brought his tape recorder and recorded the party, hoping there might be enough good performances to create a decent souvenir recording. The room was not filled with jazz fans; it was filled with overt and covert people from the CIA. But it all worked out and there were no complaints.

I was scheduled to relocate to New York City the following June in 1967, and the only people I would know in the city were Jimmy and Marian, Eddie Condon, and a used record dealer who also had a shop in Washington. Jimmy was in Merrick, New York, on the south shore on Long Island, Marian was on Eighty-Sixth Street on the east side of New York City, Eddie was on the north side of Washington Square, and Max Draisner, the record guy, was in a shop about a block from where the wonderful and much missed traditional jazz joint The Cajun used to be.

Before I moved to New York City in June, I made a one-day trip in May. The purpose was to go to a performance of the Royal Ballet at the newly opened Lincoln Center. Marian had called and said it was imperative that I attend a specific performance with her. She said she knew I would enjoy it, one that was featuring the hottest couple in the world of dance at the time, Margot Fonteyn and Rudolph Nureyev. I agreed to make the trip, but said I had to be back at my CIA desk the next morning.

And so, during the evening of a workday I was with Marian in a barely used orchestra seat at the Metropolitan Opera waiting for Fonteyn and Nureyev to astound us in *Paradise Lost*, a newly choreographed ballet that had been created for these two dancers by Roland Petit. It may have even been the premiere performance in the United States.

I was no expert in matters of dance and still am not, but even a rank amateur such as myself could tell this was not a production that would find its way into the repertory of any company, unless the company had two stars of the caliber of Fonteyn and Nureyev and they insisted on performing it. I remember the audience cheered and cheered, but I was pretty sure they would have cheered if the two stars had come on stage and danced the hokey pokey. Later I would learn *The New York Times* dance

Ashtray from Eddie Condon's 56th Street. (Author's collection)

Rudolf Nureyev and Margot Fonteyn, *Paradise Lost*, 1967. (Author's collection)

With various CIA officers, Eddie Phyfe, Steve Jordan, Billy Taylor Jr., Bill Potts, Charlie Butler, and Squirrel Ashcraft. (Author's collection)

critic Clive Barnes had trashed the piece and summed up the performance with the words: *The stars shone brightly in an otherwise empty sky*.

When the dancing was done and I was thinking about the long drive back to Washington, it turned out I wasn't leaving anytime soon. As we made our way up the aisle, Marian said something like, "We have to go backstage. We have our choice, fifteen minutes with Nureyev and fifteen minutes with Margot or half an hour with Margot." I was surprised and blurted out, "Half an hour with Fonteyn," which is exactly what happened. I don't remember all of the details, but Marian was born in 1918, Margaret Hookham (i.e., Margot Fonteyn) was born in 1919, and at some point they were classmates together as teenagers somewhere and had remained in touch.

Fonteyn was charming and wonderful, the two old friends had a nice chat, I may have said a few words more than "Please sign my program," but I did say those four and she did. I had the picture framed and fifty-eight even further years later it still looks good.

But we still weren't done. Marian insisted we head over to Eddie Condon's and have a listen to the band, and so we did that as well. She had arranged for a car that whisked us to East Fifty-Sixth Street, where she was treated like royalty. I don't remember who was on stage, only that Eddie wasn't that night, but I do remember we were seated at a table down front, next to one where Joe DiMaggio was having a serious listen. We stayed until the set ended, Marian said something to the guys on stage, but before we left, she grabbed an ashtray off our table and stuck it in her purse, a black-and-white plastic ashtray with the words EDDIE CONDON'S 330 East Fifty-sixth Street N.Y.C.

That was my first night of up close and personal music and dance in New York City. There would be many more. Somehow, I made my way to wherever I'd left my car, headed south, and arrived back in Washington in time to continue my New York City transition training. Whatever the lesson was scheduled for that day, my training the night before was far more instructive.

One of the reasons it was suggested I transfer to New York City was that it was a place to which no one wanted to be assigned. It was a city that was costly, crime-ridden, and difficult for a young government employee on a modest salary. It was impossible for one who had a wife or family because the rules of the game were that the younger officers such as myself had to live in Manhattan so as to be able to get to the office quickly if the need arose.

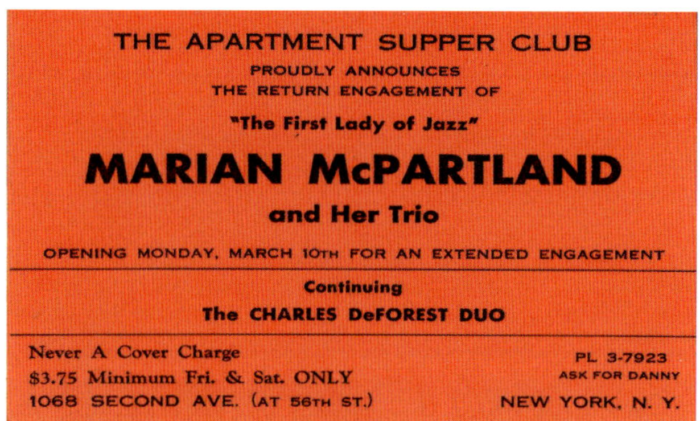

Flyer from The Apartment Supper Club. (Author's collection)

One of the first things I noticed when I arrived in New York was there was almost no interest whatsoever in musicians like Eddie Condon or Jimmy McPartland, and there were few places for them to play that offered even a subsistent wage. In fact, jazz joints of a certain sort were on their last legs, just like Broadway, struggling to get to the next month. The lights were still on at Eddie Condon's when I arrived in June, but they turned them off for good at the end of August. Marian McPartland's old haunt The Hickory House remained open long enough for me to visit it a single time; Billy Taylor was in residence, but it closed in 1968. But in mid-1967, very little was going on, and I was thrilled when one day Marian called and suggested a dinner date. She said, "Please meet me at Chan Kibbee's apartment" at such and such time and at such and such address. Chan was the CFO of Philip Morris at the time. What I didn't know was that Marian was using the dinner as an excuse to pair me up with her stepdaughter, Dorothy. She'd casually introduced me to Dorothy a month or so earlier at her apartment uptown and later told me a bit about her. A year or so later, Dorothy's former husband designed the Halcyon logo and label we used on our first record releases.

It was a lovely dinner, and the conversation bounced around nicely. Dorothy wasn't exactly a stranger, and Marian had clearly told her as much about me as she'd told me about her. And then after more chit chat and desert, Marian announced she and Chan were going out to have a listen to Charles DeForest, a wonderful pianist who often shared the bill with Marian during her long residencies at The Apartment on Second Avenue. As Marian and Chan exited, her parting words were something like, "You kids have a good time."

After a few looks and some conversation, we decided the

With his daughter, Dorothy.
(Author's collection)

In his backyard in Merrick, New York, 1968.
(Author's collection)

best place to do that would be where we were, and we continued to have a good time well into mid-1968, whenever Dorothy's business or other commitments brought her from Chicago to New York City. We probably both assumed that night would be a onetime brief encounter, but we were wrong and enjoyed one another very much in the coming months. I have no idea if either Jimmy or Marian were aware of what was going on, but then sometime in June 1968 the telephone rang. Dorothy was on the other end. She said she wasn't coming to New York any longer, and while it had been wonderful being together when she was in New York, she was going to Mexico with "Mr. Right" and would probably stay there forever.

I was surprised. I knew Dorothy had been married twice in the past, and I said I hoped number three would be the charm. We chatted a bit more about nothing in particular, good luck and that kind of thing, and this was the last time I ever spoke with her. A few weeks later at the end of July the telephone rang again, and it was Jimmy this time, crying and mumbling, upset and barely intelligible. I didn't get the whole story from Jimmy, he was far too upset to tell me, but the bottom line was Dorothy was dead. I didn't know what to think or even how to react. I certainly didn't want to say anything that would further upset Jimmy, and I didn't really have any details other than she was dead in Mexico; the first woman I'd ever been with in my inexperienced twenty-eight-year-old life who had died unexpectedly or otherwise. I later learned some of the details from Marian.

Dorothy was troubled and had a turbulent relationship with various men, at least one of whom was Mexican. They had married but things didn't work out, and at some point in late July Dorothy had swallowed a bottle of sleeping pills at a remote location in Mexico. By the time she was taken to a local hospital it was impossible to save her. This tragedy was the beginning of a series of other complicated events with Marian and Jimmy that would ultimately resolve in the fall.

A few months before the tragedy of Dorothy unfolded, much to everyone's surprise, a club calling itself The Downbeat opened at Forty-Second Street and Lexington Avenue. Even more surprising, the club was to have a mainstream jazz policy, and one of the mainstreamers it booked was Jimmy McPartland. He was excited to get a booking at the new club and was working hard to get in shape for what all hoped would be a triumphant return at a fancy venue.

Marian had encouraged Jimmy to become a wagoner and it was working, but then one day there was unexpected trouble. Marian called on a Saturday morning and asked if I would take a drive with her to visit Jimmy in Merrick. My date book was empty, so I was happy to take a ride but wondered what was up and asked. It seemed as though Jimmy had fallen off the wagon, and Marian had not been able to reach him for a week or so. She was worried about what she might find on Webster Avenue.

She was driving her old New York City street clunk, but it made it to Merrick. We pulled up in front of 41 West Webster. Nothing looked out of place from the street, and Marian said, "I'll take the front, you go around back." I did as I was told, climbed the steps to the back porch, and looked in the kitchen door. Jimmy was standing in the kitchen, maybe he was moving around, maybe he wasn't, but movement wasn't the issue. He was wearing nothing but boxer shorts, had the 1968 equivalent of a 7-Eleven Big Gulp in one hand, filled with something other than Coca-Cola, and a pistol in the other. It was not a pretty sight.

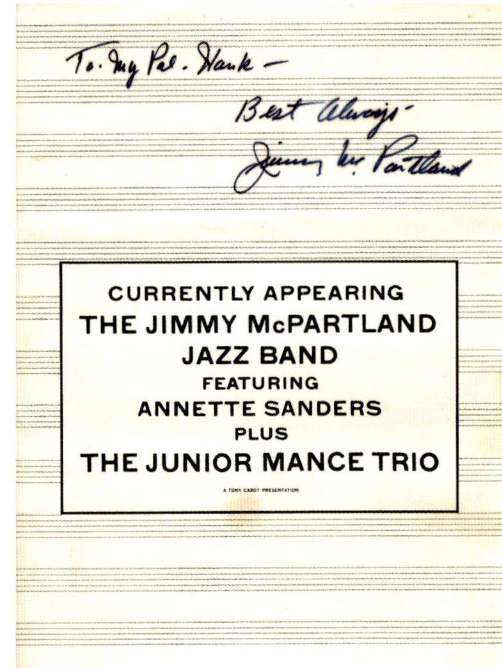

I tapped on the window, mustered up a smile, waved cheerfully, and went in. Jimmy wasn't in good shape but handed me the pistol without too much encouragement. Marian appeared a few moments later and managed to commandeer what was left in the faux Big Gulp, maneuvered him into a chair in the living room and before worrying about what had caused him to fall off the wagon, made a call to a tank that had been used in the past, requesting an emergency treatment for a returning customer. Jimmy was due to open at the Downbeat in less than ten days.

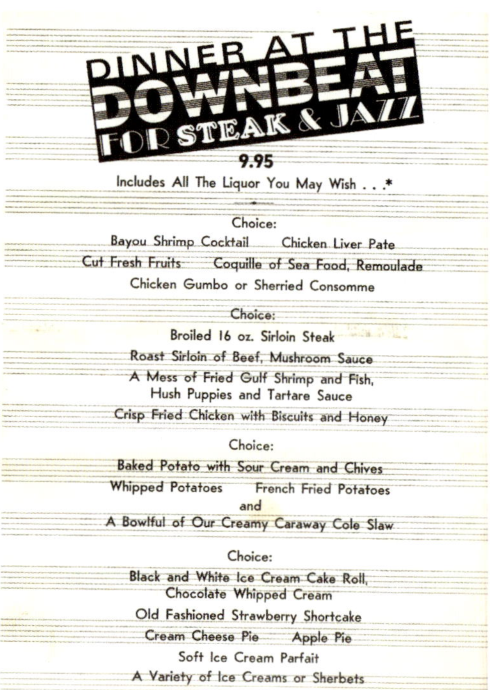

Downbeat program and menu. (Author's collection)

It all worked out. With the help of the tankers, Jimmy got back in shape and played the date without a hitch. Marian was a little worried going in, so Pee Wee Erwin was hired as a second cornet for the Tuesday night opening. It was nice to hear Jimmy and Pee Wee together, but Jimmy was in full control.

It was a crazy couple of months, first with Dorothy's death and then Jimmy's collapse, but when the story came out about what had happened to Jimmy it was more remarkable. He was a bit of a fitness and exercise nut and was serious about getting in shape and staying there. Jimmy's home in Merrick was just a few miles from Jones Beach, and there were a couple of places that were even closer. He'd been going for a swim each morning, then returning home, exercising, push-ups, and that kind of thing, and then getting down to serious practice with the horn.

One morning he got up, went to the beach, had his swim, came home and exercised like crazy, and then grabbed his horn. But he had exercised a little too much, a few sets too many of real push-ups, and when he put his horn to his lips his arms were trembling and he couldn't stop the shakes. It never occurred to him it was over-exercise, he assumed it was under alcohol, took a drink and pretty soon he was not just off the wagon, he was under it. But the cure to make the Downbeat date worked; he never had another drink for over twenty years. He never played the club again because by 1970 it had become a rocker's venue.

I do not have any recollection of Jimmy's vocalist, Annette Sanders, but this was when I first became aware of Junior Mance. Some years later he became a regular performer at the Floating Jazz Festival; we worked together a great deal beginning in the early 1990s, all the way through his retirement in the 2010s. I also have no recollection of what happened to the pistol I took from Jimmy in his kitchen. In those days there were very strict rules about handguns in New York City. I may have violated them for a minute or two, but at some point the pistol went away. Maybe I stashed it in the vault at my office.

I spent far more time with Marian in the late 1960s and early 1970s than Jimmy because she was very active in town, and the more I learned about her and the various activities in which she was involved and the obstacles she'd overcome to do so, the more impressed I became. What obstacles? Just think about it. In 1967, jazz was for guys. Sure, there were a handful of females, but very few stars. Plus, Marian was white, non-American, and married to a very traditional musician who came to prominence in the 1920s. She'd overcome all these problems and had become the celebrated artist, Marian McPartland. I thought this was remarkable.

There was also another reason; we were also involved together because of the legendary Sherman Fairchild. Marian had known Sherman for many years because he was a piano fan and a super fan of hers. I knew Sherman because one of his many companies was involved with highly classified work that was important to certain activities of the CIA.

There is no easy way to verify the exact day I met Sherman at his home at 17 East Sixty-Fifth Street, but it was probably in early 1968. At the time my interest was in Fairchild Camera and Instrument, an outgrowth of Fairchild Aerial Surveys, a company he'd launched in the late 1920s. I was unaware he'd also started a company called Fairchild Recording Products in 1931–32, and in 1968 some of the equipment this company made was still the gold standard in the recording industry, notably its compressors and limiters. I was also unaware he had a recording studio and two Steinway pianos at the Sixty-Fifth Street address. But we hit it off beyond the overhead cameras and within a few months I was teaching myself how to use all the equipment in his home studio.

Interplay LP jacket. (Author's collection)

I don't remember the first time Marian and I met with Sherman together, nor do I remember the first recording project I undertook at Sherman's studio, but sometime in 1968 Marian sat down at the piano, I sat behind a console in the control room, and the ultimate result was completing a wonderful record she had begun some months earlier at another studio. Marian had picked out a name for her own label, Halcyon, and this new recording was to be its first release. It was a duo, Marian accompanied by Linc Milliman on bass. Someone had the idea to call the album *Interplay* and it stuck.

Marian had a terrific photo of her hands she wanted to use on the cover and that stuck as well. Everyone had so much fun with the project we decided to launch a new record company, one that would use Marian's label name, and would be a three-way partnership between Sherman, Marian, and myself. We each contributed $500 to the enterprise, and while this didn't impact Marian and certainly not Sherman who funded everything a zillion times beyond the $500, I was saddled with the CIA salary shorts and I'm sure I took the subway home, where I managed to cobble together the $500 entry fee. One of our first projects was a trio date with Michael Moore on bass (his debut recording) and Billy Hart on drums. This album was released as *Ambience* and fifty-three years later, in May 2023, I gave a still-sealed copy to soon to be eighty-

Marilynn Danitz, Marian, and myself as seen by Sherman Fairchild in his living room in 1970.

three-year-old Billy Hart. He was pleased to have it.

We got to work and ultimately released four LPs and recorded material for two additional releases. All the recording for the released LPs was done at the Sixty-Fifth Street studio, except for Willie "The Lion" Smith, which was done at Blues Alley in Washington, DC. We were very proud of our accomplishments and created a flyer to announce our four new releases.

It was amazing; everyone from Duke Ellington to Bill Evans to Count Basie were rolling logs for us. Plus, John Hammond, who'd brought Bobby Henderson to our attention, and George Simon, the big band authority who dipped his toe into the world of solo piano for a minute, also weighed in. It seemed to be going very nicely, and all parties were happy, but in the background the blues were brewing.

The three of us had a common goal, but each of us also had a separate agenda and all were perfectly legitimate. Marian wanted to record herself in a variety of different

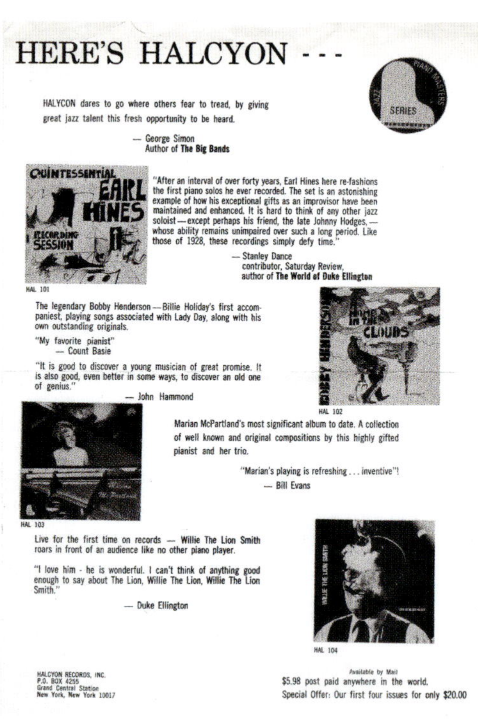

HERE'S HALCYON - - -

JAZZ PIANO MASTERS SERIES

HALYCON dares to go where others fear to tread, by giving great jazz talent this fresh opportunity to be heard.

— George Simon
Author of **The Big Bands**

"After an interval of over forty years, Earl Hines here re-fashions the first piano solos he ever recorded. The set is an astonishing example of how his exceptional gifts as an improvisor have been maintained and enhanced. It is hard to think of any other jazz soloist—except perhaps his friend, the late Johnny Hodges,—whose ability remains unimpaired over such a long period. Like those of 1928, these recordings simply defy time."

— Stanley Dance
contributor, Saturday Review,
author of **The World of Duke Ellington**

HAL 101

The legendary Bobby Henderson—Billie Holiday's first accompaniest, playing songs associated with Lady Day, along with his own outstanding originals.

"My favorite pianist"
— Count Basie

"It is good to discover a young musician of great promise. It is also good, even better in some ways, to discover an old one of genius."

— John Hammond

HAL 102

Marian McPartland's most significant album to date. A collection of well known and original compositions by this highly gifted pianist and her trio.

"Marian's playing is refreshing . . . inventive"!
— Bill Evans

HAL 103

Live for the first time on records — **Willie The Lion Smith** roars in front of an audience like no other piano player.

"I love him - he is wonderful. I can't think of anything good enough to say about The Lion, Willie The Lion, Willie The Lion Smith."

— Duke Ellington

HAL 104

HALCYON RECORDS, INC.
P.O. BOX 4255
Grand Central Station
New York, New York 10017

Available by Mail
$5.98 post paid anywhere in the world.
Special Offer: Our first four issues for only $20.00

The first Halcyon flyer, 1970.
(Author's collection)

settings and advance her career. I wanted to record every good pianist in town, from the famous such as Earl Hines and Marian to the unknown like Bobby Henderson. And Sherman, who was funding all our activities, just wanted to hear some good music and have a good time, and then suddenly he wasn't because Marian was unhappy that I was reaching out to too many other pianists and even bands. Of course, she was right; I thought one out of four was a good mix (actually two out of five if you count *Interplay*), but she didn't and voiced her frustration one time too often.

Sherman decided the best thing to do was put things on hold in the fall of 1970, return to Marian her label name, all the master tapes, and rights to HAL 103, *Ambience*, the master tapes for the as yet unreleased duet album featuring Marian with Teddy Wilson, and her initial investment of $500. Then the two remaining partners would go it alone, reissue the other three albums with another label name and move forward in an as yet undeveloped business plan.

How this plan developed is long and complicated and is completely documented in the book *The Chiaroscuro Story*. The initial driving force in the unraveling is that Sherman underwent a minor surgery in February 1971, became infected in the hospital, which was undetected, and died in March. It is a tragic story, one told elsewhere, but I wound up with what was left of the record company for $500.

Marian clowning at the piano, 1970.
(Author's collection)

I had limited contact with Jimmy or Marian for the next two decades. I wasn't angry but Marian was, and since Jimmy was struggling, I kept my distance. Then something peculiar happened. In February 1991, almost twenty years to the day when Sherman had his fateful surgery in 1971, the New Jersey Jazz Society decided to give both Marian and me a lifetime achievement prize at the annual Pee Wee Russell Memorial Stomp. The traditional jazz Jersey Boys had no idea we were supposed to hate one another and put us at a table together for the stomp on February 24. There were no fireworks; in fact, all was very cordial. The only downside was that Jimmy wasn't present. He was feeling poorly.

Then something even more unusual happened; less than a week after the stomp and the prizes, Marian and Jimmy remarried. And about a minute or two after that, the telephone rang; it was Marian, who told me the news and that Jimmy wanted to say hello. It had been a long time. We chatted for a while and caught up about this and that, and then Marian returned to the telephone. We spoke a bit more and she told me Jimmy was failing and the cancer was galloping. He died a week or so later on March 13.

Marian and I stayed in touch sporadically during the 1990s. I tried to convince her to be part of a Floating Jazz Festival, but there was always an excuse. Never a no, just an excuse; it was legitimate, she was very busy towards the end of her career. The last time I heard her perform in person was the spectacular tribute to Oscar Peterson in Carnegie Hall on June 8, 2007. She was only eightnine, and in very good form that day. She lasted another six years, and her performances and hosting of NPR's *Piano Jazz* continued until November 2011. She had a long run as a radio host. I was with her during the broadcast of some of her shows from the WBAI studios in 1967 and 1968. I was even on one of her broadcasts probably saying something inane.

I have always wondered what would have happened if we hadn't gone in different directions. Maybe she did as well. It all worked out for both of us in the end, and one result is there is still a great deal of good music to listen to, music that came out of a fair amount of turmoil. But when Earl or Bobby or Willie or Marian begin to play, the turmoil goes away pretty quickly. At least it does for me.

19

Gerry Mulligan

April 6, 1927 – January 20, 1996

GERRY MULLIGAN was the last person who ever sang "Happy Birthday" to me. He's lucky he played his saxophone better than he sang. So am I.

I'm not sure when I first became aware of Gerry in terms of hearing him on record. I had copies of at least two of the Capitol 78 rpm discs from what has become known as the *Birth of the Cool* date, and I'd read a bit about him because by 1956 I had one book, Hugh Panassie's *Guide to Jazz,* and a booklet, *Jazz Americana* by Woody Woodward. Gerry was mentioned in both, and many of his records were listed in the Woodward booklet. But the record that really got my attention was the soundtrack of a nasty melodrama, *I Want to Live!*, in which Gerry led a band that played the music Johnny Mandel had written

I saw the film at a long-forgotten theater in Troy, New York, loved the music, and bought an LP entitled *The Jazz Combo* from *I Want to Live!* The now sixty-seven-year-old album I bought when I was a freshman at Rensselaer Polytechnic Institute is tattered and split at the bottom. I just pulled it off the shelf where it has lived all these years and noticed for the first time the cover illustration was designed by Paul Bacon, who would later become a friend and design CD booklets for Chiaroscuro and dust jackets for my books and posters for the Floating Jazz Festival, a yearly event we produced and at which Gerry made his last public appearance in 1995. The LP I bought sixty-seven years ago is still filled with the great music I first heard in 1958, and even though I've never revisited the movie, I've heard the music frequently. I downloaded a CD to my computer and the main title is playing as I write these words, and the cover designed by Paul Bacon is featured in a chapter in this book.

I saw Gerry and his Concert Jazz Band in 1960, but until 1976, I only knew him through his many recordings. Then things changed. This was a transitional year for Chiaroscuro, Downtown Sound, and my life in general. This was the year I resigned from my position with the Central Intelligence Agency, met Gerry Mulligan, and made a recording of his "New Sextet," all in the month of October. I don't remember what came first, the resignation or the recording. This is how the meeting and recording came about.

In late summer of 1976, New York City's then-busiest drummer, Bobby Rosengarden, was at Downtown Sound with a client. After the session, we began talking and Bobby suggested he was working with a new group, and they needed a rehearsal space and wondered if my studio might be available. I said Downtown Sound wasn't available for rehearsals unless it was for a group I wanted to record. He said the group was Gerry Mulligan's "New Sextet." That was different; I was a fan first and being a studio owner was in a distant third place, after the record company. Gerry and his new sexteters came in a few minutes or weeks later, and we had a good time for the next twenty years. A few days ago, a post turned up in my inbox from the Gerry and Franca Mulligan Foundation,

OPPOSITE

Gerry Mulligan liner portrait, 1976. (Author's collection)

Guide to Jazz. (Author's collection)

Jazz Americana. (Author's collection)

and it still features my nose-to-nose portrait of Franca and Gerry. Some things don't change, and that is nice.

One thing led to another, and Gerry's new group made a spectacular recording, one that took much longer than any of us anticipated. In some ways, however, this worked out nicely for everyone because it enabled me to see Gerry at work over a sustained period, get to know him better, and prove to him I wasn't an idiot.

About the same time Gerry was creating the music for the album we later named *Idol Gossip*, I was developing ideas with George Avakian about the possibility of launching a new record label in the not too distant future. The future came faster than any of us anticipated when I sold Chiaroscuro to Audiofidelity Enterprises in 1978, and by 1979 George and I embarked on a series of projects with an array of exceptional artists. The most exceptional of artists was Gerry, and he brought six projects to the table. He even had a name for his records, *The Sunflower Series*.

Gerry had four existing masters he wanted to release and two new projects he wanted to undertake. The older projects were a concert from the Olympia (Paris) Theater in 1957 with his piano-less quartet, with Bob Brookmeyer, Joe Benjamin, and Dave Bailey; a forty plus minute encounter from 1962 with Paul Desmond; a live quartet date from 1973 with Junior Mance, Bill Pemberton, and Oliver Jackson; and one or more LPs from live material he recorded with his "new sextet" in 1975. This group was slightly different from the *Idol Gossip* group. It featured John Scofield on guitar and Bill Goodwin on drums.

The most interesting project Gerry and I undertook was a big band project that began on May 18, 1978. The entry in the studio log for 1:00 p.m. that day reads, *Gerry Mulligan (big band rehearsal)*. The rehearsals and, ultimately, recording and remixing continued until the album was released.

Idol Gossip LP jacket. (Author's collection)

The project grew out of a conversation Gerry and I had one day during which he lamented that he had never won a Grammy. Oscar Peterson won for soloist that year and Chick Corea won for best jazz group. Saxophonists Al Cohn, Dexter Gordon, Stan Getz, and Phil Woods had been nominated. The previous year Oscar and Phil had won, while John Coltrane and Dexter had been nominated. He thought his own *Idol Gossip* was very good and wondered why it wasn't even nominated. "What do I have to do to win a Grammy," he asked and without too much thought, I blurted out, "Make a record just to win a Grammy." He was intrigued and probably asked something like, "How do you do that?" and I suggested he should make an exceptional record that could be nominated in a category that wasn't crowded. I said he should put together a version of his old Concert Jazz Band with great younger musicians, write some terrific originals, and when the time comes it can be nominated for the Best Jazz Instrumental Performance: Big Band.

Gerry thought this was a fine idea, and because of the availability of Downtown Sound, we were able to get to work immediately. The first rehearsal to the final recording took nearly two years. The various discographies and even a CD release claims the recording date as September 1980, but this is incorrect; it was much earlier in the year. The studio logs show between January 4 and February 23 Gerry was at Downtown Sound recording and mixing for fifty-eight hours. Later, he spent the afternoon and early evening at the studio on March 1 and March 8 doing some patches and beginning and completing the second of our joint projects, a solo piano album, which in 2025 remains unissued.

There was a bonus to all this activity in 1979 and 1980, and that was a photo session one afternoon that led to a portrait of Gerry and Franca Rota that remains one of her favorites to this day. It is the nose-to-nose picture on the "wall of clouds" at the studio. Johnny DeVries, a skilled artist, as well as fan and acquaintance of René Magritte, painted the wall, and I used it as a backdrop for portraits for almost four years. He also designed many LP and CD covers for me, including *Idol Gossip*, and later created the cover design for Gerry's big band adventure.

Pegasus Records and the Gerry Mulligan Sunflower series didn't work out. It failed because in 1979–80 George Avakian and I couldn't find anyone at a major or semi-major record company who cared enough about what we were doing to offer us a pressing and distribution deal. I knew in early 1980 the record Gerry was creating would have to find a home elsewhere, which he ultimately did with Hugh Fordin's DRG Records. Hugh issued the record in 1980, in time to make the cutoff for Grammy nominations.

When the five nominations were announced for Best Jazz Instrumental Performance, Big Band they were: Gerry Mulligan, Toshiko Akiyoshi/Lew Tabackin, Panama Francis, Rob McConnell, and Don Menza. Gerry Mulligan and *Walk on the Water* won. I was not surprised, and Gerry even got over the mistake in the album's title pretty quickly. His composition was entitled *Walk on Water*, not *Walk on the Water*. Copies can be found here and there, but it is no longer in print.

In the spring of 1981, my new record venture, Hammond Music Enterprises, got an unexpected infusion of cash that was substantial enough to allow both John and me to begin working on a project. John wanted to undertake a solo project with the Czech/Polish pianist Adam Makowicz, and I wanted to do a small band date with Gerry and Dave Grusin. John eventually turned the Makowicz date over to me, and I turned it into a trio date with Adam, George Mraz, and Jack DeJohnette.

The Gerry/Grusin date was far more complicated, expensive, and took forever. It began rather modestly in April 1981, a session with Gerry, Dave, Jay Leonhart, and Butch Miles, but it grew exponentially, with horn and saxophone sections. I came to think of it as just how many studios can we use to complete one CD? At one time or another we found ourselves at A&R, Right Track, Electric Lady, and The Review Room. The label and inlay card says it was produced by Gerry Mulligan and Hank O'Neal, but that is an exaggeration; it was an eighties overproduction with almost every track overdubbed and extremely

With Franca Rota at Downtown Sound, 1979. (Author's collection)

Clowning on wedding day. (Author's collection)

Walk on the Water, LP jacket. (Author's collection)

Little Big Horn, LP jacket. (Author's collection)

complicated. Only one track from the under-produced acoustic session in April 1981, "Sun on the Stairs," made the cut.

By the time Gerry and Dave were satisfied with all the music, HME had the shorts, and the master tapes were sold to Dave Grusin to pay the rent or the telephone bill or whatever. *Little Big Horn* was released on GRP, the label Dave and Larry Rosen owned jointly. Like *Walk on Water*, it is also out of print, but depending on the day, if you check eBay there are copies available. On the day I'm writing this, there are thirteen copies of *Walk on Water* ($3.99–$29.87) and thirty copies of *Little Big Horn* ($4.00–$95.95).

Then it was June 5, 1982, and Gerry and Franca had decided to get married at the home of a close friend, the art dealer Marisa Del Re. I was scheduled to be both in the wedding party and to be introduced to someone they thought I should know and was encouraged to come solo that day. It was quite a party, and introductions were made, music was played, mostly by an elegant string quartet, and lots of photographs were taken. One of my favorites was one of Gerry clowning with one of Marisa's sculptures.

Gerry was in an expansive mood that day, and at one point he stopped the proceedings and stood with the string quartet. I expected him to offer a toast or a loving remark to his new bride, but instead he had prearranged for the piano-less quartet to play "Happy Birthday," which he aimed in my direction and even sang to me. When he finished, and I managed to crawl out from under the rock to which I'd retreated when he began crooning, I eventually gathered up my camera bag and what was left of my dignity and went home as I came, solo.

And the years danced by, and we talked and laughed and socialized. Then one weekend in early January 1985, Shelley and I went up to visit Gerry and Franca at their home in Darien, Connecticut. It grew late and they suggested we stay over, and we did. At some point Gerry asked what our plans were for the next day, and I said we were going to an afternoon concert at the Church of Heavenly Rest, that it was just a trio, but one made up of Zoot Sims, Al Cohn, and Dave McKenna. He recognized immediately that those three guys would be making musical magic that afternoon at the church, that all those in attendance would be resurrected in one way or another, and asked sheepishly, "Do you think they'd let me sit in?" I said something like, "What do you think?"

We drove down the next day. It turned out it was the last time the legendary duo of Zoot and Al played together. Zoot was frail and failing, but he sounded like a million bucks. I was lucky; he always did when I heard him. So did Gerry, he played the entire second set, and it was a unique musical adventure. There had never been a quartet like that one. I grabbed a few photographs for my scrapbook.

It was like Louis and Bix and Jabbo and Earl in a band, all together, making it up as they went along and astounding one another as they did. And the good news was that it was recorded, and maybe one day someone will issue it. I know where the master tape lives and it's safe.

After the concert we returned to 830, but the music wasn't over, except the music that was made was completely unexpected. Gerry, Franca, Shelley, and I were talking about something when Gerry said he had to make an urgent telephone call, something he'd forgotten to help someone with. I suggested he go into my little office where he could have a bit of privacy. He vanished into my cubbyhole and, I presume, got on the telephone and called whomever.

Franca, Shelley, and I resumed discussing the upcoming Floating Jazz Festival at which Gerry was scheduled to appear with a specially assembled 1985 edition of the Concert Jazz Band when suddenly we heard music coming from my office. It wasn't the radio or a record; it was live and rather nice. It was Gerry playing a clarinet, but not just any clarinet. It was Shelley's clarinet, one I kept as a prop, a joke. It was made of real rubber, a kid's clarinet from when she was in grade school. It was dirty and dusty, there was but half a reed, and it was twenty years hardened. And here was Gerry, making it sound just fine. I had once taken silly pictures of him playing a cornet inside a large plastic garment bag. My guess is Gerry could have found a way to make music out of the toothpick Valery Gergiev used to hold in his hand when conducting the Metropolitan Opera Orchestra.

Then there was the day the scrapbook turned up, a remarkable, totally unexpected occurrence. 830 Broadway is located next to 828 Broadway, the address of The Strand, the finest bookstore in New York City. The third floor has both offices and The Rare Book Room. At the time, Craig Anderson was in charge of rare books, and he telephoned and said something had come in he felt I should see. I went next door and had a look.

Craig pulled out an old scrapbook, the kind sold at five and dimes in the 1940s and 1950s, the ones with cheap, crumbling acid-laced paper and an equally crumbly cardboard binding. He said it had come in downstairs where people sell used books; downstairs had priced it at $20.00 and sent it up to him to deal with. It was a Gerry Mulligan

With Carson Smith, Chico Hamilton, and Chet Baker, as seen by William Claxton.

With Dave McKenna, Zoot Simm, and Al Cohn. (Author's collection)

mid-1940s through mid-1950s scrapbook, filled with pictures, programs, clippings, copyrights, flyers, tickets, and whatever pieces of paper he decided to keep at the time. The only thing I could figure was that sometime in the mid-1950s Gerry may have suddenly terminated a relationship and left the scrapbook behind, and now thirty years later it was brought to The Strand. I paid the $20.00 and carried the scrapbook to 830.

I looked at every page carefully and was astounded. There were multiple copies of original photographs of Gerry and Chet by Bill Claxton, original copyright documents from the copyright office in Washington, and programs for concerts as far back as the late 1940s. There was even a ticket to a dance at a high school somewhere in Pennsylvania. I decided to have a little fun. I picked out three or four items that had a date attached to them and called Gerry. After some chitchat I tossed out a question like, "Hey, Gerry, where were you on October 23, 1947?" or "Tell me about the time you played a dance at such and such a school," or "Do you remember when you got your copyright on 'Walkin' Shoes?'" And when he didn't know the answer, I'd tell him the date.

He got very excited very quickly, and I told him what I'd found next door. He went nuts. He hadn't seen the scrapbook in thirty years and couldn't wait to revisit the past. A week or so later, we drove up to Darien and I gave him the book. He in turn gave me a couple of pictures he already had. The famous one of him with the Three "Cs," Chet, Chico, and Carson, is on my office wall about three feet away. He never told me how the scrapbook got away from him, but it was probably a lot simpler than how it made its way back to him.

Later that year, Gerry stepped aboard the *S/S Norway* and stayed for two weeks, performing with his big band, with his quartet, and almost everyone else on board. There was one set with the legendary much older eighty-year-old Art Hodes that was particularly wonderful. Another night, he added Al Cohn to his quartet, and every saxophone player on the ship got a lesson. The big band played concerts in the theater, and Gerry relaxed on sun deck when we were anchored in the Virgin Islands.

Then time passed, and we weren't on a ship with Gerry for almost ten years. But when we lured him back to sea, it wasn't on the *S/S Norway* but on the *Sovereign of the Seas*. We had organized an alternative spring festival we called the Ultimate Caribbean Jazz Spectacular, and we wanted Gerry to help us launch it. He was happy to do so; we shared a table at dinner for seven nights and had a wonderful time together.

Concert Jazz Band at The Floating Jazz Festival, 1985. (Author's collection)

Aboard the S/S *Norway* 1985.

Gerry was onboard with his working quartet that featured Ted Rosenthal, Ron Vincent, and Dean Johnson. All the music they made was remarkable, but that wasn't the most remarkable music Gerry made that week at sea. What happened was totally unexpected.

In the early 1990s, I'd managed to convince a legendary big band leader from the 1930s who had not led a big band for almost forty years to come aboard the *S/S Norway* for one of our annual Big Bands at Sea festivals. The man was Erskine Hawkins. He'd been in residence at the Concord Hotel since the mid-1950s, where he served as the hotel's music director. He had broken up his big band in the early 1950s; the big band era was over, he was tired of the road, and he opted for the security offered by the Concord. But the Hawk was intrigued by the possibility

The Erskine Hawkins Orchestra, 1994. (Author's collection)

of standing in front of a big band again and seeing people dance to "Tuxedo Junction" and other hits he'd had in the 1930s and 1940s. He had so much fun he came back regularly to Big Bands at Sea and the Floating Jazz Festival. We asked him to be a part of our new festival in 1994. But what we didn't count on was that the Hawk would die in late 1993.

We had never had a headliner die that close to a festival and discussed the situation with his niece and star vocalist, Asa Harris. She said she hoped the band could come on and perform; she would lead it for her uncle, and she had access to all the charts. We agreed to this, and when we set sail on April 2 all the men and women who were to be part of the Hawk's big band were onboard. But there was a problem. Asa was perfectly capable of standing in front of the band, counting off songs and singing them when appropriate, but she had never rehearsed a band in her life. Many of these men had never even seen, let alone played, any of the arrangements. It was a sticky situation but one that was solved in a flash when I mentioned the

With Asa Harris aboard the *Sovereign of the Seas*, 1994. (Author's collection)

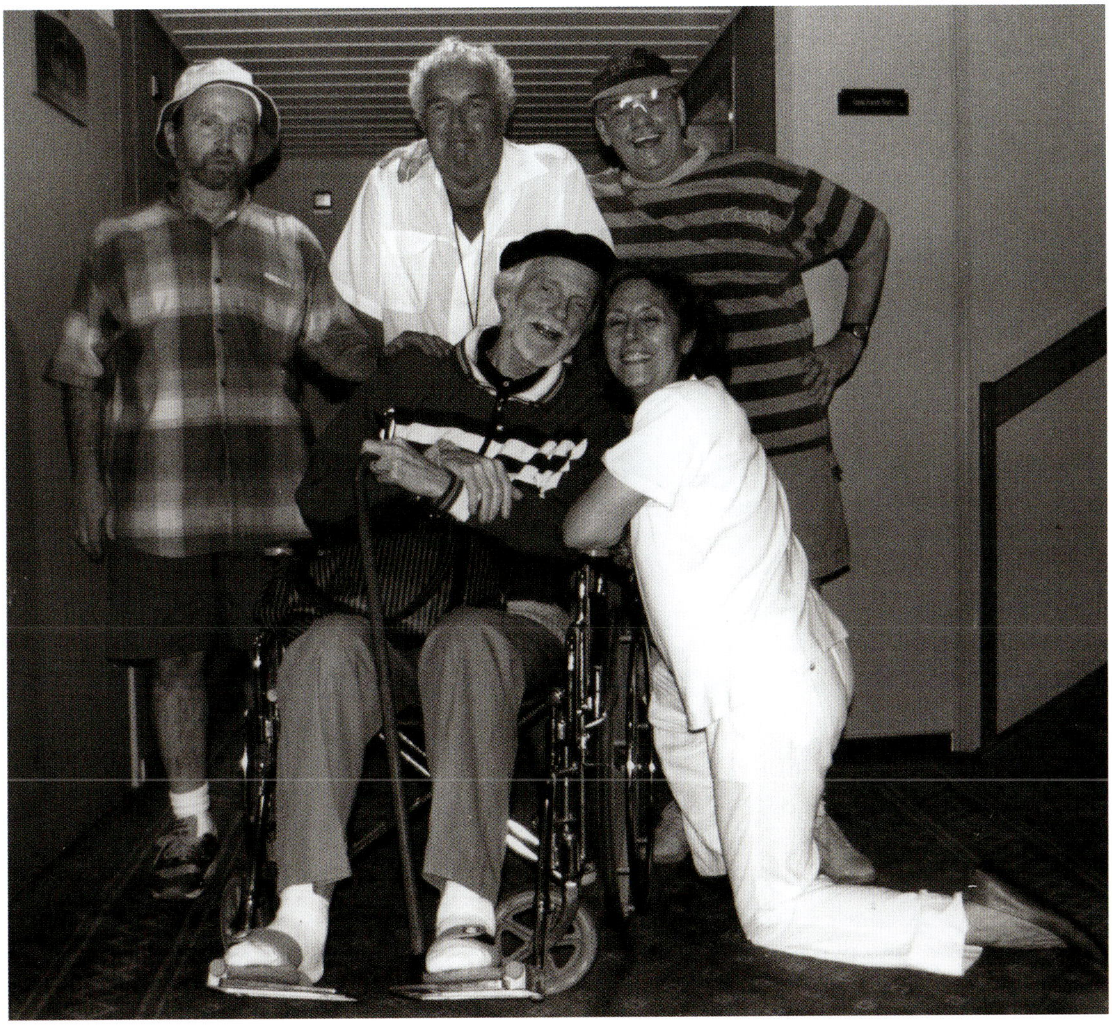

With Johnny Mandel, Gene Lees, Phil Woods, and Franca Rota aboard the S/S *Norway*, November, 1995. (Author's collection)

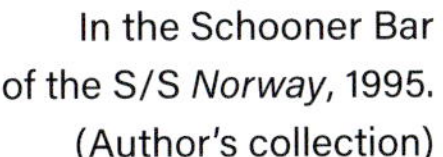

In the Schooner Bar of the S/S *Norway*, 1995. (Author's collection)

problem to Gerry. He said he'd not only rehearse the band but would really enjoy doing it. He loved nothing more than playing older big band charts he had never seen but had probably heard in his youth. And if necessary, he might even sit in with the band. As it turned out, the last performances of the Erskine Hawkins Orchestra were led by his niece, performed by a band that was rehearsed and structured by Gerry Mulligan. It was a lovely moment, and those at the festival were thrilled to witness such a unique occurrence.

A few months later we began to assemble the artists for the 1995 Floating Jazz Festival aboard the *S/S Norway*. We planned to call the 1995 festival "Celebrations" and invite musicians with special birthdays, Clark Terry at seventy-five, Flip Phillips at eighty, and Milt Hinton at eighty-five. We thought it would also be appropriate to ask Gerry; this was the tenth anniversary of his first appearance on the ship. And besides, he really liked ships. He said he'd be happy to come aboard and be part of the festivities.

What we didn't know, and Gerry probably didn't either, was that his health was becoming increasingly precarious. By the time we were scheduled to set sail in November, he boarded the ship in a wheelchair. We had discussed his failing health ahead of time, and Gerry made it very clear he wanted to be aboard, but we did arrange for a light performance schedule, just two concerts in the Saga Theater.

It was quite a wonderful week at sea; sixty of the finest jazz artists in the world were performing all day and all night long as well as interacting with one another socially. Gerry was very much a part of this mix, even though he wasn't running on a full tank. He was always thin, but in November 1995 he was positively gaunt. Yet on most days he made his way to the Schooner Bar, a tiny outpost with a piano that was pretty much soundproof, where he could work on new compositions and visit with old friends, of whom there were many. One friend who came on board unannounced was Johnny Mandel from the *I Want to Live!* days. Johnny and other pals like Phil Woods and Gene Lees often signed on for wheelchair duty to make sure Gerry had no problem getting from here to there or anywhere he wanted to be. It kind of reminded me of Percy Grainger pushing Frederick Delius around or hauling him up a mountain in Norway to see one last sunrise.

And then it was time for the two concerts in the theater, 8:45 and 10:45, November 9, a night at sea. The team onboard dressed the stage beautifully, making use of backdrops and scenery from the shows they normally presented when the Floating Jazz Festival was not on board. Gerry was seated throughout the concert, and the group played magnificently. Some people who heard the late show and were in a position to know said they'd never heard him sound better. It was his last public performance. He died on January 20, slightly more than two months later.

But the Gerry Mulligan Quartet wasn't quite done. A bit of trivia: in his last years the group was normally billed as Gerry Mulligan and the Gerry Mulligan Quartet. In the fall of 1995, there had been some discussion of a Gerry Mulligan songbook recording. It's ironic that in the early days the Gerry Mulligan quartet was often pianoless. If a piano was required and a well-tuned instrument was available, Gerry, or later Bob Brookmeyer, would sit in on piano.

For the last decade of his life, Gerry's group had either Bill Charlap or Ted Rosenthal on piano. On June 6 and 7 1996, Bill and Ted joined forces at two matched Steinway D pianos in Rudy Van Gelder's Englewood Cliffs studio, and with Dean Johnson and Ron Vincent created a Gerry Mulligan Quartet, this time with two pianos instead of none. Over two days they produced ten exceptional recordings of Gerry's compositions he had picked out in 1995. It was a day-late wedding anniversary present to Franca.

Forty years earlier, Paul Bacon had created the graphics and design for the *I Want to Live!* recording, and in 1996 he created the design for the CD booklet. We were happy he chose to include the ghost of Gerry on the cover, making certain everything was being done properly. And it was.

The last performance, November 1995.
(Author's collection)

The Gerry Mulligan Songbook CD booklet, 1996.
(Author's collection)

Gibson

20

Les Paul

June 9, 1915 – August 12, 2009

I KNEW LES PAUL for almost five decades, and try as I might, I was never able to hire him a single time. It's an amusing and complicated story that began sometime in 1975 with a telephone call from Bill Gallagher, better known in the music industry as William P. Gallagher. He suggested I come by his office a few days later so he could introduce me to someone he felt I should know. The someone turned out to be Les Paul.

Bill got to know Les in the 1960s when Les Paul and Mary Ford were over, in more ways than one, and Les made a couple of LPs for Columbia Records, where Bill was vice president of sales and marketing. And Bill was Les's pal when his life reached a low point because of circumstances regarding Mary and the subsequent divorce. And so, I showed up on the appointed day and was a fly on the wall while a powerful record executive and a legendary musical pal caught up and reminisced.

Since Bill made the introduction and it turned out we had a number of mutual friends, plus I'd known Sherman Fairchild and now had my own recording studio; we had a lot in common. Les concluded I wasn't an idiot and suggested I come out and visit him at his home in Mahwah, New Jersey.

I don't remember when I made my first trip to 78 Deerhaven Road, but it was probably about 1977 because in an old telephone book his address and telephone number, 201-327-7935, are sandwiched in between Gordon Park's and Estelle Parson's, and Gordon went in the book in 1977 when he was helping me with a John Vachon portfolio project.

Les's house in Mahwah was beautifully unique. The interior changed a bit over the years as he became increasingly famous until finally it became almost museum-like, but on that first trip the things I remember are what greeted me in the back of the house where I parked my car, as well as the unusual décor of the large room in which we chatted about this and that.

I can't prove that I saw anything; I'd messed up and hadn't brought a camera and, in fact, never took a picture of Les until 1982 and then it was only a couple of snapshots, but this is what I remember from the first visit.

Les's house was built on the side of a steep hill; the house faced Deerhaven Road but was well up the hill, and the steep driveway took you to the back of the house. First visits with celebrated people are often a lot of fun. The first time I drove up Les's driveway in Mahwah, I was surprised. I'd been told to come around to the back of the house and did as I was told. That day there was an old rusting Lincoln and a small mountain of magnetic tape of various widths in residence. The pile of used tape was maybe five feet high, perhaps twelve feet across, about the same size as the car. There was probably enough music on that tape to have launched a couple of independent record companies.

OPPOSITE

Les Paul, 2000. (Author's collection)

Chester & Lester LP jacket. (Author's collection)

There was also a beat-up and driven one mile too many Lincoln, possibly a refugee from Carl Jefferson's used car lot, a battered car that Les had perhaps once used when he was on tour. Twenty plus years later, there was still a battered old Lincoln in the back; I'm not sure if it was the same one. I exited my equally battered old Volkswagen, banged on the back door, was greeted by Les, and we started a conversation that rambled along off and on for the next thirty or so years.

Once inside, I was given the grand tour of a remarkable house. The only room that didn't contain a recording system was a bathroom I visited, and I wasn't too sure about that because Les had told me he'd once wired an outhouse out back up the hill so he could frighten anyone who used it.

I have a lasting memory of a stack of beer cases in the living room. The stack was floor to ceiling. This may not seem like much, but my guess is the ceiling in the living room was about twenty-five feet high. I have no idea how the last few cases made it to the top, but Les isn't called the Wizard of Waukesha for nothing. I wish I'd taken a picture of that, but I didn't.

It was a good time to get to know Les. He'd just finished up *Chester and Lester*, a "comeback" record of sorts, one that had been suggested by Chet Atkins. I don't remember if he told me about the recording sessions during my first visit in Mahwah or a subsequent one, but it was a good story. And so sitting in his "sitting" room, next to the floor to ceiling Brancusi-like endless column of beer cases, in-between bites of a peanut butter sandwich on white he'd also offered to me but I'd declined, he told me how Chet Atkins had approached him and suggested he come to Nashville and the two would make a record together.

This wasn't to be a country record; Les was not going to resurrect his Rhubarb Red character, put on a funny hat and appear at the Ryman and the Grand Ol' Opry, no, this was going to be two super guitarists playing nothing but standards from the American songbook, oldies like "It Had To Be You," "Moonglow," "Lover Come Back to Me," and "Someday Sweetheart." And playing them like no one had in the past.

Les told me at the recording session they selected a number of tunes they both knew and slowly worked all the way through them. They could afford to take their time since Chet was the head of RCA A&R in Nashville at the time, so studio costs were of no concern. And because these two guys knew their way around a studio and what was possible, there was complete separation between the two guitars, at least on tape.

Once they'd had a casual try with all the tens tunes that made their way to the finished LP and subsequent CD reissue, Chet was pleased with what they'd done and told Les it had been a great rehearsal. And it did sound like a casual rehearsal; there is talking and friendly banter throughout the recordings that was issued. But it wasn't a rehearsal in Les's mind. This was the finished recording as far as he was concerned; he'd done his part. Apparently, Chet wanted to do some fixes with his tracks and fussed with them for a few months but finally came up with something he liked, and the record was released. It won the Grammy the following year as Best Country Instrumental. It was an instrumental record, and it was certainly a "best" recording of some sort, but "country" it was not.

In terms of what Chester and Lester sounded like, it didn't sound much different from the way Les's shows sounded on the Monday nights at Fat Tuesdays or Iridium for the next quarter of a century. The music Les made on that record and the years that followed on his magic Monday nights was basically just a pretty, relaxed, jazz and American songbook, a mixture infused with melodically improvised excursions into the recesses of his mind where he'd stored a lifetime of musical memories.

Practicing at home, 1977.
(Author's collection)

The long abandoned, battered Lincoln.
(Author's collection)

And the story about his one-take session with Chet in Nashville? Why not? About the same time, one of the most interesting stories he ever told me was about playing duets with Charlie Christian in Harlem around 1940. I assumed it was a tall tale, but then one day I was talking with Erskine Hawkins and I asked him about his most remarkable memory of Harlem in the old days. He replied, "Did I ever tell you about the time Les Paul came up to the Golden Gate and played duets with Charlie Christian all night long?" It made me wish Jerry Newman had been at the Golden Gate that night instead of sticking close to Minton's and Monroe's. So much for my skepticism, and I never doubted anything Les ever told me again. I shouldn't have in the first place. He certainly didn't have anything to prove.

Monday nights with Les started out slowly but grew into the world of legendary things you must do if you are in New York, events happening at either Fat Tuesday early on in the 1980s until 1988 or Iridium from until about ten minutes before his death in 2009. There are a number of very good reasons why this Monday night gig lasted so long, but how it got started is interesting.

In the late 1970s and early 1980s, Astrud Gilberto and I were very close, and in 1978 or early 1979 Astrud agreed to do a club date in New York City to support her new recording, "That Girl from Ipanema," and the lucky club was Fat Tuesdays.

Fat Tuesdays launched in 1970 and lasted eighteen years. It was an above-average room with a decent piano. Later, Kenny Barron made a live recording on it. The guy in charge of booking the club was Steve Getz, the son of that tenor player who was in charge of the Ipanema date in the early 1960s. One day when Les and I were just talking, he said he thought it might be nice if there was a place in New York where he could play once a week on a regular basis with some like-minded musicians. I immediately thought of Fat Tuesdays because it was downtown, modest in size, was usually not busy, if open at all on Mondays, it wasn't a hustling joint, and I knew Steve would take my call, so I did. He was initially puzzled but eventually spoke with Les, and it turned into a quarter of a century, not for Fat Tuesdays, but for Les.

Initially it was quiet and intimate, low-key and casual. Les just played pretty tunes with a trio, a rhythm guitar, Wayne Wright as often as not in the early days, and an acoustic bass. Adding to the musical mix were Les's stories, charming, amusing, and informative, and Monday nights at Fat Tuesdays soon became filled with a rapt hear-a-pin-drop kind of audience. As time passed and the word spread, Les was joined at one time or another by every guitarist on the scene, with the possible exception of Segovia and Julian Bream. There were many magic nights downtown, then uptown in the basement of the Empire Hotel, and finally midtown, when Iridium made the move to Seventh Avenue.

The first Floating Jazz Festival set sail in September 1983, and we didn't ask Les to be on board. But by 1984 we knew what we were doing, and we asked him to appear on the *S/S Norway.* Shelley Shier and I made a trip to Mahwah to make our case as to why he should be aboard. It was a successful trip; Les agreed to be part of the festival and even showed us around his home, which featured a recording device of one sort or another in every room.

Time passed and we printed a program for the festival, but as time was passing so were more and more customers, crowding into the basement of old Scheffel Hall where every Monday night every chair was filled. Les began to love his Monday nights so much he didn't want to give up one to go out and jam with Dizzy Gillespie or Benny Carter. And neither did Fat Tuesdays. So he canceled. And we asked the next year and the next, but the next year never worked out.

One day we were talking about his adventures recording people at his old studio in Los Angeles in the 1940s, and I remembered my Swedish friend Anders Öhman had told me about a rumor that Les had recorded the late and legendary Swedish clarinetist Stan Hasselgard a year or so before his tragic death in an automobile accident. I asked Les if there was any truth the to the rumor, and he said something like, "Yeah, in the late forties, and the tapes are up there," pointing in the general direction of an upper level of the house. I knew that Anders was keen on issuing a Hasselgard tribute album, and this would be very good news.

Anders Öhman was a prominent lawyer in Sweden; he was also at one time president of the Royal Swedish Music Academy. As a sideline he created Phontastic, a label that specialized in recordings devoted to the clarinet, both classical and jazzical. He urged me to do whatever I could to help Les find the Hasselgard tracks and allow him to issue them.

Les looked and I helped, and finally we found a reel of tape with four tracks featuring Hasselgard that were recorded in late 1947. There may have been a modest fee involved, or perhaps Les just gave them to Anders, but in 1988 four tunes, "By the Fireside," "Lullaby in Rhythm," "A Cottage for Sale," and "All the Things You

LES PAUL

(guitar)

The legendary Les Paul makes one of his rare personal appearances with the Floating **Jazz** Festival. He began his career as a teenager on Chicago radio stations in the thirties, played with various orchestras and finally settled in California in the mid-forties. He became a highly respected **jazz** guitarist, toured with **Jazz** at the Philharmonic and won several Downbeat polls. In the late forties, however, he became even more well-known as an inventor, engineer, pop recording star and television personality. He invented the solid-body electric guitar (the LES PAUL is still the most popular Gibson model) and a host of electronic devices and concepts that revolutionized the recording industry. Along the way he gathered twenty-five gold records, Grammy winning LPs and recently became one of a handful of members of the National Academy of Recording Arts and Sciences Hall of Fame. He will be featured with his own quartet and with his long time guitarist/ friend, Bucky Pizzarelli.

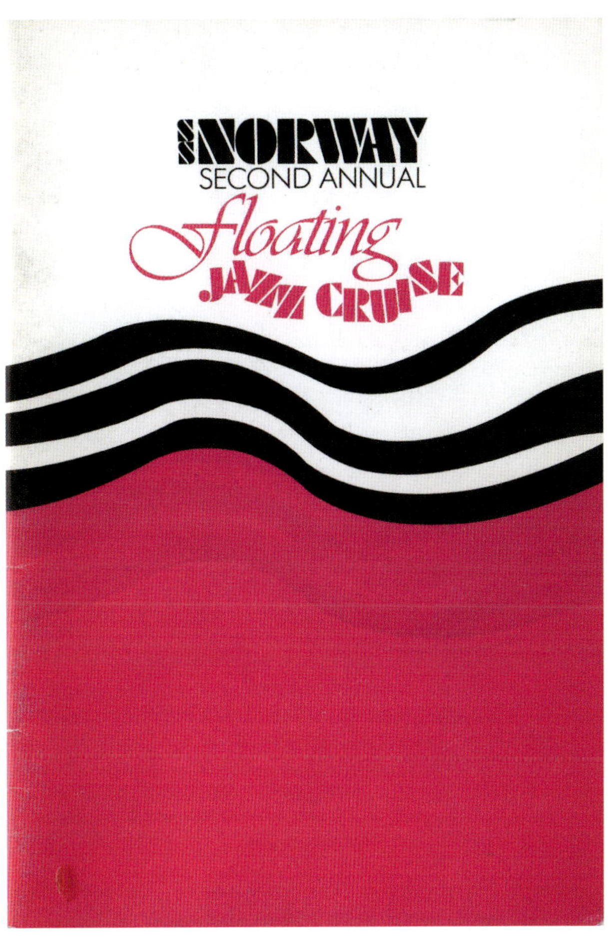

The Floating Jazz Festival 1984 program. (Author's collection)

The Permanent Hasselgard LP jacket.

The original hand made 8-Track.
(Author's collection)

Are" turned up on a Phontastic CD, *The Permanent Hasselgard.* Louise Tobin, who just died in 2022 at the age of one hundred four, sang on "Lullaby in Rhythm" and "All the Things You Are." I always wondered what else might be hidden away on all those shelves or what was on the discarded tapes that sometimes made mini mountains in the back of the house.

One of my great regrets is I never took a picture of one of the tape mountains, nor did I climb up the hill and photograph the wired-for-sound outhouse. He loved that outhouse and the pranks he could do with it. It would have been fun to have combined Les with Joe Venuti to see who could come up with the best prank. Les's idea was to talk about his outhouse up the hill and someone, the fancier the better, someone who wanted an outhouse experience and had never had one, would make their way up the hill to the outhouse, pick a hole and have a seat and proceed to do their business, when suddenly with the flip of a switch, Les would fill the outhouse with something he had overdubbed or underdubbed or whatever and the sitter would possibly be transported into a permanent state of constipation or even worse.

One picture I did manage to take one day was Les with his eight-track before it was shipped off to the Smithsonian to be installed in some kind of an exhibition. I think he had more than one, but he told me this was the original one he put together, and it still worked just fine.

And then more time passed, and we talked and talked, and Iridium moved over to Seventh Avenue, and the legend grew and grew, and Beatles and Stones and many others came by and sat in, and the lines were longer, and it was a new century, and everything was new again, even things that were very old, like Les Paul.

One of the new things was a magazine called *Madison,* and the most talented thing to turn up in my family since my mother's sister in the teens was Jennifer Stroup, a young lady who became an associate editor at the magazine while still in her very early twenties. And it just so happened that one of the things she wanted to do for the magazine was to interview Les Paul and do an illustrated article that would feature his own words and ideas.

"Do you know Les Paul?" she asked one day, and I said I did, waited until midnight, made the calls, a date was found when everyone was available, and Jennifer and I made the trip to Mahwah, turned off Deerhaven Road, chugged up the driveway to the back of the house, parked near the old abandoned Lincoln, went inside, and things got underway. It was July 15, 2000. It worked perfectly; lots of pictures, lots of words, and five months later Jennifer had condensed Les's remembrances into a wonderfully coherent statement for *Madison.* These are Les's words, as transcribed by Jennifer:

Why did I do what I did? I did it because it was my next day's work. And "work" was never a bad word in my life. It gave you a reason to get up and do something. It made you look forward to tomorrow. Working with the Bing Crosby's and the Sinatras and people like that, I learned so much. And if you don't do it, if you're not working constantly, you lose it. It's a hard thing when people say,

"Well, I wouldn't be here if it wasn't for you—you made all these toys to play the music with possible." That's hard for me to handle. Yeah it's heavy. I'm very grateful for it. But I never believe it.

The question you ask is very interesting—why? It's very hard to answer. Why did Andrés Segovia practice till the last day he was alive? He got up, he practiced right till he dropped over. I can understand that. The guitar is such a friend. Say you're depressed and you want to go to the doctor—maybe it's because you're lonesome, that's really

The interview, 2000, with Jennifer Stroup. (Author's collection)

The interview, 2000. (Author's collection)

With his funny violin.
(Author's collection)

The electronic archive. (Author's collection)

why you wanna go. If you go to your guitar, you got not only a guitar, you got a psychiatrist, you got a wife, you got your best friend. And he's a great bartender, too. He just does everything. And that's what I love about the guitar. If ever you find that you're out of step, if something is breakin' your heart and you're about to cry, what better fix would there be to pick up your instrument and play it? That's your friend.

I was about ten or eleven years old when I started playing guitar and harmonica and singing at a barbecue stand—in those days it was a drive-in—halfway between Waukesha and Milwaukee. I was smart enough then to hook up my mother's radio so it made a PA system; I had a broom handle stuck in a cinder block, and at the top I taped the magnetic coil from the telephone and sang into it. Well. This fellow sitting in the backseat of one of the cars sent a note to me that said RED, YOUR GUITAR'S NOT LOUD ENOUGH. So I went home that night and I thought Jeez, I have to get another telephone and put it in front of my guitar. Well, that didn't work very good. So I took the needle from the record player and pushed it into the wood of the guitar, and lo and behold, I got an electric guitar. But it was feeding back—the hollow resonance of the instrument was working against me. So I put socks, shirts, anything I could find in the guitar, and it was better, but it wasn't right. So finally I filled it up with plaster of Paris, and that was a lot better.

Eventually I made this thing I call the log in 1941 and took it to the Gibson people. They laughed at it. Many years later, the president of Gibson says, "Les, I gotta tell you something. For ten years we laughed at you—you were known as the character with the broomstick with the pickup's on it. Little did we know that we'd be sitting here having sold not one guitar, but millions."

At one time I decided to manage other people. It was 1962, I think, and I was driving down Route 46 in New Jersey. We pulled off to the side of the road and I went in this saloon to see who was there, and here's this big black guy, playin' a left-handed Les Paul guitar. He's got that amplifier turned up 2,000 decibels, and there is nobody in there but the bartender—he was auditioning. I had to go take

The electronic archive.
(Author's collection)

The office. (Author's collection)

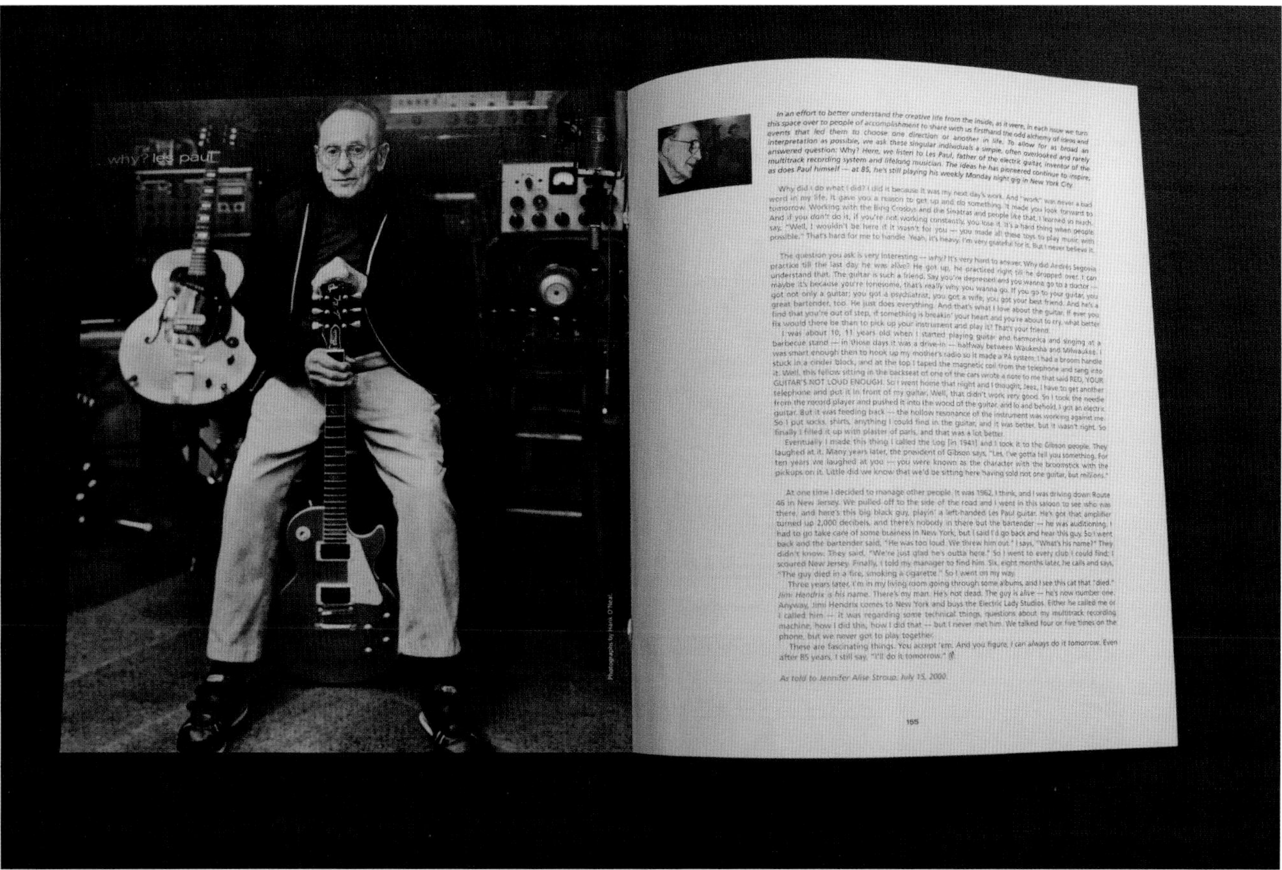

why? les paul

In an effort to better understand the creative life from the inside, as it were, in each issue we turn this space over to people of accomplishment to share with us firsthand the odd alchemy of ideas and events that led them to choose one direction or another in life. To allow for as broad an interpretation as possible, we ask these singular individuals a simple, often overlooked and rarely answered question: Why? Here, we listen to Les Paul, father of the electric guitar, inventor of the multitrack recording system and lifelong musician. The ideas he has pioneered continue to inspire, as does Paul himself — at 85, he's still playing his weekly Monday night gig in New York City.

Why did I do what I did? I did it because it was my next day's work. And "work" was never a bad word in my life. It gave you a reason to get up and do something. It made you look forward to tomorrow. Working with the Bing Crosbys and the Sinatras and people like that, I learned so much. And if you *don't* do it, if you're not working constantly, you lose it. It's a hard thing when people say, "Well, I wouldn't be here if it wasn't for you — you made all these toys to play music with possible." That's hard for me to handle. Yeah, it's heavy. I'm very grateful for it. But I never believe it.

The question you ask is very interesting — *why?* It's very hard to answer. Why did Andrés Segovia practice till the last day he was alive? He got up, he practiced right till he dropped over. I can understand that. The guitar is such a friend. Say you're depressed and you wanna go to a doctor — maybe it's because you're lonesome, that's *really* why you wanna go. If you go to your guitar, you got not only a guitar; you got a psychiatrist, you got a wife, you got your best friend. And he's a great bartender, too. He just does everything. And that's what I love about the guitar. If ever you find that you're out of step, if something is breakin' your heart and you're about to cry, what better fix would there be than to pick up your instrument and play it? That's your friend.

I was about 10, 11 years old when I started playing guitar and harmonica and singing at a barbecue stand — in those days it was a drive-in — halfway between Waukesha and Milwaukee. I was smart enough then to hook up my mother's radio so it made a PA system. I had a broom handle stuck in a cinder block, and at the top I taped the magnetic coil from the telephone and sang into it. Well, this fellow sitting in the backseat of one of the cars wrote a note to me that said RED, YOUR GUITAR'S NOT LOUD ENOUGH. So I went home that night and I thought, Jeez, I have to get another telephone and put it in front of my guitar. Well, that didn't work very good. So I took the needle from the record player and pushed it into the wood of the guitar, and lo and behold, I got an electric guitar. But it was feeding back — the hollow resonance of the instrument was working against me. So I put socks, shirts, anything I could find in the guitar, and it was better, but it wasn't right. So finally I filled it up with plaster of paris, and that was a lot better.

Eventually I made this thing I called the Log [in 1941] and I took it to the Gibson people. They laughed at it. Many years later, the president of Gibson says, "Les, I've gotta tell you something. For ten years we laughed at you — you were known as the character with the broomstick with the pickups on it. Little did we know that we'd be sitting here having sold not one guitar, but *millions*."

At one time I decided to manage other people. It was 1962, I think, and I was driving down Route 46 in New Jersey. We pulled off to the side of the road and I went in this saloon to see who was there, and here's this big black guy, playin' a left-handed Les Paul guitar. He's got that amplifier turned up 2,000 decibels, and there's nobody in there but the bartender — he was auditioning. I had to go take care of some business in New York, but I said I'd go back and hear this guy. So I went back and the bartender said, "He was too loud. We threw him out." I says, "What's his name?" They didn't know. They said, "We're just glad he's outta here." So I went to every club I could find; I scoured New Jersey. Finally, I told my manager to find him. Six, eight months later, he calls and says, "The guy died in a fire, smoking a cigarette." So I went on my way.

Three years later, I'm in my living room going through some albums, and I see this cat that "died." *Jimi Hendrix is his name.* There's my man. He's not dead. The guy is *alive* — he's now number one. Anyway, Jimi Hendrix comes to New York and buys the Electric Lady Studios. Either he called me or I called him — it was regarding some technical things, questions about my multitrack recording machine, how I did this, how I did that — but I never met him. We talked four or five times on the phone, but we never got to play together.

These are fascinating things. You accept 'em. And you figure, *I can always do it tomorrow.* Even after 85 years, I still say, "I'll do it tomorrow."

As told to Jennifer Alise Stroup, July 15, 2000.

195

Madison Magazine, October 2000. (Author's collection)

care of some business in New York but I said I'd go back and hear this guy. So I went back and the bartender said, "He was too loud. We threw them out." I says, "What's his name?" They didn't know. They said, "We're just glad he's out of here." So I went to every club I could find; I scoured New Jersey. Finally, I told my manager to find him. Six, eight months later, he calls and says, "The guy died in a fire, smoking a cigarette." So I went on my way.

Three years later I'm in my living room going through some albums, and I see this cat that "died." Jimi Hendrix is his name. There's my man. He's not dead. The guy is alive—he's now number one. Anyway, Jimi Hendrix comes in New York and buys the Electric Lady Studios. Either he called me or I called him—it was regarding some technical things, questions about my multi-track recording machine, how I did this, how I did that—but I never met him. We talked five times on the phone, but we never got to play together.

These are fascinating things. You accept 'em. And you figure, I can always do it tomorrow. Even after eighty-five years, I still say, "I'll do it tomorrow."

Les had a lot of tomorrows still to come, but except for an occasional visit to Iridium, I didn't catch up with him again until late 2022 when a group from The New School was debating about who we should select to receive the 2003 Beacon in Jazz Award. After going around for a couple of hours, we selected two legendary musicians and one outstanding industry figure. One was just down the street on Fifth Avenue, one was across the big river in New Jersey, and the other was across the other big river in Kansas City. Les was the one in New Jersey, and this was the closest I ever came to pinning him down for an event, and the only reason he did is because he didn't have to perform and it wasn't a Monday night. Thank God the ceremony was on April 1, a Tuesday, but because it was Les, who was known to pull an occasional prank, it took a little doing to convince him it wasn't an April Fool's prank. An article in *Downbeat* set that straight.

At 830 Broadway with Qi the Pup.
(Author's collection)

On April 1, New School University's Jazz Program will honor Bruce Lundvall, Jazz visionary and President of Blue Note Records, guitar virtuoso Les Paul and blues master Jay McShann with the Beacons in Jazz award. The Beacons award recognizes living legends in Jazz whose vision and talent have significantly influenced the music.

Hosted by Allan King, the gala will take place at The Supper Club, 240 West Forty-Seventh Street at 6:30 p.m. In addition to the awards ceremony, many renowned Jazz artists will be performing to pay tribute to the honorees and many leading figures in jazz will be in attendance.

Founded in 1986, New School University's Jazz Program has produced some of the leading voices in Jazz today. The Beacons raises scholarship funds for the New School's Jazz BFA students and is the single-most important fundraiser of the school's year.

As I recall, the car we sent to pick up Les in Mahwah got lost, but finally found him and got to 830 Broadway in time to get him to the The Supper Club almost on time. The only delay was Les wanted to have a word or two with Qi, the Cavalier King Charles Spaniel, before we headed north and into formality. Qi was in charge of all comings and goings at 830, including guitar wizards. But a bit late or not, there was time for him to sign a fancy model of a Les Paul, which was auctioned for the scholarship fund.

We didn't get a piano for Hootie to sign, but he did play a couple of tunes, and Bruce Lundvall appeared with his latest and possibly first Blue Note zillion record–selling superstar, Norah Jones. Her first record was already multi-platinum, and I'm sure Les would have been impressed if he'd known, but he'd been there fifty or sixty years earlier. There were a number of great musicians in the room that night, and we'd asked Pat Martino to play some special things for Les, who just had to sit back and take it.

Les still had six more good years, as did the legions of men and women and boys and girls and guitar players of all ages and genders who got to sit in on a Monday night, and maybe even an occasional puppy dog, who got to hear him at Iridium, but other than an occasional night at Iridium or a late night telephone call to 201-327-7935, that was the only contact I had with him. There were no more photographs, no more trips to see piles of tape in the backyard in Mahwah, or PB&J on white, or rummaging on a shelf for a tape recorded in an earlier century. But all these things did happen for thirty years, and these were special times I'm lucky to have had.

OPPOSITE
Les Paul X 49. (Author's collection)

21

Mel Powell

February 12, 1923 – April 24, 1998

MEL POWELL may have been the most intelligent person I have ever met. He may have also been the finest jazz pianist, at least once upon a time, but because he performed in public so infrequently after his mid-twenties, we'll never know. In the world of jazz in 2025, he's largely forgotten, almost all of his contemporaries are long dead, and those who worked with his contemporaries as younger artists are fading fast.

But fast was how Mel Powell emerged in the mid-1930s. By the time he was fifteen, he was studying simultaneously with Willie "The Lion" Smith and Nadia Reisenberg and had been smitten by his first exposure to Teddy Wilson at the Paramount Theater. He was also being smuggled into Nick's in Greenwich Village, often hidden in the men's room when a union representative showed up, but was also given a shot as a solo intermission pianist. In a 1983 interview with Loren Schoenberg, he recalled one night Art Tatum came in and did what Tatum always did, make all the other pianists in the room wish they played the drums or saxophone. Little Melvin Epstein from the Bronx was slated to follow Tatum as the intermission guy, and he was terrified. He recalled he hoped Nick (Rongetti) would let him off the hook, but Nick insisted Mel do his intermission set, with Tatum sitting close to the piano.

He did as best as he could and when he finished the first selection Tatum growled at him something like, "How old are you?" and Mel replied, "Fifteen and a half, almost sixteen." Tatum replied, "You gonna be one of the real ones." And he almost was.

The following are extracts from an essay I wrote for a catalog celebrating Mel's work as a painter, presented at the Sordoni Gallery in October 1987, when he was very much alive and the smartest guy in the gallery. They provide a brief historical overview of the beginning of his career in the 1930s and early '40s, when he burst onto the jazz scene as a teenager.

Sometime in early August 1942, there was a special gathering of musical talent at the uptown branch of Barney Josephson's legendary Café Society. Teddy Wilson was there, along with his band, which, among others, featured Edmund Hall and Sid Catlett. The pianist Hazel Scott was also there, handling intermission duties. At some point in the evening, the two resident pianists were joined by Duke Ellington and Count Basie. The four crowded behind the piano and urged the evening's guest of honor to join them. The guest of honor was Mel Powell, a teenaged object of much obvious affection and respect, just a kid who was scheduled to be inducted into the army the following day, along with hundreds of other nineteen-year-olds. There were probably farewell parties for many other young men that night, and on other nights throughout 1942, but the party at Café Society was decidedly different.

OPPOSITE
Mel Powell at the 1986 Floating Jazz Festival. (Author's collection)

With Count Basie, Teddy Wilson, Hazel Scott, and Duke Ellington. (Author's collection)

Mel Powell was anything but an ordinary nineteen-year-old inductee; his prodigious talents were well defined by the time he became part of the Benny Goodman Orchestra in June 1941. He was only eighteen but had trained as a serious pianist since childhood. He heard Teddy Wilson as early as 1935, and discovered it was amusing to improvise on the themes of the Beethoven sonatas he was studying. His teacher looked on such behavior with dismay, but she was unable to do anything about it as her young pupil continued to stray, listening with care to the work of Jess Stacy and Earl Hines. Within a few years of his introduction to jazz, he found himself playing at Nick's in Greenwich Village, alongside many of the outstanding musicians associated with that legendary jazz club.

It was with Benny Goodman, however, that he began to make his mark and during the fourteen months between June 1941 and August 1942, he quickly became recognized as the new pianist in town. He not only held down the piano chair with the big band, and the various small ensembles, but also contributed many arrangements and original compositions to the Goodman book, eighteen of which were recorded by the band during his brief tenure. He also managed to secure a recording date for himself with Milt Gabler's Commodore label, and four exceptional sides were released featuring Powell and some of his

The first recordings, *The World Is Waiting for the Sunrise*. (Author's collection)

musical associates, including his boss, participating as a sideman named "Shoeless John Jackson." Given Powell's early endeavors as a semi-professional baseball player, it is puzzling why he didn't refer to Goodman as Shoeless Joe, instead of John.

These months of crowded activity with Goodman led to a third-place finish in the Metronome All Star poll, finishing behind Jess Stacy and Count Basie, but ahead of his first idol, Teddy Wilson. He made a lasting impression; he remained in the top five of the Metronome Poll throughout the war years, even though he was part of the Glenn Miller Army Air Force Band, a group that never released a commercial recording during the years it was active and rarely performed in venues or even countries where the average Metronome reader might encounter it.

With Danny Kaye, Lionel Hampton, and Virginia Mayo. (Author's collection)

Mel returned from the war and dabbled in jazz for the next ten years, primarily in the recording studio. He made a handful of wonderful recordings for Capitol, Vanguard, and Columbia. Particularly notable and never reissued was the Columbia *Jam Session at Carnegie Hall*, a live recording of a concert to benefit the Lighthouse for the Blind. He worked for a minute in Hollywood studios and also undertook occasional forays with Benny Goodman, often to beef up his bank account. It seemed that whenever Benny had a special project, like a movie such as *A Song Is Born*, or an important recording or television special, Mel would get the call and be persuaded to forsake academia for a shining moment or two. The last time Benny managed to convince him to do this was in 1957, when Mel appeared with him on a series of television shows, culminating with one with Perry Como in October. In that same year, I heard my first Mel Powell recording, and he taught his first class at Yale.

With Benny Goodman and Perry Como. (Author's collection)

Mel left jazz and the big band business for the same reason Artie Shaw did. Just as Artie didn't want to play "Begin the Beguine" night after night, Mel didn't want to play "Mission to Moscow," or anything else, every night for the next forty years. That last performance with Benny in 1957 was a case in point. It was just a nice quartet; the first few songs were American songbook standards, and Mel actually had a couple of short solo breaks on "If I Had You" and "I Know That You Know." But then Perry Como comes on stage, and the quartet plus Perry launch into "Sing, Sing, Sing" and after a few seconds Tony Bennett joins in and then a few more singers and then all of the Mitchel Ayers Singers, and then the curtain rises and half the musicians on the NBC staff are on stage blaring out the song and a moment or two later ten dancers enter the fray.

A nice quartet and a boy singer had swelled to fifty or sixty people on a television soundstage in less than a minute, and it was just awful. So Mel happily retreated into the arms of academia. The only difference was, he first dropped out at the age of twenty-two, long before he developed a career and large following, and when Artie Shaw called it quits, he was one of the most celebrated musicians in America. Artie withdrew to write novels and stories with little success; Mel became part of academia, first at Yale and then the California Institute of the Arts, and achieved much success in his newly chosen field.

In 1985, Ruby Braff suggested, or to be precise, told me to call Mel and invite him to be part of the 1986 Floating Jazz Festival aboard the *S/S Norway*. He gave me his number to make sure. I said I thought it was about as

With Joe and Jill Williams during the 1986 Floating Jazz Festival. (Author's collection)

With Joe Williams and Buddy Rich during the 1986 Floating Jazz Festival. (Author's collection)

likely the ship would fly, but I did as I was told, and much to my surprise, after a bit of give and take, Mel agreed to leave the secure confines of CalArts for a moment and dip his toe back into the wicked world of jazz. He hadn't played jazz on a regular basis in years, but, somehow, I wasn't worried. I'd seen a video clip of him playing "Body and Soul" and "Avalon" with Benny on *The Merv Griffin Show* in 1976 and he was terrific. He may have been playing on muscle memory, but Benny couldn't keep up with him. I was pretty sure the same thing would happen in 1986, and it did.

Once the word got out that Mel Powell was onboard the *S/S Norway*, everyone wanted to play with him, and they pretty much did. Since we couldn't fit everyone onstage, some of the musicians had to sit in the audience. During one concert, Mel told a wonderful story about Buddy Rich, who happened to be sitting in the audience, and then suggested to Buddy that he come on stage and be part of the band, which he did, to the delight of everyone in the theater. Not many people could tell Buddy what to do, but Mel could and did and got away with it. He had a way with words and was so charming no one could refuse any request he might make.

Joe Williams was also on board that week, and because of Mel, poor Joe had to do double duty. He not only presented his concerts but was also required to look after Mel as well because as a young girl in wartime London, Mrs. Joe Williams, Jill Williams, was smitten from afar by the dashing young pianist with the Glenn Miller Army Air Force Band and now, after a forty-year wait, here was the object of her wartime affections.

Because he loved to talk to the audience, Mel's concerts were often very long. It wasn't unusual for Mel to speak for fifteen minutes before the concert and take another five or ten between each selection. No one seemed to mind, because he spoke as well as he played, and while what he said was not necessarily as stimulating as what he and his pals played, it still gave the listener a perspective they might not otherwise have had.

His level of musicianship was remarkable. He was usually up early every morning, even if he'd stayed up all night discussing musical matters with Dizzy Gillespie. One of my great regrets is that I didn't get to hear these conversations, and they weren't recorded. In the mornings, he'd make his way to a small, out-of-the-way room with a piano and play Bach. Other musicians on board, leaders and sidemen alike, would also get up early, hoping to find a seat in the small Windjammer Lounge just to listen to each and every note he played. Sometimes they'd ask questions, sometimes, if they were old enough and had been around or had mutual acquaintances, they'd reminisce. And once I photographed him with violinist Svend Asmussen. After sharing a few wartime stories, they played a little Bach.

With Svend Asmussen in the Scooner Bar during the 1986 Floating Jazz Festival. (Author's collection)

With Dizzy Gillespie during the 1986 Floating Jazz Festival. (Author's collection)

Mel had such a good time, both playing and socializing with old friends from the 1940s and 1950s, that he returned to the festival as often as possible and performed in many different groups and surroundings. But as the years passed, it became increasingly difficult for him. He suffered from an unusual muscular disease that prevented him from walking without assistance. He managed to make his way around the ship on a little electric scooter.

In his home studio, 1987.

In conversation with Roland Hanna and Tommy Flanagan.

With Howard Alden and Ruby Braff in Club Internationale during the 1986 FJF. (Author's collection)

At the piano in Club Internationale aboard the S/S *Norway* in 1986.

His condition was something of a mystery, and it was later discovered it had been misdiagnosed, but in the late 1980s it was a struggle for him to get around. We built a ramp so we could get him on stage in Club Internationale; there was an elevator in the theater, so it was easy to get him to the piano in that room. Then came the day when the elevator was thrown overboard during a fit of remodeling, and for one concert in 1987 Mel had to perform on one level while the rest of the band was four feet higher. It sounded fine but looked terrible.

In that same year, he said that in his view one of the most profound statements of the twentieth century was made by the Czech composer Ernst Krenek who said, "What we understand no longer interests us and what interests us we no longer understand." The philosophical implications of this statement clearly guided Mel's thinking and actions for many years. In hindsight, it seems clear: he had a simple lack of interest in the kind of music he was playing in the 1940s or on the *Perry Como Show* in 1957 or even the new directions jazz was taking after World War II. It is even possible that had not the war and the Glenn Miller band intervened, Mel might have ceased being an on-the-road-again full-time jazz musician in 1942.

He understood the technical facility of his playing, dazzling inventions at the keyboard were not difficult, and the skill and originality he brought to his compositions and arrangements for Goodman and Miller seemed to come with ease. It was exciting to sit next to and perform with some of the most creative men in jazz, but the problem was at the age of eighteen, Mel was at the pinnacle. There was no place to go except to accomplish more of the same.

Yet, he loved his weekly jazz sojourn each year, when he was able to abandon academia and the composition of minimalist and electronic music. I listen to the tapes we made of the concerts, hear the sparkling piano, but more importantly, I hear the tone of his voice and what he said. He was having the time of his life. One evening I teamed him with Benny Carter, Howard Alden, Milt Hinton, and Louie Bellson. It was magic, and the tape recorder was running. *The Return of Mel Powell* also announced the return of Chiaroscuro Records after a nine-year absence.

One night, Mel asked that we assemble a special band for a concert. One of the people he asked to be included was Don Menza, the wonderful saxophonist then usually working with Louie Bellson. Somehow Mel had found out that Don loved Verdi's operas above all others. Before the first set, Mel told Don he had a surprise for him. He played a selection from act 3 of *Othello* and sang it to him, in Italian. Italian opera was about as far from Mel's normal musical interests as was the Grand Old Opry, but the depth of his musical knowledge was so profound he could bring off a song (I can't say aria, because Mel didn't sing very well) from a Verdi opera.

The muscular disease that plagued his legs eventually reached one of his fingers and sufficiently weakened his hands. He couldn't play; at least he couldn't play at the level he felt appropriate. The last two years he came to the festival, he didn't play at all; he was just an honored guest. But he continued to compose and consider other projects. He once told me he had enough commissions to last through 2005, and he even managed to complete some of them.

In early 1987, I thought of something a little different that might stimulate Mel. Why not try and arrange to have an exhibition of Mel's watercolors in conjunction with a concert based on various aspects of his life in music. I bounced this idea off Andrew Sordoni and Andy jumped on board in a single bound.

The reason I began painting was a shift in my function at Cal Arts. In 1972 I was asked to become Provost and I accepted because the place was teetering. I didn't know what a Provost was or what one should do, but I quickly learned and that sort of thing seemed to me to be very easy to do, but I soon found myself removed from composition, removed from music. Dull, absurd and unchallenging as provostal chores might be for a composer, they nevertheless made it impossible to compose and sustain over an extended period of time an undistracted focus on musical thought. Some felt a good deal of compassion for me and one day someone suggested that it might make sense for me to lecture to the institute as a whole . . .

With that as background I decided to give a lecture on some very advanced music . . . The lecture was a good chance for me to talk to people who knew nothing technically. The painters didn't know anything about it nor did the writers or the actors . . .

I sat at my desk in my office wondering what to do and, while sitting there, decided to attempt to illustrate what certain twelve-tone manipulations are in a visual way. I used color-coding to show different transformations of serial techniques and, while I was working on them, my secretary came in and said that one of the Cal Arts designers had arrived for his appointment. He came in and when he came over to my desk he looked down and noticed what I was doing. He said, "What is that? It's lovely." I then looked at it for the first time and said, "My good-

Tone (14″x11″). (Author's collection)

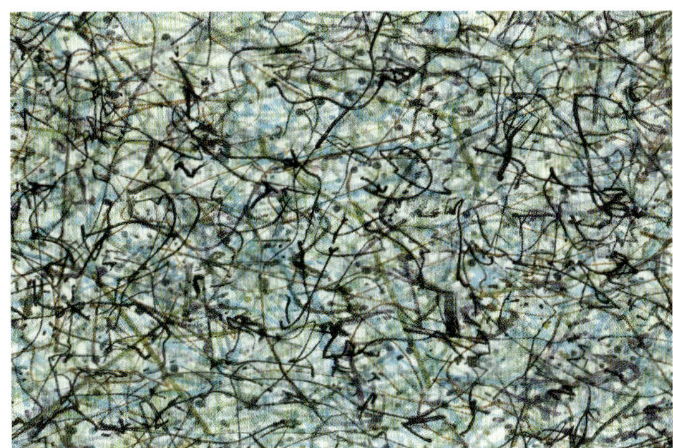

Little Pollock (4.5″x 6.4″). (Author's collection)

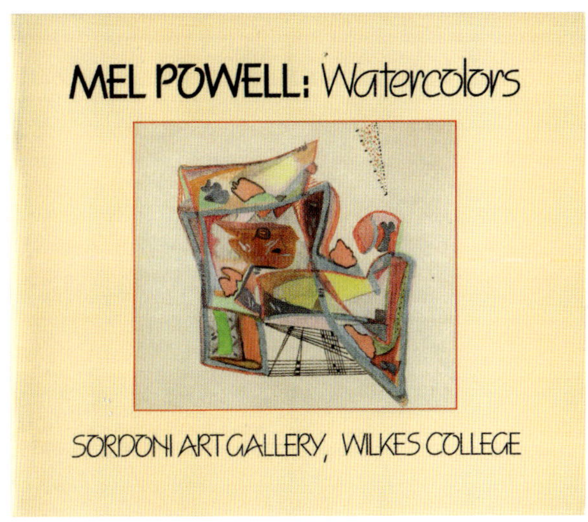

Mel Powell watercolors catalog. (Author's collection)

Here and There (12″ x 16.5″). (Author's collection)

ness, you're right. It is lovely." I was stunned because it had to do with the formal structure of music. This was the actual beginning.

And so we began working on an exhibition in early 1987. A trip to Los Angeles was in order to meet with Mel and his wife, the noted actress Martha Scott. We picked a total of sixty-four watercolors for the show, I photographed them, and because they were small, transported them back and turned them over to Judy O'Toole, the director of the gallery. I also gave her a number of other photographs to illustrate various aspects of Mel's life and work. I then set about writing what eventually emerged as *The Artistry of Mel Powell*, excerpts of which have appeared in this essay.

The exhibition was scheduled to open October 10 and remain up for a month. I'd finished my essay, and Andy Sordoni and Judy O'Toole arranged for a fine catalog to be printed, one that listed all sixty-four watercolors and illustrated seven of them. Mel and Martha Scott flew in for the opening, there was a concert and dinner, and all was right with the world.

There were no more Floating Jazz Festival events from the end of the decade, but in 1989 the newly resurrected Chiaroscuro Records issued its first release, CR(D) 301, *The Return of Mel Powell*. He was very happy with it, as were we, but there was an even more exciting "first" that was to occur in 1990.

One of Mel's most ambitious new compositions was *Duplicates, a Concerto for Two Pianos*, which had been commissioned by the Los Angeles Philharmonic Orchestra. The soloists were to be Mel and the orchestra's then music director, André Previn. Unhappily, when the piece was completed, Mel's illness prevented him from performing, and André Previn had moved on to another orchestra. But *Duplicates* was quite wonderful, and the premiere on January 28 went off without a hitch but with two other pianists.

When Mel told me about the piece and how well it had been received, it occurred to me that it might be possible to do the same thing with Mel that I'd done with Gerry Mulligan a decade earlier. Just as Gerry was due to win a Grammy, Mel was due to win a Pulitzer Prize, and the timing for the 1990 prize couldn't have been better. Unbeknownst to him, I spoke with Martha and told her what I wanted to do, but to pull it off I had to have a recording of the performance, a score, and letters of recommendation. She thought it was a terrific idea, and although she didn't know how to keep it a secret from Mel, she agreed to help.

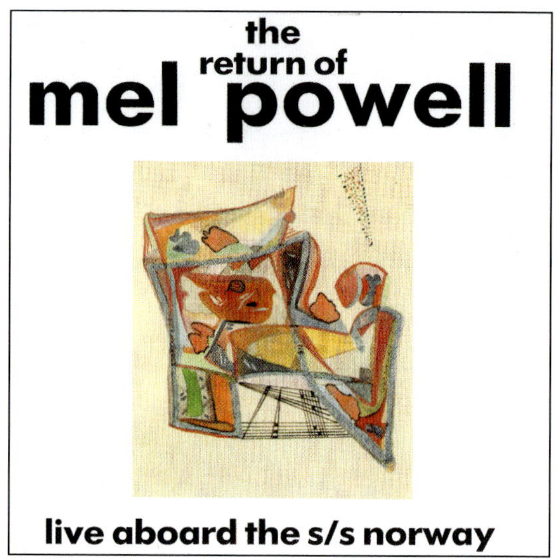

The Return of Mel Powell CD, 1989.
(Author's collection)

The Return of Mel Powell CD liner, 1989.
(Author's collection)

There was a tape of the January 1990 performance, but Mel had stashed it somewhere. Martha had no idea where it was located but said she would try and get one from the orchestra, which she eventually managed to do. We also managed to turn up the score, but we were running out of time. I wanted the letter of recommendation to come from André Previn, but he was out of town, and when he returned to the US he was ill and none too eager to write anything, even to sign his name for his old MGM

Judy O'Toole and Andy Sordoni at the 1987 exhibition.
(Author's collection)

Susan Sordoni, Mel, Bente Løwendahl, and Stein Øvrebo.
(Author's collection)

colleague. But when he rested and was feeling better, he said to get the paperwork to him, which I did.

Jon Bates hand delivered the nomination forms to André in Bedford Hills. Once everything was signed, Jon FedExed it to me with next day delivery, which was the final day to submit everything to the Pulitzer committee. The paperwork from Andre arrived on Saturday, midmorning. I rushed it to Columbia University, made the deadline by a few hours, and some months later, someone telephoned and said, "Did you hear, Mel won the Pulitzer Prize." I wasn't exactly surprised, and it turned out he never even knew he'd been nominated. To say he was surprised is something of an understatement, and for me it was fun to have manipulated the system.

The press descended on Mel, his students at CalArts were dancing in the classrooms, André gave interviews about the commission, but Martha was not very good at keeping the secret, and not too long after the announcement Mel telephoned and told me he was sending me a little souvenir. It arrived a few days later, a cassette marked simply *LAPO 1/28/98, Powell: "Duplicates" (31:18).* This was his copy that had been hidden away. When I telephoned to thank him, he jokingly referred to it "our" prize.

Mel Powell is one of the great musical mysteries, one of the more important "what if" artists of this century. And he knew it. He told me any number of times he knew he was writing music that would be appreciated by very few, that he wasn't sure he'd made the right decision in turning his back on more accessible forms of music. Maybe jazz was just too easy for him; success came so quickly, with so little effort, and there was little musical challenge. His comments about returning after the war to hear Charlie Parker and Dizzy Gillespie in full bloom and being frightened to death just don't stand up. He could have assimilated everything they were doing in a heartbeat. His decision remains a mystery.

Towards the end, in late 1997 or early 1998, we had a short conversation that touched on it. A new composition of his had been performed at a CalArts concert; I seem to recall it featured a clarinet. He said it was well received, and after the performance, he was greeted by many well-wishers. He told me that a young man had come up to him and complimented him on the new piece, but added, "I like 'Mission to Moscow' better." To which Mel said he replied, "So do I."

Mel's health deteriorated rapidly in 1998, and he was hospitalized. He'd been elected into the American Academy of Arts and Letters and was due to be inducted in May, but it was clear he wouldn't last that long. Precedent was broken and there was a bedside ceremony in April, a few weeks before he died. A moving tribute was offered at the formal ceremony by his old friend and colleague Milton Babbitt. Mel would have enjoyed Babbitt's remarks, but would have been even happier if Benny Goodman could have said a few things as well, but Benny had been gone for over a decade.

Time passed. Martha Scott died, and their possessions were then dispersed to children and grandchildren. Some wound up with their daughter, Kati. One day she telephoned and said she'd found something she thought I might like. A dusty plaque arrived a few days later. *Downbeat magazine* awarded it to Mel as the outstanding pianist in jazz for 1947, probably based on the few months he spent with Benny Goodman in 1946, and the handful of records he made under his own name. He didn't win in 1948; he'd left the jazz world by then.

The plaque hangs on my office wall next to a small watercolor he did in the 1970s. He told me he called the abstract painting of what is clearly a pianist in action, *Jelly Roll*. He always came back to the music of his youth.

Downbeat Award, Piano, First Place.
(Author's collection)

Cassette tape, *Duplicates*. 1990.
(Author's collection)

B
Brunswick
One-Step
JAZZ BATTLE
Batalla de Jazz
—Smith—
THE RHYTHM ACES
4244
THE BRUNSWICK-BALKE-COLLENDER COMPANY
MADE IN U.S.A.
REG U.S. PAT. OFFICE. M. de F. MARCA INDUSTRIAL REGISTRADA

22

Jabbo Smith

December 24, 1908 – January 16, 1991

Jabbo and the Jazz Foundation of America

There are a lot of jazz musicians named Smith. There was only one with the surname Cladys, and he wasn't really ever known as Cladys. In fact, I never heard of anyone named Cladys, and I certainly never knew of anyone who was named Jabbo. But he was called that all his life, at least that was what he was still called when he died in 1991. He was born in 1908 and named Cladys, after his mom who was named Gladys, a fairly conventional and common name at the time, but no one was ever named Cladys.

Nobody paid much attention to Jabbo until he got out of the orphanage when he was about sixteen, and not many people paid any attention to him when he died in 1991 or when he lived his ragtime life over his eighty-three years. Sure, there was a little buzz in the late 1920s when his sensational trumpet playing had him on deck to be the next Louis Armstrong, but that wasn't to be. What was to be were years of struggle just to stay alive and make it to 1991.

But in a funny way Jabbo has had a positive effect on the lives of thousands of jazz musicians he never knew and made their lives immeasurably better. This is a roundabout story, one that began in the mid-1960s and involves many, many people, mostly people unknown to the ultimate beneficiary of Jabbo's convoluted legacy: the staff, board, and thousands of clients of The Jazz Foundation of America. As best as I can recall, here's what happened.

In the mid-1960s, one of the foremost dealers in obscure and rare original 78 rpm records was Robert Altshuler, better known as Bob. He had a day job as the executive VP for corporate promotion at CBS. He would later become a good friend. At the same time, one of the foremost collectors of rare original 78 rpm records was Richard Spottswood, who had a day job as a music librarian. I knew Dick as part of a circle of jazz enthusiasts in the Washington, DC, area where I had a day gig with the Central Intelligence Agency.

One day Dick telephoned and said he was going to New York to buy some rare records and would I like to tag along. It was a weekend and I was happy to make the trip. He said he had a friend named Bob who had managed to acquire almost all the 78 rpm file copies in the Decca warehouses for a dollar apiece. It was never clear if it was a bribe or a sale or whatever, but the bottom line was Dick's friend Bob had the mint file copies of all twenty recordings Jabbo Smith made for Brunswick in 1929 leading his small group, The Rhythm Aces. None of these records were in print on an LP, and Dick's intention was to reissue these twenty selections, along with other equally rare recordings, on which Jabbo appeared in those years, with bands led by Alex Hill, Charlie Johnson, Lloyd Smith, and Banjo Ikey Robinson, and make all these recordings available on two Melodian LPs.

OPPOSITE
Jazz Battle, The Rhythm Aces.
(Author's collection)

With Tommy Lodge, Beale Riddle, Billy Taylor, Dick Spottswood, Johnson McRee, and Louisa Spottswood, Arlington, Virginia, 1966. (Author's collection)

Everyone associated with the project thought it would be a good idea to bring Jabbo to Washington to celebrate the release of his now thirty-six-year-old records, and with the help of the legendary John Steiner, Beale Riddle found Jabbo in Milwaukee in December 1965, where he was eking out a meager living cleaning returned cars at an Avis rental agency. He was largely inactive in music, long forgotten by most but remembered by a few, including himself. After some cajoling, he agreed to come to Washington and relive his once glamorous past, if only for a moment. He arrived on January 16, 1966. I don't remember why, but I was nominated to meet him on the banks of the Potomac River, at what was then called National Airport.

Roy Eldridge and Jabbo Smith, Washington, DC, 1966. (Author's collection)

I was nervous about fetching Jabbo. I was just a kid of twenty-five, but I was game and smart enough to round up a sidekick to keep me company. I knew that Roy Eldridge was in town playing at Blues Alley, and a friend was then a co-owner of the soon-to-be legendary club. He told me where Roy was staying and I made the call. I was very nervous when Roy answered. He didn't know me, but I asked him to go to the airport. He probably said something like, "Why would I go to the airport with you?" and I blurted out, "To meet Jabbo Smith." He said, "Jabbo is coming to Washington?" I thought I could hear him putting on his pants and getting ready. Roy remembered what the 1929 Jabbo sounded like and how that had influenced what he sounded like a few years later and still did today, many years later.

A couple of hours later I found myself at the airport with Roy Eldridge, waiting for Jabbo to arrive. I took my little cheapo 35mm Kodak and took a picture of Roy looking sharp and Jabbo looking kind of raggedy but smiling. The original slide was lost somewhere along the way, and all I have today is a fading print. But it was a great reunion, and I'm sure both men were thrilled with the encounter. Later, we gathered everyone together at the home of Dick and Louisa Spottswood, where Jabbo was treated like long lost royalty, which is many ways he was.

The people who gathered were Tom Lodge, a jazz fan who made films for the Department of Agriculture (his mother had been J. Edgar Hoover's personal secretary for decades), Beale Riddle, a longtime fixture on the DC jazz scene, Jabbo, bassist Billy Taylor Jr., Dick Spottswood, Johnson "Fat Cat" McRee of Blues Alley and Manassas Jazz Festival fame, and Louisa Spottswood. The conversations were recorded; I can see a microphone sticking out next to Billy Taylor in the photo I took on that January day.

This casual gathering and the release of the two records produced one significant outcome. From this point onward, Jabbo was no longer cleaning cars for Avis; he was back in music on a modest scale and for the next quarter of a century had a decent career, performing in the United States and Europe and recording with revival bands. His renewed career culminated with his appearance as a featured artist in Vernel Bagneris's hit show *One Mo' Time* in 1980.

One Mo' Time was presented at New York City's The Village Gate, and it had a good run. Set in New Orleans in 1926 and premiered in that city in the late 1970s, the New York City version of the show was altered, and a special part was created for Jabbo to play and sing his composition "Love," as well as playing in the pit band. One of the producers of the show was Jerry Wexler, who arranged for an original cast recording of the album to be issued by Warner Bros. Records. Jabbo is featured on the recording and pictured on the album jacket. But then there was trouble; one evening in the early 1980s, as the band relaxed in the dressing room at intermission, Jabbo had a stroke, putting the brakes on his twenty-five-year comeback. Then there was another stroke that impeded his speech. But these two strokes would set in motion a series of events that would culminate in a 1991 concert that took place a few months after Jabbo's death that same year.

When Jabbo was stricken in the basement dressing room of The Village Gate, there was no Jazz Foundation of America and its predecessor, the Jazz Musicians Emergency Fund, didn't even exist. There was no program dedicated to helping ailing, elderly, and possibly indigent jazz and blues musicians. Social Security was a possibility, but he would have qualified for about ten cents a month.

Jabbo was luckier than most old and infirm jazz musicians. He had a friend and patron in the form of Lorraine Gordon, who, while making certain Jabbo didn't fall between the cracks, also managed to run the Village Vanguard, the most famous jazz club in the world. She remembered Jabbo from her teenage years in Newark and the Newark Hot Club, which celebrated Jabbo all those years ago.

While I was working on *The Ghosts of Harlem* in 1987, when it was time to interview and photograph Jabbo it was at Lorraine's Charlton Street apartment. When we invited Jabbo to be an honored guest at the 1989 Floating Jazz Festival, we invited Lorraine as well to make sure he didn't get into too much trouble. He was still a ragtime kind of guy.

The interview in 1987 didn't work out; the stroke had robbed Jabbo of his speech, but by 1989 he'd managed to get enough of it back that he was able to sing one song at a special performance during the jazz festival at sea. And he continued to sing occasionally; the last time I heard him was at the Village Vanguard, probably sometime in 1990, when he sat in for a song or two with Don Cherry's group. That may sound ridiculous, but Jabbo was as out there in 1929 when he burst on the scene as was Don Cherry when he was teamed with Ornette Coleman in the late 1950s. In 1990, his voice wasn't strong, barely more than a whisper, because he now had advanced lung cancer.

Scene and time change: Once upon a time there was a terrific hospital in New York City's Greenwich Village: St. Vincent. It is where Berenice Abbott didn't die on the roof in 1918 where she'd been left to do just that because the staff didn't think they could save her from the Spanish flu and gave the scarce empty bed to someone they thought

At Lorraine Gordon's New York City apartment in 1987.
(Author's collection)

they could. It is also where Earl Davis found himself in May 1990, waiting for his wife, Suzanne, to give birth to their son, Joshua. Earl was an old friend, the son of the noted American artist Stuart Davis, who had named his only son Earl (for Hines) George (for Wettling) Davis. In those years, the hospital was still a landmark on Seventh Avenue, about fifty yards from the entrance of The Village Vanguard. And this proximity to the Vanguard has a great deal to do with what transpired over the next eighteen months. In the words of Earl Davis:

> *Between hospital time and baby visits with friends and family, during the next few days I was invited by a jazz-world friend, Hank O'Neal, to attend a concert Tribute to Cab Calloway, at The New School (where my father had long taught), which conveniently happened to be located right down the block from St. Vincent's Hospital. Suzanne excused me for this special purpose. After the performances and presentations, Hank introduced me to Lorraine Gordon, the widow of Max Gordon, who owned and managed the famous jazz club, The Village Vanguard, which also happened to be diagonally across the street from the hospital, on Seventh Avenue, two blocks down from my father's long time studio. She proclaimed herself to be a great fan of my father's work and remembered him coming to the Vanguard often. I told her about the upcoming show at The Metropolitan and about my idea for an appropriate jazz concert. She was instantly enthused and invited me to stop by while I was staying at the hospital to talk with her about it. The next day, I did so. Lorraine was full of excitement and supportive spirit. She knew everyone in the jazz world and the best pianists still playing. In particular, she told me about and invited me to come hear a woman I had never heard of, named Dorothy Donegan, who she considered to be one of the greatest jazz pianists of all time and who she happened to have booked to play at the Vanguard at the end of that month. As I was about to leave, she told me about this old jazz trumpeter, named Jabbo Smith, who I had also never heard of, and who at that very moment was suffering with lung cancer in St. Vincent's, a couple of floors below my wife and baby's room. She told me that he had no money and that she was paying all his medical bills, something she was regularly called upon to do for many musicians when they were sick or couldn't afford their rent. But Jabbo was special to her and she asked if I wouldn't mind going to visit him, just to show him that someone knew who he was and that he was there.*
>
> *Before heading back up to our hospital room where Suzanne was preparing to be discharged and for me to drive her home with our baby boy, I stopped off to honor Lorraine's request to visit with Jabbo Smith. Since I was embarrassed I had never heard his music and he was barely able to whisper, after telling him that Loraine sent her love and that my baby had just been born upstairs, I didn't have much else to say. In light of the obvious contrast and poignancy of his own condition with that of my son's birth, we just sat together in silence. No words seemed appropriate or necessary. At some point, he reached out his beautiful old leathery hand and clasped my own with appreciation that I had come to visit. His gentleness made me think of how it must have been for Sonny Greer when he ended up in the hospital, no one would have known what made him special or how much joy and spirit he had brought into the world. As we held hands like that in the silence, I was suddenly struck with the fully formed and simple idea that it would be appropriate for me to make my father's jazz concert tribute into a benefit to establish some sort of Jazz Musician's Emergency Fund! He would have loved to be honored in such a way.*

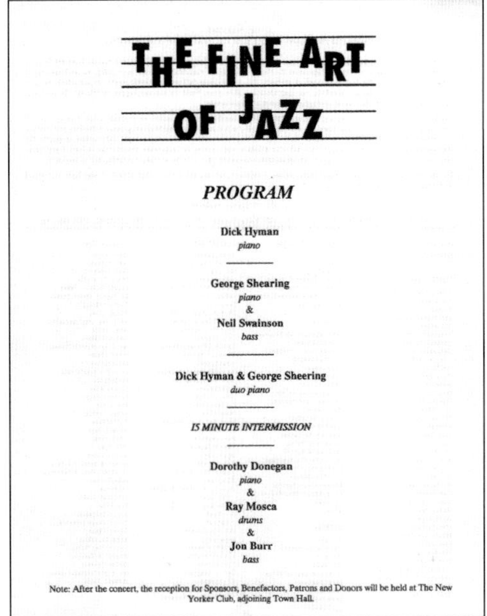

THE FINE ART OF JAZZ

PROGRAM

Dick Hyman
piano

George Shearing
piano
&
Neil Swainson
bass

Dick Hyman & George Sheering
duo piano

15 MINUTE INTERMISSION

Dorothy Donegan
piano
&
Ray Mosca
drums
&
Jon Burr
bass

Note: After the concert, the reception for Sponsors, Benefactors, Patrons and Donors will be held at The New Yorker Club, adjoining Town Hall.

The Fine Art of Jazz program, 1991.
(Author's collection)

And this is how the concert that was later called *The Fine Art of Jazz – A Stuart Davis Centennial Celebration* began. Jabbo died on January 16, and Lorraine had a memorial for him at the Village Vanguard on February 3. I don't remember exactly when I first spoke with Earl about the concert; it may have been at the Village Vanguard memorial event. But at some point early in the year we talked about the circumstances surrounding Jabbo's last years, and Earl was eager to do something to help musicians who found themselves facing difficult circumstances and at the same time honor his father. He asked me if I knew of any organization that helped musicians in need, and I said I'd just been asked by Herb Storfer to become involved with a modest nonprofit called the Jazz Foundation of America, and it had a division called the Jazz Musicians Emergency Fund that was to be used to assist musicians just like Jabbo. I said I'd accepted the invitation. The timing almost seemed too perfect, and we agreed there should be a benefit concert to help this new organization. A concert in Town Hall was scheduled for November 21.

Time passed and legions of people worked and worked and then it was October and then November. October and November 1991 were filled with events that seemed to be eerily interrelated. Our Floating Jazz Festival was scheduled for October 19 through November 1 and featured two of the three artists scheduled to perform at the Town Hall concert, Dorothy Donegan and Dick Hyman. It was remarkable how the upcoming Town Hall concert on November 21, the Stuart Davis exhibition at the Metropolitan Museum of Art scheduled to open on November 23, and our own festival seemingly were synergistically linked.

The concert involved three great pianists, many of the most celebrated American visual artists, a hundred or so of the most prominent nonperforming jazzers in New York City, and major record companies and art galleries. Even better, every seat in The Town Hall was soon to be filled to hear Dorothy Donegan, Dick Hyman, and George Shearing.

On the back of the program of performing artists was a listing of all the sponsors, benefactors, patrons, and donors, as well as a note from the JFA president, Herb Storfer that in part read:

It is my pleasure and privilege to welcome our guests to a rare program of superlative jazz piano, one that we hope will become the forerunner of many events that will epitomize the best of this uniquely American art form . . . And because this is a benefit for our Jazz Musicians Emergency Fund, we are carrying out our pledge to assist jazz musicians in coping with their social, medical and career development needs.

We have ambitious plans for our organization . . . If you would like to be placed on our mailing list, please fill out an address form and place it in the special membership box in the lobby.

AN OPEN LETTER
FROM THE PRESIDENT OF THE JAZZ FOUNDATION OF AMERICA, INC.

It is my pleasure and privilege to welcome our guests to a rare program of superlative jazz piano, one that we hope will become the forerunner of many events that will epitomize the best of this uniquely American art form. In so doing, we are beginning to realize the mission of The Jazz Foundation of America, Inc. *"to stimulate and promote public interest in jazz music and jazz history..."* and, because this is a benefit for our Jazz Musicians' Emergency Fund, we are carrying out our pledge *"to assist jazz musicians in coping with their social, medical and career development needs"*

We have ambitious plans for our organization. Within the foreseeable future we expect to establish a Jazz Center that will become a mecca for jazz fans and future fans from far and near- with lectures, rare jazz films, programs for children and students and other features. We are in the process of planning jazz tours, that we expect to be most unusual and excellent in quality. We are organizing a membership jazz club which will offer delightful ways to enjoy and appreciate the art form we love. If you would like to be placed on our mailing list, please fill out an address form and place it in the special membership box in the lobby.

Finally, we would like to thank our generous sponsors, benefactors, patrons, and donors and all volunteers who have contributed to the realization of this inaugural event.

Cordially,
Herbert F. Storfer, President

THE JAZZ FOUNDATION OF AMERICA / 1200 BROADWAY (7/D), NY 10001 / TELEPHONE: (212) 685-5206

SPONSORS

Gilbey's Gin
The New Yorker Magazine, Inc.

BENEFACTORS

Armand Pierre Arman
Arts Magazine
Baldwin
Bark Frameworks, Inc.
Will Barnet
Nanette Bearden
Andrew Bolotowsky
Chiaroscuro Records
John Crawford
Earl Davis
Terry Dintenfass Gallery
Rackstraw Downes
Dallas Ernst
Gagosian Gallery
Sam Gilliam
The Harrington Press
Hecht and Company, P.C.
Irwin Hollander
Jasper Johns
Donald Judd
Kennedy Galleries, Inc.
Sara M. Kuniyoshi
Sol Lewitt
Roy Lichtenstein
Cady Noland
Kenneth Noland
Nathan Oliveira
Pace Editions
Elena Prohaska
Mrs. Eleanor Quirt
Marcus Ratliff
Robert Rauschenberg
Larry Rivers
Courtney Sale Ross
Salander-O'Reilly Galleries
Kendall Shaw
Candida Smith

BENEFACTORS (cont.)

Rebecca Smith
Sotheby's
William Steig
Muriel & Herbert F. Storfer
Thorner Sidney Printing
Warner Bros. & Reprise Records
Jack Youngerman

PATRONS

The Louis Armstrong Educational Foundation, Inc.
Associated American Artist
Blue Note Records
Mario Buatta
Concord Jazz, Inc.
Elektra Records
Festival Productions, Inc.
Susan and David Horowitz
Phoebe Jacobs
Sidney Janis Gallery
June Kelly Gallery
Barbara & Jon Landau
Marlborough Gallery
Musicmasters Records
Mr. and Mrs. Roy Neuberger
Gloria F. Ross Tapestries
Mary Ryan Gallery
Barbara & Larry Salander
I. B. J. Schroder Bank & Trust Company
V'Soske

DONORS

Peg Alston
Robert & Jan Anderson
Jean Bach
Jean Banks
Dorothea & Laurence Berger
David Blumberg
Linda Bodner
Leslie G. Brennan

DONORS (cont.)

Martin Bressler
Dr. Judith M. Burton
Kim Carter
Andrew Clunn
Eileen & Michael Cohen
Gylbert Coker
Sylvan Cole
Mr. & Mr. Fred C. Collins
Helen & Leo A. Corbie
Evelyn Cunningham
Lester Dembitzer
Michele & Frederick Doner
Marjorie F. Downey
Selma Ertegun
Mr. & Mrs. Neal Fellenbaum
Anne & Gary Fisketjon
Judith Garson
Henry Geldzahler
Lorraine Gordon
William Grossman
Mr. & Mrs. James Harithas
Fred Hechinger
Ruth Houghton
Edgar B. Howard
Michelle Hyk
Yuka Inomata
Sandy Williams Jordan
Sidney Kahn
Dr. Alfred J. Kaltman & Ricelle Grossinger
Stanley King
Burt Korall
Anna Kosof
Robert A. Krasnow
James Levy
Dr. Trevor Lindo
Linda & Ted Lynn
Terry Mansky
David I. Margolis
Claudia Marx
Muriel & Lawrence Mayers
Ronay & Richard Menschel

DONORS (cont.)

Daniel Meyer
Solveig Miesen
Frank Military
Juliette M. Moran
Juliette McGinnis Nelson
Ina Engel & Vincent Norrito
William O'Reilly
Mrs. Sy Oliver
Mr. & Mrs. Jerry Oppenheim
Jimmy Owens
Loriann Palkimas
Mr. & Mrs. James R. Palmer
Robert Panzer
Francine Port
Dr. & Mrs. Donald Reis
Bruce Ricker
Stephen Riker
Lawrence Rivkin
Jane Roche
Betty J. Roemer
Clifford Ross
Gloria F. Ross
Ann Ruckert
Mary Ryan
John Schreiber
Barbara & Robert Schwartz
Mr. & Mrs. Peter W. Schweitzer
Bebe Sheehan
Iris Shorin
Edward G. Shufro
Ben Sidran
John A. Silberman
Toni & Martin T. Sosnoff
Seymour Stein
Annie Stinchfield
Lynn & Glen Tobias
Kenneth R. Todd, Jr.
George Trescher
Mr. & Mrs. Nathaniel Usdan
Robert J. Vanni

Donors to Jazz Foundation of America. (Author's collection)

There were eighty-nine individual donors, twenty patrons (Blue Note & Elektra Records, Festival Productions, Sidney Janis Gallery, Marlborough Gallery to name a few), forty-four benefactors (Will Barnet, Jasper Johns, Don Judd, Sol Lewitt, Roy Lichtenstein, Robert Rauschenberg, Bill Steig, and others) and two major sponsors (Gilbey's Gin and *The New Yorker Magazine*). The art auction featured works by thirty-five prominent artists, including not only works by the benefactors but Romare Beardon, Stuart Davis, Willem de Kooning, Jacob Lawrence, Robert Motherwell, Louise Nevelson, Larry Rivers, and Ben Shahn.

A beautiful souvenir booklet was also produced. It was filled with photographs and biographies of the performing artists, but also illustrations of works by Stuart Davis, photographs of jazz greats associated with jazz and Davis, artists like Duke Ellington, George Wettling, Eddie Condon, Earl Hines, and Art Tatum, letters of support from Mayor David Dinkins, who was later to serve on the JFA board of directors, and Governor Mario Cuomo. Earl Davis wrote about his father and how jazz inspired his work in *Stuart Davis: A Celebration In Jazz*, Dan Morgenstern penned *The Golden Age of Jazz Piano,* and trombonist/actor/gallery owner Conrad Janis provided *Taking Care of Our Own*. Plus, there were a bunch of ads from those who cared, all the way from the Louis Armstrong Educational Foundation to George Wein and Festival Production. For those who would like to see a souvenir program in person a couple of years after the fact, in February 2025 there are three copies in "good" condition available from various dealers associated with ABE Books for less than $20 each and one for $75 that is in better condition.

The Fine Art of Jazz

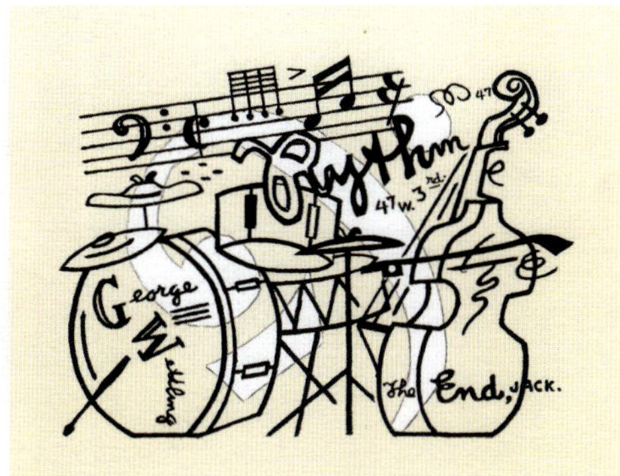

A Stuart Davis Centennial Celebration

Cover, *The Fine Art of Jazz* program. (Author's collection)

When Dorothy Donegan's last notes had faded away and receipts were counted and expenses were deducted and the last bid had been entered and results tallied for the silent auction across the street, the fledgling JFA found itself with it first four- and probably even five-figure payday, with as much as $65,000 to be added to its possibly overdrawn bank account. And from that point onward, especially after JFA hired Wendy Oxenhorn as executive director in 2000, followed by Joe Petrucelli in 2018, JFA began growing into the remarkable organization it has become today.

It is now thirty years later. Instead of assisting a handful of musicians a year, JFA normally handles more than seven thousand cases a year and not just in New York City, but in New Orleans, Puerto Rico, and points north, south, east, and west. Its fundraising events, such as A Great Night in Harlem and its annual loft party, are equally legendary. In February 2025, JFA announced that in partnership with the Mellon Foundation twenty older musicians would be given unrestricted fellowships in the amount of $100,000 each, part of a $35 million Mellon project to support the cultural preservation of jazz.

And if you look up Jabbo Smith on Google on a day like today, you will find he gets many thousands of hits. Every note of music he ever recorded can be found on hundreds of LPs and CDs listed on Amazon, most of it also streams on YouTube, and mint or new copies of his original recordings like "Michigander Blues" on a lightening Brunswick can sell for many thousands of dollars, instead of the $35 Dick Spottswood paid Bob Altshuler fifty-five years ago.

The music sounds just as good fresh as ever; Jabbo was never old-fashioned, and his 1929 recordings don't sound old today, whether on a computer or a "new" original 78 rpm disc. But what sounds even better than Jabbo's music are the words "thank you" that our new executive director, Joe Petrucelli and his dedicated staff hear every day from the ailing and struggling musicians they assist. And in a small way some of these words of thanks should be directed towards the memory of an ailing and struggling musician JFA was in no position to help when he needed it, but who in retrospect, even though he didn't know it, was, however indirectly, able to help JFA when the new organization needed it almost as badly as he did.

Clark Terry

23

Clark Terry

December 14, 1920 – February 21, 2015

ON DECEMBER 14, 2014, I wrote a short essay about my friend Clark Terry. Everything in it is still true and more relevant than ever, but I thought if I expanded it slightly and added some illustrations it would be an ideal entry in *More Than the Music*. This is the revised essay, circa 2025.

Today is Clark Terry's ninety-fourth birthday. It is late in the afternoon in Arkansas, where he lives these days, and his home and mailbox and computer screen are probably already jammed with happy birthday wishes from all corners of the world. The telephone has been ringing all day, and friends and neighbors come and go nonstop for a week or so. It wasn't too long ago that Wynton Marsalis diverted the Lincoln Center Jazz Orchestra tour bus and headed south to Clark and Gwen's home and gave them a concert for two.

Clark is not only one of the oldest jazz musicians still making a contribution to the music but possibly the most beloved. And certainly the most honored. He's the guy who negates the "nice guys finish last" remark attributed to baseball's legendary Leo Durocher. Clark is the best example I know of a nice guy finishing first.

As I look back on my involvement with various aspects of jazz since the mid-1950s, it occurs to me that Clark Terry has been part of that journey almost every step of the way, from the first LPs I acquired as a teenager all the way through today, as I write an entry about him for this book, *More Than The Music*. Just off the top of my head, he was a featured player on either the second or third LP I ever owned in 1955, and I've been listening to him ever since. When I arrived in New York City and built my first recording studio and began producing my own records, Clark was there, first recording for others but then appearing on Chiaroscuro as a leader on many CDs and a featured sideman on countless others. But even before that, he was part of the Composer's Showcase concert series at the Whitney Museum that we recorded for the producers, and that is where I first worked with him.

I've been associated with The New School since 1969 and the Jazz and Contemporary Music program since the mid-1980s. Clark was one of the first to whom we presented the Beacons in Jazz Award, and he then continued to come and perform at subsequent Beacons concerts, raising thousands of scholarship dollars for needy students. He also participated in the long-running Party for Zoot fundraising events at the same school. He was always on the short list of someone we wanted to be an adjunct professor, but his schedule was such it never worked out.

He was an eager participant at the very first Floating Jazz Festival in 1983 and through 1999 was featured at eleven subsequent festivals, the last of which was dedicated to him. When we began to organize US musicians for the annual Oslo Jazz Festival, Clark was perhaps the first and most often requested artist. We snared him in 1992 and 1999.

OPPOSITE

Clark Terry's flugelhorn and personalized chair. (Author's collection)

When I began work on *The Ghosts of Harlem* in 1987, he was almost my first call and he helped me at various stages of completing that book. He didn't need any assistance in the earliest days of the Jazz Foundation of America when it was getting off the ground, but as he became more grounded in the later years of his life, the JFA was there to help and did. I hosted *Christmas Music: The Jazz Feeling* for twenty-five years, and we played Clark's music at various times. Then in 2002, he appeared as my special guest host. We just kept intersecting over the years.

I don't really remember when I first met him, sometime in the 1970s at Downtown Sound when he was recording for someone else, but the earliest I can document, because I took some pictures, was in February 1976 at the Whitney Museum for a Composer's Showcase production that somehow involved Clark, a big band, and Vanessa Redgrave. But I distinctly remember the first time I heard him, sometime in 1955 on a $1.00 EmArcy sampler LP in 1955 called *Jazz of Two Decades*. There was a track entitled "Swahili" that knocked me out as an innocent teenager and still does today sixty-eight years later.

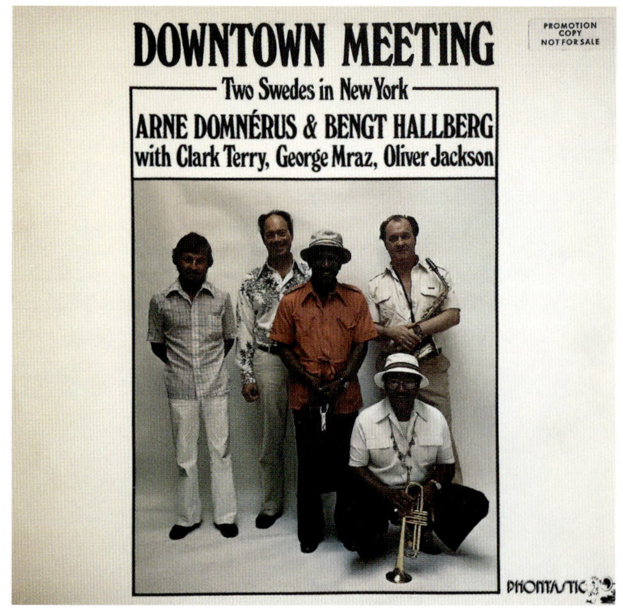

Downtown Meeting LP cover. (Author's collection)

I played "Swahili" over and over again and stopped just short of wearing it out. It was a lucky day for me because from 1955 until today he has been one of my favorite musicians and as years passed, best musical friends. It was a good way to start; just look at who else was on that track, Cecil Payne, Wendell Marshall, Oscar Pettiford, Art Blakey, Horace Silver, and Jimmy Cleveland. And on the rest of the *Jazz of the 50s* side of the album were just as amazing. Sarah Vaughan with Roy Haynes, Erroll Garner, then CT's track, followed by Dinah Washington, where Clark is featured again, and then the side is concluded with Cannonball and Nat and an all-star band playing Quincy Jones's arrangement of "This Song Is You." Like I said, what a way to start! A few years later I scraped together enough to buy the LP *Introducing Clark Terry* in 1958 or so. It was one of his first as a leader. There would be more.

Jazz of Two Decades LP cover. (Author's collection)

Time passed and I kept listening but other than the concert at the Whitney, somehow our paths never crossed until September 5, 1978. My friend, the noted Swedish lawyer, jazz fan, and amateur clarinetist Anders Öhman owned and managed Phontastic, a modest record label in Sweden that released both jazz and classical chamber music. He had business in New York and decided to combine work at the United Nations with a musical excursion into Greenwich Village. He had called ahead and said he wanted to record two of his favorite Swedish musicians, Arne Domnerus and Bengt Hallberg, and combine them with three guys based in New York City: Oliver Jackson, George Mraz, and Clark Terry. I recently looked at the production credits on that album, and I am listed as "Recording Supervisor" and "Photographs By." If true, it must be one of my last efforts at a mixing console, a place I loved to be but had less and less time to be at. But what did happen that day was I met Clark Terry. We hit it off and stayed in touch.

In the early 1980s, I was struggling with John Hammond and John Moore to make a go of it with Hammond Music Enterprises. It was not going as well as we had hoped. I had some casual conversations with Clark about projects that never materialized, but then in the spring of 1983, one did, but it had nothing to do with recordings; it had to do with a music festival at sea. It was the beginning of what for the next twenty years would become known as The Floating Jazz Festival.

Peter Martin Associates, acting on behalf of Norwegian Caribbean Line, asked Shelley Shier and myself to organize a musical event on the then pride of their fleet, the old *S/S France*, now converted to a cruise ship and known as the *S/S Norway*. They were having a hard time selling cruises during hurricane season and were looking for something to distract seasick passengers, or better still, lure them onboard. It was a hard sell; forty years ago, the *S/S Norway* was the largest ocean liner now cruise ship afloat. We suggested jazz might draw passengers who were less worried about stormy seas than a typical cruiser, they bought it, and that was the start of a two-decade adventure that for some cruise lines and other producers continues to this day.

NCL and Peter Martin Associates didn't pull the trigger until April or early May. Most music festivals book many months, if not years, in advance. We were way behind schedule even for a club date, let alone a festival. We had almost no time to pull things together and no reputation for booking artists for festivals, especially a festival on board an ocean liner. So it fell to me to call musicians I knew, men and women who knew I wasn't an idiot because what I was suggesting sounded idiotic. Many years later, in 1999, we dedicated the festival to Clark, and looking back to the beginning, I wrote:

> *Clark Terry has been part of the Floating Jazz Festival from the very beginning. On the day in April 1983 when we made the decision to produce the first Floating Jazz Festival, we made two calls, one to Clark, the other to Earl Hines. In retrospect, it is easy to see the direction the festival was to take, just based on those two calls. Earl, of course was eager to take part, but he was not in good health and died two weeks later. Clark, on the other hand, was on board as an integral part of the festival for the next eight years.*
>
> *There were a handful of artists who defined the festival in those early years, and Clark, along with Dizzy Gillespie, Joe Williams, Mel Torme, Benny Carter, Cab Calloway, and Woody Herman, was one of those people. The difference, however, was that Clark was there every year, either as a soloist or leading his own group. He was the great artist everyone could count on; if there was a Floating Jazz Festival, Clark would be there. It was that simple, and it was this kind of tradition that made the festival special.*

The first year out, Clark had a group with Zoot Sims and they were so popular, we kept them together in 1984. Well in advance of the 1985 festival, we asked Clark to come aboard the ship for four weeks and to bring his big band book with him. The *S/S Norway* had a big band on board that was filled with some of the best studio guys in Miami. They mostly played for dancing, and we'd been told they'd be thrilled to be able to play Clark's big band jazz book. But how did we manage to go from a week at sea in 1983 to four weeks in 1985? This is the story.

In 1985, Norwegian Caribbean Line, astounded that jazz music, as presented by the likes of Clark Terry and his pals, had filled the ship first in 1983 and then for two weeks in 1984, in hurricane season no less, were willing to take a chance on four weeks. We asked Clark to be onboard for all four weeks, but he was only available for three of them. The first week he was onboard, he gave his all for five days and then on the sixth got to relax one afternoon on the beach while the ship was anchored off a Bahamian island, Little Stirrup Cay. He liked the beach and told me he planned to go the next week and relax a little more. I asked him if he'd bring his trumpet along so I could take a picture we could use as a poster the following year. He thought that was a fine idea, and the next week we went to the island, found a spot where the *S/S Norway* was in the background, he walked into the water, and I took the picture. Clark then relaxed for the rest of the day, returned to the ship and either led the big band or performed with his own group.

With Mel Torme, 1985 Floating Jazz Festival. (Author's collection)

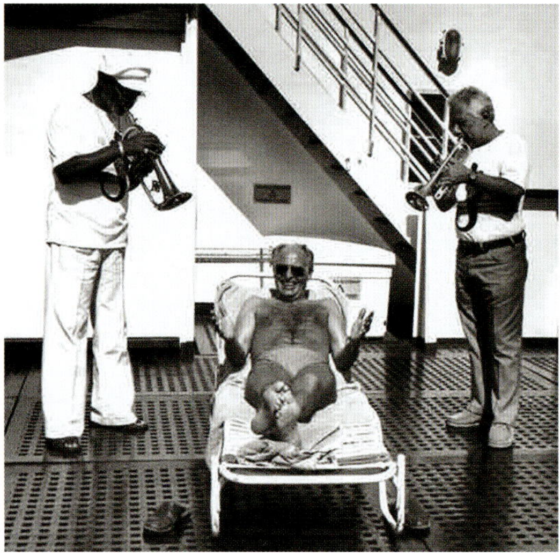

With Ruby Braff serenading Captain Haugassen, 1984 FJF. (Author's collection)

The picture turned out and we used it many times. And for those interested in such things, if you look carefully, in addition to the *Norway* in the background there is a small boat with a red sail. The sailboat was being navigated by the pianist Eddie Higgins, who sailed as well as he played piano. He was the only other musician who challenged CT for most weeks as part of a Floating Jazz Festival.

Even more fun than playing in the Caribbean Sea was the night there was a late night session in Club Internationale where I found Clark singing a duet with Mel Tormé, with Mel doing double duty on drums. This was probably a night when Mel did his big show in the Saga Theater, after which he ditched his tuxedo and prowled around looking for a group he could join for a few numbers as a session drummer. He was pretty good, and no one ever said no.

Things were not only bubbling around at sea with Clark, but they were getting active on land as well. In 1987, he was one of the first people I interviewed for my book *The Ghosts of Harlem*, and then two years later, as the new incarnation of Chiaroscuro Records was getting off the ground, I asked him to bring his reconstituted group, The Clark Terry Spacemen, into Rudy Van Gelder's studio in Englewood Cliffs, New Jersey. There were only two of the original "Spacemen" in the band, Clark and Britt Woodman, but ringers like Al Grey and Haywood Henry and Phil Woods filled in nicely for the long departed Ellingtonians who made up the original group. I tried to get Jimmy Hamilton to come join the band, but he wouldn't budge from his happy and relaxed life in St. Croix. The recording was a great success. It was issued with a cover design by Johnny DeVries and reissued with a cover designed by Clark himself. Except for *The Return of Mel Powell*, this was the only Chiaroscuro release that featured a cover designed by the leader of the recording.

The Ghosts of Harlem interview was at Clark's home in Queens and took place on February 16, 1987, just as I was getting into the project. He not only answered all the questions but gave me sound advice on how I should approach my subject matter and how to best deal with some of his peers. When I told him that a few weeks earlier Milt Hinton had expressed concern about me doing this book, his exact words being, "Why does a white guy like you have to write this book about Harlem? Aren't there any young black writers who care? In my classes I try to talk about things like this." And Clark had much the same feeling. He didn't try to dissuade me; just the opposite, he encouraged me, but it made him sad all the same. He had experienced racial prejudice and animosity all his life, and it still surrounded him in his Whitestone

Clark Terry on the beach, Little Stirrup Cay, Bahamas. (Author's collection)

With Doc Cheatham. 1984 FJF. (Author's collection)

The Clark Terry Spacemen CD, Version #1. (Author's collection)

The Clark Terry Spacemen CD, Version #2. (Author's collection)

Relaxing at home, 1987. (Author's collection)

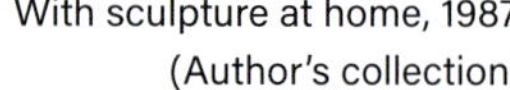

With sculpture at home, 1987. (Author's collection)

With Gwen Terry in Oslo. (Author's collection)

With Gwen on the S/S *Norway*. (Author's collection)

neighborhood. Yet he was determined to do whatever he could to combat it, on the bandstand and off, in the classroom with his students, or in a hot, sweltering rehearsal studio he kept in Harlem just to tutor and mentor young musicians.

That first day at his home was a revelation to me, because he told me he was experiencing nasty racial harassment at that very moment. He had a neighbor who didn't like the idea of a black guy on his block, especially one who had a white girlfriend who was far more attractive than his wife, or someone who turned up as a featured soloist on late night TV as part of *The Tonight Show* orchestra. And this guy did all sorts of things to annoy Clark; petty things like sneaking out at night and piling up trash cans in the back of his car. We brainstormed a little and came up with some novel ideas to get back at this creep and did.

And then the years whizzed by, and it was 1991. That was the year back surgery slowed Clark down for a minute, but not too many of them. It was going to be a special week at sea. We had often presented Gary Burton leading a group of his finest students that we called The Berklee Ensemble, but this year we were expanding things. Clark had put together a big band made up of the best students from his classes at the University of New Hampshire. We scheduled the band for three evenings of performances, but at the last moment the leader had back surgery and was unable to even sit, let alone lead the band. But we brought the band on anyway, and it was led on different nights by Dizzy Gillespie or Jon Faddis or Red Rodney, and nobody complained.

Clark recovered nicely, and we managed to snare him in 1995 and 1997 for our festival at sea and even produced a record in 1995 he called *Top and Bottom*, named for a drink he'd once enjoyed in Harlem. We wanted to have a special *Top and Bottom* cover, and to accomplish this we gave a copy of a photo I'd taken of Clark to one of Hugh Hefner's favorite Playboy artists, the legendary Buck Brown, who embellished the photo with very appropriate tops and bottoms. Clark told me Buck's tops and bottoms were far superior to any drinks he had in Harlem.

And then suddenly it was 1999 and the seventeenth Annual Floating Jazz Festival aboard QE2, which was billed as *A Tribute to Clark Terry*. I asked Clark who he wanted to be on board and he gave me a list. The first man I called was Oscar Peterson who dropped whatever he was doing and signed on immediately, as did fifty other musicians, with a dozen leaders to keep them in check.

With Oscar Peterson on the QE2, 1999. (Author's collection)

The Clark Terry Quintet Live on QE2 CD, 1995. (Author's collection)

The Clark Terry Quintet Top and Bottom CD, 1999. (Author's collection)

There were written and musical tributes for ten days at sea. Two of his best pals, Oscar Peterson and Quincy Jones, said it all in a few sentences. Oscar: *To me Clark Terry epitomizes the culmination of everything I want to hear and realize from a jazz musician. He is the epitome of true talent. But perhaps above all he is a very warm and treasured friend of mine.* Quincy: *At fifteen years old, you showed me the right way to put the horn to my lips. Then twelve years later, you left Duke's band to come play with my band in Europe. If you hadn't been there, I wouldn't be here. I always have, and always will love you, and thank you from the deepest part of my soul.* That was twenty-six years ago, and it's all still true in 2025, at least as far as the ghosts of Q and OP are concerned. And there are hundreds if not thousands of others who feel the same way. If you need to see why this is the case, simply have a look at the film about CT mentoring a young blind pianist, Justin Kauflin. The year *Keep On Keepin' On* was released it made its way to the short list for an Academy Award for Best Documentary.

With Shirley Horn, 1999 FJF. (Author's collection)

We recorded all of Clark's performances that week on the QE2, and the best one was perhaps the last night of the festival. One aspect of the CD we were producing was to have Clark accompany each of the female vocalists on board that week on at least one song. It was working perfectly; at one performance Etta Jones did "Fine and Mellow," at another Carrie Smith sang "Everyday I Have the Blues," and Vanessa Rubin teased everyone with "Just Squeeze Me." But we were missing Shirley Horn. She was singing and playing wonderfully but was tired, frail and their performance schedules just didn't align very well. But finally on the last night at sea, the stars did line up, and Shirley arrived at the theater in a wheelchair. We managed to get her on stage, and the two great artists teamed up for a moving duet, just Shirley with her unique voice and piano and Clark on flugelhorn for a suitably beautiful "But Beautiful."

A Tribute to Clark Terry poster, 1999 FJF. (Author's collection)

That same year Clark was a major part of the Oslo Jazz Festival, and for some reason his wife, Gwen, was unable to accompany him, so we traveled together. By this time his diabetes was kicking in pretty good and he also had some vision issues; when he'd use that little pin prick device to check his blood sugar level he had a hard time reading the number, so I took charge and did my seeing eye dog duty as best as possible.

Clark was scheduled to do a special concert with Teri Thornton, but at the last moment Teri had to cancel and was replaced by Vanessa Rubin. The restructured concert went well, and the following day I took Clark to the new airport at Gardermoen; he had to be somewhere else in Europe for a concert the following day. It was a long ride and along the way we chatted about many things, including his eyesight, but I'll never forget when we reached the airport and an extremely attractive lady exited the car in front of us. Clark had no trouble seeing her and describing her various attributes in exacting detail. Perhaps he only had trouble with the small print.

Relaxing at the Oslo Jazz Festival, 1999.
(Author's collection)

With Randi Hultin and Vanessa Rubin at the Oslo Jazz Festival, 1999.
(Author's collection)

My next out-of-the-ordinary close encounter with Clark was in 2002 on the radio. Since the mid-1980s, I'd been the on-air host of an NPR holiday show produced by Andrew Sordoni and WVIA-FM. The one-hour program was presented annually for twenty-five years and broadcast by upwards of one hundred NPR affiliates around the country. In 2002, Clark Terry was the celebrity musical guest. It was always an adventure to put the show together, the right musician, the right music; it was a lot of fun, but this year we got a late start. Sometimes we did the show as early as September, but this year because of festivals and assorted commitments we didn't get to create the show until November 27, and this left very little time to not only get everything ready to be put up on the NPR satellite to send it all over the country but to manufacture and distribute a few hundred special CDs of the program to friends and family of NPR, WVIA, Clark and Gwen Terry, Andrew Sordoni, and myself.

Christmas Music The Jazz Feeling, 2002. (Author's collection)

Clark was based in New Jersey at the time, and WVIA sent a truck outfitted with a remote recording studio to his home. We had selected eleven Christmas tunes that had been jazzed up by the likes of Oscar Peterson, Louis Armstrong, Terry Gibbs, Duke Ellington, and Clark himself. This was also the year when we included the famous Charlie Parker version of "White Christmas." It was from a radio broadcast on Christmas Day in 1948 from the Royal Roost and somehow it was recorded. It has appeared on countless LPs over the years, but I had somehow managed to acquire the private 78 rpm disc that John Steiner had issued in the late 1940s. After a couple of tunes by Clark's pal Oscar, and Louis Armstrong doing "Christmas Night In Harlem," we switched to Parker and "White Christmas." When asked if he'd ever played with Parker, Clark replied:

After the show. (Author's collection)

We were up at The Band Box, and Bird was at Birdland next door opposite the Basie band. And Duke said, "I'll hook up a set with the 'hip boys.' He called us the "hip boys," me, Jimmy Hamilton and Paul Gonsalves. So Bird said, "What do you want to play?" He was such a beautiful person too, so humble and he said, "Whatever you fellows would like to do." So I said, "Let's do 'Scrapple From the Apple,'" and he said, "So you fellows like my little ditty, oh that's good, I'd love to do that with you," so we played that and he was such a sweet person. It was just unbelievable.

In retrospect I wish we hadn't been recording the radio show because I should have followed up and asked a bunch of questions that didn't have anything to do with *Christmas Music – The Jazz Feeling.*

Then I ran into him by accident in Bern, Switzerland. He wasn't physically there but I was, and his presence was all around because he been a frequent and major participant at the annual Internationale JazzFestival in Bern on many different occasions and had also turned up with some frequency at Marians Jazzroom in that city. Marians is the finest venue for live jazz in the city, if not in all of Switzerland. Located in the unique Innere Enge Hotel, the finest jazz and blues artists perform there or have performed at the annual festival on a regular basis. The finest of those artists, Oscar Peterson, John Lewis,

The Young Titans of Jazz CD booklet cover, 2004.
(Author's collection)

Louie Bellson, Milt Hinton, Lionel Hampton, and a host of others have been honored with a named room in the hotel. Clark's room is No. 1, dedicated when the hotel opened in 1992.

In May 2004, Clark had assembled a sixteen-piece big band to perform at that year's festival in Bern. He called it The Young Titans of Jazz and it was everything the name suggested. The band was mostly young and younger, and they played for an entire week and almost every note was professionally recorded. In the booklet that accompanied the CD that featured the best of the performances I wrote in 2005:

> *When Clark asked if Chiaroscuro would like to release a CD of the best of his performances at the Bern festival, we jumped at the chance, but we wanted to add something we thought might make the release even more special. We felt in addition to presenting the music, we should also present Clark, sharing his thoughts about music education, all the way from those who gave him his first lessons, through his fifty plus years of training others. This remarkable story, condensed to fifty-plus minutes, is presented on a supplemental CD. Nat Hentoff and I asked the questions. Clark's answers have been slightly rearranged because the questions we asked weren't in chronological order and the narrative flows much better with a little judicious editing.*

We also asked one of his more famous students to write the liner notes. Quincy Jones's notes are as perfect as the best of his arrangements and productions.

> *When I was a teenager, the Count Basie Band came through my town—Seattle. I somehow got Clark to agree to give me several trumpet lessons. In spite of the fact that he was working late at night and I was going to school early in the morning, he managed to find a couple of hours before school for my lessons. He was always loving, inspiring, and motivating.*
>
> *While listening to this tape, I discovered that he still takes the time to encourage, inspire, and motivate young musicians. The album is great and the talent is fantastic. I'm sure you'll love it. I do.*
>
> *He is a giant, as a musician and as a human being. Keep on keepin' on. CeeTee. There will never be another you. With all my love and gratitude and big time props!*

And CeeTee kept on until the very end, mostly in Arkansas in his last days, mentoring young musicians who would have their lessons in his bedroom. Clark died February 21, 2015. His funeral/memorial service at Harlem's Abyssinian Baptist Church was not only standing room only but spilled onto 138th Street. Reverend Calvin Butts was in charge of the service and dozens of musicians were on hand to perform and offer their tributes. When the formalities were over, Wynton Marsalis and the Lincoln Center Jazz Orchestra gave Clark the best New Orleans-style sendoff ever seen in Harlem.

QUINCY JONES

When I was a teenager, the Count Basie Band came through my town - Seattle. I somehow got Clark to agree to give me several trumpet lessons. In spite of the fact that he was working late at night and I was going to school early in the morning, he managed to find a couple of hours before school for my lessons. He was always loving, inspiring and motivating.

While listening to this tape, I discovered that he still takes the time to encourage, inspire and motivate young musicians. The album is great and the talent is fantastic. I'm sure you'll love it. I do.

He is a giant, as a musician, and as a human being.

Keep on keepin' on, Cee Tee. There will never, ever be another you.

With all my love and gratitude and big time props!

Quincy

A note from Quincy Jones, 2004.
(Author's collection)

In the Abyssinian Baptist Church, 2015. (Author's collection)

On the street with Wynton Marsalis.
(Author's collection)

24

Joe Venuti and Zoot Sims

Septmber 16, 1903 – August 14, 1978

October 29, 1925 – March 23, 1985

THE OTHER DAY an email arrived from someone interested in the legendary violinist Joe Venuti and concerned a 1928 recording on Dinah. One paragraph read as follows:

> *This recording was made in New York City on March 8th 1928 by "Joe Venuti's Blue Four"* featuring Joe Venuti violin & leader, Eddie Lang guitar, Rube Bloom piano, Don Murray baritone sax, and Justin Ring bell. *"Dinah"* was composed by Harry *Akst, with lyrics by Sam M. Lewis and Joe Young.*

This notice set off a chain reaction of thoughts about Joe and this particular song and took me back to the mid-1970s when Joe Venuti and a bunch of his pals assembled at Downtown Sound and recorded "Dinah" fifty years ago. It had exactly the same instrumentation of violin, piano, guitar, and bass saxophone, and the arrangement Joe structured for the group was similar to the one in 1928. You can listen to each version via YouTube and the Internet.

I was very lucky because when I began producing records over fifty years ago there were still a handful of great musicians from the 1920s, the first golden age of jazz, who could still play their instruments with as much skill, passion, and inventiveness as they could and did as young men and women fifty years earlier. Extraordinary artists, incomparable musicians like Joe Venuti (b. 1903?), Earl Hines (b. 1903), Mary Lou Williams (b. 1910), and even Eddie Condon (b. 1905) and Gene Krupa (b. 1909) all turned up on Chiaroscuro, as did many of their friends and associates from those years, Bud Freeman (b. 1906), Jess Stacy (b. 1904), Spencer Clark (b. 1908), Eubie Blake (b. 1887), Wild Bill Davison (b. 1906), Willie "The Lion" Smith (b. 1893), and Milt Hinton (b. 1910).

But the two artists who appeared most frequently at my recording studio in those years were Earl Hines and Joe Venuti. Joe was leader or co-leader on six LPs plus one reissue, and Earl was the leader or a featured sideman on twelve. And Joe almost appeared on a seventh, as a rather unusual leader, but that's a story I'll tell later because first I have to tell the story of what happened in 1973.

Every so often you get lucky; the sun comes up, it's a nice day, you meet someone special, and you wind up working or socializing with this person for years to come. Sometimes the person turns out to be unique, even a legendary person, perhaps someone you've known of forever but never thought you would meet, but then suddenly there they are, they are wonderful, and it all works out just as it should.

OPPOSITE

Joe Venuti and Zoot Sims, 1973.
(Author's collection)

September 27 was a Thursday in 1973, and I don't remember how the day started but I remember how it went from about 1:00 onward at my barely one-year-old recording studio, then known as WARP Studio, and how it ended four or five hours later. And I remember working with two legendary musicians together for the first time that day, a recording session that didn't change my life or theirs, but one that did lead to a great deal of good music being made for the next decade plus.

This was not the first time I'd met and worked with Joe Venuti, that had happened a few years earlier in 1970 at Sherman Fairchild's studio, but it was the first time I met the equally legendary Zoot Sims. Most of what I knew about either of them up to then was from records, books, and tall tales seemingly told by everyone who had worked with or known either man. And the most recent tales I'd heard were about how the unusual combination of a hard-charging 1920s-era violinist and an equally hard-swinging saxophonist from the 1940s was the most exciting "new" act on the block or at least the jazz party scene in 1973. It wasn't my idea to get Joe Venuti and Zoot Sims together musically, but it was my idea to get them recorded. The idea to team Joe with Zoot Sims had first been done in the late 1960s at one of Dick Gibson's legendary jazz parties.

Dick Gibson brought Joe Venuti and Zoot Sims to one of his Colorado jazz parties in 1968 but failed to program them together. But Zoot watched Joe dazzle everyone and in 1969, Dick brought them back to his party and programmed them together. Overnight their stars were born and quickly the word began to spread. *The New Yorker* ran a brilliant story by Whitney Balliett, and soon everyone was talking about this unique musical combination. It was a union of two strong musical personalities and, on the face of it, one so unlikely that only an inspired super-enthusiast would have considered recording them. An ordinary, faint-hearted bottom liner A&R man at a major or even minor record label would have never taken the chance.

But this was the state of the record business in 1970 and beyond; no one cared except for a tiny, obscure label with but a few releases to its credit. In those days there were almost no indies; John Hammond was throttled at Columbia; Norman Granz hadn't launched Pablo; Joe and Zoot weren't anything for Creed Taylor, Bob Thiele, or either Ertegun; and George Avakian was still on hiatus, more concerned with the family business than hot jazz, so it fell to tiny Chiaroscuro to come up with a few dollars to get one of the hottest bands of the decade on tape and it worked out perfectly.

Joe and Zoot were brilliant, but I only had them together at my studio on five different days, September 27, 1973, May 28 and 29, 1974, and one day in May 1975. There was a photo call on September 29, 1973, for an album cover. Joe brought his violin and some cigarettes, which he smoked one time too often, and Zoot brought his soprano saxophone; the tenor was too heavy for a noon call. As I think about it today, I find it puzzling that no one else jumped in after the release of the first LP, but they didn't and I got to make two more.

But I wasn't done with Joe. He came back for his duo session with Earl Hines on October 22, 1975, and I recorded a duo session with Joe and Dave McKenna at Albany's Palace Theater over two days, April 27 and 28, 1977. In August 1976, I visited Joe in Seattle and arranged to purchase some master tapes that I issued the following year.

And so, over the course of about five years I spent part of a day on about twenty occasions in the company of Joe Venuti; not a lot of time, but enough to get to know him a bit, enjoy his company, and enjoy watching him create a lot of exceptional music.

It lasted longer with Zoot because he lived until 1985. He not only recorded with Joe but was at the studio for a number of other sessions as well, was part of the Floating Jazz Festival on two occasions, and we even got to socialize a bit because he was local and could come down for dinner or even pop in my office uptown. But here's a day by day with both of these remarkable artists. It's a peculiar chronology, but in the end it all makes sense.

1970
Joe Venuti at Sherman Fairchild's

This is a lost recording and my first meeting with the guy many people simply called "the old man," and it took place at Sherman Fairchild's home/studio in New York City. I was doing a favor for George Buck, the owner of Jazzology, a record company he'd founded many years earlier. He had called and said he wanted to record and release an LP featuring Joe Venuti in a quartet setting and wondered if I could help. He had a low or no budget for a studio, and he'd heard I could help with things like that and I did.

George had hired Venuti, and Joe rounded up the rest of the group. Not only was it my first time working with Joe, but Milt Hinton and Lou Stein as well. I knew Cliff Leeman because of the Bobby Hackett Roosevelt

At Sherman Fairchild's home/studio, 1970. (Author's collection)

Grill recordings. The only thing that survives from this recording session are a handful of photographs I took with my then-new Pentax 35mm SLR. We recorded for the better part of an afternoon and there were at least four, perhaps as many as six, good takes but not enough for an LP. I shipped the tapes off to George, but there was no follow-up session to complete the project. To the best of my knowledge, none of this material has ever been issued. I was not to see Joe again for three years.

September 27, 1973
Joe & Zoot

This was the first session with Joe and Zoot. It was just a quintet, and it was clear from the outset Joe was in charge. The rhythm section for the recording was chosen by Joe; indeed, virtually everything including tunes and tempos was chosen by him. Dick Wellstood, a relative newcomer to working with the legendary violinist, was admittedly terrified and he told me so. George Duvivier and Cliff Leeman were ideal choices; each man had worked with both Joe and Zoot many times in the past. All the performances were simple head arrangements, worked out by the participants in the studio, with Venuti making most of the decisions. Joe would ask, "How about such and such?" and Zoot might nod and everyone would noodle around for a bit and they'd find a solo order and a tempo and then away they'd go. Each selection was either pretty or hot and the session couldn't have been easier. This loosely structured jam session-like recording was over in four or five hours. There were a couple of false starts, but no breakdowns or alternate takes.

The date was full of musical surprises, not the least of which was the last number, "C Jam Blues." It began with a spirited ensemble; Zoot soloed after the introduction, followed by Dick and then Cliff Leeman and Joe. As Cliff was working his way through his drum solo, Joe began to disassemble his bow. My engineer Fred Miller, a classically trained musician (oboe and English horn), was shocked and had no idea what was happening and then almost collapsed when Venuti began bowing from underneath the violin, playing all four strings (à la "Four String Joe") at once. We were lucky that the microphone placement didn't have to be changed. But no one missed a beat, and it was a perfect way to end the day. As I recall, there were no second takes or a need to repeat anything. Joe and Zoot were so happy with what they'd accomplished they each promised to do it again the following year.

Joe & Zoot & More CD booklet. (Author's collection)

With Zoot Sims and Dick Wellstood, 1973. (Author's collection)

March 25–26, 1974
A Buck Clayton Jam Session

Buck Clayton, March 1974. (Author's collection)

This was totally different circumstances; Zoot was part of a four-man saxophone section, surrounded by six other all-star musicians, all improvising within the confines of Buck Clayton's arrangements. The other saxophones were Earle Warren, Budd Johnson, and Joe Temperley. This was the first Buck Clayton jam session to be recorded since those organized by George Avakian in the 1950s, and to make sure all was in order George was on hand, as was John Hammond. It was the first time these two guys had been in a studio together in a minute or two.

Ping Pong with Joe Newman, Budd Johnson, and Joe Temperley, 1974. (Author's collection)

Since Buck was in charge of wrangling the ten all-stars, I handled the secretarial chores that consisted of writing the solo order on an old portable blackboard. The first tune was called "Boss Blues," and Buck wanted Earl Hines to start things off, but it turned out no one was willing to follow Earl. There was some discussion, and everyone but Zoot agreed he should follow Earl. He did, spectacularly, setting the stage for a remarkable two-day recording session.

May 28–29, 1974
The "Lost" Joe & Zoot Session

I didn't have to wait a year, only eight months, but this turned out to be a very peculiar, almost disastrous session. This time, some care had been taken in selecting songs and structuring different combinations of musicians. In fact, we planned five different instrumental combinations, all the way from duets to a six-piece group, and I had flown Spencer Clark in to become Adrian Rollini on bass saxophone for the day. This is what happened.

One day the telephone rang and it was Joe. He suggested I join him for lunch at the Berkshire Hotel to go over a few loose ends before the recording. Joe always stayed at the Berkshire because they had clean rooms and the manager was an amateur violinist to whom Joe gave lessons in exchange for a really nice room at an even nicer price; no charges for the violin teacher.

With Bucky Pizzarelli, Spencer Clark, Oliver Jackson, and Dill Jones, 1975. (Author's collection)

I arrived at the hotel dressed down, coming directly from a session at the studio. I was refused entrance to the dining room because the rules were I was required to have a jacket and tie. Remember, this was 1974, and even though the Berkshire wasn't the St. Regis, it was close enough to have a snooty maitre d'. Joe was outraged. He stormed out of the dining room and told me to follow him upstairs to his on-the-house room, #1217. Once there, he went to a closet and grabbed a jacket and tossed it to me, theb said, "Put that on." I did, but I am a forty-two long and this jacket was a fifty-four short. It looked as though I was wearing a tent with arms that ended at my elbows. He tossed me a nasty looking tie and once again said, "Put that on." I did, and we went back to the restaurant where I was seated and served even though I looked like Bozo the Clown. But we managed to fill in the loose ends and our stomachs.

The next day everyone arrived on time, including an honored "guest" photographer, the legendary André Kertesz. He was a neighbor I was now visiting with frequently, and I'd invited him to come by and take photographs. He got along well with Joe, who was happy to have him around because it meant he wasn't the oldest guy in the room. How old was Joe? Who knows? The most up-to-date Wiki says he was born in 1903, and so does a memorial plaque in Philadelphia. But others say he was born in Italy in 1898. At one of the recording sessions some of Joe's relatives came up from Philadelphia, and I asked an older guy who had a no-nonsense look if it was true that Joe was born on the ship coming to America. He gave me

With Bucky Pizzarelli, Spencer Clark, Oliver Jackson, and Dill Jones, 1975. (Author's collection)

a look and said, "Yeah, and he was playing pretty good when he got off the boat." That was good enough for me.

The first group we recorded was the sextet with Joe, Zoot, Spencer Clark, Bucky Pizzarelli, Dill Jones, and Oliver Jackson. As the group rehearsed, André began working his magic. A nice side story: A number of other photographers were there that day because the word had gotten out about Joe and Zoot and all wanted to grab a picture of the two men together. At one point one of the other photographers asked me, "Who is that old guy in the corner?" I replied, "André Kertesz." He or she gasped, and the word spread quickly. Soon all the non-André photographers left the room to allow him to not have to work around them.

But the recording itself was a disaster because of a phasing problem we didn't discover until the session was over. By accident we had been listening in the control room off the record head instead of the playback head, and what was coming in wasn't what wound up on tape. It was the only session that was ever lost at the studio. All we recorded that day was light on a few rolls of film. But Joe was undeterred. He and the other bands returned the following day, and we completed the album with a tasty quintet in which Dick Hyman replaced Dill Jones. This was the group that recorded the song "Deep Night," one that I'd suggested to Joe. Zoot was hesitant, but he was game and was suitably spectacular. Once he'd heard the playback he wanted me to make him a copy of the sheet music. I didn't have a copy machine so I gave him the sheet.

The Dave McKenna Quartet album cover, 1974.
(Author's collection)

October 27, 1974
The Dave McKenna Quartet

A monthlong quartet gig with Zoot at Michael's Pub may have been the longest engagement Dave McKenna ever had in New York City. He was camped out at the Condon apartment on Washington Square, and I was often camped out at Michael's Pub. I decided early on I wanted to record the quartet, and because of the way things worked out it may have featured Dave's name but it was Zoot all the way. Dave was much too shy and modest to be a bandleader.

Everyone recognizes that recordings from long ago can become important many years later, and one track on this album proves the point many times over. It was called "One Good Turn," which on my take sheets I'd simply written as "Erroll's Tune."

Zoot was in tremendous form that night. The night went on and on, and there were breaks along the way, the kind of thing you can do if the clock is not being watched. One of the tunes we did that night was a ballad Eddie Condon had written in the 1940s, "Wherever There's Love." Dave wanted to do it as a thank you for Phyllis Condon, his then landlady, but Zoot not only didn't know the tune, he'd never even heard it. But he was game and after a little rehearsal with Dave, the quartet recorded two five-minute masterpieces and then we had a playback. The playback wasn't for the band; we put the telephone by a speaker and let Phyllis Condon have a listen. She picked take one, and then we moved on to the next selection.

But the highlight of the night was the previously mentioned "One Good Turn," but nobody knew it at the time. And they don't know it today. But more about that a few pages and years down the road.

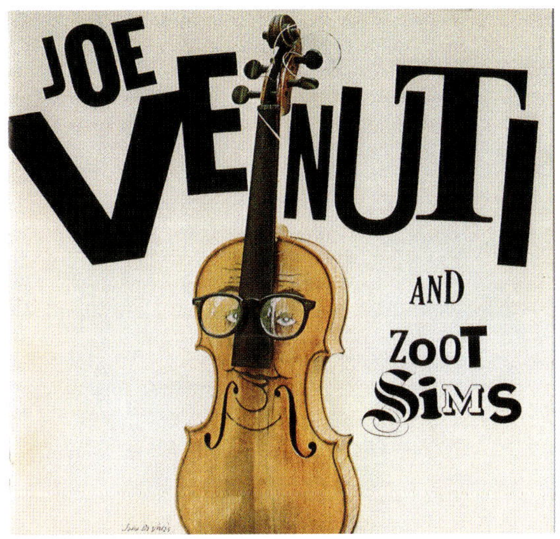

Joe Venuti and Zoot Sims album cover, 1974.
(Author's collection)

May, 1975
Joe Venuti & Zoot Sims

And then it was a year later, and we assembled a totally different rhythm section to accompany Joe and Zoot as well as a special guest from Joe's past. John Bunch, piano; Milt Hinton, bass; and Bobby Rosengarden, drums were the rhythm section. I'm not sure but Bobby and Milt may have been in Joe's group at Michael's Pub. The special guest from the past was trombonist Spiegel Wilcox; the two men had performed together as part of the Jean Goldkette band in the mid-1920s.

There was nothing left to chance other than how Joe and Spiegel might get along after all those years apart. I probably had seen Spiegel more recently than Joe; I'd actually tracked him down many years earlier at the Wilcox Oil and Coal Company in Cortland, New York, and was amazed to walk into an office filled with Bix Beiderbecke

Rehearsal, 1974.
(Author's collection)

memorabilia and Jean Goldkette posters from the 1920s. But the two old guys hit it off, and Spiegel continued to work with Joe until Joe ran out of gas in 1978. And Spiegel sent me the craziest letters I'd ever seen until his tank emptied out in 1999. He had a great second act after he gave up the coal company.

October 22, 1975
Hot Sonatas with Joe Venuti and Earl Hines

Once upon a time, a violin and piano sonata was one of the most popular and frequently composed musical formats. That time was in the 1700s when a violin/piano combo was the new kid on the block. It is much less popular today.

In the 1970s, I was always searching for an exciting, unusual combination of players or instruments. In October 1975, I decided to attempt a recording of some hot piano/violin sonatas with Joe and Earl Hines. I knew it was a long shot, and it was a combination rarely recorded in jazz, but my feeling was that Joe and Earl performing Ellington was just as interesting as Perlman and Levine performing Mozart.

In 1975, both Joe and Earl were legendary figures, but they did not know one another; if they had met, it was only in passing. They had never even thought of recording together, nor had anyone else had the idea. I suggested it to each man separately and both, while possibly mystified, accepted the offer. On the appointed day in October, they greeted one another formally at the recording studio and got down to the business of agreeing on songs to perform. There was no show of ego, no strained moments; an old videotape of part of the session shows how smoothly everything went that day. It was just a meeting of two highly professional musical giants tending to the business at hand.

Creative sparks flew all afternoon. There were no bad takes, just outstanding takes and then some that were even better. It was one of the few instances in the studio where Hines made more than a single take of anything, but only because of the videotaping. A guy with a primitive Sony reel-to-reel videotape recorder captured five selections. It was almost as if we used them for rehearsals because as soon as the bright lights required for the video were turned off, we recorded the real takes. The final

Hot Sonatas album cover, 1975. (Author's collection)

Alternate portrait, 1975. (Author's collection)

performance, "C Jam Blues," was a masterpiece, and this time Fred Miller was not surprised with the four-string-Joe routine.

Joe really enjoyed the date. It was an unusual experience for him, and afterwards we took some pictures of the two men with Earl fiddling with the painted fiddle John DeVries had created for the Joe and Zoot album recorded earlier in the year. The expressions of the two men in these photographs point to the success of the date, especially the one used for the album/booklet cover. Outstanding as the combination was, their paths never crossed again.

April 27–28, 1977
Joe Venuti and Dave McKenna
Alone at the Palace

This is one of my favorite recordings from the decade of the 1970s, and I took care fashioning the liner notes, probably more words than were needed but I never counted them. As I recall they were all included in a long *JazzTimes* feature about Joe when that publication still looked like a newspaper. This what I said in the first two paragraphs:

> *The Palace Theater is a three thousand seat movie house; a relic of the past when three thousand people were likely to go to the picture show on Saturday night; a somewhat more dignified way to spend an evening than standing in line in the rain to cram into little places with names like Cinema-One-Two-Three or going to a movie at the mall. The theater failed a few years ago and was taken over by the city of Albany but unlike many of the older buildings in the central city, Albany didn't let the Palace fall down; some enterprising people got a direct line to the Palladium and the Bottom Line. Pictures of all the current pop acts are hung all over the box office wall, but prominently displayed in the manager's office is a dusty tin sign in a copper frame announcing Joe Venuti's Orchestra and The Andrew Sisters. A reminder of the once upon a less frantic time when a guy with a violin could be "popular."*

With Dave McKenna, 1977.
(Author's collection)

Alone at the Palace album cover, 1977.
(Author's collection)

> *Joe was back at the Palace in April 1977, sitting behind a massive, shiny-new nine foot grand. He plays piano well, but not as well as Dave McKenna, for whom he was waiting, to begin recording an album of duets. He hadn't been in the theater since 1941, and wouldn't have even remembered if Evelyn Knowles, who runs the place now, hadn't remembered and dug out the old sign. Joe was a little embarrassed by it; you can forget a lot in thirty-six years, especially if you've been on the road the whole time, a couple of thousand weeks, maybe a thousand different places. Perhaps that's an exaggeration; Joe was based in Los Angeles for a few years in the 1950's, but for 90% of the time he's been on the road. I've seen a lot of him in the last six years, and except for one visit to his home in Seattle, I've never known him to be anywhere except in a hotel. A frantic existence for someone sixty years younger, but he's holding up OK and is booked through 1980.*

It never occurred to me in late April 1977 as I drove back to New York City after completing this record that I'd never make another one with Joe Venuti. In fact, we began planning others when he came to town a few weeks later. What I didn't know was his lung cancer was already moderately advanced by then. He didn't either, but when I listen to the Albany session tapes today I can hear him coughing between takes.

May 5, 1978
Chiaroscuro CR 203
The Best of Joe Venuti

The final Chiaroscuro record I organized in the analog era was *The Best of Joe Venuti;* it was just a sampler of my favorite tracks from previous releases. Because of issues with the new owners of the label, it was barely circulated and sold perhaps as many as a dozen copies to friends and family. Some of the producer notes I wrote at the time have not been seen since then and tell a good deal about Joe. Here in a slightly jumbled fashion are a few of the thoughts I had in 1978.

After his engagements in Albany, Joe was scheduled for his spring residency at Michael's Pub. He was at the Berkshire, and we were in touch about other projects. It was toward the end of a two- or three-week engagement. He was playing extremely well and on Friday, May 5, Margaret Whitton and I went to see *Dracula* at the Martin Beck. She was scheduled to play Lucy for about a year in the road company version of the play and was doing homework. She also loved Joe Venuti, and I told her he might help her with the play. She was still puzzled by my suggestion when we wandered into Michael's for a post-theater dinner/musicale. After a romping set, Joe came over and, of course, had any number of suggestions about *Dracula*. No, he hadn't seen the current version of the play but fifty-one years earlier he had seen Bela Lugosi in the original production any number of times. He regaled us with stories about the play and Bela Lugosi, who Joe had known in his Hollywood days with Bing Crosby. After the lecture and answering questions, I hoped we could find time to talk about a recording session we'd planned a couple of days later.

So Joe excused himself and rejoined his group onstage. In his nearly eighty(?) years, Joe had been here and there forever, and I don't mean just to that old play he'd seen with Bela Lugosi in the 1920s. And that night, that last set I ever heard, he was still there, playing just as well, with as much vigor and vitality as anyone in town; he boiled through the set, never let up for a moment and just a few moments before had enough energy to charm the pants off the newest Miss Lucy in town, someone young enough to be his great-granddaughter. At one point, he would be ripping merrily through "That's a Plenty"; then he'd turn to a sugar sweet ballad. He played "Tenderly" in that set, and when he thought the customers were getting out of hand, he stepped to the microphone and growled "Tenderly" into the microphone as loud as possible. The audience was noticeably quieter for the rest of the set. I didn't notice anything different about the growl, but I should have.

The Best of Joe Venuti album cover, 1978.
(Author's collection)

And what recording sessions were we cooking up? Joe was very fond of Itzhak Perlman and wanted to ask him about a possible collaboration. It would have probably worked; Perlman had come to hear Joe at Michael's Pub, as did Ruggiero Ricci, and a couple of years ago Joe did some wonderful duets with Stephane Grappelli. This was a long shot, but the most "typically Joe Venuti" project that we had planned was actually scheduled for recording two days later, on May 7, 1978. But it was not going to be an ordinary record, and we had been talking about it for years.

I went to see Joe the next day to talk about our "special" record. He was a bit low-key, but one of the last things he said to me as I was leaving was, "If you need some dough, let me know." I replied that I needed about $200,000. He frowned and said, "That's too much." We both laughed and that was that.

The next day, early Sunday morning I called Joe at the Berkshire, and he growled into the telephone that he just wasn't up to a recording session. And I understood because this wasn't to be an ordinary recording session. It was all vocal, not vocalizing, but talking, Joe telling all the terrible stories, all the pranks, the Roy Rogers and

1973. (Author's collection)

The 1975 Christmas Record

Trigger tale, the flour in the tuba, at the bar with Jack Teagarden, the Sousaphones at The Plaza, the most awful of the Whiteman stories and the best of the Crosby stories. All of the tallest tales, the naughtier the better. And then the best tale of all: This record. Our plan was to make a relatively small edition and sell them all for $25 apiece, not much in 2025, but plenty in 1978. And why was it going to be the best prank/tall tale? This was because the only way you could buy the record would be to write a check to Sister Annette's convent. All those nasty stories benefiting a nunnery. How nice was that? But it didn't happen because the next thing I learned was the cough wasn't a cold, and the lung cancer was kicking in full force. All those cigarettes had taken hold.

But there was one of Joe's pranks that had already been recorded and lives on for a minute or two. It happened at the end of the third Joe and Zoot session. The date was over when suddenly it was decided a Christmas carol was in order. Joe wrote some hurried words to "Good King Wenceslaus" and the result measured up to Joe's previous outrages and mangling of other innocent songs. The playback revealed the truth to the participants, and all agreed it was as bad a bit of musical nonsense as they'd ever heard. Needless to say, it became the 1975 Chiaroscuro Christmas release and a few hundred lucky(?) listeners got to have a listen. A few may still be breathing. He sang part of the song in Yiddish and shouted, "Zoot, Zoot, Zoot!" when he wanted him to take a chorus. That pretty much sums up what the tune was all about.

I wrote many of these words in mid-May 1978. Joe died three months later on August 14. Very little is known about Joe's personal life other than occasional tall tales, but two years earlier in August 1976 I had flown to Seattle and visited him at his home, which turned out to be a bedroom he had been given in the home of a doting fan and her husband. The fan in question was Helen Fisher; I don't remember her husband's name. I have a note in my diary that four days after Joe's death I sent her a box of Joe's records to 10215 13 South, Seattle, Washington, 98168. But I carried on with his partner in crime, Zoot Sims, and, interestingly enough, Zoot is still carrying on and making a difference in 2025. He just doesn't know it. More about that later.

September 3–10, 1983
The First Annual Floating Jazz Festival
Zoot Sims and Bucky Pizzarelli

In the spring of 1983, what was then known as Norwegian Caribbean Line made up their collective minds and asked HOSS to produce a jazz festival aboard the *S/S Norway*. That was wonderful, and though it was a minute or two too late in the day from a booking standpoint, it was a success. It was also the first festival in what would be a twenty-year run. It was scheduled to kick off in early September, the 3–10 to be exact, to coincide as closely as possible with the launch of that year's hurricane season.

1983 Floating Jazz Festival program.
(Author's collection)

With Doc Cheatham, 1984.
(Author's collection)

Most jazz festivals are planned a year or more in advance. We were looking at appearing a few months later in an unproven, usually nonmusical venue. We resorted to calling friends, and Zoot was one of the first calls. He looked at his appointment book and said four words, "OK, but get Bucky." So with the next call I did, and in a couple of minutes had one of the preeminent jazz duos set for our inaugural cruise. And he was all over the ship, sitting in where appropriate. In retrospect, I wish I'd had the courage to suggest to him that he do a couple of numbers with Astrud Gilberto, who was also on board. It would have been fun to see him trying to outdo Stan Getz.

Zoot Sims and Bucky Pizzarelli with other artists and passengers at the 1983 Floating Jazz Festival. (Author's collection)

October 20 – November 3, 1984
The Floating Jazz Festival
Zoot Sims with Everyone

Such was the popularity of Zoot Sims that for the second edition of our festival at sea Zoot was scheduled to be on board for two full weeks. It was the policy for twenty years that we would rarely have anyone on board for more than one week, but Zoot was special. We all knew he was in poor health and felt two weeks without travel would be good for him. Then the day before we were to set sail, we learned Zoot's doctors felt he needed another week of treatment, but they were certain he could travel a few days later and board the ship on October 27. He did and boarded the ship looking a bit haggard from all his medical excursions, wearing a large floppy hat that made him look like a refugee from a banana boat. As anticipated, Zoot was frail but optimistic and musically spectacular, usually playing in a sextet with Clark Terry, Dave McKenna, Bucky Pizzarelli, Michael Moore, and Bobby Rosengarden.

And Zoot didn't just play with those guys. He sat in with Chip Hoehler's big band just to try out some of the charts and was reunited in a quartet setting with his old friend Jake Hanna. And jammed a bit with Doc Cheatham and Clark Terry during an outdoor photo session.

A highly anticipated feature of the Floating Jazz Festival was something we called Meet the Stars. Three times a week, on days at sea, we would wrangle a group of musicians into the North Cape Lounge and a moderator would ask them questions, as would members of the audience. On October 29, we had an all-star lineup, and how I'd like to have recorded that band, Clark, Zoot, Bucky, Dave, and Bobby. I don't know why Michael Moore wasn't on stage; maybe we ran out of chairs. But there was a surprise guest who showed up to make a special appearance.

Everyone was in a good mood that day. In a small book entitled *Norwegian Caribbean Lines Floating Jazz Festival 1985* I wrote:

> . . . *It was his (Zoot's) birthday and we arranged a surprise for him. Donn Lewis, the Ccruise director, asked Zoot a loaded question and before he could reply Mel Torme stepped from behind a curtain and sang "Happy Birthday." The audience quickly joined in, and a large cake, complete with saxophone decoration, was presented. Donn asked Zoot how old he was and Zoot replied, "I'm fifty-nine (pause) but have the body of a fifty-seven-year-old man." It was his last birthday, but a good one. At five o'clock that day he was surrounded by five hundred people who cared about him very much.*

The book I wrote in 1985 about the first two years of the Floating Jazz Festival was dedicated to Zoot who very much wanted to be on board but knew this was not to be.

December 5, 1984
830 Broadway

In late November or early December, Zoot called and suggested we get together and chat about 1985. I knew 1985 was a long shot, but I jumped at the idea because I had no idea how many times I'd get to be with Zoot again. It was an early dinner at 830, and as fate would have it on the same day a messenger had brought me the proposal David Levy and Arnie Lawrence had cooked up that eventually became the outline for what now exists as the Jazz and Contemporary Music department at The New School's College of Performing Arts. Allen Austill, then the dean of the school, wanted my opinion, and I was happy to have a look.

One thing jumped out to me. There were to be many adjunct teachers, a laundry list of who was who in jazz were to be part of the part-time faculty, and Zoot was featured prominently on the list. It even listed courses, and I showed it to him. I should point out that Zoot's academic credentials were a bit thin, as were those of almost everyone else in his generation. There is the funny story about when he once supervised a saxophone master class at a college level institution, and when all the students had performed for him the person in charge asked Zoot if he had any specific suggestions. Zoot replied, "Play better."

When he looked at The New School Proposal he simply said, "I don't think so." I then asked him if he decided he was going to teach a course at the school, what kind of a course he'd like to teach. His reply became legendary and is probably floating around the school somewhere. He said, "I'd like to have a course that would teach them how to scuffle." But his association with The New School program didn't turn out the way anyone expected.

Before the Church of Heavenly Rest concert with Gerry Mulligan. (Author's collection)

Jimmy Heath, Arnie Lawrence, Bob Wilber, Al Cohn, Lew Tabakin, Harold Ashby, Lee Konitz, and Gerry Mulligan, 1986. (Author's collection)

A Noise Reduction EQ Normal : 120μs
B Noise Reduction EQ Normal : 120μs

1. I CANT BELIEVE (DAVE) 3:49
2. ALICE BLUE GOWN (DAVE) 5:29
3. MEDLEY (TALK, PLEASE DON'T) 7:37
4. SUNDAY (DAVE / ZOOT) 3:57
5. MY OLD FLAME " (INC) 7:36
6. I HEAR A MELODY ? " 5:02
7. WILLOW WEEP FOR ME " 5:10
8. THEM THERE EYES (DAVE & AL) 4:32
9. EMBRACEABLE YOU " 6:36
10. UPTEMPO BLUES 4:20
11. WHEN YOUR LOVER HAS GONE CUT

TDK D60
SIMS/COHN/MULLIGAN/MCKENNA I
HEAVENLY REST
NO.
DYNAMIC CASSETTE
TDK NORMAL POSITION TYPE I D60

The lost recording, 1985.
(Author's collection)

January 13, 1985
The Church of Heavenly Rest

January 13 was a Sunday, and on January 11 Shelley and I were in Darien with Gerry Mulligan. At one point Gerry asked me what I was doing for the weekend, and I replied I was looking forward to a concert Paul Weinstein had organized at The Church of Heavenly Rest on Sunday afternoon featuring Zoot and Al Cohn with Dave McKenna. His eyes brightened and he said, "Do you think they'd let me sit in?" I gave him a long look, and we agreed we'd come into New York and we'd go up together.

It turned out to be a remarkable concert, just a trio, Zoot, Al Cohn, and Dave McKenna plus Gerry on the second half. If you closed your eyes, it was Zoot and Al circa 1955 or 1965 or even 1975 at their very best. But Zoot was thin as a rail and not ready for a close up in *GQ*. It was professionally recorded, but the tapes have never been released. I have a cassette of the first half of this remarkable concert. This was the last time I heard Zoot; he died two months later.

The family of

Mr. John "Zoot" Sims

deeply appreciates

your kind expression of sympathy

Invitation, memorial concert at The New School, 1986. (Author's collection)

Dear Hank,
It was so thoughtful of you and Shelley to write me as you did and I am grateful indeed for the photographs and for your willingness to make VCR copies for me of the Norway tape & the one or two I will have of the tribute. It is friends such as you two who are making the pain more bearable and I am comforted by so many friends who cared for Zoot and who now share in my loss. Thank you, dear friends.
Much love, Louise

Note from Louise Sims, 1986. (Author's collection)

December 14, 1986
Zoot Sims Memorial Concert
The New School

And then it was time for the first of many memorial concerts, and it turned out to be a great one because it was not just the first and best one, it was for a perfect cause, to establish a scholarship in Zoot's name at The New School's newest department, the one concerned with jazz and contemporary music, where possibly one young saxophonist wouldn't have to scuffle.

It was a big deal and as Bobby Rosengarden always used to say, "I guess you couldn't get anybody." Everybody turned up. *The New York Times* had reported:

> *It will be a party and concert held in the New School Auditorium, 66 West Twelfth Street, from 7 to 11 P.M. on Dec. 14, with musicians who, as Mrs. Sims says, "were really Zoot's friends." They will include Al Cohn, Gerry Mulligan, Red Rodney, Bob Brookmeyer and Jim Hall as well as Lionel Hampton, George Masso, Sylvia Syms, Warren Vache, all five members of Scott Hamilton's quintet, the pianists Tommy Flanagan, John Bunch, Ben Aronov and Don Friedman, the bassists Ron Carter, George Mraz, Frank Tate, Bill Crow and Major Holley, and the drummers Akira Tana and Bobby Rosengarden.*

I took about two rolls of film and can add that based on the negatives Ted Curson, Arnie Lawrence, Lew Tabakin, Clark Terry, Bob Wilber, Lee Konitz, Red Rodney, Joe Wilder, and Jimmy Heath were also on stage. It was a great success and set the stage for the next dozen years when every year The Party for Zoot was used as a fundraiser for the scholarship fund.

April 18, 1997
The Father of Jazz Violin

Mary Cianfrani Park, Philadelphia, PA

In 1996, Andew J. Sordoni got the ball rolling to get a memorial historical marker installed in a prominent place in Joe Venuti's old neighborhood in Philadelphia. He knew the correct political strings to pull and after a few appropriate pulls the Pennsylvania Historical & Museum Commission authorized a memorial maker to be created and installed on the northeast corner of Mary Cianfrani Park at Eighth and Fitzwater Streets. Joe wasn't there to play, but Lou DiCrescenzo of WJZ and WRDV radio was on hand, as were Congressman Thomas Foglietta and Henry "Buddy" Cianfrani. With a name like O'Neal, I'm surprised I was allowed to attend!

Historical marker, Philadelphia, 1997. (Author's collection)

The handsome oversized marker read *JOE VENUTI (1903–1978) "Father of the Jazz Violin." Classically trained as a child, Venuti went to grade school here. He introduced new string techniques, worked with his close friend, guitarist Eddie Lang. 1921–33. Led his own band, 1935–43; was on screen and radio. Major comeback in 1968*. They could have added that Eddie Lang was also from Philadelphia, born a year "before" Joe in 1902, and his name was really Salvatore Massaro, but there wasn't enough room on the marker. Maybe someone will create a marker for Eddie one day.

1987–2001
A Party for Zoot
The New School

For fifteen years or so, we threw an annual Party for Zoot to raise money for the scholarship fund. Many people worked to make this event a success, but Paul Weinstein was often the primary moving force behind the party. It was a wonderful event serving a worthy cause and was a good excuse to gather together many old friends and musical associates. In 2000, *The New York Times* reviewed the party before it happened, giving it a bit of free publicity. The paper of record was always nice to Zoot; Louise Sims, who married Zoot in 1970, was the longtime assistant to Clifton Daniel, the equally longtime managing editor of the paper.

(October 16, 2000 – New York, NY) New School University's Jazz and Contemporary Music Program will host a benefit evening for the John Haley "Zoot" Sims Scholarship Fund on Sunday, December 10 at 6:30 PM at The Jazz Standard restaurant and jazz club located at 116 East Twenty-seventh Street in Manhattan. "A Party for Zoot" honors the memory of Zoot Sims and raises scholarship money for talented, young artists in the New School Jazz Program. Tickets are $200, which includes cocktails, dinner and the show at 7 PM. For further information, call (212) 229-5896, ext. 309.

Past performers at the Zoot Sims benefit have included Walter Blanding, Jr., Jane Ira Bloom, Joe Chambers, Andrew Cyrille, Kenny Davern, Jon Faddis, Tommy Flanagan, Barry Harris, Jimmy Heath, Milt Hinton, Junior Mance, Cecil McBee, Bucky and John Pizzarelli, Benny Powell, Rufus Reid, Clark Terry, Warren Vache, and Reggie Workman. Many of those artists are expected to return for this year's event at The Jazz Standard.

The Zoot Sims Scholarship was established in 1986 to memorialize one of the most gifted and original voices in jazz. Tenor saxophonist Zoot Sims (October 29, 1925 – March 23, 1985) worked as a professional musician from the age of 15, touring with dance bands. In 1943, he toured with Benny Goodman and was a member of Woody Herman's big band from 1947 until 1949.

One Good Turn CD, 2022. (Author's collection)

One Good Turn Throughout 2022 and Beyond

And time continued to pass until suddenly it was 2022, and this made me and some of my pals at Jazz Foundation of America think about possibly revisiting the past. In 2002, I put together a CD to benefit the JFA, on whose board I have been and remained on since about 1991. I selected a potpourri of tracks from various Chiaroscuro releases, and because of the primary mission of the JFA to assist elderly jazz musicians in need, I called this special issue CD *One Good Turn.* This tune was the lead selection. The CD was a success and raised needed funds for JFA when it needed all the help it could get. "One Good Turn" was a selection that originally appeared on the *Dave McKenna Quartet Featuring Zoot Sims.*

It was now twenty years later, and the JFA was in much better shape, and *One Good Turn*, though aging, is still in the good shape it has always been. Duke Ellington once said if music sounds good it is good, and since most of the music Ellington created and played throughout his long and distinguished career is/was jazz and blues oriented, it can be assumed that he was probably talking about jazz and blues, music that when it is good is perhaps more often enduring and timeless than your average pop/rock/rap hit on the current billboard charts. And forty-eight years after we recorded it on a cold Sunday night at Downtown Sound, *One Good Turn* still sounded good. And since it still sounded good and the musicians on the CD were even more legendary twenty years later, a few of whom had actually been helped by JFA, Joe Petrocelli and his associates at JFA had the idea to reissue the CD.

The upscale clothing emporium, 32 Bar Blues, a company that has long supported JFA in many ways, thought this was a good idea. So good, in fact, they wanted to create a new design for the CD, feature the design on a tee shirt, launch a promotional campaign, and include it in all their Christmas catalogs. In October 2022, they funded a reworked and enhanced version of *One Good Turn*, launched a media blitz in print, on radio, and the Internet, and Zoot and Dave will possibly be heard by millions and hopefully will raise even more funds for JFA. This is why Zoot is still smiling after all these years.

A word about this final photograph of Zoot. It was taken during a playback break. Fred Miller had recorded Zoot on a number of occasions and knew Zoot was a passionate player who didn't just sit erect in a chair and play the notes. He often got up and really *played* the notes, and Fred didn't want to miss any of them. One of the microphones is a Neumann 67; the other is an 87. I can't tell which is which. The studio is long gone, but I'm sure those two microphones are doing just fine somewhere, as is the music Zoot and Dave and Major and Ray made that night.

Doubled miked, 1977. (Author's collection)

25

George Wein

October 3, 1925 – September 13, 2021

THE LIVES of all creative artists are precarious, and it doesn't matter the nature of the art form. Performing artists, actors, dancers, vocalists, musicians of all sorts, or visual artists, painters, sculptors, photographers, illustrators, or artists of the written word, poets, novelists, philosophers; they are all in the same army of the self-employed, looking and hoping for the next gig, the next spark of inspiration, the next grant or fellowship. There is no regular paycheck, no health insurance unless self-provided, no safety net, no free phone or anything else. So life is precarious, and when it becomes too precarious, creativity slips between the cracks. A crack that all too often swallows up the artist as well.

To prevent those cracks from swallowing too many artists it often falls to non-artists to organize and structure circumstances where artists can thrive, either as promoters, producers, publishers, gallerists, or a guy like George Wein, who was a little bit of all these things in the course of his seventy-plus year career. He was also a fine pianist and occasional vocalist.

I know of no other producer/musician who provided so much employment and artistic opportunity for other musicians, particularly jazz/blues/folk musicians, as George Wein. In a career that lasted over seven decades, he enabled many thousands of musicians, from the most famous to the most ordinary, a way to earn a living, first through work in clubs in the late 1940s, then in theaters and concert halls, jazz festivals, national and international tours, audio and video recordings, and, more recently, through charitable and philanthropic activities. Along the way, these musicians were able to entertain and stimulate millions and millions of people at concerts, festivals, in clubs, on television, on recordings, and, as technology has advanced, on DVDs, Internet streaming, and probably social media platforms I still don't know about. George also managed to play piano, as opportunities presented themselves, as a sideman in the early days in Boston and with his own Newport All Stars for the last fifty years of his life.

Look at it this way. Name a great leader, big band guys like Benny Goodman, Duke Ellington, or Count Basie, or leaders of small groups like Dave Brubeck, Miles Davis, and any of a hundred others. These leaders all put bands together, often for decades. They hired a lot of musicians, but George has hired *all* these leaders and their bands for almost six decades. He's the guy who found a way to offer these leaders additional employment options beyond clubs and occasional concerts, notably in the development of the large-scale jazz festival. It would be difficult to name a major jazz artist, or even a minor one, who has not been featured at one of the thousands of events George has produced over the years.

OPPOSITE

George Wein video shoot

I never knew George Wein in the olden days when he was opening and running his clubs in Boston and founding the Newport Jazz Festival and the folk festival a few years later and hiring everyone from Sidney Bechet to Charlie Parker and Billie Holiday to Lee Wiley and everyone else in between for his clubs and festivals. No, I never knew him for the first half of his legendary career. I knew of him but didn't get to know him until 1981, when he turned up on the board of a company I'd founded with two Johns, Hammond and Moore. It was called Hammond Music Enterprises, and George was on the board because he was really fond of John Hammond, not because of John Moore or myself. He didn't know us from a couple of lampposts. But he knew and respected John Hammond because when some of the people associated with the Newport Jazz Festival in its first years wanted to sack George, it was John Hammond who stood up for him when it really mattered, made certain everything worked out just fine, and for the next sixty-five years, except a little bump in 2007–8, it did and George remembered.

George Wein video shoot

George always remembered, and I watched and listened to him do so for the second half of his life, and very closely for the last quarter. He was a guy with a lot of dreams, and in the seventy years since his inauspicious beginnings, he's managed to realize most of them.

I didn't really get to know George well until 1998–9, when first the Floating Jazz Festival transferred from the *S/S Norway* to the *Queen Elizabeth 2* and then when various people became interested in possibly acquiring George's music festival business and quite by accident I became involved with some of the people interested in the acquisition. It was a decade-long adventure, one involving millions of dollars, Wall Street brokerage houses, many of titans in the world of finance and entertainment, thousands of hours of work, even more thousands of telephone calls and meetings, and a pile of emails and assorted memos a couple of feet high. And the funny thing is that after the sale of Festival Productions and many of George's other holdings, at the end of his life in 2021 he was still in control of his jazz and folk festivals in Newport. This is what happened.

In 1998 when we switched the Floating Jazz Festival from the *S/S Norway* to the *Queen Elizabeth 2*, it seemed as if we had usurped the festival at sea George had presented for the past few years. In the mid-1990s, he produced an event on the *QE2* while it was anchored off Newport during the weekend of the Newport Jazz Festival. It was an elegant way for jazz fans to hear jazz on land and sea and use the ship as a hotel during the festival itself. But sometime at least two or three years earlier, Cunard had decided to change the scheduling of the QE2 and reposition the ship bypassing Newport. They informed George sometime later.

We presented the Floating Jazz Festival on QE2 in November 1999, a ten-day festival that sailed from Miami and wound up in Southampton. George always jokingly maintained that we "stole" his festival on the QE2, and he told people this all the time, as often as not in my presence. He'd also say we were the only people who ever managed to "steal" one of his festivals, but if I was present, I'd add a tag line that it had nothing to do with anything other than the people who planned routes and sailings at Cunard decided they no longer wanted to stop at Newport. We had nothing to do with it; it was simply a matter of the cost of fuel, the color of autumn leaves in New England, and many other nonmusical considerations. But this switch put me on George's radar screen.

In 1999, things changed more directly when I was asked to meet with two Johns, my old partner from Hammond Music days, John Moore, and John Phillips, then the president of George's company, Festival Productions (FPI). It was the beginnings of a decade-long adventure and a story that has rarely been told and the parts that have are largely forgotten or fabricated.

In 1999, John Phillips, though president of FPI, was concerned about his future; if anything was to happen to George the company might cease to exist. Indeed, a few years later George told me that if he were no longer associated with his company, he'd give it no more than a year or two at best. I was certain Phillips was exploring the possibility of an acquisition without George's knowledge. We had three cordial meetings at which both Johns presented various scenarios dealing with possible acquisition. The bottom line was that Phillips wanted John Moore to raise the money to buy the company from George. This didn't seem to be a likely possibility at the time. After these three meetings there were no more meetings, but I never forgot about them and filed the encounters away in the back of my mind.

At some point in early 2001, John Moore suggested that it might be interesting to have a meeting with his cousin Chris Shields. He said his cousin, who had once worked for George, was interested in developing financing to purchase FPI and perhaps this might fit in with John Phillips's interests. A meeting was set, there were discussions, and Shields and I had some lively conversations. I told George I had met with Shields, and his reaction was not entirely positive.

Shields was a well-born young man in his early thirties who loved music, was properly educated, had extensive social connections, and had the personality of a born salesman who could talk you out of your pants if you weren't careful. Moore told me that his only reservation was that he thought his cousin was "a little slippery." He didn't elaborate. I came away from our initial meetings with Shields feeling that he had an all-consuming desire to purchase FPI and expand it. He also needed someone such as myself, who was respected in the music industry and didn't have any negative baggage to carry into a meeting with George. He was confident he could secure some initial financing from, among others, two men associated with Enron, J. Clifford Baxter and David Wallace Cox. I was initially unaware that George and Shields had a history beyond the fact that Shields had worked briefly for FPI a few years earlier, a relationship that did not end positively. George was still on the fence regarding the sale of FPI, but he was pretty sure he didn't want to sell it to Shields.

By 2001, my interest in the possible acquisition of FPI became more serious, as it began to appear more and more likely the Floating Jazz Festival would no longer be floating on the QE2 after 2002 and because there were no other ships in service that were appropriate venues, the festival as we envisioned it was coming to an end. But because it was still floating in 2001, a bit of good luck came my way because of one regular passenger, a man named Israel Asper.

The Floating Jazz Festival passenger list was very diverse. Old jazz fans, young jazz fans, captains of industry, and plumbers, and many races from many countries around the world. I tried to interact with as many of the regulars as possible, and one of those I met with more often than not was Asper, a man who loved jazz. It was my mother-in-law who tipped me off about him.

Israel Asper, better known as Izzy, was a prominent Canadian businessman, the chairman of CanWest Global Communications, one of the largest media conglomerates in that country. He was also a serious jazz enthusiast and was in the process of launching a twenty-four-hour jazz radio/TV station to prove it. At one of our casual meetings on the ship, Izzy asked me what other jazz projects I was involved with and during a meeting in the Queen's Lounge aboard the QE2 I told him FPI might possibly be for sale. He was interested and suggested we should continue to be in touch. I relayed Izzy's potential interest to George.

Shields and I continued our discussions and even began to write some tentative business plans. There was a minor setback when Enron collapsed; it was clear that people associated with this company would not be a likely source of any kind of funding. At the time, Shields had no other alternative suggestions, so this left Izzy Asper as the only possible active source.

In November 2001, I sent a letter to Izzy outlining my discussions with Shields. The letter included, among other things, Shields's written outline of the responsibilities and positions of each of us and the team that would be required to run the company.

On December 10, 2001, I introduced George and Izzy, who had just bought an apartment in the Trump International Hotel. We wandered downstairs and met George at Jean Georges, one of his favorite restaurants. The two men hit it off very well; Izzy was a real fan as well as a billionaire. He'd just come from a meeting with Sumner Redstone, and George recognized he was dealing with someone of substance. After a couple of hours of fan talk and pleasantries, we agreed to meet again in early 2002.

In January, J. Clifford Baxter was so messed up by the Enron scandal he killed himself. I wondered at the time how well Shields had known his potential investor, and I should have taken this as an indication that Shields was possibly a guy who knew people who played fast and loose, but didn't know them that well. With Shields's potential investors bankrupt or dead, Izzy Asper remained the primary funding possibility. And it still wasn't clear if George really wanted to sell his company. One day, I had a fax from Izzy asking me to telephone him later that night. I made the call from a telephone booth at the Metropolitan Opera. I asked him if he was in or out. He said, "I'm in."

And then nothing happened. All was on hold. George wasn't sure he wanted to sell, things were going well for his company, and he was planning for the fiftieth anniversary of the Newport Jazz Festival. So things drifted, despite many positive conversations. The primary hurdle that had to be overcome was that George didn't trust Shields; he'd fired him for insubordination a decade earlier. It was over a minor matter, but he never forgot and he never let me forget it was always on his mind. George always remembered and time passed. Then Izzy Asper died suddenly in October 2003, and everything stalled and remained so until 2005 when another potential investor entered the picture. Shields had convinced Joe Stanislaw to become involved with his pursuit of FPI.

Stanislaw was a successful businessman and scholar. With various partners he founded Cambridge Energy Research Associates in 1984, built it into one of the foremost think tanks related to oil and energy, and then sold his interests for many millions of dollars in 2004. The timing was right for him to invest some of his money in an exciting new venture that dealt with a different kind of energy. Shields had clearly sold Stanislaw on the viability of the project and possibly sold him on a concept that was markedly different from the plans we had formulated in 2002. I have no idea if this was the case, but my guess is Shields told Stanislaw whatever he thought he wanted to hear.

I met with Stanislaw at the Knickerbocker Club on February 1, 2006. He encouraged me to do what I could to bring George on board. He was genuinely excited about acquiring FPI. When asked, I explained to him my desire to be involved with the new company as a senior executive, but one who didn't punch a time clock. I added that this was the understanding I had with Shields, who planned on being involved on a day-to-day basis. I added that I saw my primary role as acting as the link between George and the group of younger individuals who would ultimately run the company in the future. I told Stanislaw that the most important asset Shields and his group would be purchasing was George Wein himself. He said he understood, but it turned out he didn't have a clue.

A few months later, another investor with even deeper pockets appeared on the scene: Richard Sands, the CEO of Constellation Brands, the largest distributor of distilled spirits, beer, and wine in the United States. There were now two major investors on board, but it was still not clear that George actually wanted to sell his company, and even if he did, he was reluctant to sell it to a group that included Shields. Shields and his investors wanted me to convince George that they were the best choice for him, both financially and to protect his legacy. I agreed to try, but by now my primary loyalty was to George because we'd embarked on a couple of other projects together.

At the same time I was meeting with Shields and Stanislaw, George was thinking of other ways to expand his company, particularly in Newport. He was afraid he might lose some of his sponsors after 2007 (he turned out to be correct), and he looked at Newport as a tourist destination that could be used for more than a simple jazz and folk festival each year. I discussed this with John Moore, and he suggested the ideal person to help George expand his activities was an old friend: Michael McMahon, who had decided to leave the rat race in New York and act as a special counselor to the governor of Rhode Island. McMahon's portfolio included developing programs specializing in economic growth. Moore arranged for a luncheon at The Brook Club and introduced George to McMahon.

Over the next couple of months, I expended a good deal of energy working on developing a concept for a "new" Festival Productions. There were meetings with various people in Rhode Island, all the way from the governor's office to the Department of Environmental Management and the Newport Chamber of Commerce. We talked about a dozen different festivals in Newport so the city could better compete with Foxwoods and other tourist destinations in Connecticut. We even discussed building new performance venues and hotels. I produced charts and plans, and there was interest on both sides. Then, almost as suddenly as it had begun, everything vanished when McMahon was offered a major position with a billion-dollar hedge fund in New York City. He took the first flight back to New York, no one picked up any pieces, and that was the end of this initiative.

Meanwhile, Shields and his team wanted to press on, but George still didn't want to have anything to do with Shields. His ideal scenario was to be bought by the concert and entertainment production giant AEG, and at the same time sell his share of the New Orleans Jazz and Heritage Festival to the same company. The problem was that AEG was not particularly interested in FPI; they only wanted the festival in New Orleans. I told George I might have one other person to ask about the sale of his company and he said to go ahead.

In the spring of 2006, I telephoned an old friend, Warren Spector, who was co-president of Bear Stearns. We had a brief conversation and within a few weeks he had identified someone he thought might be interested. Tom Lee, formerly of Thomas H. Lee Partners and now head of Lee Equity Partners. It looked like a possible match; Lee loved music, sang a little bit, sponsored good projects on PBS, had once raised money for one of George's sponsors, Dunkin' Donuts, and had bags of money.

I met with Lee, who expressed interest one day and then bailed the next. I was very puzzled. He kept saying to call him later, but he was never there later. I learned later that he was a guy who didn't like to say no. This wasted a lot of time.

The Shields team kept pressing, and George and I continued to talk to them. In August I was at the Oslo Jazz Festival and one night the telephone rang. It was Warren Spector, who asked if FPI was still for sale. I said it was for the right price and to a group or person George would consider a qualified buyer who would strengthen his company while protecting his legacy. He said to call him when I returned, which I did.

Later in August, I met with Liz Barron at Bear Stearns, an entertainment company specialist, who thought she could put together a deal. I then arranged for George to meet with the Bear Stearns group, and we waited and waited. This was the only time in my experience George failed to make a meeting he'd scheduled to attend. I was very puzzled, and later he told me he was concerned that his company could not withstand Wall Street scrutiny and had decided to pass. Bear Stearns, however, didn't want to quit and pursued me into late September, wondering if a deal could be put back on track. I told them it couldn't, and they finally believed me.

George was now left with the Shields group. AEG had passed, he didn't think he could pass Wall Street scrutiny with Bear Stearns or any other Wall Street firm, there were no new opportunities in Newport, and he was certain he would lose some sponsors in 2007 and more in 2008. He was also looking at a large payroll and a potential loss in both years. Suddenly the Shields group looked better and better.

In the summer and early fall of 2006, I had hundreds of meetings and telephone calls and emails with Shields, members of his group, various lawyers from Akin Gump, the firm representing Shields, and George and his lawyer Elliott Hoffman, trying to move the project forward. There was still no commitment from George himself, but he never suggested to me that I should back off. He kept the door open. Finally in September, after AEG passed, George told me he'd meet with Joe Stanislaw and Richard Sands, set a price that wasn't negotiable, tell them everything that was wrong with FPI, and if they still wanted the company, he'd sell it. The meeting was arranged to be held on Richard Sands's private jet at Teterboro airport on September 22.

George did as he said and painted the sorriest scenario he could imagine. He also asked for $4.1 million and tough employment contracts for his business and personal staff, as well as personal guarantees and protection of his trademarks and legacy if the purchasing entity failed to meet its obligations. Stanislaw and Sands said they wanted to do the deal. It took a month to draft a suitable Letter of Intent and an additional month to get to a finished contract, but as far as George was concerned, the deal was done in the airplane when he said he'd sell the company. He made it clear to me he'd made the decision with great misgivings because he thought Shields's business plan was deeply flawed, but he knew he'd be there to offer guidance and experience and I'd be there to interact with the new owners. I felt the business plan Shields had shown me earlier in the year was ambitious but possible, providing there was adequate financing, sound fiscal controls were maintained, the business plan was followed closely, and the new company, now called Festival Network, was lucky. This was the plan, but it was not to be.

The purchase agreement was complicated. George had many demands but two of the most important related to insuring that he and select members of his staff had iron-clad three-year employment contracts and that if Festival Network defaulted on any aspect of the contract or declared bankruptcy within the three year period, all of the trademarks and assets covered by the purchase agreement would revert to Wein. My position within FN was not specified in this contract; it had only been covered in the original Letter of Intent.

After dozens of revisions, a final purchase agreement was signed by George and Shields on December 7 at the Akin Gump offices in New York. There was almost a hitch at the last moment, and Shields was beside himself with worry. It was all I could do to calm him down and it worked; the lawyers, Elliott Hoffman on behalf of George and Channing Johnson (on video conference) working with Shields, went through the contract line by line, made a few minor adjustments, the purchase agreement was signed, I took a few photographs when George and Shields shook hands, and then George and Elliott left. Shields and I followed a few moments later.

We walked up Madison Avenue together; I was heading to the subway, the fastest way to reach my downtown office, and Shields was going somewhere else. George drove by in his car, and Shields said, "There goes my car." We stopped at Sixtieth Street and Shields extended his hand and said, "Thanks, I couldn't have done it without you." He had no idea. It was now thousands of telephone calls, emails, meetings, and memos after that first meeting in 1999, and with two signatures on a contract Shields was now in charge of Festival Network, technically the supervisor of a man who didn't want to sell him his company, a man who had serious doubts as to whether his new "boss" was up to the job and capable of running a staff made up of a dozen plus people who were suspicious of one another.

I knew it would be rough going but never anticipated how it would play out. Everyone associated with the project was hopeful and enthusiastic, even George. Later he told me that despite his misgivings, he hoped it would work out to everyone's advantage. And I should have had misgivings as well when I saw that the twenty people Shields had brought into the company were late to work, over-confident, usually-bullshitting early-thirty-somethings who wore a uniform that, starting at the bottom, consisted of good, conservative wing-tip shoes, blue jeans, an untucked dress shirt, and a blazer. At least most of the time.

I have no idea what Shields was thinking about after the contracts had been signed, but he may have already been planning on how he was going to marginalize George and in so doing marginalize me even more, because that is what ultimately happened. The contracts were signed in December 2006, and toward the end of January a payment of $4.1 million was made to George. The check cleared, after which George compensated me for what I had done to facilitate the sale.

Festival Network was up and running in early 2007, and the festivals produced that year were successful largely because George and his team already had them in place. But the new team at Festival Network was both inept and inexperienced, and the best word to describe what happened over the next eighteen months was "debacle." By 2008 the company was on the ropes despite burning through nearly $20 million in working capital. By the end of the year they were out of business, despite a website that indicated they had festivals scheduled through 2014.

I had helped George sell his company but also helped write the contract that stipulated if the purchaser defaulted in any way within three years, all trademarks associated with Festival Productions reverted to George. Festival Network didn't even last two, and the Newport Jazz Festival and Newport Folk Festival were produced by George in 2009. George had managed to have his cake and eat it too, and the world is better off for it.

It all began to fall apart quickly; first for me, then for George and his staff, and finally for the new company. It wasn't immediately apparent, and truthfully, for the first six months it looked like things were going well. But it only looked that way if you didn't look very carefully. Guggenheim Partners didn't look very carefully and invested $10 million in the Festival Network. This infusion of capital made things look better than they were, and despite their investment, it appears the Guggenheim people didn't really exert any meaningful fiscal control. In 2007, things were still hot and there was a lot of money around, seemingly an endless supply, to invest in companies like Festival Network, which was becoming little more than a concept built on dreams.

The average age of the Shields team was less than thirty, and no one had ever produced a major music festival from start to finish. They had been involved with festivals from the booking and production standpoint, but they'd never been in charge. Fortunately for the Shields team,

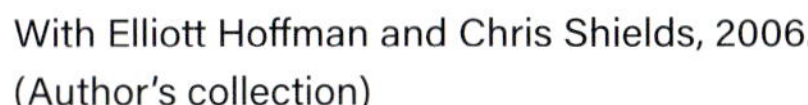

With Elliott Hoffman and Chris Shields, 2006.
(Author's collection)

With Chris Shields, Marie Daulne, (aka Zap Mama) and Ian Zaider, 2007. (Author's collection)

the Wein team had already organized most aspects of the 2007 festivals. There were a few holes that needed to be filled but nothing major. The only problems that existed were for new festivals, particularly one on Martha's Vineyard, the first of what was to be new destination-based music festivals. The artists for the festival were secured with less than a month to spare, which left scant time to publicize the event. It turned out procrastinating about talent was to become the norm. The event was a semi-disaster from an artistic standpoint and a complete financial failure.

George spent the spring organizing his affairs, selling the building that had once housed FPI, and selling his share of the New Orleans Jazz and Heritage Festival. I visited the new offices three or four times a week, primarily to meet with Shields, but I didn't have a place to hang my hat and neither did George. We were supposed to have adjoining offices, but somehow it never worked out. There were construction delays, problems with the lease, and any number of other excuses. As summer approached, Shields became annoyed with George over some minor matter and said he didn't deserve a large office. As more and more people were hired, space became more dear, and George was relegated to a cubbyhole. I was relegated to nothing at all.

The summertime festivals went well and attendance was good. JVC New York was just as it always was, and Newport jazz and folk were as well. To the new owners, this was a problem, and they began accelerating the business plan, particularly in terms of "buying" existing festivals and becoming producers of others in exotic places. The existing festivals were deemed "old-fashioned" and soon various members of the Shields team were flying all over the world, from Monaco to Dubai to Mali to Thailand to England and other locations, looking to buy or become involved with new events, most of which had little or nothing to do with the type of music featured at the core events that had been presented for so long and with such success by FPI. The Festival of the Desert in Mali is a long way from the Newport Jazz Festival in miles, but it is tenfold further away in terms of concept and sustainability. And while there may have been occasional trouble in Newport with rowdy patrons, notably during the major riot in 1960 and the minor one in 1971, none were on the level of the armed Islamic militants who shut down the Festival au Désert in 2012.

But the new owners were more interested in the new and the exotic and rapid growth rather than the core events that had sustained FPI's business for so many years. They were also intent on doing it on their own, apart from Wein's staff, with whom they were usually at odds. By following such a path, they lost the company's most valuable asset: George Wein.

My situation with Festival Network became untenable, and I began to pull away, with George's blessing. He was pulling away as well, just not as obviously. There were new employees, even a new CEO, a man named Tom Shepard, a former executive at VISA, but none of the new hires had any experience in organizing or presenting a music festival. But the two festivals in Newport went well in 2007, because they were already in place. I rarely set foot in the office for the remainder of the year. Other than attending the jazz festival in August, I spent the rest of the year planning a course of action to take against FN. I kept George informed of everything.

In early January 2008, I pricked the boil in an email to Shields and created a bit of a stir and a flurry of telephone calls. The last thing Festival Network wanted was for anyone to sue them. There were a few steps taken to address my concerns, but nothing came of them. I was offered a modest six-figure settlement and refused it. This was a mistake, but I didn't know how close the company was to collapse. The projections were it would run out of money by August 2008.

I worked with my friends Bruce Ricker and David G. Berger throughout the summer and put together a lengthy position paper. This paper, with supporting documents, was sent to Channing Johnson at Akin Gump in August, who in turn forwarded it to Shields. The thinking was to simply put all my cards on the table and show them what we could present in court. The call from Shields came in a day or so later, and he said we should get together and settle the matter. He sounded sincere; he wanted to sort things out, but we never did. It turned out he was trying to keep the lights on.

Shields never told me that the problems at the company were as profound as they were, but by the end of the summer the money had run out, the financial crisis in the US was just getting into gear, money was tight, and Festival Network had bills coming due all over the United States and Europe with a staff of thirty-seven that had to be paid on a weekly basis.

I didn't know the staff hadn't been paid when I had my last meeting with Shields in late November, or that the COO of the company had resigned because he hadn't been paid since August. Shields told me he was still working on securing a contract to produce the Dubai Jazz Festival and was planning to fly to Dubai to finalize arrangements. I asked him when the festival was to be presented, and he said early 2009. It seemed to me the Dubai adventure was unlikely, and everything finally just collapsed, setting the stage for marginalized George to come roaring back and take control of his copyrights and forge a new relationship with the City of Newport. He also had whatever was left of the $4.1 million to fund the festivals in the summer of 2009.

The employees of Festival Network drifted away in the early part of 2009. Some stayed on longer than others, hoping there might be a payday, but it never came. There was just too much owed to far too many people. Bills from all over the world went unpaid. JVC had paid a fixed fee for all the festivals that had their name on it. The earlier festivals paid for the later festivals, and the later festivals had bills that couldn't be paid. The primary subcontractor in Martha's Vineyard, a local man, wasn't paid, so he couldn't pay others he'd contracted. He was so embarrassed he wasn't even seen on the island in 2009.

Various contractors and government entities were owed in excess of $500,000 in Newport, and the City of Newport cancelled their agreement with Festival Network. The company tried to pay down various bills with the funds it had secured by selling the old FPI audio and video archive, even though there were no rights associated with any of these recorded performances. In other words, someone could buy the tapes, but they had no rights for broadcasting or issuing the content unless they were cleared with artists or their estates. The party to whom they were sold, Wolfgang's Vault, apparently had no qualms about such inconvenient legalities and in 2025 is still offering material from Newport and other Wein-related venues on its Internet site.

The funds derived from the sale to Wolfgang's Vault were to be used to pay off debts in Newport, with the hope that in so doing the City Fathers might be persuaded to grant Festival Network a license to present a jazz and folk festival in 2009. FN even went so far as to "hire" a city councilman to plead their case, but the City Fathers were not convinced. The damage had already been done, and the license to put on a jazz and folk festival in August 2009 was issued to old, out-of-date George Wein.

George had no intention of letting his festival die and fought hard to get the license. He hired a skeleton staff, reassembled his team in Newport, and was prepared to fund the festival himself. Then something fell out of the sky and a sponsor appeared for the jazz festival. One week after the fiftieth anniversary of the Folk Festival was presented, George Wein's CareFusion Jazz Festival 55 was a triumph in every way. When the dust settled, about fifteen thousand attended folk and thirteen thousand turned out for jazz; it was just as it had been in earlier years, and there wasn't an Escalade in sight. The sponsor was happy, and so was the world of jazz and music festivals, except possibly for the Islamic militants who were plotting to scuttle the Festival au Désert to insure the sonic purity of Timbuktu.

In 2010, George began working on a plan to create a nonprofit foundation and fold both Newport festivals into it. By 2011, a good board had been assembled and the jazz and folk festivals have been presented as nonprofit events ever since, benefiting the Newport Festivals Foundation.

Meanwhile, the thirty-seven festival networkers, from top to bottom, have scattered with ill-will swirling about them; $20 plus million investor dollars vanished, the company website remained up until about 2015, advertising nonexistent events and stating "new site coming soon." I wrote a piece about FN I called "Debacle," and its

With Ahmet Ertegun, 2007.
(Author's collection)

existence is probably only remembered by those whom FN failed to pay for their services.

The New York State lottery has an advertising slogan about a dollar and a dream. Festival Network was twenty-two million dollars and a dream. The difference is that with the dollar and a dream scheme, even though the odds are long, there is usually at least one winner. With Festival Network there were only losers, and the old guy who wasn't with it, whose advice and counsel was largely ignored, was still in business until his death in 2021. While the debacle that was Festival Network was underway, I was involved with another project involving George. In 2003, documentary filmmaker Bruce Ricker suggested he'd really like to make a good *American Masters*–like film about George. He'd just completed *Clint Eastwood–Out of the Shadows* and he was on a roll. He asked David G. Berger and myself if we'd like to be involved. In mid-2003, we agreed to embark on a project to produce *A Man for All Festivals*. It was agreed that Bruce Ricker would direct the film, and Berger and I would act as producers and writers. Clint Eastwood agreed to serve as consultant.

In our role as producers, Berger and I agreed to play, and in fact did play, a major role in developing the content for the film. We each wrote rough treatments, decided on talking heads to interview, and searched for archival material. David and I raised sufficient personal funds to begin filming in January 2004. Our initial idea was the possibility of filming during the fiftieth anniversary of the Newport Jazz Festival, but that proved to be overly ambitious.

As we were collaborating on creating the content for the film, David and I intended to create a joint work of authorship; in other words, to jointly and equally own the copyright in the raw footage as well as in all cuts of the film, including but not limited to the final version.

There were multiple film shoots between 2004 and 2007, including five days of filming in New York City during the annual International Association of Jazz Educators (IAJE) convention, January 21–26, 2004; three days of filming in Los Angeles, including a shoot at a public library where George discussed his newly released book, *Myself among Others;* and shoots at press conferences and meetings related to the 2004 Playboy Jazz Festival, February 29–March 4, 2004; a one-day shoot featuring other festival producers in New York City on November 12, 2004; and one-day shoots with George Avakian (2005), Wynton Marsalis (2006), and Ahmet Ertegun (2007). In late 2007, the project was put on hold because of financial difficulties as well as Bruce Ricker's health concerns, and it stayed on hold until Bruce Ricker died in 2011.

With his Newport All Stars in 2008, Bern, Switzerland. Espenranza Spalding, Jimmy Cobb, Anat Cohen, and Howard Alden. (Author's collection)

George with Esperanza Spalding, Jimmy Cobb, Anat Cohen, Howard Alden, Randy Brecker, Glory Van Scott, Hans Zurgruebb, and Marian Gauer. (Author's collection)

All of the footage that had been compiled for this project was on the shelf for almost a decade. In 2019, there was a flurry of activity when the noted director Oren Jacoby expressed an interest in possibly completing the film, but George was in no hurry to do so and the board of the Newport Festivals Foundation had no interest in an outside party completing a film that they would have no control over. They were convinced a film about George could be created using in-house personnel. Of course, they were

With Dave and Iola Brubeck, 2006.

wrong, and no such film has even been undertaken, let alone completed. But all of the footage featuring George and dozens of others has been digitized and transferred to the George and Joyce Wein Foundation. The footage in the foundation's archive exists as it was originally shot; it was never edited, and no version or "cut" was ever created from the raw material.

In the 2010s, I no longer talked to George a couple of times a day or saw him four days a week, and neither of us were in touch with any of the people associated with Festival Network, either those who funded it or those who ran it into the ground. But we were in touch with one another frequently because our lives continued to overlap in so many ways. George remained one of the biggest supporters of The Jazz Gallery and the Jazz Foundation of America, two charities I also support. And, of course, he knew if he mentioned Frankie Newton or Ruby Braff, I'd know what he was talking about.

He was at musicales at my house and I was at his, and there was even a musical book launch at his 150 East Sixty-Ninth Street home for his close friend Dr. Glory Van Scott, and countless dinners or performances at the opera or special birthday parties (his ninetieth was quite remarkable at City Winery) or performances at the Apollo uptown, or just a drive around town looking at old locations or helping Ryszard Horowitz with his remarkable book of jazz reminiscences and photographs or helping Hans Zurbrügg organize the two special "George Wein" rooms at his Innere Enge Hotel in Bern Switzerland, rooms that are filled with memorabilia related to George's career as a festival producer and musician or any number of other fascinating projects.

A few years ago, we were at Dizzy's Club Coca-Cola together to hear Christian McBride's Big Band. Christian had been hired by George to help lead his festivals in the coming years. The band was terrific. After the first set and before Christian and the guys in the band came over to say hello, a man almost as old as George came by and sat down next to him. The lady sitting next to me asked, "Who's that old guy talking to George?" I said, "Lee Konitz." She asked, "Who's Lee Konitz?" I replied, "In 1954, Lee Konitz beat out Charlie Parker as the best alto player in the Metronome poll, was a headliner at George's first Newport Jazz Festival, and is still playing great." Suddenly, Lee wasn't just an old guy talking to George but was a piece of jazz history. I only had my iPhone but took a picture anyway.

As I've written earlier, he called one day in November 2012 and asked if I wanted to take a drive. I never said no to one of his suggestions, but I did ask what he had in mind. He said, "To say goodbye to Dave." George really loved Dave, as did almost everyone who knew him well. An example: When Jazz at Lincoln Center finally got around to asking Dave to play a concert at Rose Hall, it was only because George funded the concert. So Andrew drove us to Wilton, and we sat around Dave and Iola's kitchen table and ate chocolate chip cookies and said goodbye. We were very sad, and then the years passed and suddenly it was 2020 and the COVID-19 pandemic got us. But somehow there was a bit of a Newport Jazz Festival to be had by anyone who had a computer and knew how to use it. At the time I wrote a note to myself that read:

> *Last Saturday night I spent an hour watching my computer screen. It was the Newport Jazz Festival Gala, streaming from George's Sixty-ninth Street apartment and wherever Wynton Marsalis, Diana Krall, and Christian McBride stream from. There was no Newport Jazz or Folk Festival in 2020; Covid-19 wiped both out, so there was a steaming gala with live performance and video clips. But if the world gets it's act together there will be festivals in 2021, and if I know George, he's already got most of the shows booked. He'll turn ninety-five on October 3.*

With young musicians and Dr. Glory Van Scott
at 830 Broadway, 2020

And I don't think he ever thought about when the time would come when he couldn't do this, couldn't remember and run things. The last time I saw him, in August 2021, a month or so before he died, he was in pretty punk shape, confined to a wheelchair with most parts of his ninety-five-year-old body failing, everything except his brain. We talked about all the things we always did and who was good and who wasn't and who would be playing at Newport in 2022 and how well the box office was in 2021 and how many tickets were sold and did Frankie Newton really play at that funny venue on MacDougall Street in the 1940s? All those kinds of things, and he was right on top of everything.

EDDIE CONDON'S
47
GEO. WETTLING

26

George Wettling

November 28, 1907 – June 6, 1968

I NEVER MET George Wettling. I never saw him perform. He's the only person I got to know pretty well, but only after his death. Because of a series of unusual circumstances that began in the summer of 1968, I became involved with Wettling from the standpoint of preserving and protecting one aspect of his legacy, one that continues to this day. Because of this involvement I was called up to write an essay about the part of his legacy that dealt with his paintings for an exhibition in 1986. Portions of this 1986 essay are still relevant, especially those that deal with his life in music, and, slightly modified in 2025, this is what I wrote all those years ago. Not a great deal new has been unearthed regarding Wettling in the last thirty-seven years, but a good deal has probably been forgotten. If I were to try and assemble a small book about his life and work, it is unlikely I could find a single person who actually knew him or heard him in person. But in 1986 I wrote:

> *August 6, 1954. Celebrity Service's Celebrity Bulletin picks its celebrity of the day. George Wettling. Listed along with William Holden, Louis Lamour* [sic], *Fred Allen, Ella Fitzgerald, Yvonne DeCarlo, and Portland Hoffa. George Wettling, the multitalented painter, writer, photographer, and highly skilled jazz musician was the celebrity of the day. He died in Roosevelt Hospital thirteen years and ten months later, remembered by a few but not many. It was a bad time for a jazz musician of his kind to die, a sort of in-between time in terms of the historians and scholarly types.*

It's a pity how quickly he's been forgotten; I don't mean by young jazz fans or even jazz fans who emerged in the 1970s who have had little or no opportunity to hear his music, let alone know about him, but by the current batch of writers, critics, and educators who should be somewhat better informed. Wettling's oblivion is, however, much more complicated than simple sloppy scholarship and the ill-informed listeners who really believe Spyro Gyra plays jazz.

George Wettling was born in Topeka, Kansas, in 1907, the same year as Dave Tough and two years before Gene Krupa, the others in the triumvirate of exceptional white jazz drummers from the Midwest. He was active in Chicago by 1921, the right place at the right time, able to be influenced by the influx of great musicians from New Orleans and some equally great young musicians growing up in Chicago. By the time he was twenty, he had already formed lifelong friendships and recorded with Muggsy Spanier, Frank Teschmacher, Joe Sullivan, Eddie Condon, and a host of others. He was not only an exceptional drummer with small jazz ensembles but was also sufficiently versatile to later handle big band chores with Paul Whiteman, Chico Marx, and Bunny Berigan in the 1930s and the ABC staff in the 1940s and 1950s. There was even talk in the early 1950s that ABC was going to launch a symphony orchestra to compete with Arturo Toscanini and the NBC Symphony, and Wettling was slated to be one of the percussionists.

OPPOSITE
Eddie Condon's, 47 East 3rd Street, New York City.

Big band and studio jobs like these paid the rent, but the musical friendships he made in the 1920s always led to his finest performances and the best working conditions. But the good jobs were never sufficient to provide a steady income, even during the 1940s and 1950s when the music that flowed from Eddie Condon's Greenwich Village club was moderately commercial.

As the 1950s became the 1960s, there were fewer and fewer jobs for a drummer like Wettling, with his old friends, who were less and less active, or anyone else. There were reunions at festivals, a special gathering, or perhaps a private party, but by and large he was lucky to get a job with the Dukes of Dixieland or a piano trio date. His last steady job was in Clarence Hutchenrider's Trio at Bill Gay Nineties, a place that still operates on East Fifty-Fourth Street in New York City, serving hamburgers to harried businessmen for lunch and martinis to the same crowd after work. The trio played in a room on the second floor; it was a long climb up the stairs, and in the spring of 1968 Wettling found he could no longer climb them. He was already ill; this was the last nudge he needed. He gave up and died in June. A few weeks later, I became aware of his paintings. I'd never met him or heard him in person.

Two of Geo. Wettling's treasured recordings. (Author's collection)

Marian McPartland telephoned me sometime in mid-June 1968, told me Wettling had died, that his drums were at Bill's Gay Nineties, and the owners would be cheered if they were quickly removed. She added that it was my duty to help her; I loved the music he had made over the years, had a strong back plus an automobile in Manhattan. I agreed with her on all points, and we did the job on a sunny Saturday afternoon. She had not warned me that the elevator was out, and I would get to haul everything to the fifth floor.

When Marian and I arrived at Jean Wettling's Fifty-Seventh Street apartment, I was not surprised to see everything in a state of disrepair; Marian had warned me beforehand that housekeeping was not Jean Wettling's strong suit, but she had not warned me about the paintings. I knew that Wettling painted; Eddie Condon had one at his apartment, but I was unprepared to see all that were hanging on or leaning against walls in most of the rooms; they looked remarkably like copies of Stuart Davis's work, which, I later learned, was not surprising.

I placed the drums and assorted hardware in a small room and then spent some time consoling the widow Wettling. She was not having a good day. In fact, it appeared she hadn't had a good one in years, but one thing that registered was she said she planned to "sell" all the paintings to a guy who owned a saloon in the neighborhood for a couple of months credit or $300, whichever came first. I urged that she not do anything so foolish, and Marian quickly agreed. I told her it was likely the paintings could be sold to jazz fans, and she could realize something better than a few months of free drinks. I came back a few days later and took photographs of most of the paintings, made a list of people I thought might be interested in acquiring one, and got on the phone. It wasn't that difficult a chore. I bought one, Marian bought one, Squirrel Ashcraft bought two, and an art collector at the New York CIA office bought one featuring McSorley's Old Ale House. I spotted a signed Stuart Davis print in an inexpensive frame on the wall; it was in color, and Roselle Davis was happy to acquire it. It took a few months but eventually, most of the paintings were sold. The going price in 1968 was $300 apiece. Maybe I should have asked for more, but I had just turned twenty-eight, was inexperienced, and there was not a booming market for Stuart Davis–like paintings by a recently deceased mostly-Dixieland drummer.

I stayed in touch with Jean Wettling throughout the 1970s. I tried to give her advice on how to sort out her ragtime life. I paid her telephone bill every so often, and I suggested to Bob Altshuler he should buy all of George's original 78s. He did, plus he gave her a new Columbia record player/console. The same one William Paley had sent to Eddie Condon about the same time.

She ignored almost everything I said, especially if it involved her live-in boyfriend, a guy I felt was a bit of a brute. She finally got the point of my suggestions when he threw her down the subway steps at Fifty-Seventh and Eighth Avenue. Somebody saw him do it, the police were called, the brute was busted and sent to Rikers for a few months and wasn't let back into Chez Wettling.

Occasionally, Jean would "find" a painting in the back of a closet or under a bed and as often as not I'd wind up buying it from her; better me than the guy at the saloon. Then one day in early 1981, the telephone rang; it was a woman who lived in Jean's building. Jean had died in Roosevelt Hospital and when the super went into the apartment he found a telephone book next to her bed. It was open to the page with the "Os" and mine was the only name. I got the call.

The woman on the telephone didn't know what to do, who to call, if there were any relatives, if there was a will; in short, there was nothing. I later learned the story was even worse than it appeared. Jean had some kind of galloping cancer; it was untreated and became worse and worse. At some point she made her way to the emergency room of Roosevelt Hospital on Fifty-Ninth Street, but without any identification. She didn't live long enough to even check in. Later, I was told by the building's super that Jean remained at Roosevelt unclaimed for some while before she was identified. I have no idea how the identification was accomplished, but here I was on the telephone with a frantic lady.

Left-Handed Study (oil on canvas board).
(Author's collection)

I telephoned Phyllis Condon and we went up to that sad little apartment on West Fifty-Seventh Street only to find ourselves confronted by a number of people in the hallway on the fifth floor. They all had their eye on a piece of furniture or bric-a-brac. In the same address book where I lived under "O," I found the name of Jean's brother in New Mexico or Arizona. I placed a call, and the conversation was very brief. Upon learning of his sister's death, he strongly suggested he didn't want to be bothered and would I please arrange to have everything thrown into the street.

I had never experienced such a response. I noticed the crowd in the hallway was growing and appeared to be increasingly impatient, eyeing the furniture as well as Phyllis and me. We hurriedly searched the apartment and filled a large box with all the letters, photographs, clippings, sketchbooks, memorabilia, and scrapbooks related to George Wettling. We also found two small paintings that I later titled *My First Piece* and *Left Handed Study*. To avoid being claimed by the neighbors and hauled off to their apartments along with the furniture, we left Chez Wettling to the bargain hunters and headed south to

My First Piece (oil on board).
(Author's collection)

Gene Krupa.
(Author's collection)

Greenwich Village, much saddened by the day's events. I recall that unhappy day very vividly, but despite the unpleasant aspects I'm glad I made the trip. We managed to save scrapbooks, sketchbooks, and photographs. George was a good photographer.

There were not then, nor are there now, many people who can shed any light on Wettling. Other than the comments of a few people, old jazz books, and discographies, all I know about him comes from that small box of letters, photographs, scrapbooks, and ephemera that Phyllis and I collected. As of 2025, this is about all I know.

George Wettling began drumming in his teens, but he began to paint and pursue assorted intellectual matters in the early and mid-1940s. The small portrait of Maggie Condon as an infant dates the beginning; this was his second painting. She was born in 1945. In 1970 Eddie Condon recalled, "George Wettling learned to paint at our apartment in 1943. We were moving out and to get back at a pesky super we decided to have a wall painting party. George was our most enthusiastic painter. When he ran out of walls at our apartment, he left immediately for Stuart Davis's where he found lessons and encouragement."

Buddha Wettling.
(Author's collection)

Duke Ellington. (Author's collection)

Stuart Davis. (Author's collection)

Stuart Davis. (Author's collection)

Norlyst Gallery program, 1947. (Author's collection)

Jazz Is In (oil on canvas).
(Author's collection)

Stuart Davis on Oil Cloth.
(Earl Davis Collection)

Self Portrait (oil on canvas).
(Author's collection)

Wettling's relationship with Stuart Davis was critical in his development as a painter; within a few years, his paintings began to resemble his teacher's. From the correspondence that has survived, as well as photographs and assorted memories and memorabilia, it is clear the two men were very good friends who admired the other's accomplishments. Painting became important to Wettling; jazz was equally important to Davis, who once wrote, "Recently I had occasion to inquire of a little boy what he wanted to be when he grew up. Without breaking the Chicago style beat of his bubble gum he replied, 'Eddie Condon.' Conference had been fogging my vision a bit of late. It was clear that the little boy had hip boots well clasped up to his navel. This was the jolt I needed. I played an old Punch Miller record with a George Wettling backing I had recently dubbed in, added a configuration to my current painting, *The Mellow Pad*, and forgot all about Sir Alexander Cadogan and Gromyko. For a brief moment I thought I was Eddie Condon too, but that passed." Add to this that Wettling was intellectually on Davis's wavelength. One only had to look at the books on Wettling's shelves; no useless books, no pulp, nothing trendy. He had everything Henry Miller, John Steinbeck, and Kenneth Patchen had ever written and many others as well.

With painting from 1940s.
(Author's collection)

Wettling was sufficiently accomplished by 1947 to have produced a body of work that was of interest to a New York City gallery. A one-man show was mounted at the Norlyst Gallery, and the advertising flyer contained a special tribute by Stuart Davis. Two of his paintings from that show, *Stuart Davis on Oil Cloth* and *My First Piece,* were still at his apartment when I delivered the drums in 1968.

Wettling's paintings fall into four distinct stylistic periods; the first period is characterized by limited technique and lack of direction, as may be observed in *Maggie Condon* and *My First Piece*. These paintings are charming but very primitive. He entered his second phase well before the 1947 show, exhibiting a much better technique and the beginnings of a strong dependence on Stuart Davis, shown in *Stuart Davis on Oil Cloth*. This really is a painting on oil cloth, a red-and-white checkerboard tablecloth of the sort found in Italian restaurants in New York City that sell pizza, heroes, and other tasty Italian specialties.

Wettling's third phase, perhaps his best, began in the late 1940s and lasted into the early 1950s where the complete dominance of Davis is apparent, as is a secure technique. *Jazz Is In*, my $300 acquisition in 1968, is a painting that tells about a recording session and was the focal point of a 1951 article about Wettling in *Collier's* magazine. It is a prime example of his work at this time and is perhaps his finest painting. Later on, I bought *Road Graders* from Jean, and Marian McPartland bought one titled *High as a Kite*. Both of these paintings, exhibited at the Philadelphia Museum of Art in 1952, are also from this period. This exhibition, as well as the possibility of being part of the ABC Symphony Orchestra, indicates the level at which Wettling's artistic accomplishments were viewed in 1952.

The final phase, which lasted into the late 1950s, shows the influence of Davis but here Wettling also presented a more personal vision, as may be seen in the *Self Portrait* and *McSorley's*.

It is likely Wettling did not continue to paint after 1960, even though his sketchbooks continue to 1967. It may well be the sketchbooks took the place of larger works for, beginning in the early sixties, he began to date and locate many of his tiny drawings; *Albany 62, Toronto 63,* and *Gay Nineties 67*. It also appears he stopped taking photographs about the same time he gave up painting. There is nothing in his scrapbooks after 1960, and his album of clippings ends in 1955.

It is unclear why he stopped, and probably no one can supply a definitive answer. It may have been he was no longer interested but this seems unlikely. The death of Stuart Davis in 1964 was probably demoralizing, but he had stopped well before his friend's death. It is apparent he never had any particular commercial success with his paintings; he rarely sold them and for the most part they were given to friends. I don't think lack of commerciality would have stopped Wettling; he doesn't seem to have been the kind of person who was only concerned with that aspect of his art. A more likely reason is that he stopped because of personal disasters and serious health problems.

Wettling's health deteriorated in the early 1960s. His personal life, which was never particularly stable, became intolerable about the same time. When he was dying in the hospital in mid-1968, Eddie Condon went to visit him. Wettling told him the doctors had said he was just about done, there was nothing they could do for him, that he should just go home. He then told Eddie he'd asked the doctors not to send him home, "Anything but that," he said, and they let him remain at the hospital.

But what about the paintings and paintings he abandoned? Various factors mitigated against his painting, personal, financial, lack of meaningful employment, and lack of artistic expression. As gloomy as these circumstances might have been, it might have been possible to overcome them on some level. I think the real answer lies elsewhere; at some point Wettling seems to have suffered a severe case of lack of confidence in creating new work on canvas, and this condition was exacerbated by some very poor guidance.

Hidden away in the back of Wettling's large scrapbook of clippings I found three sheets of "critiques" and a letter from the Famous Artists School, one of those dreary organizations that advertise on matchbooks and in cheap magazines, snaring the unwary with promises of untold success. They snared George Wettling; he sent in a dime to be turned into Michelangelo in a minute, and it is tragic to see an employee of this "school" offering all sorts of manufactured suggestions on how Wettling might improve.

Apparently Wettling would submit a painting and then the "instructor" assigned to him would repaint the picture, showing him how it might appear if properly executed. Perhaps it would have been best had someone executed the instructor; one of the criticism sheets deals with a painting of Eddie Condon's club and the suggestions are so pretentious and overtly scholarly it is sickening. Here is an academic hack, someone who probably exhibited at county fairs and sidewalk events or public parks and has been reduced to working for the matchbook school of art and he's telling Wettling how to paint.

There is even a letter, dated 1960, from these bandits advising Wettling one of his paintings has been selected from thirty-two hundred entries to tour the United States. In addition, the letter announces a prize for the lucky artist; $25 worth of art supplies from the Famous Art School store plus a $10 bonus for a "professional" photographer to take a picture to travel along with the painting. How sad; a man who was one of the finest jazz drummers, a student and close friend of one of the finest painters this country ever produced. And $10 for a photograph? George Wettling had been photographed by Weegee, Gjon Mili, Lisette Model, Charlie Peterson, and goodness knows how many other photographers of note. Wettling started painting the walls of the apartment from which Eddie Condon was being evicted and ended fumbling about with the Famous Artists School; both events equally ridiculous, but in-between he produced some exceptional work.

Eddie's Guitar (ink on paper).
(Author's collection)

George Wettling was not a great painter, but he was a more than adequate disciple of Stuart Davis. He certainly painted better than Davis drummed. He was also a fine photographer; it is obvious he used his camera as a sketchbook in the same manner as did Ben Shahn and Reginald Marsh. His writing was inventive and witty. Every artistic endeavor he approached, music, painting, photography, and writing, showed a genuine creative flair. And as a drummer/percussionist he was in the top tier of American jazz drummers, something he began doing over a century ago. Much has been made recently about the death of Charlie Watts who kept the Rolling Stones under control for so many years. Charlie Watts knew about George Wettling and said so, in print and if anyone chose to ask.

With Eddie Condon, Max Kaminsky, Pee Wee Russell, and Frank Orchard. (Author's collection)

PeeWee Russell (ink on paper). (Author's collection)

But there was a flaw somewhere in Wettling's personality: his personal life was in shambles, and he was unable to cope with the way in which our society often treats some of its more creative, though distinctly less commercial, citizens. Had his personal affairs been better organized he could have perhaps overcome the difficulties caused by his lack of commercial success, but each of his problems fed on the other. Had it not been for Phyllis Condon, Marian McPartland, and myself all the nonmusical aspects of his very creative life would long ago have been scattered along West Fifty-Seventh Street or gracing the walls of a dingy saloon.

Most of Wettling's paintings are dispersed, destroyed, or abandoned in long forgotten attics, but those that survived are quite wonderful. That his life was topsy-turvy is a pity. He was a good painter and his work deserves better treatment. Thank goodness, the musical aspects of his life were better documented and preserved. You will see them if you look in one of the many discographies that detail the recordings made by jazz musicians, and since he recorded with the best and often most legendary musicians, there are a lot of entries. And he also painted with them when not recording.

It is now 2025. I still have all the material produced by and about Wettling I rescued from the hallway crowd in the early 1980s, as well as seven paintings. There are hundreds of photographs by and of Wettling, even more drawings and sketchbooks, letters, cards, and memorabilia. I was once offered $35,000 for *Jazz Is In* twenty years ago. I saw a Wettling painting at an Armory Show about the same time, and the price tag was $28,000. These prices are not based on who he is; these days no one remembers or cares about George Wettling. The prices are based on the fact that they are extremely good.

I have always wanted to create a small book about Wettling, one that would feature his paintings, drawings, photographs, and writings as well as a bit of his history. I suspect this will probably never happen unless an angel appears before I audition to become one. The last person I know of who actually worked with Wettling died two years ago. The one person still alive who may have worked with Wettling is Dick Hyman, who is ninety-five and increasingly forgetful. I can think of no other firsthand sources.

George was pretty much forgotten by the jazz and artistic community in 1968, when I first encountered his widow. It is not fifty-five years later and I'm sure he's fifty-five years more forgotten and sixty-eight from when he was celebrity of the day. There were six other people on the list that day, and all are deceased and the only person on the list who might be recognized in 2025 is Ella Fitzgerald. And I started writing this thirty-five years ago. Maybe it is about time to call it a day.

JAZZ

27

Three for the Road

John Moore, Andrew Sordoni, and Hans Zurbrügg

THE FOUNDING, elevation, flowering, and now codifying of jazz has been liberally populated by hundreds and maybe thousands of nonmusicians and amateur musicians, and often these men and women, mostly working behind the scenes or in the shadows, have made important and far-reaching contributions to the world of jazz.

It is so much more than just the men and women who blow the horn or hit a drum or sing a song. It is also the people who provide the funding and work opportunities and are behind the scenes in many different capacities. We all know and recognize the name at the top of the LP jacket or CD or DVD booklet, but the names on the back in little print and a zillion others who are not well-known or important enough to even warrant a small, printed notice have helped make it all possible.

When I was in my early and mid-twenties, first Squirrel Ashcraft and then Sherman Fairchild appeared, followed in rapid succession by John Hammond and George Avakian and then a few years later by George Wein and later still Clint Eastwood. They helped me immensely, but all along the way there were dozens, maybe hundreds of others. Almost always nonmusicians, but men and women who loved the music and made it possible for guys like me and the girls I liked to be with to have something to listen to now and again and be active in many different ways within the music business and on its fringes as well.

Sid Smith, a noted live television producer, occasional lyricist, and Eddie Condon's brother-in-law introduced Shelley Shier and myself to Peter Martin, an advertising executive who was struggling to help Norwegian Caribbean Line fill its big blue ocean liner the *S/S Norway* (formerly the *S/S France*) during hurricane season but with little success. This led to the inaugural presentation of the Floating Jazz Festival aboard an ocean liner in 1983, where it continued aboard the *S/S Norway* and *Queen Elizabeth 2* for the next two decades.

Stanley Dance, and by extension, Helen Oakley, introduced me to Earl Hines and convinced him to humor me and undertake a recreation of his eight legendary piano solo recordings for QRS in 1928. This in turn led to Earl appearing on eleven additional Chiaroscuro recordings, LPs that formed the backbone of the Chiaroscuro catalog in the 1970s. I recently came upon a lengthy review of the record, part of which stated: *However, this is not only one of Hines's greatest recordings, but it is also one of the greatest Jazz Piano recordings of all time.* The person who wrote this is the kind of enthusiastic listener who helps make the music possible.

Another jazz hero who receives far less credit than he should is Father Peter O'Brien, S.J. He was Mary Lou Williams's spiritual advisor, and without Peter's help and encouragement, none of Mary Lou's recordings for Chiaroscuro (or any other label) would have been possible without divine intervention. He also managed to collect and organize her massive musical archive and, working with Dan Morgenstern, arrange for it to be transferred to the Institute for Jazz Studies at Rutgers University.

OPPOSITE

Hans Zurbrügg, 2008 (Author's collection)

Fr. Peter O'Brian, S.J., and Mary Lou Williams, 1973.
(Author's collection)

Dan Morgenstern

Dan Morgenstern was the editor, first of *Metronome* and then *Downbeat*. He had more knowledge of jazz in his head than anyone alive and more than the files of the Institute of Jazz Studies at Rutgers, which he ran for so many years. We shared musical interests, and his lucid commentary spread the word about a tiny record company with but a handful of releases and gave a bunch of them terrific reviews and made sure others wrote about them as well. In fact, of the first ten releases all got four- or five-star reviews in *Downbeat*. And all these years later, at the age of ninety-four he was still doing as he always had, trying to move the music forward while remembering the importance of the past but being careful to make certain he was both accurate and positive. He died peacefully on September 7, 2024. Two days later, I delivered these remarks at the gravesite:

In late 1963 and early 1964, at twenty-three I was the youngest member of the Office of National Estimates. I was naïve, inexperienced, and ill-prepared for the position in which I found myself, but somehow something I had written had made its way to the desk of a senior official who asked to see me to discuss what I had written. I entered Abbot Smith's spacious living room-like office only to find him not hard at work, but stretched out on a couch reading a small book. He asked me to bring my paper to him, and I did as I was told. As I brought the paper to him, he noticed me looking at the book he was reading and said, "It's Mahler's Fourth, do you know it?" I probably mumbled something like, "I've heard it, sir, but I don't really 'know' it."

Dr. Smith was a wise, cultured, and experienced man, everything I was not, and when he was not reading a Mahler score for relaxation he was gathering facts, sorting them out and arranging them in a way that made sense and used this information to form a coherent and honest narrative, one without preconceived ideas or prejudice and then present them to his primary client, President Kennedy up to November 22 and Lyndon Johnson thereafter.

And this is what Dan did on a daily, if not hourly basis, in the field of music, jazz music in particular, and I was fortunate enough to witness this from 1967 onward. I don't remember the exact circumstanced of our first meeting, and I'm sure I was still naïve and inexperienced, but he

Dan Morgenstern, 2021.
(Author's collection)

didn't treat me as a newbie, and later he reviewed, or made certain others did, my first recordings in the early 1970s and even introduced one of my earliest concerts at The New School in 1972. It made a difference to me and to so many others with whom he interacted. He was the wise, cultured, and experienced man I always turned to first and put a pin on the word experienced.

Fifty plus years later, in May of this year, The Jazz Gallery, a fine organization with which I'm associated, honored Dan with a special Contribution to the Arts award. Just a few weeks ago, we had a conversation about a Newport Jazz Festival presentation in the 1950s when George Frazier made his introduction in Latin. Dan could discuss this because he was there. And this is just one of the things that made him so very special. He was the guy who was there and remembered. As he aged, I used to tell him he had to hang in there, to live until the ability to download one's brain became a possibility. I'm sad he didn't quite make it.

Then there are the engineers and recording people like Rudy Van Gelder, Wally Heider, and the not nearly so well-known Bob Fine, or the completely forgotten John Steiner. Or even the men and women who worked with me at Downtown Sound, Fred Miller, Jon Bates, Aimie Chiarello, and Bruce Gerstein, or the musicians who learned to record their own sessions, artists like Phil Clendeninn, James Mason, and Borah Bergman.

Recording a spontaneous, ever creative, always improvising jazz artist or jazz group requires a far different sensibility from that required for pop or rock or hip hop or even classical and Broadway shows. In 2025, a skillful iPhoner can make a decent recording, but you can rarely make a great one. Today, as yesterday, a great engineer can still make a big difference. The best ones make a difference on a daily basis and make the music possible.

Rudy Van Gelder

Rudy Van Gelder was in a class by himself. A unique and legendary figure in the world of music but especially in the world of jazz, there was simply no one like him. Even though I had stacks of recordings that first emerged from the horns of plenty in his New Jersey studios, I didn't get to know him until the second incarnation of Chiaroscuro. The first date we recorded at his Englewood Cliffs studio was a solo piano date with John Eaton, followed closely by projects featuring Al Grey's new quintet, Jay McShann and Ralph Sutton, as *The Last of the Whorehouse Piano Players*, Clark Terry's revitalized and reassembled *Spacemen*, an extremely complicated Milt Hinton project, Flip Phillips with strings, Kenny Davern and Bob Wilber, back together after a decade plus apart, but now working as *Summit Reunion*, and a bunch of others. The last was in June 1996, *The Gerry Mulligan Songbook*, with Bill Charlap and Ted Rosenthal. By then Rudy was in his seventies and slowing down a step or two.

We got on well, possibly because, to pinch the title of this book, it was more than just the music. Sure, I followed the rules with no drinking, eating, smoking, or touching the equipment, rules that were pretty strict, and the bills were paid on time without any haggling, but it also had to do with many friends in common, technical recording matters, photography, and, strangely enough, birds. I had built a couple of studios and knew how to plug in a tape recorder and where to place a microphone, and I had more cameras than he did and knew how to use them, but it was birds that sealed the deal.

I am not a birder and never had much interest in them but knew a little. Rudy, however, knew a lot about birds, which is not well known, except possible to the birds he watched with such enthusiasm. Many of his happiest summer vacations were those he spent in Maine photographing birds. One morning I was at the studio, and he was mixing and mastering a session he had recorded for us a few days or weeks before. There were large windows in the control room that faced north, and there was plenty of foliage outside; a perfect landing strip for birds in need of one and a cute little Yellow-Bellied Sapsucker did so. I said something like, "Oh look, a Yellow-Bellied Sapsucker," and he stopped mixing, looked at the visiting woodpecker and asked me how I knew that. I have no idea how I replied, but I was more than OK after that.

The recordings Rudy did for us (and for everyone else) are among the best in our catalog. And we always gave him projects that we were pretty sure would interest him from a musical and technical standpoint. Flip Phillips and a room full of strings, two dueling pianists, where we had to import an extra piano from Steinway Hall. It was always an adventure with Rudy, but one we always knew would come out perfectly in the end.

Rudy Van Gelder in his Englewood Cliffs studio, 1992.
(Author's collection)

Clint Eastwood and Dr. John.
(Author's collection)

THE WHITE HOUSE
WASHINGTON

June 1, 1994

Mr. Joseph Phillips
Bradenton, Florida

Dear Flip:

It gives me great pleasure to join your friends and colleagues in honoring you for your extraordinary lifetime of musical achievements.

Music has always been a unifying force in our world, bringing people together across vast cultural and geographical divisions. For over fifty years, millions have gained tremendous enjoyment from your brilliant talent as a saxophone player. With such memorable works as "Apple Honey" and the famous solo from "Perdido," you have broadened the scope and appeal of jazz, helping to make it one of America's most important and original offerings to the arts. You have touched countless lives in the course of your distinguished career, and I am delighted to commend you for your many wonderful contributions to the rich legacy of our nation's music.

Best wishes for every future happiness.

Sincerely,

Bill Clinton

Letter from Bill Clinton, 1994.
(Author's collection)

An informal session at Blues Alley in 1967 with Clancy Hayes, John Phillips, Steve Jordan, Squirrel Ashcraft, and Tommy Gwaltney. (Author's collection)

The people who write about the music, especially those whose attitude or mantra is to do no harm, are particularly important. What they write about an always fragile art form, one that is often marginalized and frequently dismissed, particularly commercially, that needs all the help it can get and the men and women who make this music, who are often equally fragile can often make the difference between success and failure. Men and women who had or have the passion to write about the music with words filled with as much passion as the music they were writing about. And almost all of them required a day job, writing about something else as well or in an office or whatever. Most of today's members of the Jazz Journalist's Association are moonlighting elsewhere to pay their rent, just as Otis Ferguson, George Frazier, George Hofer, and many others did so many years ago.

There are also celebrities who take an interest in the music. It is well known, especially to me, that Clint Eastwood put his artistic talent to work on behalf of jazz, but so did TV guys like Norman Lear, an actor/comedian like Billy Crystal, a publisher named Hugh Hefner, presidential jazz fans like Jimmy Carter and Bill Clinton, or people who worked for them like the legal scholar Len Garment, who before he left government service found a way to gather together the funding that led to the establishment of the National Jazz Museum in Harlem, and the basketball Hall of Fame guy Kareem Abdul Jabbar and baseball Hall of Famer Bob Lemon, who actually once wrote notes for a Chiaroscuro CD featuring his pal Flip Phillips. The list is long.

Or the people who formed the small record companies recording jazz of all sorts, from New Orleans and traditional music on Jazzology to the furthest reaches of the avant-garde on ESP, both formed in the 1950s and 1960s when jazz of each type was largely being ignored. Or the people at major record companies, secret jazzers at heart, who could be called upon to contribute. Men like Ahmet and Neshui Ertegun and Jerry Wexler at Atlantic,

Bruce Lundvall at CBS (later Blue Note), Bob Altshuler and even Bill Paley at CBS, Ken Glancy at RCA, or Norman Granz at Clef/Verve and later Pablo. In 2025, an art gallery/performance space in Chicago, Corbett and Dempsey, not only shows exceptional artwork but produces equally exceptional concerts and CDs that explore the deepest reaches of avant-garde jazz and American music.

Businessman and women also make a difference. They fill the boards and bank accounts of countless nonprofits with which they are affiliated, and without them many fine organizations might wither. I am associated with three jazz and music-oriented nonprofits: The Jazz Foundation of America, The College of Performing Arts at The New School, and The Jazz Gallery. Richard Parsons was chairman of the JFA for years, while he was also chairman of Time Warner and then Citi Group. The current chairman is Jarrett Lillien, formerly the head of E-Trade. The chairman of the Advisory Board at COPA is Sheila Johnson, the cofounder of BET, and though hardly in the same league, I've been chairman of The Jazz Gallery for over twenty-five years and we are thriving.

And simple fans and jazz party hosts and hot club enthusiasts like Dick Gibson or Matt Domber or the countless men and women in out of the way places that launched their own jazz festivals hire hundreds of jazz musicians and make a difference. Guys like Johnson "Fat Cat" McRee, who created a festival in an unlikely former railhead now turned DC bedroom community once known only for the Battle of Bull Run, now known as Manassas, Virginia. He kept the festival going from the mid-1960s until his death in 1990. Less well-known is that in 1965, along with his friend Tommy Gwaltney, he founded Blues Alley in Washington, DC. In 2025, it is still going strong, and is possibly the oldest continuously operating jazz supper club in the country. This is what it looked like in 1967 after a recording session that took place on a Sunday afternoon. I was fortunate enough to know and work with many of these people, from the 1960s up through today, and each made their own distinct contribution.

There were hundreds of dedicated men and women with whom I interacted during the years 1963 through 1980, but in early 1980, the first of three encounters with three amateur musicians who loved music in general and jazz in particular came along, very unexpectedly. The first was in 1980, John Chandler Moore III, proud piano-playing member of whatever American Federation of Musician's local is responsible for Sun Valley, Idaho; the second, in 1985, was Andrew J. Sordoni III, a saxophone playing businessman based in northeastern Pennsylvania who, in his dreams, when not overseeing his construction and telecommunications businesses, would rather have been playing in a hot rock band on the Jersey shore in Wildwood or a jazz joint in Philadelphia; and the third was in 2005, Hans Zurbrügg, a cornet-playing hotelier based in Bern, Switzerland who, when not tending to his two hotels in that city and Marians, the finest jazz club in Switzerland, and producing the annual Internationale JazzFestival Bern since 1974, led a hot little ensemble known locally as the Wolverines, named after Bix's band in the 1920s. All of these men had a day job; they played music for fun and supported it in every way they could.

John Moore, Tony Bennett, Danny Bennett, and Chuck Gregory, 1981. (Author's collection)

John Chandler Moore III

John Moore was the first of the three with whom I interacted and, happily for him and his wife Susan as well as a barn full of cats and a stable full of racehorses, I can still call or text him on his birthday. The way we worked together in the formation of Hammond Music Enterprises in the early 1980s is detailed in the "John & George" chapter, and there is no need to duplicate it here, other than to say that for the first half of the 1980s the events that transpired illuminates the influence nonmusicians or well-meaning amateurs can have on the business in a positive manner.

After the complete collapse of Hammond Music Enterprises in 1985 to 1986, I was in a completely different space, as was John Moore. HOSS, Inc., the production company Shelley Shier and I had founded in 1983, was

John Moore, 1981.
(Author's collection)

Andrew Sordoni. (Author's collection)

increasingly successful, both on the high seas and with the Oslo Jazz Festival, I had contracts with both the Justice Department and Internal Revenue Service to work with them in tracking down abusive tax shelters and other shenanigans in the music business, a contract with Doubleday to deliver a book entitled *The Ghosts of Harlem*, the Jazz and Contemporary Music Department was just getting off the ground at The New School, and the acquisition of Chiaroscuro Records was just a year or so away.

John phased out of the music business and still played and listened, but to the best of my knowledge never used his Sun Valley, Idaho, union card. After a very successful career in various capitalistic adventures in the United States and the Middle East, he combined business and matrimony and entered the world of thoroughbred racing. I don't know how many horses he and Susan have owned over the years or how many races these horses have won, I lost count many years ago, but suffice to say his similarly named silver-smithing father and grandfather, each either in charge of design and manufacturing or president of Tiffany, would be proud of the amount of silverware that fills his home. He no longer runs races, but his horses do. He remains as the chairman emeritus of the Thoroughbred Retirement Foundation. In 1983, he introduced me to Shelley Shier, and, much to everyone's surprise, we are still together.

Andrew Sordoni

In 1973, at the end of Dave McKenna's first Chiaroscuro recording session, I asked Dave to record two Christmas tunes. Nice versions of Mel Torme's "The Christmas Song" and "Jingle Bells Stomp" were the result. My idea was to send out a 45 rpm Christmas record at the end of the year instead of a traditional Christmas card. I don't remember how much Christmas cards cost in 1973, but a 45-rpm disc cost a dime and media mail was cheap. It was my idea for a musical Christmas card, something that wouldn't wind up in the trash after January 1.

I made up a few hundred or so for myself and an equal number for Dave. He was happy to have a unique record to send out and so was his wife, Frankie. And so were a few hundred recipients of a special, unexpected Dave McKenna recording. Remember, in 1973 there had not been a solo Dave McKenna recording released in over a decade.

I continued to make annual Christmas records through 1977, the last was with the Welsh pianist Dill Jones, and in between were Earl Hines, Joe Venuti and Zoot Sims, Bucky Pizzarelli, and a few others. One or two of them that didn't wind up with the Christmas cards in a trash can or fireplace or dumpster or a collector's shelf wound up in the hands of Andrew Sordoni, better known as Andy or simply "AJ."

Though nominally retired in 2025, in 1986 Andy was the CEO of Sordoni Construction Services and Commonwealth Telephone Enterprises. In his spare time, he had organized a jazz concert series at Wilkes University, established an art gallery at the same school, and was doing whatever he could to assist the local NPR/PBS station, WVIA.

At WVIA, he had produced and launched a holiday radio program he called *Christmas Music the Jazz Feeling*. He used his friend Bob Wilber as the musical host for the inaugural broadcast. At some point the two men were discussing the program and each remembered my 1970s Christmas 45s, one thing led to another, and Andy booked passage on the *S/S Norway* to be part of the 1986 sailing of the Floating Jazz Festival.

At the same time, I was still occasionally in touch with whatever was left of Audio Fidelity Enterprises, the then-owner of all the Chiaroscuro masters. I had sold Chiaroscuro to AFE a decade earlier and they were still following the playbook used successfully by Herman Gimbel, the man who had purchased the company in 1965 from the founder, Sid Frey. This playbook being simply don't pay anyone until they come after you and then pay as little as possible.

But by 1986, things were catching up with them. They were now based in Rahway, New Jersey, just a few blocks away from the East Jersey State Prison, which to me seemed only appropriate. They had not released any new recordings in years and were primarily in the reissue business, with lines of both audio and video products, many of which they were not authorized to sell. Some of these releases led to some pesky lawsuits and constant battles with the Harry Fox Agency, to which they owed as much as a million dollars in unpaid royalties, and these problems were taking their toll. The company was then run by the always affable but equally dicey Dante Pugliese.

Christmas Music the Jazz Feeling cassettes.
(Author's collection)

Christmas recordings 1973. (Author's collection)

Christmas recordings 1975. (Author's collection)

30 Chiaroscuro CDs. (Author's collection)

Christmas Music:
The Jazz Feeling

Steve Allen
the most versatile entertainer in history, appears as your station's guest this December on WVIA's 11th annual Christmas Music, The Jazz Feeling. In this entertaining hour Steve Allen will present NPR listeners with jazz interpretations of familiar holiday tunes and share his uniquely intelligent and humorous observations.

Steve Allen, *Christmas Music: The Jazz Feeling*. (Author's collection)

With Julia Knaus, Jon Bates, Hank O'Neal, Junior Mance, and Bill Kelly. (Author's collection)

Andy and I spent time together on the *S/S Norway*, enjoying the music and the musicians, talking about the music we both loved, and getting to know one another. When the ship returned to Miami, we made plans to continue talking about the music, *Christmas Music the Jazz Feeling*, and a new topic, the possible acquisition of the Chiaroscuro masters and the label name and trademarks.

The *S/S Norway* returned to Miami on October 25, and Andy and I got to work. I was in Wilkes-Barre on October 31 where, instead of trick or treating, we strategized. I then contacted and met with Dan Pugliese a few weeks later on November 19 and the possible purchase of the masters was set in motion. Andy and I were both concerned about timing. My feeling was AFE was in trouble and might not be long for this world and Andy agreed. This might work to our advantage regarding a lower purchase price but depending on circumstances, if the acquisition of the masters was too close to a bankruptcy or out and out failure, it might impact on the sale.

But it all worked out. The masters were purchased, and AFE hung on for about seven months, one more than they needed to, before they went down in 1988. Andy arranged for a truck to be sent from Wilkes-Barre, where we planned to headquarter the second incarnation of Chiaroscuro. I met the truck in Rahway, was shown to a room where all the company master tapes were located, and pulled all the masters and bogus safeties off the shelves.

No one supervised me. I could have emptied the room and no one would have noticed for weeks and months, and, strangely enough, someone did just that. The handful of treasures, the masters for Louis Armstrong dates supervised by Sid Frey, and Elmo Hope and Al Hirt and Lionel Hampton and the marvelous classical material the company once possessed just vanished and have never turned up. Even the Dukes of Dixieland and the Mexican bullfight music I really liked, it all vanished. When the company failed, its assets were seized and put into a secure location, but when those assets were unfrozen and sold some years later, the room that once contained thousands of reels of master tapes had been reduced to two small boxes. But the Chiaroscuro masters were safely stored elsewhere and are still being used effectively thirty-five years later.

The second incarnation of Chiaroscuro, the digital version, got underway and the hundred or so CDs Andy and I produced during the years 1987 to 2011 are the equal of the one hundred analog LPs that were produced in the 1970s. It was quite an adventure and was so much more than just producing the one hundred CDs. There were concerts, radio shows, art exhibitions, new offices, a home in Pennsylvania, an as-yet-unpublished book describing all we were doing and did, working toward reestablishing the label, creating award-winning jazz-related video productions with the team from WVIA, coordinating Chiaroscuro with the activities of the Floating Jazz Festival, and then eventually donating the company to the National Public Radio affiliate, WVIA-FM. And then, once the donation was made, expanding Chiaroscuro beyond CD production and sales into the realm of fulltime radio and Internet steaming, as well as an Internet presence second to none. And all these activities were made possible and created alongside the music that appeared on the CDs and occasional vinyl release and were almost exclusively funded by either Andy or one of the foundations or nonprofit institutions with which he was affiliated.

Christmas Music the Jazz Feeling was presented for a quarter of a century, from 1984 through 2008. It was a simple concept; a noted jazz artist and an announcer and from 1986 onward, myself, to interact with the celebrated jazz artist. We would play jazzy recordings of Christmas or seasonal or *Winter Wonderland*–like songs, talk about them a bit, and see where things went. In some instances, if the celebrity was a pianist, like Steve Allen or Junior Mance or Bill Charlap, they might do a live, new recording of a Christmas standard. We always had a well-tuned Steinway on hand. In addition to Steve, Junior, and Bill, the guest artists were Bob Wilber, Don Watt, Nick Niles, Doc Cheatham, Milt Hinton, Teo Macero, Michael Moore, Flip Phillips, Joe Williams, John Bunch, Paul Bacon, Joe Temperley, Derek Smith, Frank Foster, Bucky Pizzarelli, Clark Terry, Andy Sordoni, Phil Woods, Dave Brubeck, Billy Taylor, and Chevy Chase.

Once the songs had been selected and there was a one-hour show in the can, it was readied for broadcast, loaded onto the NPR satellite feed, and transmitted to affiliates all over the country for broadcast by as many as one hundred stations. Meanwhile, WVIA was arranging to have cassettes and inlay cards created so all parties would have a supply of Christmas treats to send out to the faithful. Beginning in 2003, these cassettes were replaced by CDs.

The Sordoni Art Gallery celebrated its fiftieth anniversary in 2023 and is still going strong today. Named after Margaret Barnard Sordoni, the gallery is part of Wilkes University and has long been a jewel in the university's intellectual crown. It has featured five exhibitions throughout the years that have ties to jazz and jazz artists, some of whom were associated with Chiaroscuro Records.

Christmas Music the Jazz Feeling, Dave Brubeck, Billy Taylor, Phil Woods, Chevy Chase, Clark Terry, and Bill Charlap. (Author's collection)

MEL POWELL:
Watercolors

Sordoni Art Gallery
Wilkes College
Wilkes-Barre, Pennsylvania

October 10 through November 8, 1987

Hank O'Neal, *Guest Curator*
Exhibition organized by the Sordoni Art Gallery

THE GRAPHIC ART OF PAUL BACON

Exhibition Curated by
Stanley I Grand

Essays by
Hank O'Neal
Stanley I Grand

Introduction by
Bob Greene

THE ART OF

PEE WEE RUSSELL
AND
GEORGE WETTLING

Sordoni Art Gallery, Wilkes College
Wilkes-Barre, Pennsylvania

April 27 through June 1, 1986

Essays by Hank O'Neal and Dan Morgenstern

Exhibition Organized by the Sordoni Art Gallery

Programs for three exhibitions. (Author's collection)

Pee Wee Russell Ditto (oil on canvas). (Author's collection)

George Wettling, *The Queen Mary* (oil on canvas). (Author's collection)

Mel Powell, *Little Miro*. (Author's collection)

Paul Bacon dust jacket designs. (Author's collection)

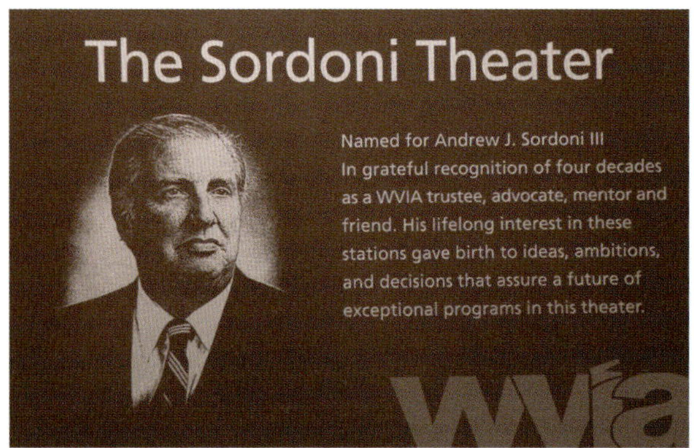

Plaque outside the Sordoni Theater at WVIA. (Author's collection)

There were celebrations of jazz and art featuring the paintings of Bob Haggart (1984), George Wettling and Pee Wee Russell (1986), Mel Powell (1987), Paul Bacon (1999), and myself (2000). Beautiful posters were created for the Haggart, Russell/Wettling, and Powell exhibitions, and catalogs were created for the last four. The opening of the exhibitions that featured paintings by musicians were followed by a special concert that showcased music associated with the artist being celebrated.

There were also concerts at Wilkes University featuring Chiaroscuro artists, as well as seminars and classes that dealt with jazz and related topics, largely conducted by Bob Wilber. The concerts were recorded by WVIA-FM and constitute an important part of the station's musical legacy.

In the early 1990s, Chiaroscuro took up residence at 180 Mundy Street in an industrial building, from which CDs were sold, inventory was stored, master tapes were preserved, and historical items and business records were maintained. For the next twenty years, CDs, concerts, exhibitions, DVDs, newly commissioned artwork and catalogs, and publicity of all sorts were both created and presented. Hundreds of musicians were hired who played millions of notes on thousands of selections that pleased legions of listeners. Each project was unique and there is an interesting backstory to every one.

All because a group of nonmusicians or, on occasion, amateur musicians, were assembled and spurred into action by one or two forward-thinking people who recognized that even though jazz and blues are not the most commercially viable entertainment options for most people, it is important that opportunities should be made possible for this music to not only exist but to develop in every way possible and be accessible to all.

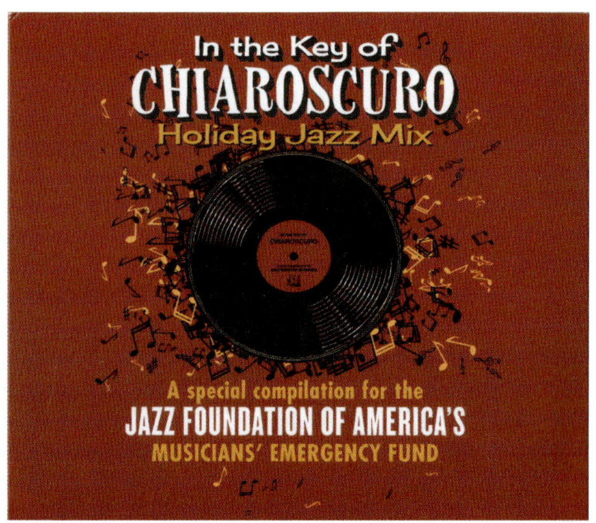

Special JFA Release 2023. (Author's collection)

WVIA Chiaroscuro website design. (Author's collection)

Special JFA release 2025. (Author's collection)

The Wilkes-Barre/Scranton metropolitan area has a population of nearly 600,000. It ranks #100 in the United States, in between Jackson, Mississippi, and Chattanooga, Tennessee. There are some deficiencies in this modest metropolitan area, but one thing it does have is the local NPR/PBS affiliate, something to balance the political pie fights, sporting events, and scripted reality that dominate networks and cable. Plus, on the NPR side, thanks to the Internet, you can listen to The Chiaroscuro Channel twenty-four hours a day, seven days a week, and on the PBS side, in 2023, a documentary film about legendary jazz and blues guitarist/trombonist/arranger Eddie Durham was completed. At the time, it was unclear where the premiere would be, in Texas near Eddie's home in San Marcos or elsewhere, but the unofficial premiere took place at the theater Andy built at WVIA.

And Chiaroscuro still issues and reissues new CDs. The catalog is also used in many different ways, most recently in 2022 and 2023 in partnership with the Jazz Foundation of America and the fine apparel company 32 Bar Blues to create special CDs to benefit the good works of the Jazz Foundation of America. There will be another release for the holiday season in 2025.

This is how much of the art world works in 2025. A handful of enthusiastic men and women make it possible, people in government, successful businessmen and women, trustees of foundations, and countless others. Chiaroscuro was never meant to be a company that sold hundreds of thousands or millions of LPs and CDs. It was more of a preservation society. Taylor Swift will sell more records in an hour than Billy Taylor and Cecil Taylor will sell in a lifetime. That's reality. So is the music that has been preserved that continues to both please listeners and serve musicians in need.

JazzFestival Bern 2023. (Author's collection)

JazzFestival Bern 2025

Hans Zurbrügg

It works the same way all over the world. In 2004, the latest addition to the nonmusicians trio was Hans Zurbrügg. Of course, like the other members of the trio, Hans is a musician, but also like the others, he's not a professional one. He would be the first to tell you that he is possibly the finest cornet-playing hotelier in Switzerland, but it has been many years since he paid for a meal or anything else from his earnings as the leader of the Wolverines, a fine amateur band that has been active in Bern for almost half a century.

50th Anniversary Wolverines Scrapbook. (Author's collection)

20th anniversary book celebrating The JazzHotel (2012). (Author's collection)

I should add that in addition to owning and managing the finest hotels in Switzerland and playing cornet with the Wolverines, Hans has also produced the Internationale JazzFestival Bern since 1974, one of the finest and longest-running jazz festivals in Europe. He produced the festival in every way, financially and artistically.

And how did Hans and I connect? It was because of someone else I have written about earlier, the four-string guitar virtuoso Eddie Condon. This is the story:

In 1991, Hans and his partner in crime Marianne Gauer, who happens to be his wife, began work on what would become the Innere Enge Hotel, a charming boutique hotel in Bern, Switzerland. The property they purchased in that city had been frequented by fancy folks beginning in the 1760s, rebuilt in the 1860s, but was no longer in tip-top shape. But that all changed when the new hotel opened and a few years later, Marians Jazz Room made its debut.

Once open, the Innere Enge Hotel became the focal point of the annual Internationale JazzFestival Bern. The hotel was not only a gathering point for the festival, but it was a unique venue, a "jazz" hotel in many different ways. Most of the guest rooms in the refurbished building were named for noted jazz musicians, artists like Clark Terry, Lionel Hampton, Ahmed Jamal, Dizzy Gillespie, Louie Bellson, and Oscar Peterson. Not only were the rooms named after and dedicated to the musicians, but they were filled with memorabilia celebrating these musicians, much of which had been donated by the musicians themselves. As often as not the musicians had been able to be a "guest" in their own room! Milt and Mona Hinton were in #32, Louie and Francine Bellson were in #34, Mariana and John Lewis were in #27, George Wein was in #32, and Ahmed Jamal was in #6. Over the years I slept in six or seven different rooms, surrounded by drums, vibes, trumpets, and original recordings, photographs, programs, and posters. But no ghosts allowed.

In 2004, Hans decided he would break precedent and open two new rooms dedicated to a single musician. In this case, it was Eddie Condon; Room 25 was for Eddie's contribution as a promoter and club owner and Room 26 was for his contributions as a musician. He began to accumulate photographs, recordings, books, and memorabilia of all sorts linked to Eddie. Then in May 2005, he accumulated Maggie Condon and myself for the official opening of the two rooms. He also organized appropriate musicians who played what was once called "Americondon" music each evening at Marians Jazz Room as part of that year's jazz festival. I cut the ceremonial ribbon on Room 25; Maggie took care of Room 26. We both enjoyed the festival, the hospitality, all the people involved, and Bern and Switzerland as well.

I enjoyed it a little more than Maggie and returned to the festival many times, sometimes to accompany musician friends, other times just to enjoy the music and take as many photographs as possible. Then, in 2007, I became involved in a way I never expected. Hans had produced his festival since 1974. It was successful from the beginning, both artistically and financially.

But in the early 1980s, Hans wanted to expand the reach of the festival and in 1983 negotiated an arrangement with the Swiss equivalent of PBS in the United States and for the next twenty years all of the festival's primary concerts were televised and broadcast nationally throughout the country. It was just a coincidence that Hans's festival broadcasts were presented during the same years that Shelley Shier and I produced the Floating Jazz Festival aboard the *S/S Norway* and *Queen Elizabeth 2*, 1983 to 2002. We each used many of the musicians in the same year and, in many cases, ensembles and groups of musicians.

In those twenty years, Swiss television created an incredible archive of recorded material and Hans was determined to find a way to release these concerts to as wide a public as possible. After much thought, Hans decided to produce a set of approximately two hundred forty DVDs, accompanied by twenty hardcover books, that would be housed in a stand-alone, specially designed metal "Art Box." It would become the most complete record of a jazz festival ever to become commercially available. Some years ago, I wrote:

In 1983, Hans made an agreement with Swiss Television to record and broadcast every performance of the Internationale Jazzfestival Bern. And, taking it one step further, it was determined the concerts would be filmed with full production values, with the highest quality technological standards of the era. Perhaps unaware of what they were preserving for posterity, for the next twenty years Zurbrügg and Swiss TV created one of the most extensive and lasting visual records of those years.

Gil Goldstein and Bobby McFerrin (2009). (Author's collection)

Russell Malone, Monty Alexander, and Junior Ranglin (2007). (Author's collection)

Hiromi (2008). (Author's collection)

Esperanza Spalding (2008).
(Author's collection)

James Moody (2006).
(Author's collection)

Since all the music was already recorded to the highest standards and the plan was to issue all of the concerts, there were no editing or artistic decisions to be made and my part in this enormous undertaking was to make certain all the essays and written material in the books and printed material associated with the project were grammatically, stylistically, and factually accurate. I was also in charge of creating a roughly 320-page oversized "scrapbook" that would be an overview of the festival to be included with what came to be call the Art Box, as well as advising on a special edition of the Art Box that, in addition to the 240 DVDs and booklets, would also include signed, limited-edition photographs, my portraits of George Wein and Bobby McFerrin and a portrait of Wynton Marsalis. There was also a 180-gram LP of an otherwise unavailable Ella Fitzgerald concert included with the limited edition of one hundred special sets. It took ten years and many trips to Bern and elsewhere in Germany and Switzerland before it was complete. The "Art Box" was one of the most complicated projects I've ever been involved with and along the way I became close with both Hans and Marianne.

What came to be called The Jazz and Blues Art Box was launched in New York City at an event at The New School in June 2017. This was only appropriate since a program we had developed at the school in conjunction with Hans had been sending as many as six student ensembles a year from the university's College of Performing Arts to perform at the Internationale JazzFestival Bern for ten years. The press release prior to the official presentation of the Art Box, in part, read:

> *Hans Zurbrügg, Founder/Producer, International JazzFestival Bern; Wynton Marsalis, Trumpeter/Composer/Artistic Director of Jazz at Lincoln Center; George Wein, Founder of the Newport Jazz Festival and Chairman of Newport Festivals Foundation; and Hank O'Neal, Photographer/Author/Music Producer unveiled The Jazz & Blues Art Box this evening before a group of collectors, jazz fans, industry leaders, musicians and media at a world-premiere event at The New School.*
>
> *Archived from the storied International Jazzfestival Bern, The Jazz & Blues Art Box offers what Hank O'Neal calls the "most remarkable collection of jazz and blues performances on video ever assembled." For universities and libraries, it is an educational research tool of unparalleled value. For music fans of all stripes, it's a front row seat for watching some of the greatest musicians who have ever stepped on a stage.*

The Art Box contains over four hundred hours of exceptional recordings of 230 concerts over a twenty-year period, featuring hundreds of the finest blues and jazz performers then active. In 1958, a film entitled *Jazz on a Summer's Day* was created, based on just two afternoons and evenings of performances at that year's Newport Jazz Festival. A small team of inexperienced filmmakers led by Bert Stern and Aram Avakian pulled off the impossible, and a film of lasting importance was the result. The Art Box features ten times as many concerts, flawlessly recorded, featuring artists of equal caliber. It was also one of the most expensive jazz and blues objects ever released, with a list price of $8,400.

In March 2025, the Internationale JazzFestival Bern celebrated its fiftieth anniversary. Hans and I still talk weekly, and this month, a group of students from the New School's College of Performing Arts will be performing at the festival. Marians' Jazz Room is filled almost every evening nine months a year and now that the COVID pandemic is a thing of the past, so are the rooms dedicated to Louis Armstrong, Dizzy Gillespie, Oscar Peterson, and so many others. Josephine's, the brasserie dedicated to Josephine Baker, is filled as well. And the 2026 festival is already being planned.

With George Wein and Wynton Marsalis at The New School (2017).
(Author's collection)

The debut of The Jazz And Blues Art Box on stage at The New School 2017.
(Author's collection)

Acknowledgments

There are thirty-plus remarkable individuals discussed in this book, and any number of equally remarkable people have assisted me in one way or another during my musical journey from the early 1950s until today. And they will be noted later. But since 1983, one person's contribution has been special and noteworthy.

My partner, Shelley M. Shier, was a co-equal and co-conspirator during all the jazz festivals on land and at sea, all the concerts in areas as unlikely as Martha's Vineyard, various cities in Norway, New York, and assorted ports of call and even special events that we hosted at 830 Broadway, benefiting The Jazz Gallery, WBGO, Jazz Foundation of America, and Music on the Inside.

I look at the list of names and there are many I knew and worked with when Shelley was an infant or maybe a teenager, but since 1983 she's been deeply involved with most of the artists in this book, in many instances far more so than I. Whereas my job was to make schedules and suggest when and where they play, it was her job to make sure they got to the job on time, were comfortable when they got there, and paid properly. Just ask Buddy Rich or Flip Phillips about that. She was even there when Buddy and Flip made up after feuding all those years.

Shelley Shier and Dizzy Gillespie in St. Thomas, USVI. (Author's collection)

The picture with Tony was after he'd just finished a special concert at The Fairmont Hotel in San Francisco in 1996, and Dizzy is giving her a squeeze in St. Thomas just before he boarded the *S/S Norway* in 1990.

She had special relationships with both these guys, as with Paul Bacon, who not only designed the poster for her first *Broadway Bound* production but all special tickets for passengers when the show was presented on the *Queen Elizabeth 2*. Clark Terry's nickname for her was "Muscles," Allen Ginsberg was the photographer when we were married in 1985, George Wein never failed to send her a box of chocolates on Valentine's Day, and Gerry Mulligan played her Rubber Maid high school-era clarinet one afternoon. And not to leave out John Moore, who introduced us in 1983.

One night, a year or so after this picture was taken in 1983, Zoot Sims came down to dinner, the last time he was at 830 Broadway. I hadn't made a print of it, or I would have asked him to sign it. Unhappily, he didn't last as long as Dizzy and Tony, but Les Paul did; I just can't find the signed picture.

The point is, however, that Shelley was instrumental in making many of the interactions I've written about in *More Than the Music* possible. Had it not been for her, many of them might not have happened at all, or they wouldn't have happened as nicely as they did.

Tony Bennett and Shelley Shier in San Fransisco. (Author's collection)

Zoot Sims and Shelley Shier aboard the S/S *Norway*. (Author's collection)

But there were many others, particularly on the production side, in Texas and New York. In Texas, Dan Williams made the decision to go forward with *More Than the Music* and his skilled production manager, Adrienne Martinez, first made certain Savannah Childs had the correct text to copy edit and Bill Brammer had all the text, photographs and illustrations to create a wonderful layout and dust jacket. Savannah caught all my errors and fixed them up and Bill skillfully organized five hundred-plus photographs and illustrations in a sensible fashion. Then there was the copy editing of the layout pages that were checked and fixed by Irina du Quenoy. Once this was accomplished, Adrienne, aided by Marco Roc, sprang back into action and coordinated all the work done by the printers, binders, packagers, and shippers. But even before she had a book in hand, Jennifer Watson was planning on how to best publicize *More Than the Music*. Many thanks are offered to this fine team at the TCU Press.

In past years in New York City, Ian Clifford restored faded and shifted colors in old 1960s–70s vintage photographs and fixed assorted imperfections in many older and even contemporary black-and-white images. And elsewhere there were hundreds if not thousands of others who created the events and circumstances that led to the interactions and experiences that formed the memories I've detailed and provided the opportunities to take the photographs with which I've used for illustration. All of these people, beginning with that first unknown salesman in Kilgore, Texas, in 1938 get a tip of the hat and a heart-felt thank you.

Index

These are some of the people, places, companies and songs you will find in *More Than the Music.*

About the Author

Hank O'Neal was born in Kilgore, Texas, in 1940. His career has included the worlds of government, education, music, photography, literature, and espionage.

O'Neal was employed by the Central Intelligence Agency from 1963 until he "retired" in 1976 and began the next phase of his life. He heard his first jazz record when he was a teenager. He liked what he heard and kept on listening. In the seventy years since that first awakening, he has formed two record companies (Chiaroscuro and Hammond Music Enterprises); built two recording studios; produced over 200 jazz LPs/CDs and produced or co-produced (with Shelley Shier) over 150 music festival and concerts; published a number of books and articles on jazz; photographed and worked with most of the giants of jazz who were active in the second half of the twentieth century and beyond; exhibited and published these photographs regularly; worked with Clint Eastwood and Bruce Ricker in the production of six documentary films; joined and continues to serve on the boards of various nonprofit organizations that serve the jazz community, including the College of Performing Arts of The New School (1985), The Jazz Foundation of America (1991), The Jazz Gallery (1996), and others. He was long associated with the Oslo Jazz Festival, the Internationale JazzFestival Bern, and various festivals associated with his friend George Wein.

In the late 1960s, O'Neal became seriously interested in photography and became active in that field. In 1972, he met Berenice Abbott, with whom he worked for nineteen years. About the same time, he met Andre Kertesz, Walker Evans, and all the living FSA photographers as well as many other exceptional photographic artists who were to influence him. His own photographs have been exhibited and widely reproduced since that time.

O'Neal published his first book in 1973, but the first to gain widespread attention was *A Vision Shared* (1976). Steidl reissued this important book in 2018. He has published over twenty-five books on various subjects, but mostly related to photography, his own or others, music, or both. In addition to *A Vision Shared*, Steidl is scheduled to release four other new books by O'Neal in the coming years, beginning with *You've Got to Do a Damn Sight Better Than That, Buster* (2026), a memoir based on his many years of working with Berenice Abbott. He was recently coeditor of the five volumes included in *The Unknown Abbott* (Steidl, 2013) and *Berenice Abbott—The Paris Portraits* (Steidl, 2015). His most recent book was *Sincerely, Ty Cobb* (TCU Press, 2020).

Since his first photography exhibition in 1973 and career retrospective at the legendary Witkin Gallery in 1999, his photographs have been widely exhibited throughout the United States in dozens of cities and in Canada, Norway, Switzerland, France, and Russia. At the age of eighty-five he continues to pursue numerous photographic and literary projects and is presently preparing *100 Jazz Pianists* for future publication by the TCU Press. He lives and works in New York City.

The Photographs and Illustrations

All of the photographs that appear in *More Than the Music* were taken by myself others than those are specifically identified as taken by someone else, notably George Wein in the John Coltrane section, the photograph of Marilyn Danitz, Marian McPartland and myself in Sherman Fairchild's living room. It was taken by Sherman Fairchild. In a few instances, older photographs in some chapters, such as those devoted to Squirrel Ashcraft and Jimmy and Marina McPartland were taken by others before I was born or even had a camera but were given to me many years ago by them and have been in my personal collection for many years.

Some of the photographs were credited on record covers and CD booklets as having been taken by Rollo Phelcks. This is a pseudonym I have used since the 1970s because I didn't want my name to appear multiple times in productions with which I was associated.

The illustrations, i.e., album jackets, book covers, record labels, posters, and assorted ephemera and memorabilia, such as the ash tray from Condon's, have all been taken from my personal collection.

JAZZ
君は横綱に勝てない!!